SECOND EDITION

TRADITION & DISSENT

A RHETORIC / READER

FLORENCE BONZER GREENBERG
ANNE P. HEFFLEY

TRADITION AND DISSENT

A Rhetoric / Reader

TRADITION

Second Edition

AND DISSENT

FLORENCE BONZER GREENBERG

ANNE P. HEFFLEY

THE BOBBS-MERRILL COMPANY, INC.
Indianapolis / New York

Printed in the United States of America
Library of Congress Catalog Card Number 76–145858
Second Printing
Design: Starr Atkinson

Preface

The motivating principle behind the Second Edition of this book remains the authors' belief that, since writing is a craft as well as an art, most students can learn to write with reasonable facility. Accordingly, we have attempted to follow throughout a sequential pattern necessary for the development of any skill: a statement of the objective to be realized, examples, practice; next objective to be realized, examples, practice, and so on. Since the book begins with simple material and progresses to more complex principles and writing assignments, the instructor can gauge the needs of the class and proceed through each section either quickly or slowly.

The book is divided into two parts: the Rhetoric and the Reader. The Rhetoric, in turn, is also divided into two sections: an Introduction to Writing and The Persuasive Essay. The first part aims at unlocking whatever verbal ability the students possess and moving them at their own speed to greater fluency.

Many students, we are convinced, find writing arduous because they are asked to begin on a level which is beyond them. Although many of these students have difficulty conceptualizing for one reason or another, they are asked not only to formulate ideas but also to analyze and record them in an organized fashion. For this reason we have begun the book, not in the traditional manner, but rather with a section that moves the students toward a heightened awareness of their environment.

The object of the introductory section is to encourage the students to verbalize about what is familiar to them in their surroundings. Because the "environment" suggested in this part of the book is specific and concrete, it is hoped by the authors that the students can achieve modest success from the very outset, no matter how slim the store of language with which they begin. This section, then, begins with observation of objects in the students' own surroundings, proceeds to written description of those objects, and then to practice in ways of organizing details.

The last chapter of the introductory section is devoted to demonstrating to the students the process of moving from description of the environment to conceptualizing about the environment. By the end of this introductory section, the student has been exposed to the concept of a controlling idea in writing.

The second section of the Rhetoric deals with the principles involved in the writing of the persuasive essay. This section is more traditional in its treatment, covering as it does the controlling idea, topic sentences, paragraph development, transitions, introductions, and conclusions. Wherever possible we have included student as well as professional examples to point up the rhetorical principles. Concluding the Rhetoric are two chapters dealing with definition and evidence. The chapter entitled *Definition* concentrates on language; the chapter, *Evidence,* deals with logical and illogical support. These chapters have been arranged so that the instructor may assign them when the need for discussion of logical development and fallacious thinking becomes evident.

The second part of the book, the Reader, has been updated, and current concerns, such as ecology and women's liberation, have been added. All selections are designed to stimulate interest and response in the students. The authors have deliberately selected readings on a number of controversial subjects since it is our experience that such subjects produce more effective writing than subjects on which there is general agreement. We have not in every case represented every point of view. We have, instead, attempted to offer points of view with which the students may be less familiar, hoping thereby to engage the readers' interest and encourage active participation in discussion. For this reason the reading section is entitled Dissent.

Consistent with our general format, the readings range from the simple to the complex, and the topics receive treatment in a wide variety of ways, from the formal essay to meaningful cartoons. Although some of the readings can and should serve as models for the rhetorical principles outlined in the first part of the book, some selections come from newspapers and magazines and, therefore, do not conform to the requirements of the formal essay. The immediate objectives of the reading section are to stimulate the students to think, to encourage them to read further, and to give them ideas and information for their writing.

Almost every selection in the Reader is accompanied by study questions. These questions are included to encourage the students to read carefully and to aid them in comprehension. They are also designed to stimulate class discussion. There are, in addition, writing assignments at the end of each reading section. These assignments, we hope, will cause the students to think through the material covered in the readings and in class discussions and help them to express their thoughts in essay form. A number of assignments refer the students to the library to give them practice in searching for information and in organizing the material logically into a summary or a report. In addition, we have added a number of writing assignments that encourage the students to express themselves in any form they wish: poetry, short story, personal narrative, description. This kind of assignment frequently frees students of their fear of writing and very often motivates them to write more readily.

We have kept the initial chapters of the Rhetoric short in order to give the students a feeling of accomplishment as they proceed rapidly from one concept to the next. Since the Rhetoric attempts to introduce and give practice in conceptualization, we recommend that it be used sequentially, with as much or little time devoted to each chapter as class needs dictate. The Reader, however, can be used effectively in any order the instructor wishes.

We gratefully acknowledge the assistance of Ed Tyson and Norma Shellada and students of past English 92 classes at San Jose City College. Special thanks go to Rachel, Michael, Randy, Gary, and Scott for their encouragement.

F.B.G.
A.P.H.

To Ed Heffley
and in memory of Mel Greenberg

Contents

THE RHETORIC

Part One / Introduction to Writing

PART FIVE / *Human Relations*

PART SIX / *Man's Inhumanity to Man*

PART SEVEN / *War and Mankind*

PART EIGHT / *The Future: What Do We Face?*

THE RHETORIC

PART ONE / *Introduction to Writing*

The desire for writing grows with writing.
(Crescit scribendo scribendi studium.)

Erasmus, *Adagia*

CHAPTER ONE

Observing and Verbalizing via the Haiku

No one can write unless he has something to say. The more conscious one becomes of his actions and the actions of others, of his feelings and attitudes, of what he sees and hears around him, the more easily he can write and the more thoroughly he knows himself and his environment.

Almost everyone is born with the ability to see and hear, accurately and sharply, the things around him. Most children are conscious of everything: they see the ant crawling up the blade of grass, they enjoy the feel of wet mud, they observe with wonder a bird's flight. As people grow older, however, this power of observation which they had as children seems to become blurred. As life becomes more routine, they often stop responding to their environment. The ability has not gone, though; it is simply not being used.

OBSERVATION OF SURROUNDINGS

You can write more effectively if you recapture this awareness of yourself and your environment. One way to heighten the ability to observe and to express this awareness on paper is to borrow an art form from the Japanese which many Americans have already found enjoyable: the haiku. In Japan the haiku follows a particular structure, but in English the haiku is normally written as a brief three-line observation or description, or, since it is an adapted form, it may even be four lines.

The haiku is so popular in Japan—and has been for centuries—that not only the scholar or poet, but even the ordinary man or woman, writes hundreds.

There is no limit to the subject matter. Anything that one can see, hear, taste, feel, or smell can be described and can therefore be the subject of a haiku.

Here are some examples of haiku from the Japanese:

1/
In a winter river
thrown away, a dog's
dead body.

2/
Waiting
A man, just one—
also a fly, just one,
in the huge drawing room.

3/
Leaves
The winds that blow—
ask them, which leaf of the tree
will be next to go.[1]

4/
Poor crying cricket,
perhaps your little husband
was caught by our cat.

5/
If the white herons
had no voice, they would be lost
in the falling snow.

6/
Snow fell until dawn.
Now every twig in the grove
glitters in sunlight.

7/
Since my house burned down,
I now own a better view
of the rising moon.

8/
A cautious crow clings
to a bare bough, silently
watching the sunset.[2]

[1] Haiku 1–3 from *An Introduction to Haiku* by Harold G. Henderson. Copyright © 1958 by Harold G. Henderson. Reprinted by permission of Doubleday & Company, Inc.

[2] Haiku 4–8 from *Cricket Songs: Japanese Haiku,* translated and © 1964, by Harry Behn. Reprinted by permission of Harcourt Brace Jovanovich, Inc.

Courtesy of Edward Shuster

EDWARD SHUSTER *Chicken Ranch—Pacheen Dam*

IMPORTANCE OF OBSERVATION

Even though these haiku are based on observations, sometimes humorous ones, they almost always have a deeper meaning than at first appears on the surface. For your purposes, however, the description itself is the important thing. The act of composing the haiku will help to heighten your powers of observation.

In the photograph above, the camera has captured an ordinary part of the environment in clear and vivid detail. The old boards of the fence are rich with a texture that time and weather have accentuated; knots make color and pattern variations; nails placed rhythmically down the boards create points of light and shadow; and an octagonal piece of metal catches the glow of the sun on its flat surface. Here are two examples of the way students have responded to Shuster's board fence:

A piece of metal all alone,
breaking into the world
of wood.

A knothole—
a piece of nature
cut short.

Now look closely at the contrasting photograph below of living wood: part of the root system, the source of life, is exposed in snake-like coils, and near it is water, another source of life.

What the camera is to the photographer, words are to the writer. However, before you can do an effective job of reproducing an object or a scene through words, you will have to train yourself to look at objects as though you were the camera, perhaps really seeing them for the first time.

Courtesy of Edward Shuster

EDWARD SHUSTER *Time Revealed*

IMPORTANCE OF A SINGLE WORD

Because the haiku is so short, often a single word makes the picture vivid or the meaning clear. In the first haiku on page 6, for instance, the word *dead* is the most powerful. It ties together the images of *winter* river and the body *thrown* away, and it also suggests a gloomy, sad picture of a dog not only dead, but no longer loved or needed.

In the second haiku the word *huge,* which is often a rather vague, meaningless word, makes the reader see a man in vast surroundings with only a fly for a companion. The word *huge* actually creates the impression of loneliness that the poem expresses.

STUDENT EXAMPLES

The following five haiku were written with class participation. Notice how, with reworking in class and with attention to choice of words, the last two haiku are definite improvements over the first three. Contrast, for instance, "Rising sun" with "Rising sun sparkles" and "Time to work" with "Footsteps crunch to work."

1/
All is silent . . .
sound of footsteps;
time to work.

2/
Rising sun,
sound of footsteps . . .
time to work.

3/
Break of dawn,
dull sound of footsteps
plodding to work.

4/
Damp grey dawn
and dull sound of feet
plodding to work.

5/
Rising sun sparkles
the icy morning;
footsteps crunch to work.

One student, when asked to write a haiku on something ordinary in his environment, actually saw his surroundings for the first time. He really observed the traffic signal that he had passed every day for months without seeing and described it this way:

Red and threatening,
the traffic light blinks
an angry warning.

Another student had quite a different reaction:

The traffic light stares
round and red:
be careful, be careful.

Here are more examples of haiku written by students:

1/
An ant
compressed
as he was stepped on.

2/
The green tomato worm—
oozing his way along the branches;
camouflaged, sickening.

3/
After a storm
in a muddy backyard,
lie a broken toy gun
and an armless doll.

4/
Wire stretched between poles
pencil thin
for Mike to call Jane.

5/
The student, discouraged—
wastepaper basket
overflowing with paper.

6/
IBM Card
Do not spindle, bend, tear, fold
or otherwise mutilate
my identity.

Courtesy of the Fogg Art Museum, Harvard University
Gift of Meta and Paul J. Sachs

BEN SHAHN *The Blind Botanist*

Sometimes it is but a single word that makes a description vivid. For example, in the haiku about the ant, the word *compressed* comes almost as a shock, and any change in that single word would change the effect of the entire poem. The tomato worm haiku is successful largely because of the words *oozing* and *sickening*.

SENSE PERCEPTION

Most people, except for the handicapped, tend to rely almost exclusively on the sense of sight for their sense perceptions, neglecting the other senses of taste, smell, touch, and hearing. But look at Ben Shahn's picture of "The Blind Botanist," above. Most think of a botanist as a scientist who depends primarily on his eyesight in order to identify and categorize and even to appreciate the beauty of plant life; yet Shahn intentionally makes his botanist blind, suggesting that the use of the other four senses can be as effective as the sense of sight.

Close your eyes and concentrate on what you hear. After a few moments, are you more conscious of the sounds you are accustomed to block out? Try the same experiment with the senses of touch, smell, and taste. If you practice heightening all your senses, not just that of sight, and then if you attempt to put your responses into words, you will understand yourself and your surroundings better, and you will find writing easier and more enjoyable.

Writing Assignments

The emphasis in these assignments is not to create poetry, but to heighten the power of observation.

1. Look at one or both photographs on pages 7 and 8. In about twenty minutes see how many haiku you can write based on what you see. You may concentrate on one or the other, or you may wish to compare or contrast them. Be prepared to read at least one aloud in class.
2. As you go about your daily routine, try to invent haiku about ordinary objects around you. Observe them closely enough so that you can describe them accurately in clear and vivid language. Write down five you think best. The purpose of this exercise is to heighten your powers of observation and, at the same time, to improve your ability to express yourself in words. Therefore, choose as the subjects of your haiku things you can actually see as you describe them. Do not rely upon your memory. The following are some suggestions:

   a car (motorcycle, bus)
   a classmate
   an animal
   a book
   a typewriter
   the sky
   shrubbery (tree, flower)
   a teacher
   your registration card
   a policeman
   a desk
   your toothbrush
3. Close your eyes. Feel an object, listen to the sounds around you, taste something, smell something; then write three or more haiku that *specifically* reflect your experiences.

CHAPTER TWO

Specific Detail via Simply Description

The success of a haiku, as we have seen, depends upon accuracy of observation and the best possible selection of words, sometimes of a single word. The same is true of longer writings. If you can train yourself to observe and to record your observations accurately and vividly, you can learn to write effectively. We hope that writing haiku has caused you to look at familiar objects and people as though you were seeing them for the first time, to perceive size, shape, color, and function. Joseph Conrad, the novelist, once wrote: "My task which I am trying to accomplish is, by the power of the written word, to make you feel—it is, before all, to make you *see*. That—and no more, and it is everything." Every writer is trying to do the same thing.

One of the criticisms leveled at student writing is that it is too general. Students who have difficulty finding anything to write will see that this problem begins to disappear when they learn to include specific details. While being specific may not in itself make a piece of writing clear or interesting, generalities which are not developed by specific detail *do* make a work unclear and uninteresting. Whenever possible, an effective writer tries to substitute a specific word or a specific detail for a vague description.

> Too general: "I have a dog."
> More detailed: "I have a large black and tan German shepherd named Gertrude."
>
> Too general: "There are two pictures in my room."
> More detailed: "Hanging side by side over my desk are two pictures, a Degas ballet scene and a Cezanne landscape."

AN EXAMPLE OF SPECIFIC DETAILS PUT TO WORK

Read the following poem, preferably aloud, and notice particularly the wealth of vivid details.

Elizabeth Bishop / THE FISH

I caught a tremendous fish
and held him beside the boat
half out of water, with my hook
fast in a corner of his mouth.
He didn't fight.
He hadn't fought at all.
He hung a grunting weight,
battered and venerable and homely.
Here and there
his brown skin hung in strips
like ancient wall-paper,
and its pattern of darker brown
was like wall-paper;
shapes like full-blown roses
stained and lost through age.
He was speckled with barnacles,
fine rosettes of lime,
and infested
with tiny white sea-lice
and underneath two or three
rags of green weed hung down.
While his gills were breathing in
the terrible oxygen
—the frightening gills
fresh and crisp with blood,
that can cut so badly—

HENRY KOERNER *My Parents*

From the collection of Mr. and Mrs. Charles Brisk,
courtesy of Midtown Galleries, New York
Reproduction courtesy of *Life* Magazine © Time Inc.

SALVADOR DALI *Persistence of Memory (Soft Watches)*

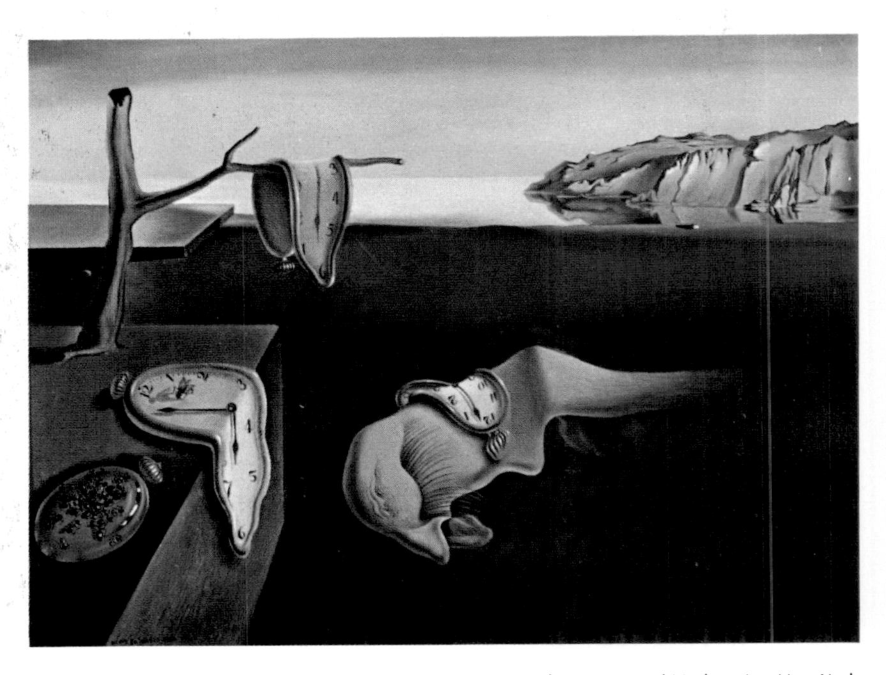

Collection, The Museum of Modern Art, New York

I thought of the coarse white flesh
packed in like feathers,
the big bones and the little bones,
the dramatic reds and blacks of
his shiny entrails,
and the pink swim-bladder
like a big peony.
I looked into his eyes
which were far larger than mine
but shallower, and yellowed,
the irises backed and packed
with tarnished tinfoil
seen through the lenses
of old scratched isinglass.
They shifted a little, but not
to return my stare.
—It was more like the tipping
of an object toward the light.
I admired his sullen face,
the mechanism of his jaw,
and then I saw
that from his lower lip
—if you could call it a lip—
grim, wet, and weapon-like,
hung five old pieces of fish-line,
or four and a wire leader
with the swivel still attached,
with all their five big hooks
grown firmly in his mouth.
A green line, frayed at the end
where he broke it, two heavier lines,
and a fine black thread
still crimped from the strain and snap
when it broke and he got away.
Like medals with their ribbons
frayed and wavering,
a five-haired beard of wisdom
trailing from his aching jaw.
I stared and stared

and victory filled up
the little rented boat,
from the pool of bilge
where oil had spread a rainbow
around the rusted engine
to the bailer rusted orange,
the sun-cracked thwarts,
the oarlocks on their strings,
the gunnels—until everything
was rainbow, rainbow, rainbow!
And I let the fish go.

If you reread the poem, you will find that the poet has achieved her effects by the kinds of details that you, too, should include when you write descriptions, details such as: **shape, color, weight, size, height, position, relationship of parts.**

STUDENT EXAMPLES: VAGUE TO SPECIFIC

Keeping in mind the difference between a general statement and a specific one, and keeping in mind, also, the use to which specific details can be put (as demonstrated in the poem "The Fish"), read the following descriptions written by students. To the right of the examples, there are relevant comments. As you read the descriptions and the comments, notice how the incorporation of specific details increases the quantity and improves the quality of the writing.

1/

I have a really nice room. It has just about everything in it I need, so I really like it.

What does the student mean by "nice"? Is it large and roomy or small and cozy? What does he "need"? A bed, chair, grand piano, portable bar? What does it look like? What sex do you suppose the writer is?

2/

My room at home is pretty. It is large enough for twin beds, a desk, two chairs, and a typing table. The rug is a soft blue that matches the curtains. The rest of the room is white, except for the bedspreads, so it always looks cool and restful.

Much more detail. We have a better impression of the room, but if we try to visualize it, we probably see only blue and white. Is the floor white, too? How is the furniture arranged? Aren't there any doors? Windows? Pictures? What makes the room "pretty"?

3/

I have had the same room since I was ten, and although it is still comfortable, it is beginning to get crowded. The room is about 12′ x 14′ and has closets running the length of the wall. The closets are pretty big, but full of junk that I never got around to throwing out. The wall opposite has a big window. Against this wall are my desk, a chair, and two bookcases. The only other furniture in the room is my bed and a big, ancient arm chair that I sit in a lot while I read or listen to records. On the wall opposite my bed are shelves I made myself to keep my record player and records on. The shelves also hold piles of paper and school books, some fishing tackle, my .22, and some empty shell boxes. Maybe the room would be big enough if I just threw some of the junk away.

Obviously more detailed than the others. We know how large the room is and pretty much what is in it, but we do not know what color anything is. Does the absence of color make it more difficult to see the room? The description even reveals the student's interests. Would it have been more effective if we also knew what kinds of recordings he enjoys and what kind of junk he has collected over the years?

Writing Assignments

1. Rewrite the following sentences by including specific details. The exercise will help you to see the difference between a general statement and a more specific one. Notice particularly how much more interesting the specific description becomes.
    a. I own a car.
    b. My friend just bought an engagement ring.
    c. There is a desk in my room.
    d. I have a younger sister.
    e. He washed his car.
    f. It was a terrible dinner.
    g. She's nice.
    h. I dropped a carton of eggs this morning.
    i. I saw a good movie last week.
    j. That's a Mickey-Mouse course.
2. Select any object, animal, or person. Observe your selection carefully. As you do, list as many specific details as you can.
3. Write as complete a description as you can of any familiar object. Be specific. If necessary, use a thesaurus to help you find more effective words. Some suggestions:

    your room at home
    your classroom
    your handbag (wallet)
    a pet

CHAPTER THREE

Logical Order in Simple Description

Once you have learned to observe your surroundings accurately and to record these observations as specifically as possible, you will find your compositions becoming longer; and once your compositions become longer, you will encounter the problem of how to organize your observations or ideas. If you write a long description of a room, for instance, you may find yourself wondering with which part of the room you should start. What should follow? With what part should you end? An examination of logical order will help you to find one method of organizing your descriptions or observations.

Every time that you look at a room or a scene, you see it from one particular point, just as you view a painting from one particular point when you stand in front of it. If a painter decides to reproduce on canvas three cows standing under an oak tree in a field, he must decide *before* he paints how he wants to depict the scene. Does he paint it as though he is sitting in the branches of a tree looking down on the backs of the cows? Does he sit far away and paint a distant scene with the cows on the left? Will he put the cows in the center of his picture, or will he put the tree in the center?

Obviously, once he has started to paint the picture as if he were standing in the center of the scene with the cows on his left, he cannot change his mind halfway through the painting. If he did, the result might be half a cow on the left, a tree in the middle, and the other half of the cow somewhere on the right! In the same way, a description of a room or a view, for example, should follow a *logical order,* as if the writer were standing in one particular spot viewing the scene. He might describe it from right to left, from left to right, from top to bottom, or from bottom to top (or even from a chandelier or the top of a tree). Or a writer may wish to imagine that he is walking through a room or an area. Whatever the writer's vantage point, he must proceed logically. If the description is haphazard, without order, the reader and writer become completely confused.

AN EXAMPLE OF A VIEW FROM A WINDOW

> . . . he heaved himself laboriously up, and, going to the window, stood looking down into the street. . . . At one end of the street McTeague could see the huge powerhouse of the cable line. Immediately opposite him was a great market; while farther on, over the chimney stacks of the intervening houses, the glass roof of some huge public baths glittered like crystal in the afternoon sun. Underneath him the branch post office was opening its doors, as was its custom between two and three o'clock on Sunday afternoons. An acrid odor of ink rose upward to him. Occasionally a cable car passed, trundling heavily, with a strident whirring of jostled glass windows.

Notice not only the order, but also the specific details which the author, Frank Norris, uses to make the reader see the same scene McTeague sees.

Writing Assignment

Keep in mind the importance of *accurate observation, specific detail,* and *logical order.* Write a description of Henry Koerner's painting, "My Parents," facing page 14. If you are not satisfied that someone could actually *see* the painting from your description, rewrite your work, being even more specific and orderly.

CHAPTER FOUR

Dominant Impression in Simple Description

In the last chapter you learned how a fairly long descriptive work can be organized by following a logical order. That is one method of making order out of a number of details. There are, of course, other methods. One of these is to organize the details around a dominant impression.

For example, in Chapter Two in student sample 3, the writer comments near the beginning of his composition that his room is crowded. He makes reference to this point again (his closet is full of junk; there are piles of paper on his shelves; the room would be big enough if he threw some of his junk away), but in the rest of the description he does not concentrate upon how crowded his room is. Instead, he simply tries to make the reader see his room, as if he were showing a photograph.

The writer may choose, however, to make the observation "My room is crowded" the central point of his description. In that case, every detail in his paragraph must contribute to this idea. The words "big window" do not contribute to the idea of crowdedness. But if the writer mentions that there are stickers on the windowpanes, a pair of gloves, a stapler, and a pipe on the window sill, and an assortment of streamers and pennants pinned to the curtains, then he is developing his dominant theme: my room is crowded. In other words, the writer chooses those details which actually make the room look crowded. He ignores everything else. He organizes all his details, therefore, around the *impression* or *mood* which he wishes to create.

This kind of organizing principle is called the *dominant impression*. Here is a student example of such a description.

STUDENT EXAMPLE

My room is just like me: disorganized. What makes it worse is that I hate to throw anything away, so anything left over from any interest I have ever had is in the room somewhere. The top shelf of my closet is piled with dolls, which I gave up when I was ten, and balanced uneasily on top of them all are the ice skates I gave up two years ago when I sprained my ankle. The year before that I had taken up taxidermy, and on the bookcases are the results: two rather odd looking owls that my brother shot in Colorado and that I stuffed with the help of a do-it-yourself book. They didn't turn out too well, though, and one looks as though he had a cold and the other one looks drunk. Next to them is the microscope I got after I gave up taxidermy. It's not a very good one, but I keep thinking I may go back to science one day, so I have kept it. When I remember to make my bed, I have to move all the stuffed animals I have received through the years as birthday and Christmas presents. All over the dresser and stuck into the mirror frame are snapshots, post cards, letters answered and unanswered, and cologne bottles. My mother has been looking very sour and muttering about cockroaches lately, and I suspect that I will have to turn over a new leaf.

This student has not tried to describe the size or actual appearance of her room. Instead, she has focused all the details on one central point: the appearance of her room is a reflection of her personality—they are both cluttered with interests. Everything in the description develops this point. The author chooses to describe those objects which reflect her interests and names them specifically. Notice, too, that her selection of those objects which develop her central theme creates the necessary organization.

All the details in this composition are organized around one idea: my room is a reflection of my personality. This dominant impression helps the writer to organize a number of details into a unified composition.

PROFESSIONAL EXAMPLE

The following brief description is written by a professional writer, Georges Simenon. Notice how he selects details to create the dominant impression.

The streets presented a more depressing sight in the light of morning than at night, because the rain had dirtied everything, leaving its dark traces on the facades of buildings, turning their colors ugly. Large drops still fell from cornices and electric wires, occasionally from the sky, which was draining itself, still in dramatic style, as though gathering strength for fresh convulsions.

The dominant impression controls what details are included in the description.

Writing Assignments

1. Develop fully one or more of the following sentences
   a. Yosemite Valley (or any other place) is one of the most beautiful (or ugly) places I have ever seen.
   b. It was one of the most depressing rooms that I have ever been in.
   c. Her (his) room is a reflection of her (his) personality.
   d. It was a place to study.

   Reread your work, and substitute specific details for any generalization. If you find any details that do not contribute to the dominant impression which you wish to create, omit them and substitute others that do.
2. Look again at the picture facing page 14. Describe what you think to be the main mood or feeling it creates. Before you begin to write, state the dominant impression in a sentence. Include specific details of the picture to support your statement.

CHAPTER FIVE

Two Kinds of Writing

Vital to effective writing is observation of ourselves and our environment. This writing may take the form of *description,* which you have practiced in the previous chapters. Obviously, writing also communicates *ideas* about ourselves and the world. Since the purposes are different, the results are different as well. To see specifically how these two kinds of writing differ, read these two student samples. Each is followed by a comment.

EXAMPLE OF DESCRIPTIVE WRITING

My mother looks like a mess in the morning. She is really pretty when she is dressed up and ready to go out, but not in the morning. When she gets up, she does nothing to herself but put on an old bathrobe that she wears especially for cooking breakfast. The color of the bathrobe is dark maroon, which makes her look older than she is; the belt disappeared some time ago, so the general effect is a rather shapeless maroon blob. Her slippers are almost as old as the bathrobe. They are the kind that cover just the front part of the foot, but she has worn them so much that the hole for the toes has stretched too wide and her toes stick out. But it is what she does to her head that is really alarming. She puts her hair up every night in the kind of curlers that have the little spikes all over them to keep the hair on the curlers. From the front she looks almost bald, and from the back she looks like a porcupine. About once a week she puts some kind of cream all over her face and then occasionally forgets to wipe it off in the morning. On those mornings the results are really frightening. In fact, I sometimes have to remind myself that I am not seeing an apparition, but just my own mother.

COMMENT. Notice that the details of the preceding paragraph develop a dominant impression: *My mother looks like a mess in the morning.* The *purpose* of the description is to create a visual image.

EXAMPLE OF WRITING BASED ON IDEAS

Most of us take for granted that a mother who does not love her children is abnormal. Even more, we believe that mother love is not only normal, but desirable. These beliefs are certainly true, but the relationship of a mother to her children is more complex than these beliefs would indicate. *Mother love can, in fact, be sometimes more harmful than helpful.*

Mother love suggests warmth, care, and protection, qualities which are in themselves desirable. Obviously a child needs to be treated warmly by his mother; he needs to be cared for, that is, to be clothed, fed, and taught; and he needs to be protected, particularly at an early age, from himself and from his environment. But these necessities, if carried to excess, can actually hamper a child's normal development. It is pleasant to feel warmth, but what happens when the warmth becomes suffocating? It is one thing if a mother picks up her child and comforts him when he falls and actually hurts himself, but it is another if she smothers him anxiously if he merely trips over the rug.

The child soon learns that the slightest excuse will bring mother's arms around him. What started as a natural reaction, the love of a mother for her child and her distress at seeing him injured, may end with the child demanding attention for the slightest discomfort, real or imagined. The final result, of course, is that the child very quickly becomes demanding of constant attention and never develops his own personality.

The same results may occur if care and protection are carried too far. Care involves, among other things, feeding and clothing. Up to a certain age, it is natural for a mother to spoon feed her child and to tie his shoe laces for him. However, if she continues performing these functions beyond the age when other children are learning to do them for themselves, she is actually slowing down the child's development. The child cannot function on his own. And although it is natural for any mother to protect her young, at a certain age the child must learn to look after himself. If a mother screams and calls him back every time her child climbs a tree or gets near the edge of a cliff, the child will eventually learn to be fearful and dependent.

Children learn by doing, by experimenting, eventually by thinking for themselves. If they are constantly picked up and hugged at the slightest injury, if they have everything done for them beyond the age when they should start doing for themselves, and if every time they start to be independent, the mother cries out in alarm, then the child will grow up to reflect these influences. He will be demanding, dependent, and fearful. Like everything else, even mother love can be carried too far.

COMMENT. The purpose of the first piece of writing is to create a visual image. The second piece of writing does not attempt to make the reader *see* a person or a scene. Instead, it develops an idea,

"Mother love can sometimes be more harmful than helpful."

This second kind of writing, the essay, is what you are called upon to do very frequently in college. Although description can be used within this kind of writing, it becomes merely one of the instruments the writer uses to try to persuade his reader to believe as he does.[1]

Since an essay evolves from an opinion, it is easy to see how important the formulation of such an opinion becomes. "Blue is an attractive color for you" is an opinion, but it is hardly a significant one, one that is worth communicating to others. The problem then becomes how to arrive at ideas that are meaningful.

Basically, ideas spring from experiences, real and vicarious. Participating in a variety of activities, meeting people, traveling, and reading are all sources of ideas. Thoughtful examination of the environment is another way to ideas. Psychologists tell us that many people, unfortunately, go through life without thinking about themselves or the world around them except in the vaguest of terms. However, college demands that students examine themselves and their environment thoughtfully and, further, that they be able to express their ideas in written form. It follows, then, that you will often be asked to write compositions about your ideas.

Until now you have been asked to observe your surroundings and record what you *see*. From now on you will be asked to formulate ideas about your environment and record what you *think*.

Writing Assignment

Find examples, in newspapers or magazines, of writing that is descriptive in nature and writing that is based upon ideas.

[1] It should be noted at this time that the word "essay" has different applications in the literature of composition. Throughout this book it will be used to refer to persuasive writing as distinguished from other kinds of writing.

CHAPTER SIX

Formulating Ideas

The main idea or primary assertion of an essay is known as *the controlling idea* since it determines what will be included in the essay. What the dominant impression does for a description, the controlling idea does for the essay. Just as you must have the dominant impression clearly in your mind *before* you begin to write a description, so you must have the controlling idea clearly in mind *before* you begin to write your essay.

Sometimes, it is true, the instructor will provide the controlling idea. More often, however, you will simply be requested to write an essay, and it will be your responsibility to arrive at a controlling idea. Here are some suggestions to help you formulate ideas.

MOVING FROM AN OBJECT TO AN IDEA

You have already seen that an object can be the source of a description and that it can be the source of an emotion or an attitude. *An object can also be the source of ideas.* For instance, in Chapter Two there are descriptions of students' rooms which simply attempt to show the reader what the rooms look like; and in Chapter Four there is a description of a student's room organized around a dominant impression: My room is a reflection of my personality. It is possible, if you think about your own room for a few minutes, to move from the room itself to an *idea* about rooms in general. In other words, thinking about a specific room can lead you to extract a statement about rooms in general. Here are some possibilities:

> Everyone should have a room in which he can be alone.
> Parents should not intrude upon their children's privacy.
> Crowded living conditions create family problems.

There are advantages (disadvantages) to living at home (away from home) during college.

OTHER EXAMPLES OF MOVING FROM OBJECTS TO IDEAS

A DESK

A desk as a source of a dominant impression:

The number of reference books on the desk suggests that the owner is a scholar.

A desk as a source of ideas:

Cabinet-making is a lost art.
A letter sometimes reveals more about the writer than he intends.
Writing can be thought of as both a craft and an art.

A CLOCK

A clock as a source of a dominant impression:

My alarm clock looks as though it belongs in an office; it is cold, efficient, and business-like.

A clock as a source of ideas:

Time eats away at life.
Adolescents and middle-aged people both try to cheat time but in opposite ways.
You can cheat time, but you can't win.
Time moves at different speeds under different circumstances.

PRACTICE. Salvador Dali's painting, "Persistence of Memory (Soft Watches)," facing page 15, portrays unusual looking clocks and watches. Write down, in sentence form, as many ideas as the painting suggests to you.

MOVING FROM A LIVING CREATURE TO AN IDEA

Just as places or objects can give rise to ideas, so can living creatures.

A fish

A fish as a source of a dominant impression (think again of the poem "The Fish"):

> The old fish in the poem is a battle-scarred but victorious veteran.

A fish as a source of ideas (thinking of fishing as a sport):

> Hunters and fishermen have a responsibility to preserve the wilderness and wildlife.
>
> What is often called sport is actually murder.

A dog

A dog as a source of a dominant impression:

> His Great Dane is one of the most aristocratic-looking dogs I've seen.

A dog as a source of ideas:

> Dogs are better companions than cats.
>
> I tend to agree with the old wives' saying that a dog knows who should be trusted and who shouldn't be.

PRACTICE. Read the following selection by James Thurber. The author observed mother dogs with their pups and in "A Preface to Dogs" relates their behavior to human mothers and their young. These observations give rise to some unusual ideas about the ideal way to bring up children. In other words, Thurber moves from observation of the animal, dogs, to ideas about parents and children.

James Thurber / A PREFACE TO DOGS

As soon as a wife presents her husband with a child, her capacity for worry becomes acuter: she hears more burglars, she smells more things burning, she begins to wonder, at the theatre or the dance, whether her husband left his service revolver in the nursery. This goes on for years and years. As the child grows older, the mother's original major fear—that the child was exchanged for some other infant at the hospital—gives way to even more magnificent doubts and suspicions: she suspects that the child is not bright, she doubts that it will be happy, she is sure that it will become mixed up with the wrong sort of people.

The insistence of parents on dedicating their lives to their children is carried on year after year in the face of all that dogs have done, and are doing, to prove how much happier the parent-child relationship can become, if managed without sentiment, worry, or dedication. Of course, the theory that dogs have a saner family life than humans is an old one, and it was in order to ascertain whether the notion is pure legend or whether it is based on observable fact that I have for four years made a careful study of the family life of dogs. My conclusions entirely support the theory that dogs have a saner family life than people.

In the first place, the husband leaves on a woodchuck-hunting expedition just as soon as he can, which is very soon, and never comes back. He doesn't write, makes no provision for the care or maintenance of his family, and is not liable to prosecution because he doesn't. The wife doesn't care where he is, never wonders if he is thinking about her, and although she may start at the slightest footstep, doesn't do so because she is hoping against hope that it is he. No lady dog has ever been known to set her friends against her husband, or put detectives on his trail.

This same lack of sentimentality is carried out in the mother dog's relationship to her young. For six weeks—but only six weeks—she looks after them religiously, feeds them (they come clothed), washes their ears, fights off cats, old women, and wasps that come nosing around, makes the bed, and rescues the puppies when they crawl under the floor boards of the barn or get lost in an old boot. She does all these things, however, without fuss, without that loud and elaborate show of solicitude and alarm which a woman displays in rendering some exaggerated service to her child.

At the end of six weeks, the mother dog ceases to lie awake at night harking for ominous sounds; the next morning she snarls at the puppies after breakfast, and routs them all out of the house. "This is forever," she informs them, succinctly. "I have my own life to live, automobiles to chase, grocery boy's shoes to snap at, rabbits to pursue. I can't be washing and feeding a lot of big six-weeks-old dogs any longer. That phase is definitely over." The family life is thus terminated, and the mother dismisses the children from her mind—frequently as many as eleven at one time—as easily as she did her husband. She is now free to devote herself to her career and to the novel and astonishing things of life.

In the case of one family of dogs that I observed, the mother, a large black dog with long ears and a keen zest for living, tempered only by an immoderate fear of toads and turtles, kicked ten puppies out of the house at the end of six weeks to the day—it was a Monday. Fortunately for my observations, the puppies had no place to go, since they hadn't made any plans, and so they just hung around the barn, now and again trying to patch things up with their mother. She refused, however, to entertain any proposition leading to a resumption of home life, pointing out firmly that she was, by inclination, a chaser of bicycles and a hearth-fire watcher, both of which activities would be insupportably cluttered up by the presence of ten helpers. The bicycle-chasing field was overcrowded, anyway, she explained, and the hearth-fire-watching field even more so. "We could chase parades together," suggested one of the dogs, but she refused to be touched, snarled, and drove him off.

It is only for a few weeks that the cast-off puppies make overtures to their mother in regard to the re-establishment of a home. At the end of that time, by some natural miracle that I am unable clearly to understand, the puppies suddenly one day don't recognize their mother any more, and she doesn't recognize them. It is as if they had never met, and is a fine idea, giving both parties a clean break and a chance for a fresh start. Once, some months after this particular family had broken up and the pups had been sold, one of them, named Liza, was brought back to "the old nest" for a visit. The mother dog of course didn't recognize the puppy and promptly bit her in the hip. They had to be separated, each grumbling something about you never know what kind of dogs you're going to meet. Here was no silly, affecting reunion, no sentimental tears, no bitter intimations of neglect, or forgetfulness, or desertion.

If a pup is not sold or given away, but is brought up in the same household with its mother, the two will fight bitterly, sometimes twenty or thirty times a day, for maybe a month. This is very trying to whoever owns the dogs, particularly if they are sentimentalists who grieve because mother and child don't know each other. The condition finally clears up: the two dogs grow to tolerate each other and, beyond growling a little under their breath about how it takes all kinds of dogs to make up a world, get along fairly well together when their paths cross. I know of one mother dog and her half-grown daughter who sometimes spend the whole day together hunting woodchucks, although they don't speak. Their association is not sentimental, but practical, and is based on the fact that it is safer to hunt woodchucks in pairs than alone. These two dogs start out together in the morning, without a word, and come back together in the evening, when they part, without saying good night, whether they have had luck or not. Avoidance of farewells, which are always stuffy and sometimes painful, is another thing in which it seems to me dogs have better sense than people.

Well, one day the daughter, a dog about ten months old, seemed, by some prank of nature which again I am unable clearly to understand, for a moment or two to recognize her mother after all those months of oblivion. The two had just started out after a fat woodchuck who lives in the orchard. Something got wrong with the daughter's ear—a long, floppy ear. "Mother," she said, "I wish you'd look at my ear." Instantly the other dog bristled and growled. "I'm not your mother," she said, "I'm a woodchuck-hunter." The daughter grinned. "Well," she said, just to show there were no hard feelings, "that's not my ear, it's a motorman's glove."

PRACTICE. Now that you have read "A Preface to Dogs" and have seen how a professional uses observation to suggest ideas, create some controlling ideas of your own. Observe a pet or use the Thurber essay as inspiration. If you have difficulty starting, here are some examples. The opposite of each statement, of course, can also be a controlling idea.

> Children, like animals, are better off "out of the nest" at an early age.
> A good deal of parental concern is sentimental rather than real.

MOVING FROM A PERSON TO AN IDEA

Just as objects and animals can be the source of ideas, so can people.

A teacher

A teacher as a source of a dominant impression:

Mr. Le Blanc, my French teacher, acted as though he hated his job.

A teacher as a source of ideas:

Teachers should have specific training in the areas in which they teach.

Some effective teachers are formal and others are informal in their attitudes toward students.

The teacher's primary responsibility is to cause his students to examine their existing ideas.

Parents

Parents as a source of a dominant impression:

My mother looks like a mess in the morning.

Parents as a source of ideas:

Parents who give their children everything for which they ask are just begging for trouble.

Children learn more from how the parents act than from what the parents say.

Parents should be forced to take formal courses in how to rear children.

PRACTICE. Using the suggestions made in this chapter and calling upon your own experience, create five significant controlling ideas about people.

Writing Assignments

Just as you use specific details to make description more vivid and interesting, so you use specific examples to support your ideas.

1. Expand one of your controlling ideas about people into three or four paragraphs.
2. Look again at the painting facing page 15. Select one of your ideas suggested by it and develop it into three paragraphs.

PART TWO / *The Persuasive Essay*

CHAPTER SEVEN

Relationship of the Controlling Idea to the Essay

In the last section you saw that observing accurately and attempting to record these observations in detail gave you material about which to write. Asking yourself questions helped you to express yourself more fully, more specifically, and more interestingly. You saw also that even ordinary items can be the source of ideas and that these ideas, in turn, can become controlling ideas, the central points of essays.

The word *essay* means literally *to attempt*. When you write an essay, you are attempting to persuade the reader to your point of view. For this reason, it is absolutely essential that you know *what* your point of view is. Obviously, then, the controlling idea, which expresses your point of view, is the most important ingredient of the essay. It either begins the essay or comes very near to the beginning. Many students write poor essays because they do not understand what elements make a controlling idea effective. Essentially, *a controlling idea makes a statement about a subject.*
Here are some examples:

1. <u>Fishermen</u> <u>often destroy, carelessly or selfishly, natural resources that they want to use for pleasure.</u>

The writer has decided to write about fishermen. Fishermen, therefore, is the subject of this controlling idea. The remainder of the sentence is the statement that the writer is making about the subject, fishermen. The statement reflects the writer's point of view toward the subject.

2. Capital punishment is a remnant of times when men were uncivilized.

Capital punishment is the subject that the writer will discuss. The double lines indicate the statement about the subject. The statement expresses the writer's attitude toward the subject.

3. Informed young people should involve themselves in contemporary problems.

Informed young people is the subject. The remainder of the sentence states the writer's viewpoint toward the subject.

Since the controlling idea determines what will be developed, it should be clearly thought out before you begin to write. If the controlling idea is fuzzy or confused, inevitably the essay will be fuzzy and confused and will not convince the reader. Remember that the purpose of the essay is to persuade the reader to your point of view. You must try to convince him, in other words, that your point of view is the correct one. For this reason, the controlling idea must be as clear as possible. Here are some of the most common weaknesses in controlling ideas.

WEAKNESSES IN CONTROLLING IDEAS

You have already read a student essay developed from this controlling idea: Mother love is sometimes more harmful than helpful. Here are some other student attempts to formulate controlling ideas on the same general subject, mother love. They are not effective. An analysis of them follows to show why they are not.

1. *"Mother love"*

This group of words is not a sentence. It has a subject, but it makes no statement about the subject. It is a general subject for which you could construct countless controlling ideas, ranging from your own experiences of mother love to the significance of mother love in the social life of Fiji Islanders. Putting your thoughts into complete sentences forces you to think them through. *A controlling idea cannot be a fragment; it must be expressed as a sentence.*

2. *"Is mother love always helpful?"*

This is a question, not a statement. Once you ask a question you have to *answer* it before you will have an idea. Asking questions is the best way to arrive at a controlling idea, but a question cannot serve as a controlling idea. *A question cannot be a controlling idea.*

3. *"I think that mother love shapes the child's character."*

The subject of the idea is mother love. The statement about the subject is the remainder of the sentence. "I think" is unnecessary. If you make the statement, you obviously think it. The same holds true of "I believe," "In my opinion," and other expressions of this nature. *A controlling idea should not contain phrases such as "I think."*

4. *"Mother love harms children."*

This is known as a blanket statement because it allows for no exceptions. Is *all* mother love harmful? Are there different kinds of mother love? Is mother love *always* harmful? The more specifically you state the controlling idea, the easier it will be to develop it into an essay. *A controlling idea should not be a blanket statement.*

5. *"My mother loves me."*

This is a statement of opinion which is undoubtedly true, but most people's reaction would be—so what? While it is true that the sentence expresses an opinion, the statement about the subject has no significance for a reader. There is no attitude expressed toward the subject. *A controlling idea should not be too narrow.*

6. *"My mother is a secretary, and she loves me."*

This sentence contains two separate statements which have no apparent relationship. If you pursue your ideas further, you might be able to write a controlling idea which includes a meaningful relationship between the two. If not, you will have to choose one of the statements and then express an attitude toward it. *A controlling idea should not contain elements that are not clearly related.*

7. *"Mothers should be nice to their children."*

The word *nice* has been used in so many contexts that it has almost no meaning (a nice day, a nice dinner, a nice cow). You saw in the haiku section how a single word could create an image or pinpoint a meaning (the ant *compressed*). The same attention to single words, choosing them to express your meaning as specifically as possible, will make your controlling ideas clear and easy to develop. *A controlling idea should not be expressed in vague language*

8. *"When one thinks about mother love, the subconscious is on a different level."*

There is perhaps the germ of an idea here, but the sentence as it stands is meaningless. Not only are the relationships among "mother love," "subconscious," and "different level" muddy, bu also the meaning of the words "the subconscious is on a differen level" is totally obscure. *A controlling idea should not contai obscure or garbled language.*

Because the above attempts at controlling ideas are weak, essay developed from them will inevitably be ineffectual. Students wh write ineffective controlling ideas often do so because they are nc really sure in their own minds of what they want to say. They ofte have a feeling about a subject, but they have not thought it throug to the point where they can express their viewpoint in precis language. If you find yourself in this position, further thought an self-questioning will help you discover what you really think on given subject, and you will be able to express a controlling idea mor easily.

It is possible that even after reflection, you will find that yo still have no views. This is the time to do some reading. Clear an simple treatments on almost any subject can be found in newspaper magazines, and books. Your school library probably subscribes over one hundred periodicals. Acquaint yourself with these valuab resources. Learn to use the *Reader's Guide to Periodical Literatur* for it will help you to find articles quickly that will be useful to you.

ABSENCE OF A CONTROLLING IDEA

All of these attempts, even though they are weak, *are* attempts at a controlling idea. An even more serious problem for the student is the essay which contains no organizing principle. The reader is left completely bewildered as to what the writer's point is. Before you begin to write, you must crystallize in your own mind the central point you want to make, then write it down in clear and concise language. If you have difficulty putting your controlling idea on paper, you probably have not really thought it through.

The following student essay demonstrates the problems which arise when there is no controlling idea. Read the essay through first, and then read the comments on the right.

TEENAGE MARRIAGE

Do teenage marriages fail? As everyone knows, the divorce rate is rising rapidly. More than one out of every four marriages fail. This produces broken homes and sometimes delinquent children.

This student begins his essay with a question, and the reader, therefore, is waiting to find an answer to the question. The question, however, is never answered. If the subject of the essay is teenage marriage, the second sentence on rising divorce rate should be clearly related to teenage marriage. The rest of the first paragraph develops the problems of divorce in general and is not related specifically to teenage marriage. Most readers by now would expect an essay on the results of the rapidly rising divorce rate.

Today, because of automation, education is a must. If you want a better job, you must have an education. When a young man marries young, he is faced with new responsibilities and financial worries. How is he going to get an education?

The second paragraph introduces two more subjects, automation and education. Is teenage marriage, divorce, automation, or education the subject of the controlling idea?

If he feels that his marriage has prevented him from getting an education and, therefore, a better job, he and his wife will begin to quarrel. She becomes resentful that she has to stay home with the children, and things go from bad to worse.

Although quarreling is tc some extent related to education, which is discussed in the previous paragraph, it is unclear by now whether education or marriage is the topic under discussion.

Sometimes their in-laws live too close, and they must visit them regularly. For instance, Friday nights they have to visit her parents, and Sunday they visit his. Sometimes the parents take sides in arguments or continue to spoil their son or daughter. If people were more careful to avoid arguments, there would be fewer divorces.

The problem of in-laws ha nothing to do with education anc is, of course, related to teenage marriage. The concluding sentence, which should tie togethe all the elements of the essay i a statement about divorce in general, not about problems facing teenagers who marry.

This essay is not develope from one controlling idea, but is series of four paragraphs on fou different ideas that have nc been clearly related. The result confusion. The student has nc thought through his subject an therefore does not know what h controlling idea is.

The following student essay contains essentially the same idea found in the preceding one. In this essay, however, there is a clearl expressed controlling idea, which is in italics. Everything in the essa is tied to this controlling idea.

TEENAGE MARRIAGES MEAN TROUBLE

The rising divorce rate suggests that all marriages, even the most ide face such enormous problems that at least one fourth of them will end divorce. If difficulties confront couples who are emotionally and financial mature, consider the magnitude of the problems faced by teenagers, n yet grown up, and not yet financially independent. *Most teenage marriages end in divorce because the partners are immature.*

When two people agree to marry, they agree also to take on considerable financial responsibility. Bills for housing, food, clothing, medical care, transportation, and even seemingly minor items like cleaning must be paid. If the teenaged boy is already working at the time of his marriage, he is faced with two choices: he can continue working and thus end his educational opportunities, or he can send his wife to work.

If he decides to keep his job to maintain his home and wife, he is faced with the possibility of a dead end in his job or replacement by machines once automation is fully realized. In each case, his lack of education cuts off any of his plans for advancement. If, instead, he decides to continue his education and send his wife to work, other problems may arise. Either his wife becomes pregnant and cannot work, or she begins to resent her position of family provider while the so-called "breadwinner" is off at school.

Whatever the situation, emotional problems inevitably arise because of the conflicts between his need for further education and his obligation to finance the marriage. It is difficult enough for any human beings to live together without emotional tension. When teenagers marry, these normal tensions are compounded by the fact that teenagers are not yet emotionally mature. They are not yet fully aware of themselves or what they really want or expect of each other, and the result is disaster: quarrels, resentment, and hostility.

To add to the difficulties, friction between the husband and wife is frequently aggravated by parental interference. Married teenagers are often financially dependent upon one or both sets of parents. This circumstance is usually accompanied by a variety of strings, all constricting the independence of the newly married couple. More important, the teenager, because of his emotional immaturity, is often not yet free of parental influence. He is often in rebellion against his parents or is still tied strongly to them. In either case, they greatly influence his emotional life. When conflict arises between the teenaged married couple, as it does predictably between all married couples, both partners may be tempted to hurl at each other insults which involve parental relationships. Since their loyalties to their parents are still firmly entrenched, and since they are still financially and emotionally dependent, they cannot cope with the hostilities and tensions which arise. Add these tensions to the other problems of education and finance, and it is not surprising that so many teenage marriages end in divorce.

SUMMARY

A controlling idea is composed of a subject and a statement about the subject. The statement about the subject reflects the writer's attitude. It is this attitude that the writer is trying to persuade the reader to believe. Since the purpose of the essay is to persuade, the controlling idea must be carefully thought out and clearly expressed. The writer then selects those ideas and examples which develop his point as expressed in the controlling idea and rejects those that are irrelevant.

PRACTICE. The following are poor controlling ideas. Analyze thei weaknesses in terms of the previous discussion.

1. Poor students tend to blame their teachers for their failures, anc they get the lowest-paying jobs.
2. A feeling to look toward a certain person who is famous has attrib uted to many fine and prominent figures of our society.
3. When reporters are sent to foreign countries to cover the new for their hometown readers.
4. The police are looking for Humphrey Nottingham, who droppe out of high school last year.
5. Education should train all young people for jobs.
6. In my opinion, I think that the population explosion is the greates problem facing the modern world.
7. The law regarding traffic offenders should be changed.
8. Mr. Farthingale, who has owned the small corner grocery store fo twenty years, has had to go out of business.
9. Since the Negro won his freedom in 1863, is it any wonder that he impatient with his conditions today?
10. The American way of life is the best.

Writing Assignments

1. Write an essay expressing your view about parental love. Be sure you *write dow* a clear controlling idea *before* you begin to write the essay.
2. What do you think accounts for the failure of some marriages and the survival others? Write an essay expressing your views. Be sure that you *write down* a cle controlling idea *before* you begin to write.
3. What is the most pressing problem facing the youth of today? Write an essay e pressing your views. Be sure that you *write down* a clear controlling idea *befo* you begin to write.

HAPTER EIGHT

The Essay: The Relationship of the Topic Sentence o the Essay

PEAKING AND WRITING

lmost everyone, in the course of a single day, expresses a number f opinions. Sometimes the opinion is so trivial that it dies without omment as soon as it has been uttered. More often, however, the peaker volunteers reasons to *support* his opinion, since most people wish to have their opinions thought valid. Or, if the speaker oes not volunteer support for his views, his friends will ask him *hy* he believes as he does. Occasionally, much to the speaker's mbarrassment, he finds that he has actually no basis at all for his pinion; it was just there. It was not arrived at because of any ought, and so it was uttered without any thought. When this happens, most people feel extremely foolish and, wishing that they had me support for their views, fall back on a feeble defense: "Well, don't know *why* I think that way. I just do."

Almost everyone finds himself in this situation at one time or nother. The intelligent person learns to take steps to avoid feeling e a fool again. First, he attempts to analyze his own opinions to scover whether they *can* be supported or whether they are simply hoes of what he has heard around him for years and has never thered to question. Second, he reads to obtain information. And ird, on the basis of analysis and reading, he either justifies his iginal opinions, or he changes them to agree with what he has learned. His discovery of the facts sometimes causes him to alter his viewpoint completely.

The unintelligent person, on the other hand, resorts to anger or resentment to cover his embarrassment. Finding that he cannot support his position, he repeats his original opinion more loudly or he changes the subject or he withdraws into silence.

The writer, unlike the speaker, cannot shout the reader down or change the subject or lapse into silence. Once he has committed his opinion to paper, he *must* support his views. He cannot use the force of his personality to persuade the reader. Obviously, the more convincing his support, the more easily he can persuade his reader that his opinion is valid.

In writing, support for the controlling idea takes the form of topic sentences and their development into paragraphs.

THE TOPIC SENTENCE

You have already been asked to develop controlling ideas, but no attempt has been made, so far, to discuss the form that this development should take. Undoubtedly, however, you have made some kind of divisions in your writing. Formally, as you know, such divisions are called paragraphs.

Each paragraph is the development of ONE supporting point. This central point of the paragraph is called the *topic sentence.* Just as the controlling idea is the central point of the entire essay, the topic sentence is the central point of the paragraph. The topic sentence should be examined in the same way that you examined the controlling idea.

Although the topic sentence may appear anywhere in the paragraph, it usually appears near the beginning. Many writers find paragraph development easier if the topic sentence is the first sentence. No matter where you place the topic sentence, however, it determines what will be included in the paragraph. Again, the topic sentence is to the paragraph what the controlling idea is to the essay.

You have already seen how a weak controlling idea or th

absence of a controlling idea results in chaotic or, at best, confusing writing. After you have the controlling idea clearly in mind, the next step is to think through the *supporting points* of your controlling idea. If the topic sentences are not effective, the essay will be weak and unconvincing in spite of your clear controlling idea. Topic sentences are vital elements of a persuasive essay.

Assume that your assignment is to write an essay of at least three paragraphs. How do you arrive at a minimum of three topic sentences? One way is to ask questions about the controlling idea. The most useful questions to ask are WHY and HOW. Here are some applications of this method.

Ask **WHY?**

1/

Controlling idea: Everyone should have a room in which he can be alone.

Question: **Why** should everyone have a room in which to be alone? *(Write down the answers as they occur to you. Your answers may be the topic sentences for your essay. Here are some possibilities.)*

Topic sentences:

Solitude helps one to concentrate on his personal problems.

Most people study more efficiently in private than with others around.

Occasionally everyone needs to escape from the stress of being with others.

2/

Controlling idea: Children are better off "out of the nest" at an early age.

Question: **Why** are children better off "out of the nest" at an early age?

Topic sentences:

They learn to make decisions for themselves.

They learn how to handle money.

They develop their own personalities, instead of mirroring their parents'.

3/

Controlling idea: Capital punishment should be abolished.

Question: **Why** should capital punishment be abolished?

Topic sentences:

Capital punishment is not a deterrent to crime.

The innocent are sometimes executed.

Capital punishment is not meted out equally to the rich and the poor.

Capital punishment is legalized killing.

Ask **HOW?**

1/

Controlling idea: Fishermen and hunters often destroy the natural resources that they rely upon for their sport.

Question: **How** do fishermen and hunters destroy the natural resources that they rely upon for their sport?

Topic sentences:

Fishermen and hunters sometimes dispose of their garbage and tin cans in rivers and lakes.

Through carelessness, they cause forest fires.

Irresponsible sportsmen try to outsmart the fish and game wardens in any way they can.

2/

Controlling idea: Both early adolescents and the middle-aged try to cheat time, but in opposite ways.

Question: **How** do early adolescents and the middle-aged try to cheat time?

Topic sentences:

Adolescents often start drinking and smoking in imitation of their elders.

Thirteen- and fourteen-year-olds copy the styles of college students.

The middle-aged also adopt college fashions.

Older men and women dye their hair or wear wigs to give an illusion of youth.

3/

Controlling idea: A personal letter sometimes reveals more about the writer than he intends.

Question: **How** does a personal letter reveal more about the writer than he intends?

Topic sentences:

The style and appearance of the paper and envelope are indicative of the writer's personality.

The handwriting itself is revealing.

The grammar, spelling, and sentence structure tell a great deal about the writer.

The contents of the letter suggest the writer's sense of values.

Some controlling ideas can be supported by asking **WHY** and some by asking **HOW.** Quite often, however, you will find that your controlling idea lends itself to division into topic sentences as a result of your asking *both* **WHY** and **HOW.**

Controlling idea: American colleges and universities are being attacked by many segments of society.

1/

Question: **Why** are American colleges and universities being attacked by many segments of society?

Topic sentences:

Many outside the educational system blame the colleges for campus dissenters.

Some students demand instant change.

Colleges and universities are often used as scapegoats for the nation's problems.

2/

Question: **How** are American colleges and universities being attacked by many segments of society?

Topic sentences:

Public officials are cutting educational budgets.

Certain student groups are destroying school property and disrupting classes.

The tradition of academic freedom, vital to the educational process, is being eroded.

If your questions result in more topic sentences than you need for your essay, select those which seem to support your controlling idea most effectively.

PRACTICE

1. Support the following controlling ideas with at least three topic sentences. Ask yourself the questions WHY and HOW.

a. Most college students conform to their own peer groups.

b. Friction between generations occurs generally because of a lack of communication.

c. College is much more challenging than high school.
d. Young people should date as much as possible before they choose mates.
e. The threat of atomic war has had an effect upon the attitudes of many people.

2. Read Anne Nichols' essay "Don't Sell Slang Short" on p. 157. Underline all the topic sentences.

Writing Assignments

1. Write an essay in which you discuss the use of natural resources by fishermen and hunters. Be sure that you write a clear controlling idea and at least three or four topic sentences *before* you begin to write the essay.
2. In an essay, discuss what you see as the greatest threat to the American college and university system. Be sure that you write a clear controlling idea and at least three or four topic sentences *before* you begin to write the essay.
3. If you could change one law, local, state, or national, which would it be? Write an essay in which you explain your reasons. Be sure that you write a clear controlling idea and at least three or four topic sentences *before* you begin to write the essay.

CHAPTER NINE

Development of the Paragraph

Once you have decided upon a controlling idea and have divided it into topic sentences, the next step is to develop each of these topic sentences into an effective paragraph. At this point, it may be helpful to examine the two most common weaknesses that appear in student paragraphs.

WEAKNESSES IN PARAGRAPH DEVELOPMENT

REPETITION

Sometimes students are at a loss as to how to develop their topic sentences. As a result, they make the same point over and over again, using slightly different language each time.

Here is an example of such a repetition of the topic sentence. Notice how this student simply restates one idea.

> *Controlling idea:* Eighteen- and nineteen-year-olds should be allowed to live away from home.
>
> *Topic sentence:* They learn to make decisions for themselves.
>
> *Paragraph:* If young people live away from home, *they learn to make decisions for themselves.* When a problem arises, they have to decide what to do. The problem may be big or small, but they alone must make the decisions. Every day they must make some kind of choice. Without fail, something crops up daily which they must make judgments about without any help from others. Thus, they learn to make their own decisions.

GENERALIZATIONS WITHOUT SUPPORT

Another common weakness in student essays is vagueness. If each paragraph contains only generalizations without any support, the writer does not succeed in convincing the reader of the point he is trying to make. Generalizations are ideas. It is not enough merely to present the reader with ideas. If the reader is to be persuaded, the ideas must be supported by specific details and examples.

The following is another student attempt to develop the topic sentence given above. This student uses only generalizations without specific support.

> If young people move away from home, *they learn to make decisions for themselves.* When they live alone, there are no older or more experienced persons to whom to turn. They must rely solely upon their own judgment. In the process, they become aware of their strengths and weaknesses, and they also learn the consequences of certain kinds of behavior. Making decisions helps people to mature.

This paragraph reads more smoothly than the previous one. The reader, however, does not know *exactly* what the writer has in mind. For instance, "certain kinds of behavior" could refer to spending money unwisely, staying out all night, or breaking traffic laws; it could also refer to saving money, planning leisure time wisely, or volunteering for YMCA work. What the writer means by "consequences" is equally unclear. The points in the paragraph could be made significant if the generalizations were supported by specific examples. Then the writer's points would be clearer, and the reader would be able to follow his line of reasoning more easily. If the reader is to be persuaded that the writer's statements are valid, the writer must keep the reader tuned to his way of thinking as closely as possible. *The writer must, therefore, support his generalizations by specific examples.*

BASIC TECHNIQUES FOR PARAGRAPH DEVELOPMENT

One of the most productive techniques for paragraph development is to ask yourself questions about the topic sentence. Your answers will provide you with both generalizations and specific examples. Most important, the questioning will help you to be *specific* in your development of the paragraph. The following are questions which are particularly productive: **how? why? where? who? what? when? in what way? examples from your own experience? examples from your reading?**

The answers you choose for your paragraph should relate to both the topic sentence *and* the controlling idea. *Each sentence in the entire essay must in some way develop the main idea of the essay, the controlling idea.* Not all of the suggested questions will produce answers that are helpful, but if you acquire the habit of asking them, you will find that you will have sufficient support for your topic sentences.

The following is a sample of the procedure to use in developing a paragraph. The topic sentence that will be expanded is the same one that was developed inadequately at the beginning of this chapter.

> *Controlling idea:* Eighteen- and nineteen-year-olds should be allowed to live away from home.
>
> *Topic sentences:*
> They learn to make decisions for themselves.
> They learn how to handle money.
> They develop their own personalities.

Always keep in mind the controlling idea as you formulate the answers.

WHY?
Why do they learn to make decisions for themselves?
Answer: There is no one to tell them what to do.

Helpful: This answer is helpful because it expands the topic sentence.

HOW?
How do they learn to make decisions for themselves?
Answer: They learn to make decisions for themselves by making decisions for themselves.

Not Helpful: For this particular topic sentence, the question "how" produces a repetition of the topic sentence and is, therefore, not helpful. Go on to the next question.

WHERE?

Where do they learn to make decisions for themselves?

Answer: They learn to make decisions for themselves in their apartments, in the supermarkets, at the cleaners. — *Helpful*

WHO?

Who learns to make decisions for themselves?

Answer: Eighteen- and nineteen-year-olds who live alone learn to make decisions for themselves. — *Not helpful*

WHAT?

What decisions do they learn to make for themselves?

Answer: They have to decide whether to rearrange the furniture, where and when to buy food, and how to take care of their clothing. — *Helpful*

WHEN?

When do they learn to make decisions for themselves?

Answer: Every time they are faced with a problem, they must make decisions. — *Helpful*

IN WHAT WAY?

In what way do they learn to make decisions?

Answer: If, when shopping for food the first few times, they buy only exotic items, they soon discover that there are no eggs for breakfast and no milk to drink during the day. The next time, they will buy essentials first. — *Helpful*

EXAMPLES FROM PERSONAL EXPERIENCE?

What examples can you give from your personal experience to support the statement that young

people living away from home learn to make decisions for themselves?	
Answer: All of the helpful answers given above are based upon personal experience.	*Helpful*

EXAMPLES FROM READING?

What examples can you give from your reading to support the statement that young people living away from home learn to make decisions for themselves?	
Answer: One of the most famous examples of someone who was forced to make decisions for himself, and thereby survived, is the hero of *Robinson Crusoe* by Daniel Defoe.	*Helpful*

These are just a few of the answers that this questioning could elicit. As you go through the questioning process, write down the helpful answers in complete sentence form. Do not include in the final paragraph any irrelevant ideas or details that popped into your mind as you used the questioning technique.

Once you have written down your answers, you will have, at the very least, a skeleton paragraph. Check the sentences carefully to be certain that they are related to the topic sentence. Now check again to be sure that the sentences *support the controlling idea.* Then rearrange them, if necessary, into a more logical order. As you think about your answers, other examples and supporting details may occur to you. Fit these in where they are clearly related.

The following paragraph is developed from answers found by asking the preceding questions. Seven of the nine questions proved to be helpful. In addition, the original answers suggested other details that help support the topic sentence.

> If young people live alone, *they learn to make decisions for themselves.* When a young person first moves away from home, he is often surprised at the number of decisions involved in the simplest acts of living. He discovers that functions he previously took for granted, like eating, require many choices long before the actual meal. Now he,

not his mother or someone else, has to decide what food will be eaten, what items will go on the shopping list, what amount of money will be spent, and, finally, how best to prepare the food. Even the minor matter of laundry requires decisions. Shirts and socks, he learns, do not wash themselves. No longer can he allow himself the luxury of being dependent upon someone else. Like Robinson Crusoe, he must make decisions for himself. In the process, of course, some foolish decisions are inevitable. Perhaps in the first flush of freedom he will spend too much on exotic food items and too little on essentials, but he learns through his mistakes. He soon finds out that all behavior has consequences and wise decisions help make life easier for himself and those around him.

PRACTICE

1. Enlarge the second topic sentence on page 53: "They learn how to handle money." As you expand this topic sentence, ask yourself the same questions used to develop the first topic sentence. *Be specific* in your support.

2. Write a paragraph based on the third topic sentence on page 53: "They develop their own personalities." *Be specific.*

Writing Assignments

1. Develop into a paragraph the topic sentence "They (eighteen- and nineteen-year-olds) learn to make decisions for themselves," developed from the controlling idea, on p. 53. Remember that somewhere in the paragraph you should relate what you are writing to the original controlling idea.
2. Write a complete essay based upon the following outline.
   Controlling idea: Many young people choose unsuitable vocations.
   Topic sentences:
   An adolescent often bases his choice of career upon his admiration for some adult.
   Parents sometimes push young people into unsuitable professions.
   Many young people decide upon a vocation solely because of the money they hope to make.
   Frequently, a young person makes his choice because of the social prestige which is attached to certain occupations.
3. Make an outline, on a topic of your choice, similar to the one in assignment 2. Develop the outline into an essay.

CHAPTER TEN

Introductions, Conclusions, Transitions, and Titles

THE INTRODUCTION

The introduction to an essay is like the label on a can. Just as the label attracts the eye and gives some indication of the contents of the can, the introduction to an essay engages the interest of the reader and establishes the general area of discussion. In other words, the introduction serves to set the stage for the discussion which will follow. The controlling idea normally comes at the end of the introductory section; therefore, the introduction must lead logically and smoothly into the controlling idea of the essay.

The length of the introduction depends upon the length of the essay. If the body of the essay contains only three or four paragraphs, the introduction should be no longer than one paragraph. In some instances, the introduction may consist of just one or two sentences which appear at the beginning of the first paragraph.

Introductions may take almost unlimited forms. The following are among the most common kinds:

Personal experience: The writer begins his essay by drawing upon an experience of his own that is related to his main point.

Anecdote: The writer relates to his main idea some short incident involving a famous or infamous person.

General background: The writer starts with one or more sentences containing general information which is related to the controlling idea.

Statistics: The writer uses significant or shocking figures which are related to the controlling idea.

Quotation: The writer uses a relevant quotation to lead into his main idea.

Question: The writer uses a question to prepare the reader for the controlling idea of the essay.

Straw man: The writer starts by presenting the chief argument *against* his controlling idea, points out the main weakness of this argument, and then states the controlling idea of the essay.

EXAMPLES

As examples of the variety of ways in which a topic may be introduced, here is the same controlling idea preceded by each kind of introduction listed above.

> *Controlling idea:* Television commercials should be shorter than they are and less frequent.
>
> PERSONAL EXPERIENCE
> When my aunt from England visited us last month, she was appalled by the commercials that interrupted, at practically every high point, the movie or program we were watching. She claimed that British television, with its absence of commercials, is infinitely superior to American television with its constant interruptions. I do not know whether British programs are better than ours, but I certainly agree with her about our annoying commercials. *Television commercials should be shorter than they are and less frequent.*
>
> ANECDOTE
> John Passmore, the movie idol of the twenties, whose pictures are currently being seen on the late, late show on television, was asked recently what he thought of the "new" medium. In a voice which seems to have lost none of its dramatic effect, he thundered, "Sir, any medium in which great acting has to compete for honors with bilious stomachs and dingy laundry can't have much of a future!" Well, there is no question that television is here to stay, but *commercials should certainly be made shorter and less frequent.*
>
> GENERAL BACKGROUND
> Television in America is a money-making enterprise, a fact which is accepted by most Americans as proper. However, when the profit motive makes serious inroads into the entertainment role of television, it is time to make some changes. Producers should give television back to the public by *making the commercials shorter than they are presently and less frequent.*

STATISTICS
The Peary Morning Call recently conducted a poll to discover the most common complaint about television. The results revealed that a whopping 83.6% of the local viewers resented the commercials, which they said interfered unreasonably with the programs. This report reflects the generally held view that *television commercials should be shorter and less frequent.*

QUOTATION
Gilbert and Sullivan's lines from *The Mikado,*

> I've got a little list—I've got a little list
> Of society offenders who might well be underground
> And who never would be missed—who never would be missed

might well be applied to today's television producers and their commercials. Few television watchers would miss the frequent and lengthy appearance of tired used-car salesmen, housewives unhappy with grey laundry, or chronic sufferers of intestinal disorders. There is no question but that *television commercials should be shorter than they are and less frequent.*

QUESTION
Who has not complained about the number and length of television commercials? Television audiences have good reason to do so. If a viewer tunes in to a Sophia Loren movie, he stands a good chance of seeing garrulous ladies comparing laundry as often as he sees Miss Loren. It is high time that *television commercials were made shorter and less frequent.*

STRAW MAN
Advertising executives maintain that the television commercials do not in any way diminish the entertainment value of the programs seen on television. This claim contradicts the experience of almost everyone who has ever watched a dramatic program, only to be wrenched from the mood by a soap or deodorant advertisement. The commercials occur so often and are so overpowering that the viewer often loses the thread of the story. Constant interruptions cannot help but spoil a program. *Television commercials should be made shorter than they are at present and less frequent.*

Other methods of introducing an essay will probably occur to you. If, however, you experience some difficulty thinking of a way to start your essay, plunge right into the controlling idea and develop it. By the time you have finished writing the first draft, an idea for an introduction will probably come to you. Then you can add it to your essay, making sure, of course, that it leads sensibly into the controlling idea.

THE CONCLUSION

Every essay, short or long, needs some kind of ending. Professional writers often conclude long essays with a brief summary; a short essay, however, should not be summarized. If the essay is from 300 to 500 words, the points the writer has made are still fresh in the reader's mind, and repetition of these points would not only be unnecessary, but boring as well. A conclusion to a short essay does serve to remind the reader of the central point of the essay, but care must be taken that the language of the conclusion is not exactly the same as that of the controlling idea.

Most writers conclude short essays with from one to three sentences. These are either added to the last paragraph developed from a topic sentence or organized into a separate paragraph.

For the most part, conclusions take one of two forms: they serve to remind the reader of the main idea, or they relate the main idea of the essay to the future.

Suppose that you have written a persuasive essay in which you maintain that continued pollution of our waters by industrial wastes should not be allowed any longer. The conclusion of your essay could be modelled upon one of the two suggestions given above. Thus:

> Pollution of our waters must cease.

or

> If water pollution is not stopped, it is quite possible that future generations will have little or no drinking water.

It must always be remembered that the last sentence of the paragraph developed from a topic sentence probably cannot serve as the conclusion. Usually, at least one more sentence is necessary to tie the threads of the essay together.

TRANSITIONS

The primary purpose of writing is communication. Once the writer knows what he wants to say, the most important way that he helps the reader follow his train of thought is by careful and logical development of his ideas. In addition, he may incorporate certain words and phrases to effect transition from sentence to sentence and from paragraph to paragraph. Just as a public transit system takes a rider from one place to another, so transitional words and phrases serve to take the reader from one point in the essay to another.

There are three techniques the writer uses to make transitions: **transitional words and phrases; repetition of a word, phrase, or idea;** and **pronoun reference.**

WORDS AND PHRASES

The second pair of sentences here reads much more smoothly because a transitional word is inserted.

> Paris is still the center of the fashion world. London styles are beginning to compete in popularity.
>
> Paris is still the center of the fashion world. However, London styles are beginning to compete in popularity.

Because transitional words and phrases show relationships, they must be used carefully. The word chosen must clearly point up the relationship the writer has in mind. If, for example, the writer's purpose is to *add* a point or an idea to the previous sentence, he would not use *nevertheless;* he might use *in addition* or *also* or *furthermore.* As an illustration, the following pairs of sentences express totally different relationships.

> Mr. Toby hates fish. Nevertheless, his wife serves it at least twice a week.
>
> Mr. Toby hates fish. Furthermore, he hates meat, poultry, vegetables, and children.

The following list contains words and phrases which are among those most frequently used by writers to effect transitions:

therefore	later	in fact
thus	at last	incidentally
consequently	finally	for example
indeed	in short	for instance
actually	however	furthermore
similarly	nevertheless	also

then	on the contrary	too
now	on the other hand	in addition

REPETITION

By word or phrase. Transition by means of repetition takes several forms. Sometimes the writer repeats in the new sentence a key word or phrase he has just used in the previous sentence, as seen in the following sentences:

> One of the solutions to the problems now faced by large cities is *slum clearance.* Although it is not the total answer, *slum clearance* is a necessary first step.

By synonym. Instead of repeating the exact key word or phrase, the writer may choose to use a synonym.

> One of the solutions to the problems now faced by large cities is *slum clearance.* Although it is not the total answer, *rehabilitation of blighted areas* is a necessary first step.

By restatement of idea. Occasionally, especially between paragraphs, the writer may make his transition by restating an important idea that he has just considered. If, for example, the writer has just devoted an entire paragraph to a discussion of the ways to solve the problems faced by modern cities, he might begin his next paragraph by using a synonym for his entire previous discussion.

> *Urban renewal* (simply another way the writer is expressing the main idea of his previous paragraph) may not be easy, but it can work.

PRONOUN REFERENCE

A third technique for making transitions from one point to another or from one sentence to another is the use of pronouns.

> Medical researchers seek new discoveries in the treatment of human diseases by *experimenting upon animals. This practice* is called inhumane by antivivisectionists.
>
> Vivisection is defended by most *doctors. They* claim that the practice is necessary if medicine is to make inroads upon human disease.

Special care must be taken when pronouns are used as transitions. The pronoun must be as close as possible to the noun or nouns to which it refers. Since the purpose of the transition is to aid the reader in following the writer's trend of thought, the writer must be especially careful that he does not confuse the reader by vague or unclear pronoun references. If the pronoun reference is at all questionable, it is better to repeat the key word or substitute a synonym instead of using a pronoun.

IMPORTANT POSITIONS FOR TRANSITIONS

Use transitions wherever they contribute to the clarity or smoothness of writing. There are some places in an essay, however, where the absence of transitions may cause the essay to be especially disjointed. Special attention should be paid to the following places: (1) movement from the introduction to the controlling idea, (2) movement from the controlling idea to the first topic sentence, (3) movement from paragraph to paragraph, and (4) movement from the last sentence of the last major division to the conclusion.

Experiment with transitions. Skillful use of transitional devices will contribute to the clarity of your writing.

THE TITLE

Titles may be imaginative or prosaic. Some people have a gift for creating titles, but if you are not among the gifted, do not be disturbed. So long as your title reflects the main idea of your essay, it will be adequate.

Every essay must have a title. The title may be a word, a phrase, or even a sentence, although sentence titles are somewhat cumbersome. Most writers prefer to make their titles short. However, there is as much variety in the kinds of titles as there is in styles of writing. The only requirement to keep in mind is that the title suggest the main idea of the essay.

An examination of the controlling idea will probably suggest several possibilities. Consider the following idea and the suggested titles based upon it.

Controlling Idea: Widespread use of the birth control pill eliminated some problems and created others.

Possible Titles
To Use or Not to Use
The Use of the Birth Control Pill
The Birth Control Pill: Boon or Bane
Is Use of the Pill Wisdom or Folly?
The Birth Control Pill and Sexual Mores

PRACTICE

1. Using the kinds of introductions suggested in this chapter, write as many introductions as you can for the following controlling idea. Be sure that your introduction leads logically into the main idea. If necessary, change the controlling idea slightly to make the transition smooth.

Controlling Idea: Many people judge a person by the clothing he wears.

2. Underline the transitional devices in the following sentences:

It was discovered accidentally that lime juice cured scurvy. Thus, life became easier for British sailors.

Mrs. Snark tried to contact her doctor and lawyer. The latter was out of town.

Many scientists believe that their only obligation is to discover truth. The layman, however, believes that the scientist has a moral obligation to his fellow men.

A friend showed me an amusing picture. It could have been taken during the flapper era; on the other hand, it could have been a photo of some modern styles.

3. Underline all the transitional devices you can detect in a newspaper editorial.

Writing Assignment

Write an essay on a subject about which you feel very strongly. Be sure that your controlling idea and topic sentences are clearly expressed. Include a title, an introduction, transitions, and a conclusion.

CHAPTER ELEVEN

Definition

English is an enormously rich language. The English vocabulary is so large and so varied that even the most delicate shadings in meaning can be expressed. There would seem to be no reason, then, why people do not understand what a speaker or writer has in mind when he attempts to communicate. Probably everyone reading this page, however, has had the experience of being involved in or hearing a heated argument which came to a sudden and amicable end when one of the arguers said, "Oh, is *that* what you meant! Why didn't you say so in the first place?"

Of course, clarification of the issue does not always bring about agreement, but once the issue has been clarified, at least it can be discussed more intelligently. Most spoken arguments become clarified as the result of questions: "What do you mean by that?" "Why?" "How?" In this case, the speaker has an advantage over the writer. When the writer presents an argument—and an essay is essentially an argument in support of a position—he has no opportunity to learn if the reader really understands what he is writing. Even more of a problem, the reader has no opportunity to ask questions of the writer. If the writer uses terms that are unclear or ambiguous, they remain unclear or ambiguous to the reader. The writer is not there to answer questions. Only the words he has already written are there.

There are many reasons why people fail to express themselves clearly. In writing, however, one of the most frequent causes of misunderstanding is the writer's failure to define terms that are capable of several interpretations.

CONCRETE NOUNS

Some words, like rose, table, or Uncle Smedley, are concrete. They refer to that which can be smelled, touched, seen, heard, or felt. Concrete words refer to everything in the environment to which any or all of the five senses can respond. These words rarely cause difficulty in communication.

ABSTRACT NOUNS

Another group, however, can cause considerable misunderstanding. This group refers to that which *cannot* be responded to by any of the five senses. Words, such as faith, hope, liberty, and justice are abstract nouns. They refer to ideas, qualities, ideals, theories, and so on. Because there is nothing *concrete* to which they refer, they usually have different meanings for different people. If a writer uses a word that is capable of several different interpretations and fails to define what *he* means by the word, he has failed to communicate to his reader.

For instance, *faith* to one reader may mean going to church every Sunday and scrupulously following the prescribed tenets of his religion. To another reader, *faith* may mean a belief in a Supreme Being. *Faith* to a third reader may mean a belief in the infallibility of the scientific method. It is possible that the writer may have had in mind still a fourth interpretation of the word *faith*. He may have meant by it that good inevitably will triumph over evil.

In this case, communication is impossible between the writer and his readers. Once communication has broken down, the writer has failed in his primary purpose—persuading the reader to his point of view. For this reason, it is essential that the writer define all terms which are capable of more than one interpretation.

DENOTATION AND CONNOTATION

Some words are capable of being understood in two different ways. One way of defining a word is denotatively, that is, the literal or dictionary definition. Other words have accumulated emotional associations; these emotional associations are called "connotations." The dictionary, for instance, says that *mother-in-law* refers to the female parent of either spouse. That is the denotation or the literal meaning of the term *mother-in-law.* The term *mother-in-law* has in addition, however, many emotional associations. For example, *mother-in-law* suggests nagging, possessiveness, and interference. Your own personal experience with mothers-in-law may be in fact very pleasant, but when you write, keep in mind that the word is loaded with negative emotional overtones, or connotations.

Sometimes words which refer to the same thing have totally different effects. For example, the dictionary or denotative definitions of *house* and *home* are essentially the same, but the word *home* has connotations which *house* does not have. *Home* implies warmth, security, and loved ones, while *house* merely suggests the image of a structure.

Adjectives, too, take on associations. If you call someone *fat,* you are asking for trouble, but if you refer to the same person as *plump,* you may get away with it. *Skinny* and *thin* create similar reactions. Think of the different reactions a person will have if you call him *thrifty* one day and *stingy* the next.

Some words differ only slightly in denotation but create very different effects in their connotations. Such pairs of words as *lady* and *woman, politician* and *statesman, opponent* and *enemy* have al-

HENRI CARTIER-BRESSON *"Cape Cod, Massachusetts, 1947. It was the Fourth of July and this woman explained to me that the flagpole over her door was broken but 'on such a day as this, one keeps one's flag over one's heart.' In her I felt a touch of the strength and robustness of the early American pioneers."*

FLAG *A piece of cloth, varying in design, usually attached at one edge to a staff or a cord, and used as a symbol of a nation, state, or organization.*

CAUSE OF ARREST *Yippie Abbie Hoffman is stopped by police as he arrived on the Capitol grounds wearing a shirt of flag design October 3 for a hearing of the House Un-American Activities Committee. Hoffman was arrested and charged with mutilating the American flag.*

Courtesy of Wide World Photos

most identical denotations or definitions; but they must be used thoughtfully because of the force of their connotations. It is important to select each word with care. It is also important to remember that abstract nouns cannot be defined denotatively, and, therefore, their connotations must be particularly kept in mind. There is no question but that the connotations words carry will, in part, determine your selection. The careful writer, then, makes use of the connotations of words to get the results he desires from his readers.

EMOTIVE LANGUAGE

Sometimes, as in the following paragraph from *The Fall of the House of Usher* by Edgar Allan Poe, a writer will deliberately use words that are intensely connotative in order to create a mood or elicit a particular reaction from the reader. Or he may select words that are inherently emotional in meaning.

> During the whole of a dull, dark, and soundless day in the autumn of the year, when the clouds hung oppressively low in the heavens, I had been passing alone, on horseback, through a singularly dreary tract of country, and at length found myself, as the shades of the evening drew on, within view of the melancholy House of Usher. I know not how it was—but, with the first glimpse of the building, a sense of insufferable gloom pervaded my spirit.

Now read "Saint Martin?" by George S. Schuyler, following, and underline those words that are emotionally charged.

George S. Schuyler / SAINT MARTIN?

The frantic drive to lift the late Dr. Martin Luther King Jr. to saintly status proceeds apace. The whole spectacle would have delighted old Anatole France and provided abundant supplementary material for a sequel to

"Saint Martin?" first appeared in the January 1970 issue of *American Opinion* (Belmont, Massachusetts 02178) and is reproduced here by permission of the publisher.

Penguin Island in which, it will be recalled, bandits and rogues in the course of time became national heroes.

As George Washington, Thomas Jefferson, and Abraham Lincoln whirled in their graves, King achieved in death a national memorial day with flags at halfmast throughout the American empire, and every politician of note trooping to his funeral in Atlanta weeping crocodile tears. While they knelt in prayer at the King bier, vandalistic blacks put a hundred cities to torch.

Before the smoke of the bonfires subsided, there came impudent demands from militant Marxists that every conceivable public building, highway, airport, and school building be named for the Atlanta preacher who had led a dozen half-wit mobs against public order and had secured financial backing from both the "white power structure" and the Communists to operate revolutionary schools to train his subordinates for the bedevilment of sundry communities.

It was only shortly after an assassin's bullet relieved the country of King's presence that his long-planned march on Washington, to plant in its center a hobo city, was led by his lieutenant Ralph D. Abernathy. Ralph resided the while in a comfortable motel as his dupes wallowed in the bog of Resurrection City. Yet this disgraceful performance was at government expense, even to the feeding of the mules who "marched" to Washington on railroad flatcars.

The King-Abernathy mob didn't quite get around to burning down the White House as had the British in the War of 1812, but they came close to it.

Nobody would have believed such an outrage could occur had there not been so many witnesses, including President Lyndon Johnson who peered gloomily at the wreckage from his front window, while his Attorney General cautioned the police and militia to treat the ruffians gently and respect their Constitutional right to rob, burn, and rape.

Incredulity soared when a few weeks ago a front-page headline in the *New York Times* declared: "King Family Halting Talks With Nixon For Memorial." The public had not known that any such talks were going on between the Nixon Administration and the King family for a giant King memorial in Atlanta! The talks were abandoned it seems "because of what the Kings say is Mr. Nixon's 'indifferent attitude' toward the black and poor people." Mrs. Coretta Scott King, the widow—and a violent, rampaging copperhead in her own right—said that "Mr. Nixon at one point had encouraged the project, but that the idea collapsed . . . after seven months of unpublicized negotiations." It had been rather like meeting secretly with the Vietcong.

Dolefully, Hanoi Coretta moaned: "We felt that to get Federal support for a memorial would have been a beautiful thing not only for our country but for oppressed people throughout the world. But President Nixon's attitude, his lack of real concern, suggests that his Administration is motivated by racist attitudes."

Nixon's attitude could also have been motivated by a concern for how Americans would react to building such a monument to a man whose personal staff had included convicted perverts, Communist organizers, and even a member of the Executive Committee of the Communist Party, U.S.A.

One might have regarded the whole thing as a figment of King family imagination had not Leonard Garment, a top White House aide, confirmed the statement, saying it was the first time he had heard that the King planned to break off the talks; that he had not been aware of any difference of opinion over Mr. Nixon's "Civil Rights" record. He whined "It would be a disservice to the cause of civil rights and the late Martin Luther King if this becomes a political football."

Mrs. King disclosed that she telephoned the President in early February to ask his help for legislation to create a Freedom Memorial Park in the two downtown Atlanta blocks that contain her husband's birthplace, the Ebenezer Baptist Church where he and his father preached, and his grave. She continued: "Mr. Nixon seemed to like the idea, he even sounded enthusiastic. He said he would send 'the best man for the job' to talk to me and promised that the plan would receive immediate attention from the White House."

Then it turns out that, according to Hanoi Coretta, Secretary of Health Education and Welfare Robert Finch visited her a few weeks later in Atlanta and offered his Department's help in setting up a Black Studies program as part of the memorial. The conspirators agreed to keep mum about all this until Nixon popped the publicity on April fourth, the anniversary of Dr. King's hurried demise. This had to be called off because of the death of former President Eisenhower.

But talks continued between Leonard Garment and Harry H. Wachter the memorial foundation's lawyer. It seems that Garment even met with the architects.

The negotiations cooled as the widow King began to propagandize for the Vietcong, and finally there came a White House letter stating that at the time the President was "not prepared" to support the proposed legislation. The Reverend Martin Luther King Sr. moaned that "Martin's memory has gotten cold."

The widow King observed between pitches for the kindly Vietcong

"We had to convince ourselves that the national Government was not willing to help us." So now the memorial foundation is going to go out and raise through a private campaign the three million dollars deemed necessary. Remembering what Phineas T. Barnum said about a sucker being born every minute, they will probably get the money, too.

One thing for which all good Americans should give thanks is that President Nixon did not dare to go through with this caper. It would have otherwise been tantamount to the government building a memorial to Benedict Arnold, who certainly did less harm to America than the sniveling, hypocritical leader of the "Communist-dominated" Southern Christian Leadership Conference.

It is interesting to note that on the board of the King foundation are such people as former Vice President Hubert H. Humphrey; Senator Hugh Scott of Pennsylvania, the new Senate Republican Leader; Senator Edward M. Kennedy of Massachusetts; former Supreme Court Justice Arthur J. Goldberg; Sidney Poitier, the Leftist screen actor; and, of course, the Reverend Ralph Abernathy, who first won fame by outdistancing an irate husband in Montgomery, Alabama, but who is now King's successor.

Well, there's no doubt they'll collect the gelt (the Rockefeller Brothers Fund has already coughed up $250,000), but it looks as if we'll be spared the disgraceful spectacle of the American taxpayer being required to honor a tinhorn Comrade.

SLANTED LANGUAGE

Another way a writer may bring forth the response he wishes from his reader is by the use of slanted language. For instance, the wife of a policeman writing to a friend about her husband might call him a *law enforcement officer;* but someone who feels he has been hustled by the police too often will probably call the same man a *cop,* or worse. Or a neighbor, describing the noisy little boy next door, may call him a *brat;* the mother, however, when referring to her son, will call him *mischievous.*

The following two news reports are about the same incident: the murder of a woman. Compare the impressions that the two reporters create of the murdered woman. Specifically, how does each reporter create the image of the woman that emerges?

Martin Gansberg / 38 WHO SAW MURDER DIDN'T CALL THE POLICE

For more than half an hour 38 respectable, law-abiding citizens in Queer watched a killer stalk and stab a woman in three separate attacks in Ke Gardens.

Twice their chatter and the sudden glow of their bedroom lights i terrupted him and frightened him off. Each time he returned, sought her ou and stabbed her again. Not one person telephoned the police during tl assault; one witness called after the woman was dead.

That was two weeks ago today.

Still shocked is Assistant Chief Inspector Frederick M. Lussen, in charg of the borough's detectives and a veteran of 25 years of homicide inves gations. He can give a matter-of-fact recitation on many murders. But tl Kew Gardens slaying baffles him—not because it is a murder, but becau the "good people" failed to call the police.

"As we have reconstructed the crime," he said, "the assailant h three chances to kill this woman during a 35-minute period. He return twice to complete the job. If we had been called when he first attacke the woman might not be dead now."

This is what the police say happened beginning at 3:20 A.M. in t staid, middle-class, tree-lined Austin Street area:

Twenty-eight-year-old Catherine Genovese, who was called Kitty almost everyone in the neighborhood, was returning home from her job manager of a bar in Hollis. She parked her red Fiat in a lot adjacent to t Kew Gardens Long Island Rail Road Station, facing Mowbray Place. Li many residents of the neighborhood, she had parked there day after d since her arrival from Connecticut a year ago, although the railroad frow on the practice.

She turned off the lights of her car, locked the door, and started walk the 100 feet to the entrance of her apartment at 82–70 Austin Stre which is in a Tudor building, with stores on the first floor and apartme on the second.

The entrance to the apartment is in the rear of the building beca the front is rented to retail stores. At night the quiet neighborhood hrouded in the slumbering darkness that marks most residential areas.

Miss Genovese noticed a man at the far end of the lot, near a seven-story apartment house at 82–40 Austin Street. She halted. Then, nervously, he headed up Austin Street toward Lefferts Boulevard, where there is a call box to the 102nd Police Precinct in nearby Richmond Hill.

She got as far as a street light in front of a bookstore before the man grabbed her. She screamed. Lights went on in the 10-story apartment house at 82–67 Austin Street, which faces the bookstore. Windows slid open and voices punctuated the early-morning stillness.

Miss Genovese screamed: "Oh, my God, he stabbed me! Please help me! Please help me!"

From one of the upper windows in the apartment house, a man called down: "Let that girl alone!"

The assailant looked up at him, shrugged, and walked down Austin Street toward a white sedan parked a short distance away. Miss Genovese struggled to her feet.

Lights went out. The killer returned to Miss Genovese, now trying to make her way around the side of the building by the parking lot to get to her apartment. The assailant stabbed her again.

"I'm dying!" she shrieked, "I'm dying!"

Windows were opened again, and lights went on in many apartments. The assailant got into his car and drove away. Miss Genovese staggered to her feet. A city bus, Q–10, the Lefferts Boulevard line to Kennedy International Airport, passed. It was 3:35 A.M.

The assailant returned. By then, Miss Genovese had crawled to the back of the building, where the freshly painted brown doors to the apartment house held out hope for safety. The killer tried the first door; she wasn't there. At the second door, 82–62 Austin Street, he saw her slumped on the floor at the foot of the stairs. He stabbed her a third time—fatally.

It was 3:50 by the time the police received their first call, from a man who was a neighbor of Miss Genovese. In two minutes they were at the scene. The neighbor, a 70-year-old woman, and another woman were the only persons on the street. Nobody else came forward.

The man explained that he had called the police after much deliberation. He had phoned a friend in Nassau County for advice and then he had crossed the roof of the building to the apartment of the elderly woman to get her to make the call.

"I didn't want to get involved," he sheepishly told the police.

Six days later, the police arrested Winston Moseley, a 29-year-old business-machine operator, and charged him with the homicide. Mosele had no previous record. He is married, has two children and owns a hom at 133–19 Sutter Avenue, South Ozone Park, Queens. On Wednesday, court committed him to Kings County Hospital for psychiatric observatior

When questioned by the police, Moseley also said that he had slai Mrs. Annie May Johnson, 24, of 146–12 133d Avenue, Jamaica, on Feb. 2 and Barbara Kralik, 15, of 174–17 140th Avenue, Springfield Gardens, las July. In the Kralik case, the police are holding Alvin L. Mitchell, who is sai to have confessed that slaying.

The police stressed how simple it would have been to have gotte in touch with them. "A phone call," said one of the detectives, "woul have done it." The police may be reached by dialing "O" for operatc or SPring 7–3100.

Today witnesses from the neighborhood, which is made up of on family homes in the $35,000 to $60,000 range with the exception of th two apartment houses near the railroac station, find it difficult to explai why they didn't call the police.

A housewife, knowingly if quite casual, said, "We thought it w a lover's quarrel." A husband and wife both said, "Frankly, we were afraid They seemed aware of the fact that events might have been different. distraught woman, wiping her hands in her apron, said, "I didn't want m husband to get involved."

One couple, now willing to talk about that night, said they hea the first screams. The husband looked thoughtfully at the bookstore whe the killer first grabbed Miss Genovese.

"We went to the window to see what was happening," he said, "b the light from our bedroom made it difficult to see the street." The wif still apprehensive, added: "I put out the light and we were able to s better."

Asked why they hadn't called the police, she shrugged and replie "I don't know."

A man peeked out from a slight opening in the doorway to his apa ment and rattled off an account of the killer's second attack. Why had he called the police at the time? "I was tired," he said without emotic "I went back to bed."

It was 4:25 A.M. when the ambulance arrived to take the body Miss Genovese. It drove off. "Then," a solemn police detective said, "t people came out."

Thomas Pugh and Richard Henry / QUEENS BARMAID STABBED, DIES

An attractive 28-year-old brunette who had given up a more prosaic life or a career as a barmaid and residence in a tiny Bohemian section of Queens was stabbed to death early yesterday.

Catherine (Kitty) Genovese, 5 feet 1 and 105 pounds, was stabbed eight times in the chest and four times in the back and she had three cuts on her hands—probably inflicted as she tried to fight off her attacker near her apartment in an alley-way, at 82–70 Austin St., at Lefferts Blvd., Kew Gardens.

Late yesterday, police said the 30 detectives assigned to the case had not come up with any clues or a possible motive for the savage murder.

HAD TEEN NUPTIAL ANNULLED

Police of the Richmond Hill precinct said Kitty had had her teen-age marriage annulled two months after her wedding and, when her large family moved to Connecticut, she stayed in New York on her own.

She worked for an insurance firm, but gave that up for a barmaid's career. In August, 1961, her travels with a "fast crowd" contributed to her arrest on a bookmaking rap.

Police pieced together this account of her last hours: at 6 P.M. Thursday, she left Ev's Eleventh Hour Tavern, 193–14 Jamaica Ave., Hollis, where she had been a barmaid and co-manager for 1½ years.

She and a male patron went on a dinner date to Brooklyn, and returned to Ev's at midnight. Her escort left (he was questioned by cops yesterday and his alibi freed him of suspicion in the crime).

GIRLS SHARED APARTMENT

Kitty left the bar at 3 A.M. and drove her Fiat sports car seven miles to her home. She parked in the Long Island Rail Road's parking lot next to the group of buildings where she and 2 other girls shared an apartment.

She walked along Austin St., instead of going more directly to her

From *The New York Daily News*, March 14, 1964. Reprinted by permission of the publisher.

apartment via a walkway at the rear of the building. Police said she apparently walked out front to have the protection of the street lights.

GASPS "I'VE BEEN STABBED!"

Neighbors suddenly heard screams and the roar of an auto driving of Leaving a trail of blood, Kitty staggered back toward the parking lot, aroun the rear of the structures, and collapsed in the doorway of 82–60 Austi St., next to her home.

"I've been stabbed! I've been stabbed!" the brunette gasped.

Kitty died in an ambulance en route to Queens General Hospita Jamaica.

POLITICAL LANGUAGE

One group of abstract nouns needs particular care in definition an use. Most words which describe political opinions or political affilia tions have been used in so many different situations that they hav taken on a wide spectrum of meanings. One man, for instance, be cause of his particular bias may call all those with whom he disagree on any subject "conservative." Another may label all who do no share his views "liberal." Countries may call those countries wi which they are currently allied by one term, and their opponents b another, regardless of the kinds of government practiced in the cou tries. We tend, for instance, to call all countries with which we a allied democracies, even though they may be in fact dictatorshi The Russians, on the other hand, tend to call all countries with whi they are allied people's republics, even though they may also b dictatorships. Either through carelessness or design, people often u the same political word to describe a variety of men and beliefs.

If the student writes an essay in which a term like conservatis socialism, communism, or democracy appears, he must be sure th the reader knows precisely what he means by the term. For examp the word *conservatism* may mean to one reader the preservation what is valuable in the existing order; to another, it may mean slavish and unquestioning devotion to every facet of the status qu The writer, however, may have had in mind the view that favors balanced government budget. If the writer fails to define the term, communication once again has broken down, and the writer has failed to persuade the reader.

Although the use of abstractions requires some thought, their use should not be avoided. Abstractions are valuable, and politics certainly must be discussed. If everyone were confined to writing only about roses, tables, and Uncle Smedley, not only would this be rather a dull world, but not very many ideas would be exchanged. *The writer must remember, however, that he has an obligation to his reader to explain exactly what he means by his terms.*

PROPAGANDA

Read E. A. Tenney's selection, following. It should be self-explanatory.

E. A. Tenney / ON READING PROPAGANDA

The greatest menace to our democracy, to our existence as a free, independent, and peace-loving people, is that insidious thing called *Propaganda.* Like the thief and the outcast it lurks in dark corners and in broken-down alleys, and like the pickpocket it stealthily insinuates its slimy, snake-like fingers into the pockets of the mind and filches from us our intellectual integrity. One touch of its corroding influence debases the purest passion, and one whiff of its breath contaminates the purest air. The stench of those thousands upon thousands of God-fearing Americans infected and diseased by it is greater than the stench that arose from the putrefying bodies of the unburied victims of the bubonic plague. The more one considers the ghastly effect of propaganda upon modern life the more one hates it for the evil thing it is and the evil it has wrought. Speak propaganda and please the devil, your master, all of you who traffic in unclean words and in foul perverted thoughts!

In the foregoing paragraph, I practiced my hand at writing some propaganda against *propaganda* just to see whether I could do it and also to give you, my reader, a chance to test yourself to see whether you are susceptible and are readily taken in. I observed the rules not for writing honest propaganda but for writing inferior or unscrupulous propaganda, insincere stuff. The difference between good and bad propaganda is the difference between good and bad persuasion—a topic treated in the next paragraph. Before turning to it, I wish to point out the principles upon which I wrote in composing the preceding paragraph. In the first place I posed the questions to myself, "How shall I prejudice my readers against this word? How shall I give to the word an evil connotation so that in the future they will feel an emotion of hate or loathing or anger when next I use it?" The paragraph itself is an answer to the question. I was insincere in that I wrote only half of what I believe to be true; I was unscrupulous in that I employed glittering generalities, appealed to the conventional stock prejudices, resorted to name-calling, personified the word into an evil thing and associated it with bad smells, unsavory places, the slimy snake, and the devil. Now it so happens that I dislike propaganda of the type I wrote—it does not play the game fairly; but I admire much propaganda, i.e., persuasion which makes no attempt to conceal its aim and which argues its case with intelligence and sincere emotion. Of late a great cry has gone up against propaganda as though it were some new evil thing which must be exterminated. In New York City a number of men have organized an "Institute for Propaganda Analysis," and each month they publish a leaflet to warn their readers against various propagandas. The paradox is that they are propagandists propagandizing against propaganda. What these men are doing is analyzing bad propaganda and striving to raise the quality.

Whenever there is an organized movement to persuade people to believe or do something, whenever an effort is made to "propagate" a creed or set of opinions or convictions or to make people act as we want them to act, the means employed are called propaganda. When the means are base, then the propaganda is base; when the means are honorable, it is honorable. The means which I employed in the opening paragraph were unworthy of a good citizen or honorable and just man, for they were intended to create an emotional prejudice against propaganda without giving the word a fair trial. On the contrary, in this paragraph I am writing good propaganda because I am honestly using what means I have to persuade you, the reader, that the word has a good connotation as well as a sinister one. The word has many synonyms—persuasion, publicity, proselytism, conversion, advertisement. Missionaries, salesmen, advertisers, publicity or public relations men—for colleges, political parties, business firms, etc., "ambassadors of good will" are all propagandists to be admired or despised in proportion to the quality of the means they use in converting others to their opinions. When Edmund Burke said that there are ways and means by which a good man will not save even his country, he meant that there are some devices of propaganda to which a sincere and honorable man will not stoop. Bad propaganda is a species of fraud; good propaganda is a process of enlightenment. The subtle, hidden, indirect lie, the lie which is intended to arouse the base passions of hate and by so doing enable the liar to achieve some unjust end—this is propaganda in its lowest, most fraudulent form. Its opposite is propaganda at its best. Between these two extremes lie all imaginable degrees of worth and worthlessness.

PRACTICE

1. See how many interpretations you can think of for the following abstractions. If necessary, consult a dictionary or encyclopedia.

a. love	hate	progress	holiness
pity	liberty	crime	power
b. socialist	democrat	liberal	conservative
communist	fascist	radical	anarchist

2. The following are examples of controlling ideas which contain terms that need definition as soon as they appear in the essay. Indicate which terms need definition and suggest ways in which they could be defined to help develop the controlling idea.

   a. Freedom is guaranteed by the Constitution.
   b. Many people do not understand that there is a difference between communism and socialism.
   c. "Beauty is only skin deep."
   d. The Negro wants equality, not tolerance.
   e. Patriotism is a virtue; chauvinism and jingoism are vices.

3. Find an editorial, a speech, or a newspaper report that uses slanted or emotive language and underline the words or phrases.

4. Find an example of what you think is propaganda. Be prepared to explain why you think it is propaganda.

Writing Assignments

1. "I don't want to get involved" is said to reflect a twentieth-century philosophy. Write an essay in which you discuss the various meanings of *involvement*.
2. In an essay, discuss why the flag may have one set of connotations for a young man from the ghetto fighting on the front line, a different set of connotations for someone brought up in wealth and safety, and perhaps another set of connotations for dissident students (or any other group you wish to include). Be sure that you make the connotations clear.
3. Attempt to write a piece of propaganda or a news report in which you use slanted or emotive language; or write a description that evokes a mood or an emotion.

CHAPTER TWELVE

Evidence

Evidence is that which serves to prove or disprove an assertion. Since the purpose of an essay is to persuade the reader to a particular point of view, it follows that the more convincing the support or evidence, the more readily the reader will be persuaded to the truth of the essay.

The most convincing form of evidence is, of course, the logical development of an idea. When you write (and the same is true of when you read), learn to examine the argument carefully. The thoughtful writer pays particular attention first to the validity of the generalization and second to the truth of the evidence given in support of the generalization. Third, if the generalization is the result of specific examples, the writer examines the steps that lead to the generalization to be certain that they are logical. If the generalization is sound and if its development is logical, the writer has supplied evidence for his argument that will undoubtedly help convince his reader. Conversely, an argument falls flat and will not convince the reader if it is illogical or illogically developed.

FAULTY GENERALIZATIONS

If the generalization is untrue or only half true, the argument itself must be untrue or, at best, suspect. A student essay on the subject of segregated housing will demonstrate this point:

> Negroes are happy to live among their own kind. Our cleaning lady, Jessie Clark, for instance, says that if she were allowed to live any place she wanted, she would still like to live among her own. Another proof is what my neighbor says. He has three Negroes driving his delivery trucks. He says they have stated often that they would prefer to live among Negroes than among whites.

The generalization "Negroes are happy to live among their own kind" is a blanket statement. A statement which does not allow for *any* exceptions is immediately suspect. The world and the human beings that inhabit it are so complex that if a statement about them is to be believed, it almost always should be qualified. Second, if a writer makes such a statement, either he is uninformed or he assumes that his readers are uninformed, since there is so much written and spoken that contradicts this assertion.

An examination of the evidence reveals that it is insufficient to support any generalization. One cannot make a valid generalization about an entire group when he knows only 4, or 10, or even 100 members of that group. The only conclusion one can draw from the paragraph is that the cleaning lady and the three truck drivers feel this way. Even this conclusion may not be valid since the cleaning lady and the three truck drivers may be saying what they think will please their employers rather than what they actually feel. Therefore, the argument is not logical because the generalization is untrue and the support is insufficient and unexamined.

Here is another student sample on the subject of car insurance:

> Insurance for teenage drivers should be the same as for adult drivers. First of all, teenagers cannot earn very much money, and therefore, if anything, they should be asked to pay less. Second, it is important that teenagers be given as much responsibility as possible. Since the insurance is unreasonably high, many are deprived of the responsibility of car ownership.

In this paragraph the generalization is a rational statement of opinion; the arguments, however, are specious. Insurance rates are determined by carefully compiled figures on accidents, not by how much the insured earns. Even if the argument for the responsibility of car ownership were valid, it has no bearing on the rates charged by car insurance companies. Therefore, it is illogical and unconvincing.

ANOTHER SOURCE OF ILLOGICAL REASONING

There is another very common form of illogical reasoning. The speaker or writer starts with what he believes to be proper examples followed by a generalization. However, when the argument is examined, it is found to be faulty for two reasons. First, the examples are insufficient to justify the generalization. Second, the speaker (or writer) is, consciously or unconsciously, hiding from himself the fact that he is not starting with the examples at all. Often he is, instead, proceeding from a generalization handed down within his culture, a kind of folk myth that has no basis in fact, and then is offering those examples that serve his purpose.

Many people are not even aware that they operate upon such assumptions as "Well-dressed people do not commit crimes" or "Redheads have terrible tempers." However, analysis of ordinary conversations, family arguments, and even formal speeches and professional writing reveals how frequently this kind of assumption is used in attempts to persuade.

The following are some familiar examples of such thinking:

THE WAY IN WHICH THE STATEMENT MAY BE SPOKEN OR WRITTEN	**THE ILLOGIC BEHIND THE STATEMENT**	
	INSUFFICIENT EVIDENCE	STARTING WITH THE FOLK MYTH
Maria is a good cook. Naturally, she's Italian.	Maria is a good cook. Mrs. Marciano is a good cook. Giuseppe is a good cook. Therefore, all Italians are good cooks.	All Italians are good cooks. Maria is Italian. Therefore, Maria is a good cook.
Boy, is old Mac stingy. Well, you know how it is; all Scotsmen are stingy.	Mac is stingy. Mary Burns, the girl who works with me, is stingy. Mr. MacIntosh is stingy. Therefore, all Scotsmen are stingy.	All Scotsmen are stingy. Mac is a Scotsman. Therefore, Mac is stingy.
The Polish are really argumentative. I should know. I married into a Polish family.	My husband argues all the time. My sister-in-law argues all the time. My husband's uncles are always arguing. Therefore, all Poles are argumentative.	All Poles are argumentative. My relatives are Polish. Therefore, my relatives are argumentative.
Jim drinks too much. That's easy to understand. He's Irish.	Mike O'Donald drinks too much. Patrick, down the block, drinks too much. Jim drinks too much. Therefore, all Irish people drink too much.	All Irishmen drink to excess. Jim is Irish. Therefore, Jim drinks too much.

Another kind of fallacious thinking is the statement composed of parts that have no logical connections. The following are examples of this kind of illogical thinking:

THE WAY IN WHICH THE STATEMENT MAY BE SPOKEN OR WRITTEN	THE ILLOGIC BEHIND THE STATEMENT
How can you be in favor of admitting Red China to the United Nations? You must be a Communist.	The Communists favor admitting Red China to the United Nations. You favor admitting Red China to the United Nations. Therefore, you must be a Communist.
Did you know that Tom Sutherland, the vice-president of Drine Corporation, actually believes that the whole system has to change? Imagine! Tom Sutherland—a radical!	Radicals are in favor of changing the system. Tom Sutherland is in favor of changing the system. Therefore, Tom Sutherland is a radical.

One can test such faulty developments of thought by visual means. Draw a circle to represent the most inclusive term of the three. Then place the second most inclusive term, also represented by a circle, within the larger circle. Finally, see if the third term falls logically within the second circle or has no logical connection and must be drawn within the largest circle but *separate* from the second.

Here is a classic logical argument that demonstrates the point:

All men are mortal.
Socrates is a man.
Therefore, Socrates is mortal.

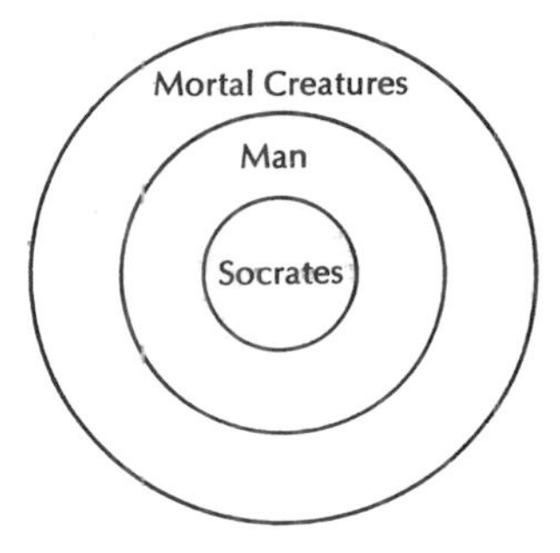

Mortals—which is another way of saying, "All men are mortal"—is the most inclusive term and, therefore, it is represented by the largest circle. *A man* falls logically within the designation *mortals* so the circle representing *man* falls within the larger circle representing *mortals*. Socrates is *a man;* therefore, the circle representing Socrates falls within the circle representing *man*.

Now examine the Red China–United Nations argument. The largest circle represents the most inclusive term, *those who favor admitting Red China to the United Nations*. Within that circle falls another circle representing *Communists*. The third circle represents *you*. But since there is no logical relationship established in this argument between *you* and *Communists*, the circles must be drawn separately, not one within the other. *You* may or may not be a Communist, but this argument has not established the fact; therefore the conclusion is illogical.

The same applies to the Tom Sutherland–radical statement.

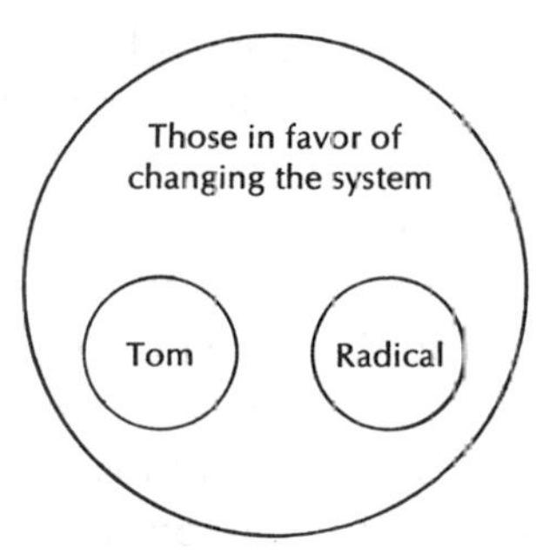

[Even though the circle technique may be successfully applied to all of the illogical arguments on p. 85, the conclusions are *still* faulty and illogical because each argument *starts* with a *false statement.*]

Education, according to one definition, is a process whereby a person develops the ability to question the validity of what he sees and hears. An educated person learns to examine very closely the support for an argument to determine if it is really valid or if it merely appears to be. In addition, he learns to analyze generalizations for indications of false reasoning. Therefore, be aware when you write that the primary way to persuade the reader to believe the truth of your point of view is to be certain that your arguments can stand up under examination.

OTHER FORMS OF EVIDENCE

Among other forms that evidence takes are the following: **direct observation; testimonial; statistics.**

DIRECT OBSERVATION. One of the most frequently used sources of evidence is direct observation. When you use examples from your own experience to support your ideas, you are using direct observation. Suppose, for example, that you wish to write an essay in which you assert that children suffer emotional disturbance later in life if their parents quarrel repeatedly in front of them. You might choose to support this assertion by noting that, because of your own experience with quarrelling parents, you still become nauseous when adults raise their voices at each other, even though they are only joking.

Almost every writer supports his ideas or generalizations by direct observation. However, not all direct observations are equally valid or equally convincing. If the writer has some training in the particular area in which he is making generalizations, his observations will obviously carry more weight than those of someone who has no knowledge of the subject. Your opinion, for instance, about college life is certainly more valid than that of your neighbor who has never been to college. On the other hand, if a child psychologist were supporting the earlier statement about children's reactions to parents who quarrel, his observations, if different from yours, would be accepted and yours rejected.

Valuable though it is in helping to form attitudes and support opinions, direct observation has a number of limitations. Everyone is aware that no two people who witness an accident tell the same story. Both policemen and psychologists know that people generally are unreliable reporters. Furthermore, if a circumstance involves a person's deep-seated prejudices or if he is emotionally aroused at the time, he is unlikely to be objective. Finally, the power of observation varies greatly from person to person. Some are trained to observe accurately and objectively; others react emotionally. Most careful readers, therefore, take into account the probable fallacies inherent in direct observation.

TESTIMONIAL. Another kind of support for an assertion or opinion is the testimonial. A testimonial is a statement, a proof, or an affirmation of fact from someone other than yourself. Testimonials come from several sources: *from people whom you know, from your reading, or from mass media such as newspapers, magazines, television, radio.*

Most people quote their friends and relatives when they wish to prove a point, and sometimes these testimonials are helpful in persuading the reader. However, the reader will be more likely to be convinced by an authority on the subject under discussion than he will by Aunt Minnie's opinions. If the writer quotes Aunt Minnie's assertion that many children of parents who quarrel grow up to become alcoholics, the reader is unlikely to be convinced. He will immediately wonder what equips Aunt Minnie to establish a relationship between alcoholism in adults and quarrelling parents.

Even more important, testimonials from friends or relatives may be contrary to what is held as truth by authorities in the field under discussion. This contradiction frequently occurs in the case of prejudice. Aunt Gertrude or Uncle Joe or Cousin Martha may claim that Negroes are lazy, that Mexicans steal, that the Scots are penny pinching. If the reader is at all educated, he will know that most scientists find no validity to the claim that personality characteristics are inherited by ethnic or national groups. The reader will, therefore, find the testimonial unconvincing, and the writer will have failed in his purpose.

Of course, if the reader is educationally limited, and if the testimonial appeals to his prejudice, he will be convinced, regardless of the source of the testimonial. This unfortunate truth accounts for the fact that the uneducated are such easy marks for demagogues who make statements supported by half-truths and falsehoods. But since college students can presuppose educated readers, and since the aim of education is not the continuation of prejudice, but rather the search for truth, the student writer should support his assertions by the most valid evidence possible.

Even the statements of so-called experts must be studied closely. Before you quote anyone in support of your generalizations, first examine the man's qualifications. Is his claim to expertise based solely on his own and his cronies' opinions? If so, a quote from such a person will not help to support your arguments. If he is considered an expert by other experts in his field, then his testimony will add weight to what you write.

Furthermore, an expert in one field is not necessarily an expert in any others. When you use testimonials in support of your generalization, be certain that you select an authority on the subject under discussion in your essay. But exercise some caution. If someone is an authority on medicine, for example, he is not necessarily an authority on social problems. Your next door neighbor, for another example, may be an authority on what is cooking in her neighbors' pots, but this expertise hardly qualifies her to be an authority on politics.

These precautions are not meant to suggest that you should avoid testimonials, just that you should be careful when you select them. By all means, add testimony to direct observation in support of your generalizations, for testimony, when it is carefully chosen, adds considerable weight to an argument. The second of the following passages is more effective because testimony has been added to direct observation.

> *The less a person knows about a subject, the more opinionated he tends to be.* I have observed, for example, that my neighbor, who knows very little about his own religion and absolutely nothing about any others, makes all kinds of dogmatic statements, almost always derogatory, about other people's faiths.

> *The less a person knows about a subject, the more opinionated he tends to be.* I have observed, for example, that my neighbor, who knows very little about his own religion and absolutely nothing about any others, makes all kinds of dogmatic statements, almost always derogatory, about other people's faiths. An article in *The Clarion,* 19 July 1965, makes the same point. A psychology professor at Symington College conducted an experiment in which he tested one hundred students to determine the strength of their convictions on controversial issues and the extent of their knowledge of these issues. He found a positive relationship: the less the student knew, the more opinionated and dogmatic he was.

STATISTICS. Statistics also add to the validity of a statement and help convince the reader that the statement is true. The following statement, for instance, becomes convincing when statistical information is added.

> *Most murders are committed by men.*

> *Most murders are committed by men.* According to the Department of Justice, Federal Bureau of Investigation, of all murders and nonnegligent manslaughters committed in cities of over 2500 in 1962, men committed 3973 and women, 945.

When you use statistics, be sure to note in your essay the source of the figures. If you do not give the source, the reader has no way of determining whether the statistics are valid. There is an old saw, "Statistics do not lie, but liars make statistics." When you obtain statistics from magazines, newspapers, or television, notice if the source is included. If no source is mentioned, the statistics may have been made up by a reporter who wanted to add a tone of authenticity to his story, they may have been doctored by an organization to serve its own purposes, or they may have been arrived at by totally haphazard and unscientific methods. If you use unverified statistics, they will not persuade the reader.

Some excellent sources of statistics are almanacs, atlases, encyclopedias, and literature from such governmental agencies as the

Census Bureau, whose sole function it is to collect and analyze statistics. Be sure to use statistics if they will strengthen your argument.

The more effectively you support your statements with evidence, the more easily you will persuade your reader.

PRACTICE

1. Find an example of faulty logic in a book, newspaper, magazine, or on television or radio. Analyze the argument, and point out whether it is illogical because of a faulty generalization, faulty development, or faulty use of examples.

2. The following sentences read as if they were statements of fact. Some are not. Check these statements against sources in your library, and if the statements are incorrect, supply the right information. Be sure to note the source from which you got the information.

    a. Heart failure was the major cause of death in the U.S. in 1963.
    b. The population of India is 36,124,369.
    c. Tokyo is the largest city in the world.
    d. *Ramparts* is a publication of the Roman Catholic church.
    e. The American Nazi Party has its headquarters in Germany.

3. Make a list of radio and television commercials that use testimonials as their basis for persuasion.

4. For one week, record as accurately as possible any illogical arguments or statements that you hear.

Writing Assignments

1. Write an essay on any controversial subject you wish in which you support your viewpoint with testimonial(s) and statistics.
2. In an essay, analyze a prejudice of your own or of someone close to you. Apply some of the principles of logical thinking discussed in this chapter.
3. Write a narrative describing an experience, either yours or someone else's, in which illogical thinking figured.

THE READER

PART ONE / *Education in Transition*

Not thine to finish the task, but neither art thou free to exempt thyself from it.
Ancient Hebrew sage

US
Ann Arbor High School, Ann Arbor, Michigan

From *How Old Will You Be in 1984?*
edited by Diane Divoky.
Reprinted by permission of Avon Books.

K. ROSS TOOLE

No Room for Slobs

STUDY QUESTIONS FOR COMPREHENSION

1. What does Toole mean by "the tyranny of spoiled brats"?
2. Specifically, what are some of the ways in which colleges can deal with revolutionaries?
3. Is Toole's anger directed against all students?

I am 49 years old. It took me many years and considerable anguish to get where I am—which isn't much of anyplace except exurbia. I was nurtured in depression; I lost four years to war; I am invested with sweat; I have had one coronary; I am a "liberal," square and I am a professor. I am sick of the "younger generation," hippies, yippies, militants and nonsense.

I am a professor of history at the University of Montana, and I am supposed to have "liaison" with the young. Worse still, I am father of seven children. They range in age from seven to 23—and I am fed up with nonsense. I am tired of being blamed, maimed and contrite; I am tired of tolerance and the reaching out (which is always my function) for understanding. I am sick of the total irrationality of the campus "rebel," whose bearded visage, dirty hair, body odor and "tactics" are childish but brutal, naive but dangerous, and the essence of arrogant tyranny—the tyranny of spoiled brats.

I am terribly disturbed that I may be incubating more of the same. Our household is permissive, our approach to discipline is an

Dr. K. Ross Toole is a professor of history at the University of Montana in Missoula. "No Room for Slobs" is reprinted by permission of the author and publisher from *The Billings Gazette*, February 8, 1970.

apology and a retreat from standards—usually accompanied by a gift in cash or kind.

It's time to call a halt; time to live in an adult world where we belong and time to put these people in their places. We owe the "younger generation" what all "older generations" have owed younger generations—love, protection to a point, and respect when they deserve it. We do not owe them our souls, our privacy, our whole lives, and above all, we do not owe them immunity from our mistakes, or their own.

Every generation makes mistakes, always has and always will. We have made our share. But my generation has made America the most affluent country on earth; it has tackled, head-on, a racial problem which no nation on earth in the history of mankind had dared to do. It has publicly declared war on poverty and it has gone to the moon; it has desegregated schools and abolished polio; it has presided over the beginning of what is probably the greatest social and economic revolution in man's history. It has begun these things, not finished them. It has declared itself, and committed itself, and taxed itself, and damn near run itself into the ground in the cause of social justice and reform.

Its mistakes are fewer than my father's generation—or his father's, or his. Its greatest mistake is not Viet Nam; it is the abdication of its first responsibility, its pusillanimous capitulation to its youth, and its sick preoccupation with the problems, the mind, the psyche, the raison d'etre of the young.

Since when have children ruled this country? By virtue of what right, by what accomplishment should thousands of teenagers, wet behind the ears and utterly without the benefit of having lived long enough to have either judgment or wisdom, become the sages of our time?

The psychologists, the educators and preachers say the young are rebelling against our archaic mores and morals, our materialistic approaches to life, our failures in diplomacy, our terrible ineptitude in racial matters, our narrowness as parents, our blindness to the root ills of society. Balderdash!

Society hangs together by the stitching of many threads. No

18-year-old is simply the product of his 18 years: he is the product of 3,000 years of the development of mankind—and throughout those years, injustice has existed and been fought; rules have grown outmoded and been changed; doom has hung over men and been avoided; unjust wars have occurred; pain has been the cost of progress—and man has persevered.

As a professor and the father of seven, I have watched this new generation and concluded that most of them are fine. A minority are not—and the trouble is that minority threatens to tyrannize the majority and take over. I dislike that minority; I am aghast that the majority "takes" it and allows itself to be used. And I address myself to both the minority and the majority. I speak partly as a historian, partly as a father and partly as one fed up, middle-aged and angry member of the so-called "establishment"—which, by the way, is nothing but a euphemism for "society."

Common courtesy and a regard for the opinions of others is not merely a decoration on the pie crust of society, it is the heart of the pie. Too many "youngsters" are egocentric boors. They will not listen, they will only shout down. They will not discuss but, like four-year-olds, they throw rocks and shout.

Arrogance is obnoxious; it is also destructive. Society has classically ostracized arrogance without the backing of demonstrable accomplishment. Why, then, do we tolerate arrogant slobs who occupy our homes, our administration buildings, our streets and parks, urinating on our beliefs and defiling our premises? It is not the police we need (our generation and theirs), it is an expression of our disgust and disdain. Yet we do more than permit it, we dignify it with introspective flagellation. Somehow it is our fault. Balderdash again!

Sensitivity is not the property of the young, nor was it invented in 1950. The young of any generation have felt the same impulse to grow, to reach out, to touch stars, to live freely and to let the minds loose along unexplored corridors. Young men and young women have always stood on the same hill and felt the same vague sense of restraint that separated them from the ultimate experience—the sudden and complete expansion of the mind, the final fulfillment. It is one of the oldest, sweetest and most bitter experiences of mankind.

Today's young people did not invent it; they do not own it. And what they seek to attain, all mankind has sought to attain throughout the ages. Shall we, therefore, approve the presumed attainment of it through heroin, speed, LSD and other drugs? And shall we, permissively, let them poison themselves simply because, as in most other respects, we feel vaguely guilty because we brought them into this world? Again, it is not police raids and tougher laws that we need; it is merely strength. The strength to explain, in our potty, middle-aged way, that what they seek, we sought; that it is somewhere but not here and sure as hell not in drugs; that, in the meanwhile, they will cease and desist the poison game. And this we must explain early and hard—and then police it ourselves.

Society, "the establishment," is not a foreign thing we seek to impose on the young. We know it is far from perfect. We did not make it; we have only sought to change it. The fact that we have only been minimally successful is the story of all generations—as it will be the story of the generation coming up. Yet we have worked a number of wonders. We have changed it. We are deeply concerned about our failures; we have not solved the racial problem but we have faced it; we are terribly worried about the degradation of our environment, about injustices, inequities, the military-industrial complex and bureaucracy. But we have attacked these things. We have, all our lives, taken arms against our sea of troubles—and fought effectively. But we also have fought with a rational knowledge of the strength of our adversary; and, above all, knowing that the war is one of attrition in which the "unconditional surrender" of the forces of evil is not about to occur. We win, if we win at all, slowly and painfully. That is the kind of war society has always fought—because man is what he is.

Knowing this, why do we listen subserviently to the violent tacticians of the new generation? Either they have total victory by Wednesday next or burn down our carefully built barricades in adolescent pique; either they win now or flee off to a commune and quit; either they solve all problems this week or join a wrecking crew of paranoids.

Youth has always been characterized by impatient idealism.

If it were not, there would be *no* change. But impatient idealism does not extend to guns, fire bombs, riots, vicious arrogance, and instant gratification. That is not idealism; it is childish tyranny. The worst of it is that we (professors and faculties in particular) in a paroxysm of self-abnegation and apology, go along, abdicate, apologize as if we had personally created the ills of the world—and thus lend ourselves to chaos. We are the led, not the leaders. And we are fools.

As a professor I meet the activists and revolutionaries every day. They are inexcusably ignorant. If you want to make a revolution, do you not study the ways to do it? Of course not! Che Guevarra becomes their hero. He failed; he died in the jungles of Bolivia with an army of six. His every move was a miscalculation and a mistake. Mao Tse Tung and Ho Chi Minh led revolutions based on a peasantry and an overwhelmingly ancient rural economy. They are the patternmakers for the SDS and the student militants. I have yet to talk to an "activist" who has read Crane Brinton's "The Anatomy of Revolution," or who is familiar with the works of Jefferson, Washington, Paine, Adams or even Marx or Engles [*sic*]. And I have yet to talk to a student militant who has read about racism elsewhere and/or who understands, even primitively, the long and wondrous struggle of the NAACP and the genius of Martin Luther King—whose name they invariably take in vain.

An old and scarred member of the wars of organized labor in the U.S. in the 1930's recently remarked to me: "these 'radicals' couldn't organize well enough to produce a sensible platform let alone revolt their way out of a paper bag." But they can, because we let them destroy our universities, make our parks untenable, make a shambles of our streets, and insult our flag.

I assert that we are in trouble with this younger generation not because we have failed our country, not because of affluence or stupidity, not because we are antediluvian, not because we are middle-class materialists—but simply because we have failed to keep that generation in its place and we have failed to put them back there when they got out of it. We have the power; we do not have the will. We have the right, we have not exercised it.

To the extent that we now rely on the police, mace, the National Guard, tear gas, steel fences and a wringing of hands, we will fail.

What we need is a reappraisal of our own middle-class selves, our worth and our hard-won progress. We need to use disdain, not mace; we need to reassess a weapon we came by the hard way, by travail and labor, firm authority as parents, teachers, businessmen, workers and politicians.

The vast majority of our children from one to 20 are fine kids. We need to back this majority with authority and with the firm conviction that we owe it to them and to ourselves. Enough of apology, enough of analysis, enough of our abdication of responsibility, enough of the denial of our own maturity and good sense.

The best place to start is at home. But, the most practical and effective place, right now, is our campuses. This does not mean a flood of angry edicts, a sudden clamp-down, a "new" policy. It simply means that faculties should stop playing chicken, that demonstrators should be met not with police but with expulsions. The power to expell (strangely unused) has been the legitimate recourse of universities since 1209.

More importantly it means that at freshman orientation, whatever form it takes, the administration should set forth the ground rules—not belligerently but forthrightly.

A university is the microcosm of society itself. It cannot function without rules for conduct. It cannot, as society cannot, legislate morals. It is dealing with young men and women, 18 to 22. But it can, and must, promulgate rules. It cannot function without order—and, therefore, whoever disrupts order must leave. It cannot permit students to determine when, what and where they shall be taught; it cannot permit the occupation of its premises, in violation both of the law and its regulations, by "militants."

There is room within the university complex for basic student participation but there is no room for slobs, disruption and violence. The first obligation of the administration is to lay down the rules early, clearly and positively, and to attach to this statement the penalty for violation. It is profoundly simple—and the failure to state it—

in advance—is the salient failure of university administrators in this age.

Expulsion is a dreaded verdict. The administration merely needs to make it clear, quite dispassionately, that expulsion is the inevitable consequence of violation of the rules. Among the rules, even though it seems gratuitous, should be these: 1. Violence, armed or otherwise, the forceful occupation of buildings, the intimidation by covert or overt act of any student or faculty member or administrative personnel, the occupation of any university property, field, park, building, lot or other place, shall be cause for expulsion.

2. The disruption of any class, directly or indirectly, by voice or presence or the destruction of any university property, shall be cause for expulsion.

This is neither new nor revolutionary. It is merely the reassertion of an old, accepted and necessary right of the administration of any such institution. And the faculty should be informed, firmly, of this reassertion, before trouble starts. This does not constitute provocation. It is one of the oldest rights and necessities of the university community. The failure of university administrators to use it is one of the mysteries of our permissive age—and the blame must fall largely on faculties because they have consistently pressured administrators not to act.

Suppose the students refuse to recognize expulsions, suppose they march, riot, strike. The police? No. The matter, by prearrangement, publicly stated, should then pass to the courts. If buildings are occupied, the court enjoins the participating students. It has the awful power to declare them in contempt. If violence ensues, it is in violation of the court's order. Courts are not subject to fears, not part of the action. And what militant will shout obscenities in court with contempt hanging over his head?

Too simple? Not at all. Merely an old process which we seem to have forgotten. It is too direct for those who seek to employ Freudian analysis, too positive for "academic senates" who long for philosophical debate and too prosaic for those who seek orgiastic self condemnation.

This is a country full of decent, worried people like myself. It is also a country full of people fed up with nonsense. We need (those of us over 30, tax-ridden, harried, confused, weary and beat-up) to reassert our hard won prerogatives. It is our country too. We have fought for it, bled for it, dreamed for it, and we love it. It is time to reclaim it.

BERTRAND RUSSELL

The Functions of a Teacher

STUDY QUESTIONS FOR COMPREHENSION

1. How, in Russell's view, is the role of the teacher different today from what it has been in the past?
2. What does Russell mean by the "decay of cultural internationalism"?
3. What distinction does Russell make between a good teacher and a propagandist?
4. Why is Russell opposed to "nationalistic feeling"?

Teaching, more even than most other professions, has been transformed during the last hundred years from a small, highly skilled profession concerned with a minority of the population, to a large and important branch of the public service. The profession has a great and honorable tradition, extending from the dawn of history until recent times, but any teacher in the modern world who allows himself to be inspired by the ideals of his predecessors is likely to be made sharply aware that it is not his function to teach what he thinks, but to instill such beliefs and prejudices as are thought useful by his employers. In former days a teacher was expected to be a man of exceptional knowledge or wisdom, to whose words men would do well to attend. In antiquity, teachers were not an organized profession, and no control was exercised over what they taught. It is true that they were often punished afterwards for their subversive doctrines. Socrates was put to death and Plato is said to have been thrown into prison, but such incidents did not interfere with the spread of their doctrines. Any man who has the genuine impulse of the teacher will be more anxious to survive in his books than in the flesh. A feeling of intellectual independence is essential to the proper fulfillment of the teacher's functions, since it is his business to instill what he can of knowledge and reasonableness into the process of forming public opinion. In antiquity he performed this function unhampered except by occasional spasmodic and ineffective interventions of tyrants or mobs. In the middle ages teaching became the exclusive prerogative of the church, with the result that there was little progress either intellectual or social. With the Renaissance, the general respect for learning brought back a very considerable measure of freedom to the teacher. It is true that the Inquisition compelled Galileo to recant, and burned Giordano Bruno at the stake, but each of these men had done his work before being punished. Institutions such as universities largely remained in the grip of the dogmatists, with the result that most of the best intellectual work was done by independent men of learning. In England, especially, until near the end of the nineteenth century, hardly any men of first-rate eminence except Newton were connected with universities. But the social system was such that this interfered little with their activities or their usefulness.

In our more highly organized world we face a new problem. Something called education is given to everybody, usually by the state, but sometimes by the churches. The teacher has thus become, in the vast majority of cases, a civil servant obliged to carry out the behests of men who have not his learning, who have no experience of dealing with the young, and whose only attitude towards education is that of the propagandist. It is not very easy to see how, in these circumstances, teachers can perform the functions for which they are specially fitted.

State education is obviously necessary, but as obviously involves certain dangers against which there ought to be safeguards. The evils to be feared were seen in their full magnitude in Nazi Germany and are still seen in Russia. Where these evils prevail no man can teach unless he subscribes to a dogmatic creed which few people of free intelligence are likely to accept sincerely. Not only must he subscribe to a creed, but he must condone abominations and carefully abstain from speaking his mind on current events. So long as he is teaching only the alphabet and the multiplication table, as to which no controversies arise, official dogmas do not necessarily warp his instruction; but even while he is teaching these elements he is expected, in totalitarian countries, not to employ the methods which he thinks most likely to achieve the scholastic result, but to instill fear, subservience, and blind obedience by demanding unquestioned submission to his authority. And as soon as he passes beyond the bare elements, he is obliged to take the official view on all controversial questions. The result is that the young in Nazi Germany became, and in Russia become, fanatical bigots, ignorant of the world outside their own country, totally unaccustomed to free discussion, and not aware that their opinions can be questioned without wickedness. This state of affairs, bad as it is, would be less disastrous than it is if the dogmas instilled were, as in medieval Catholicism, universal and international; but the whole conception of an international culture is denied by the modern dogmatists, who preached one creed in Germany, another in Italy, another in Russia, and yet another in Japan. In each of these countries fanatical nationalism was what was most emphasized in the teaching of the young, with the result that the men of one country have no common ground with the men of another, and that no conception of a common civilization stands in the way of warlike ferocity.

The decay of cultural internationalism has proceeded at a continually increasing pace ever since the First World War. When I was in Leningrad in 1920, I met the Professor of Pure Mathematics, who was familiar with London, Paris, and other capitals, having been a member of various international congresses. Nowadays the learned men of Russia are very seldom permitted such excursions, for fear of their drawing comparisons unfavorable to their own country. In other countries nationalism in learning is less extreme, but everywhere it is far more powerful than it was. There is a tendency in England (and, I believe, in the United States) to dispense with Frenchmen and Germans in the teaching of French and German. The practice of considering a man's nationality rather than his competence in appointing him to a post is damaging to education and an offense against the ideal of international culture, which was a heritage from the Roman Empire and the Catholic Church, but is now being submerged under a new barbarian invasion, proceeding from below rather than from without.

In democratic countries these evils have not yet reached anything like the same proportions, but it must be admitted that there is grave danger of similar developments in education, and that this danger can only be averted if those who believe in liberty of thought are on the alert to protect teachers from intellectual bondage. Perhaps the first requisite is a clear conception of the services which teachers can be expected to perform for the community. I agree with the governments of the world that the imparting of definite uncontroversial information is one of the least of the teacher's functions. It is, of course, the basis upon which the others are built, and in a technical civilization such as ours it has undoubtedly a considerable utility. There must exist in a modern community a sufficient number of men who possess the technical skill required to preserve the mechanical apparatus upon which our physical comforts depend. It is, moreover, inconvenient if any large percentage of the population is unable to read and write. For these reasons we are all in favor of universal compulsory education. But governments have perceived that it is easy, in the course of giving instruction, to instill beliefs on controversial matters and to produce habits of mind which may be convenient or inconvenient to those in authority. The defense of the state in all civilized countries is quite as much in the hands of teachers as in those of the armed forces. Except in totalitarian countries, the defense of the state is desirable, and the mere fact that education is used for this purpose is not in itself a ground of criticism. Criticism will only arise if the state is defended by obscurantism and appeals to irrational passion. Such methods are quite unnecessary in the case of any state worth defending. Nevertheless, there is a natural tendency towards their adoption by those who have no first-hand knowledge of education. There is a widespread belief that nations are made strong by uniformity of opinion and by the suppression of liberty. One hears it said over and over again that democracy weakens a country in war, in spite of the fact that in every important war since the year 1700 the victory has gone to the more democratic side. Nations have been brought to ruin much more often by insistence upon a narrow-minded doctrinal uniformity than by free discussion and the toleration of divergent opinions. Dogmatists the world over believe that although the truth is known to them, others will be led into false beliefs provided they are allowed to hear the arguments on both sides. This is a view which leads to one or another of two misfortunes: either one set of dogmatists conquers the world and prohibits all new ideas, or, what is worse, rival dogmatists conquer different regions and preach the gospel of hate against each other, the former of these evils existing in the middle ages, the latter during the wars of religion, and again in the present day. The first makes civilization static, the second tends to destroy it completely. Against both, the teacher should be the main safeguard.

It is obvious that organized party spirit is one of the greatest dangers of our time. In the form of nationalism it leads to wars between nations, and in other forms it leads to civil war. It should be the business of teachers to stand outside the strife of parties and endeavor to instill into the young the habit of impartial inquiry, leading them to judge issues on their merits and to be on their guard against accepting *ex parte* statements at their face value. The teacher should not be expected to flatter the prejudices either of the mob or of officials. His professional virtue should consist in a readiness to do justice to all sides, and in an endeavor to rise above controversy into a region of dispassionate scientific investigation. If there are people to whom the results of his investigation are inconvenient, he should be protected against their resentment, unless it can be shown that he has lent himself to dishonest propaganda by the dissemination of demonstrable untruths.

The function of the teacher, however, is not merely to mitigate the heat of current controversies. He has more positive tasks to perform, and he cannot be a great teacher unless he is inspired by a wish to perform these tasks. Teachers are more than any other class the guardians of civilization. They should be intimately aware of what civilization is, and desirous of imparting a civilized attitude to their pupils. We are thus brought to the question: what constitutes a civilized community?

This question would very commonly be answered by pointing

to merely material tests. A country is civilized if it has much machin-ery, many motor cars, many bathrooms, and a great deal of rapid locomotion. To these things, in my opinion, most modern men attach much too much importance. Civilization, in the more important sense, is a thing of the mind, not of material adjuncts to the physical side of living. It is a matter partly of knowledge, partly of emotion So far as knowledge is concerned, a man should be aware of the minuteness of himself and his immediate environment in relation to the world in time and space. He should see his own country not *only* as home, but as one among the countries of the world, all with an equal right to live and think and feel. He should see his own age in relation to the past and the future, and be aware that its own con-troversies will seem as strange to future ages as those of the past seem to us now. Taking an even wider view, he should be consciou of the vastness of geological epochs and astronomical abysses; but he should be aware of all this, not as a weight to crush the individual human spirit, but as a vast panorama which enlarges the mind that contemplates it. On the side of the emotions, a very similar enlarge-ment from the purely personal is needed if a man is to be truly civil-ized. Men pass from birth to death, sometimes happy, sometimes unhappy; sometimes generous, sometimes grasping and petty; some-times heroic, sometimes cowardly and servile. To the man who views the procession as a whole, certain things stand out as worthy of admiration. Some men have been inspired by love of mankind; som by supreme intellect have helped us to understand the world in which we live; and some by exceptional sensitiveness have created beauty These men have produced something of positive good to outweigh the long record of cruelty, oppression, and superstition. These me have done what lay in their power to make human life a better thing than the brief turbulence of savages. The civilized man, where h cannot admire, will aim rather at understanding than at reprobating He will seek rather to discover and remove the impersonal causes c evil than to hate the men who are in its grip. All this should be in th mind and heart of the teacher, and if it is in his mind and heart he will convey it in his teaching to the young who are in his care.

No man can be a good teacher unless he has feelings of warm

affection towards his pupils and a genuine desire to impart to them what he himself believes to be of value. This is not the attitude of the propagandist. To the propagandist his pupils are potential soldiers in an army. They are to serve purposes that lie outside their own lives, not in the sense in which every generous purpose transcends self, but in the sense of ministering to unjust privilege or to despotic power. The propagandist does not desire that his pupils should survey the world and freely choose a purpose which to them appears of value. He desires, like a topiarian artist, that their growth shall be trained and twisted to suit the gardener's purpose. And in thwarting their natural growth he is apt to destroy in them all generous vigor, replacing it by envy, destructiveness, and cruelty. There is no need for men to be cruel; on the contrary, I am persuaded that most cruelty results from thwarting in early years, above all from thwarting what is good.

Repressive and persecuting passions are very common, as the present state of the world only too amply proves. But they are not an inevitable part of human nature. On the contrary, they are, I believe, always the outcome of some kind of unhappiness. It should be one of the functions of the teacher to open vistas before his pupils showing them the possibility of activities that will be as delightful as they are useful, thereby letting loose their kind impulses and preventing the growth of a desire to rob others of joys that they will have missed. Many people decry happiness as an end, both for themselves and for others, but one may suspect them of sour grapes. It is one thing to forgo personal happiness for a public end, but it is quite another to treat the general happiness as a thing of no account. Yet this is often done in the name of some supposed heroism. In those who take this attitude there is generally some vein of cruelty based probably upon an unconscious envy and the source of the envy will usually be found in childhood or youth. It should be the aim of the educator to train adults free from these psychological misfortunes, and not anxious to rob others of happiness because they themselves have not been robbed of it.

As matters stand today, many teachers are unable to do the best of which they are capable. For this there are a number of reasons, some more or less accidental, others very deep-seated. To begin with the former, most teachers are overworked and are compelled to prepare their pupils for examinations rather than to give them a liberalizing mental training. The people who are not accustomed to teaching —and this includes practically all educational authorities—have no idea of the expense of spirit that it involves. Clergymen are not expected to preach sermons for several hours every day, but the analogous effort is demanded of teachers. The result is that many of them become harassed and nervous, out of touch with recent work in the subjects that they teach, and unable to inspire their students with a sense of the intellectual delights to be obtained from new understanding and new knowledge.

This, however, is by no means the gravest matter. In most countries certain opinions are recognized as correct, and others as dangerous. Teachers whose opinions are not correct are expected to keep silent about them. If they mention their opinions it is propaganda, while the mentioning of correct opinions is considered to be merely sound instruction. The result is that the inquiring young too often have to go outside the classroom to discover what is being thought by the most vigorous minds of their own time. There is in America a subject called civics, in which, perhaps more than in any other, the teaching is expected to be misleading. The young are taught a sort of copybook account of how public affairs are supposed to be conducted, and are carefully shielded from all knowledge as to how in fact they are conducted. When they grow up and discover the truth, the result is too often a complete cynicism in which all public ideals are lost; whereas if they had been taught the truth carefully and with proper comment at an earlier age they might have become men able to combat evils in which, as it is, they acquiesce with a shrug.

The idea that falsehood is edifying is one of the besetting sins of those who draw up educational schemes. I should not myself consider that a man could be a good teacher unless he had made a firm resolve never in the course of his teaching to conceal truth because it is what is called "unedifying." The kind of virtue that can be produced by guarded ignorance is frail and fails at the first touch of reality. There are, in this world, many men who deserve admiration, and it is good that the young should be taught to see the ways in which these men are admirable. But it is not good to teach them to admire rogues by concealing their roguery. It is thought that the knowledge of things as they are will lead to cynicism, and so it may do if the knowledge comes suddenly with a shock of surprise and horror. But if it comes gradually, duly intermixed with a knowledge of what is good, and in the course of a scientific study inspired by the wish to get at the truth, it will have no such effect. In any case, to tell lies to the young, who have no means of checking what they are told, is morally indefensible.

The thing, above all, that a teacher should endeavor to produce in his pupils, if democracy is to survive, is the kind of tolerance that springs from an endeavor to understand those who are different from ourselves. It is perhaps a natural human impulse to view with horror and disgust all manners and customs different from those to which we are used. Ants and savages put strangers to death. And those who have never traveled either physically or mentally find it difficult to tolerate the queer ways and outlandish beliefs of other nations and other times, other sects and other political parties. This kind of ignorant intolerance is the antithesis of a civilized outlook, and is one of the gravest dangers to which our overcrowded world is exposed. The educational system ought to be designed to correct it, but much too little is done in this direction at present. In every country nationalistic feeling is encouraged, and school children are taught, what they are only too ready to believe, that the inhabitants of other countries are morally and intellectually inferior to those of the country in which the school children happen to reside. Collective hysteria, the most mad and cruel of all human emotions, is encouraged instead of being discouraged, and the young are encouraged to believe what they hear frequently said rather than what there is some rational ground for believing. In all this the teachers are not to blame. They are not free to teach as they would wish. It is they who know most intimately the needs of the young. It is they who through daily contact have come to care for them. But it is not they who decide what shall be taught or what the methods of instruction are to be. There ought to be a great deal more freedom than there is for the scholastic profession. It ought to have more opportunities of self-determination, more independence from the interference of bureaucrats and bigots. No one would consent in our day to subject the medical men to the control of non-medical authorities as to how they should treat their patients, except of course where they depart criminally from the purpose of medicine, which is to cure the patient. The teacher is a kind of medical man whose purpose is to cure the patient of childishness, but he is not allowed to decide for himself on the basis of experience what methods are most suitable to this end. A few great historic universities, by the weight of their prestige, have secured virtual self-determination, but the immense majority of educational institutions are hampered and controlled by men who do not understand the work with which they are interfering. The only way to prevent totalitarianism in our highly organized world is to secure a certain degree of independence for bodies performing useful public work, and among such bodies teachers deserve a foremost place.

The teacher, like the artist, the philosopher, and the man of letters, can only perform his work adequately if he feels himself to be an individual directed by an inner creative impulse, not dominated and fettered by an outside authority. It is very difficult in this modern world to find a place for the individual. He can subsist at the top as a dictator in a totalitarian state or a plutocratic magnate in a country of large industrial enterprises, but in the realm of the mind it is becoming more and more difficult to preserve independence of the great organized forces that control the livelihoods of men and women. If the world is not to lose the benefit to be derived from its best minds, it will have to find some method of allowing them scope and liberty in spite of organization. This involves a deliberate restraint on the part of those who have power, and a conscious realization that there are men to whom free scope must be afforded. Renaissance Popes could feel in this way towards Renaissance artists, but the powerful men of our day seem to have more difficulty in feeling respect for exceptional genius. The turbulence of our times is inimical to the fine flower of culture. The man in the street is full of fear, and therefore unwilling to tolerate freedoms for which he sees no need. Perhaps we must wait for quieter times before the claims of civilization can again override the claims of party spirit. Meanwhile, it is important that some at least should continue to realize the limitations of what can be done by organization. Every system should allow loopholes and exceptions, for if it does not it will in the end crush all that is best in man.

From *How Old Will You Be in 1984?*

The following four selections are written by high-school students. They reflect a variety of attitudes expressed in a variety of forms. Which selection do you react to most strongly, either favorably or unfavorably? Does the form the writer has chosen influence your response?

Paul De Rocco / **I PLEDGE ALLEGIANCE**

I stood, facing the back of the room, my hands in my pockets, my eyes searching for something to interest me. All the other students were carrying out the mechanical pledge that somehow binds them to the United States of America.

A friend asked me why I didn't "pledguleegince." So I took him aside and together we went over the wording of the "pledguleegince."

"I pledge allegiance to the flag of the United States of America, and to the republic for which it stands . . ."

My philosophy includes the concept of a worldwide State. A world of individual nations each fighting for its own cause will never leave peace on Earth. So why should I pledge myself to a country? I pledge myself to the whole world! Why just between the Rio Grande and the forty-ninth parallel? Besides, this pledge is taken blindly by students all over America. It has lost what meaning it had, so why repeat it every morning?

From *How Old Will You Be in 1984?* edited by D ane Divoky. Reprinted by permission of Avon Books.

". . . one Nation under God . . ."

I don't believe in God.

". . . indivisible . . ."

Black versus white?

". . . with liberty and justice for all."

Except Negroes, American Indians, immigrants, the underprivileged, and minors.

I have written a pledge which follows my philosophy. It fits the rhythm of the original, and if I can remember it, I will recite it in class.

"I pledge allegiance to mankind, not the United States of America, but to the brotherhood that shall prevail, one Entity, under Love, with peace and good will for all."

Naked and Screaming
Bridgewater-Raynham Regional High School
Bridgewater, Massachusetts

A CASE OF THE STUDENT AS NIGGER AND RACIST

Racism is a frightening thing, but it's even worse when you find it in your friends or classmates. At my school, Nicolet, this is becoming increasingly apparent. When in my World History class we got to discussing civil rights, I was appalled to hear someone start talking about how all blacks (he called them "those colored people") are inherently lazy, no good, and generally less intelligent than whites.

When a friend and I started trying to tell him about the basically racist atmosphere that blacks in this country are confronted with from birth, he was joined by three or four others who started yelling about white superiority and how no black has ever done anything worthwhile. They said all this with such great conviction it was frightening.

The majority of kids in that and other classes are abysmally uninformed. I have heard people confidently telling others that all blacks are parasites on white society; while Martin Luther King, Eldridge

Cleaver, and innumerable others have done more to wake up the world to human injustice than anyone else. They believe that the American Indian is perfectly content and well off on his reservation, while he is in reality being starved by the government of land that is rightfully his, having his hunting and fishing rights taken from him, and having almost every treaty ever made with him broken. They have implicit faith and trust in anything they are told by a hypocritical government or teacher, and accept without question that the United States is liberating the Vietnamese peasants and that the NFL will trample them out of existence if they win, when in reality, it's the other way around.

This faith does not come out of stupidity, but is formed by 12 years of indoctrination in the schools where students are taught to respect and fear the authority of the establishment, represented by the teacher. By the time they graduate from high school, most students are so thoroughly brainwashed that they would never think of questioning anything they are told.

Until people are exposed to the truth and know what is really happening in this country, attitudes like these will flourish, creating a new generation of racist oppressors. It is an important responsibility of our school system to furnish the opportunity for students to learn the truth, and stop the flow of propaganda and hypocrisy with which students are now being indoctrinated.

The Open Door
Milwaukee, Wisconsin

Yvonne Criswell / MIXED EMOTIONS: MY YEAR AT WELLESLEY

Have you ever been glanced at and hated in one minute? Or talked to and not really been talked to as a person? Have you entered a room and immediately felt those walls go up? Have you ever sought something better only to find your dream at your feet? It seems strange to some of my friends that I write like this. But, I ask them, how should I write?

White America today is asking itself, "What is Black Power, and what can it do?" Through rioting and its results, White Americans have been forced to realize the full extent of the Afro-Americans' anger. I am sure some Whites felt pity and shame. On the other hand, many have been alienated from the Afro-Americans' cause. (I do not approve of the riots but I feel that they were justified.) The question of Black Power is a hard one to define. I think that Black Power means what each Black individual needs.

I believe that if we, the Black people, want respect, perhaps we should start building on the respect that is already due to us as a people. Through degeneration and propaganda by some of White America, many Afro-Americans really believe that they are inferior. For my present generation, I give a large applause. They are trying to give the Afro-Americans an identity and a culture. To a white child, it is not unusual to refer to his ancestral and cultural origins. The Afro-American, on the other hand, has no cultural link with Africa.

The day I decided to enter METCO (Metropolitan Council for Educational Development—a federally funded project which buses inner city students to suburban schools) I thought of only the pleasant side of my future experiences. I thought of making new friends, and of observing the mysterious white man. It seemed to me to be a motion of extending my hands to someone, anyone willing to grasp them. I considered it to be a positive step. Have you as a person extended your hand to another person? Have you ever thought about the dirtiness that exists in everyone? Then you know what I mean. But to those who don't—I couldn't imagine anyone hating me for being me. It seemed absurd to refuse a friendship because of color, creed, or religion. I wouldn't accept the fact that any of this existed.

When I entered my new school I thought I was prepared for all attacks.

In the short time I have been at this predominantly white school, I have found a small minority of racists, equal groups of frauds and interested persons, and a majority of apathetic, uninterested ones. To me, the most contemptible group is the group of frauds, strangely composed of the professed liberals and the ones seeking understanding. It seems odd to me that a once class of racists changes due to the presence of one Afro-American.

I sometimes wonder if the one year at this school has been worth it. Though you, the reader, may say I am a fool, I'd say that this year *has* been profitable. I have met walls, fields, and a universe in just one year. In one year, I have learned something that would have probably taken a lifetime to learn. It is something simple yet it is nebulous, and as large as the universe—that the superior White man is the same as the Black man, with worries, pains, and joys. And with pain I feel sorry for the White man.

The Searcher, Wellesley High School
Wellesley, Massachusetts

Nancy Ernst / **LONG WINTER**

The crow calls
Black and spare
Harsh

Winter of
  awakening cold
Warm skin exposed
  to the air

I hear in the morning
  the crow's voices
  cracking in the yard

A year of loneliness
Hands over weary eyes

There is nothing
More to say; a coffin

Is in the sun

So few leaves
On the graveyard tree; shivering
In the wind, sad family

The dog's howling
On and on, and still
The moonless sky

My hands are shaking with fatigue
My mind reels from emptiness
The yellow leaves that i was saving
Withered overnight
I suppose i should have pressed them
The sun goes down so early lately
And the air is very cold
My leaves rise in a gust of wind
And blow across the floor

Usually hearts don't break
But so many of them
Just die out
Over the years
From boredom
Or something

In the rooms of this dim place
We waste the last sunny days
A bird's shadow flashes
Across the window shade
And now we sit
In restless rows
Writing themes about death
Some one has carved a flower
In the corner of my desk

The only breeze is suppressed sighing in the institutions. We schoolchildren, preparing for society. Being blinded by lies and inadequate lighting. Pale feeble-souled shut-ins wasting away in the world.

Outside
A rattling can
Birds screaming

After a storm
  Fallen baby birds
    And the rainbow

I love broken things
  Dolls left in the rain
  Some one's old umbrella
And people, so wounded,
  Who mend
  But never are the same again
Like strong trees twisted
  By the wind
  Yet full of April blossoms

When you get
So bored
You begin to see
The Blankness
And you
Drink, take drugs,
Or get married.
You do something like that
You need something to label you
To pretend
You are Something
For some Reason

South Dakota Seditionist Monthly
Aberdeen, South Dakota

EDWARD SHUSTER

The Aftermath

Courtesy of Edward Shuster

JOSEPH McCORD

Evolution or Revolution?

STUDY QUESTIONS FOR COMPREHENSION

1. How does McCord describe the college generation of the 1950s?
2. What is McCord's solution to the problem of violent confrontations on the campuses?
3. Restate McCord's argument in favor of lowering the voting age.

If the study of history teaches us nothing else, it should instruct us with one inescapable fact: Institutions which do not initiate or accept or allow change peaceably will experience change forced upon them violently.

The alternative to evolution is revolution. The only place status quo can be maintained indefinitely is in a graveyard.

The story of man is replete with examples of institutions—and governments—which have toppled because they refused to accept change.

As a Californian, I am acutely aware of the physical laws governing earthquake faults: As long as we have a series of small quakes, nobody worries. But let the San Andreas Fault sit for a long period of time without a tremor, and beads of sweat begin to form on foreheads up and down the Coast. We all know that a big quake is coming, and the longer the time interval since the last one, the bigger it will be. But small shocks—which we can live with—release some of the buildup of pressure beneath our feet. In this sense, many lesser earthquakes are desirable.

From *Junior College Journal,* November 1969. Reprinted by permission of the author and the American Association of Junior Colleges.

The same thesis, to a greater or lesser degree, applies to higher education in America, or elsewhere. American colleges and universities are hit by many "earthquakes" over the years, but most of them are relatively minor, with the Richter needle barely nudging; a small amount of steam is let off, the pressure is released, and relationships settle back to normal, e.g., the dull, sometimes turgid, institutional routine of fall football, Christmas carousing, and June jubilation.

As our colleges grow, some of them become monolithic, impersonal machines which feed on ever-increasing federal research grants. They smother their opponents and critics by burying them under tons of confetti made from punched out IBM cards.

Other colleges—less favored by the federal largess—lose their more able people and become calcified; nonetheless, some do manage to graduate educated people, but this was never the problem. We know our system works—somehow. What we do not understand is how and why it works; therefore, we are not able to recognize the cracks and strains in the system for what they are.

RUMBLINGS BENEATH OUR FEET

The college and university generation of the late forties through the midfifties—the so-called "apathetic" generation—my generation—was far more interested in "getting the sheepskin" than it was in getting an education. If one word could describe us, it would have to be *nondisturbers*. Like the huge majority of Berkeley students, then and now, I was far more interested in getting through the institution than in bringing it crashing down around me. I was not unconcerned with what was happening; I just was not involved.

But there was movement beneath our feet—slow, almost imperceptible at first. The rumblings first began at Berkeley during the late fifties and early sixties. Anyone could have felt the stresses building and predicted that a "shake" was coming sooner or later. The violence and confrontation of December 1964 was a sudden, unexpected occurrence only to those people—and there were many—who had no idea of the tensions which had been building during the previous decade. Communications at Berkeley had almost completely broken down. The administration would not listen to the faculty; many of the faculty did not believe the students had anything to say; and the students distrusted both groups.

Probably most tragic of all was that the regents, for the most part, were blissfully unaware of what was happening. When the "great quake" started to bring the institution down around their ears, they were unprepared to do more than shake their heads in amazement that such a thing could happen.

Nor were the students totally innocent. Rather than consolidating their early gains, the moderates among them—and in the beginning, nearly all the leaders were moderates—bowed to the pressures of the militants who pushed them into a head-long rush toward confrontation and violence. This, of course, is the history of all revolutions, but I fault the student leaders of the late fifties and early sixties for not knowing this history and preventing its repetition.

However, the most important factor in my opinion was that the Berkeley machinery of communication broke down—or else it never was set up properly in the first place. In either case, the various sides were not talking to one another on any basis which might have prevented or diminished the later violence. What talks there were resulted only in further aggravation of the tension.

Obviously, I cannot speak with any certainty about the evolution of events at any other college where students have revolted, but because of the similarities among these confrontations, it seems safe to surmise that the same patterns may have been repeated at some of the other colleges. This surmise seems all the more accurate when one compares the recent college revolution with other types of revolutions throughout history. Over and over again when institutions fought change, they eventually were overthrown and replaced by those seeking change; whereas, those institutions which allowed change managed to survive. The Roman Catholic Church probably is the classic example which strengthens this point. The Roman Church often is pointed to as the bastion of reaction and conservatism, but any student of religious history knows that over the centuries, the church has altered drastically many of its positions, sometimes swinging back to those previously abandoned. Probably few people are aware that marriage among priests was widespread during the early Middle Ages and that vows of celibacy are comparatively recent considering the great age of the church. Now we are seeing a movement back toward a married Roman Catholic clergy—a movement which could reach completion in our lifetimes.

The Roman Empire is another example. The wonderment of Rome's history is not that it fell but rather that it lasted as long as it did. By any standards, 700 years of domination is a long time. Rome's long rule should not be attributed to any inherent quality in the stock of its people, who really were no more qualified to rule than were many of their contemporaries, but rather to the fact that the Roman system allowed outsiders to bring in new blood and new ideas. Most of the later legionnaires were not Romans at all; they came from North Africa or Spain or other far-flung provinces. In time, of course, these *barbarians* (the Latin word meant merely a *non-Roman*) took over the empire and ruled it, but the empire and its institutions stood for centuries. Even after Rome, herself, fell, the Eastern Empire lasted for another 1,000 years because it adapted to changes working from below.

The list of similar examples is virtually endless but not worth further exploring except to make the point that the world is constantly changing despite the massiveness of the status quo. A second point worth making is that this inevitable change need not be destructive to the institution involved. Like Rome, our educational institutions should allow—even encourage—the infusion of new ideas, new blood, and new ways of doing things.

THE PROBLEM

The problem, of course, is how best to go about it.

Clearly, the old methods have not worked. Violence and confrontation do not offer a solution; they simply focus attention on the problems.

Through the turmoil of the past five years, speaker after speaker—from the President of the United States to governors, senators, congressmen, college presidents, and many others—have said: "Yes, it is true that some of the student complaints are valid, but I don't like their methods; violence only makes it more difficult to meet their demands."

All right. Then we need to find other methods, other means.

If the students are sincere in wanting to improve the institution —and I believe most of them are—then the Establishment also must be sincere in wanting their help.

Let the old ways change—not overnight, simply because they will not change overnight—but let them change.

A PROPOSAL

One way I feel they should change is by including students and faculty in the decision-making process. Students and faculty should serve on boards of trustees, or boards of regents, or whatever body governs the institution involved.

The proposal is simple; the implications are complex. Putting students and faculty members on boards will open up vitally needed lines of communication to boards and administrators, so they, in turn, will recognize the ground tremors at an early stage and hopefully be able to do something to prevent the big shock which surely will follow otherwise.

The proposal has other, more political, implications. One of the greatest appeals of the Far Left to students is: "The Establishment will never listen to you until you wave your fist in front of their noses and shout four-letter words into their ears." If the students—including the militants but perhaps, excluding the radicals—can be shown that they will be listened to, then much of the Far Left's appeal will lose whatever luster it may happen to have for these students.

I do not know what effect the proposal would have on the Far Right; I have never been able to figure them out.

A further implication is that this method can and should be a way of involving our brightest young people in the political system at a much earlier age than most of them have become involved over the years. As a former deputy voter registrar, I can testify that the worst percentage of eligible voter registration is in the 21- to 25-year-old bracket. This age group should have the highest register percentage because political decisions will affect them for a longer period of time than those same decisions will affect any older group. My experience, however, is that these young people—unless they came from a politically oriented family or were, themselves, involved in politics in some way—simply were not concerned with the political process. They did not register; they did not vote.

Others have pointed out that the people who are best informed on political issues are the high-school students, and this group is not allowed to vote. Sadly, the three-year interim between high school graduation and eligibility to vote seems to be long enough to destroy the interest most eighteen-year-olds have in politics. But since more and more young people now are going to college, we might be able to fan this interest and keep it alive if we can provide a reason.

Since this is not meant to be a plea for lowering the voting age—although such action would be a logical corollary—and since the voting age is still twenty-one in most states, some other way must be found to help our young people retain a healthy interest and involvement in politics. One way would be to involve them early in the decision-making process, particularly in those decisions having a direct bearing on their lives.

At Ohlone College in Fremont, California, we have done just exactly that. Beginning later this year, we are going to bring a student and a faculty member onto our board to aid us and to involve them in the decision-making process. California law prevents these two representatives from having an actual vote in any decisions, but nothing in the law prohibits us from listening to their points of view and their ideas, and incorporating them, if we wish, into these decisions. The experiment might not work. Since the selection of both the faculty and the student representatives will be left up to the faculty and the students, respectively, there is the possibility that irresponsible people might win these ex-officio seats. There is also the possibility that either or both of these representatives will not truly reflect their own constituencies or will embarrass the institution. These are risks we must take. The important thing, however, is that we are willing to take them.

Recently, too, the lieutenant governor of California suggested that students be added to the University of California Board of Regents and to the State College Board of Trustees. In his statement,

Lt. Gov. Ed Reinecke said: "It's time we stopped hitting kids over the head."

His suggestion has not been considered yet by the California Legislature—but there is positive sentiment expressed by some legislative members, and perhaps, the idea will be carried through.

The proposal to add students to college boards is hardly new. A number of colleges in the United States and Canada have tried it and are satisfied with it as a good tool. I firmly believe the idea should be advanced and tested.

If we really are sincere in wanting to preserve and protect our institutions of higher education, then we had better give some hard thought as to how those institutions are being operated. If we are not, then we should stock up on a large supply of hard hats—and buy lots of "earthquake" insurance.

SEYMOUR METZNER

School Terrorism

STUDY QUESTIONS FOR COMPREHENSION

1. What does Metzner mean when he writes of a "power vacuum" in our educational system?
2. How does the civil rights movement affect the school crisis?
3. Explain Metzner's charge that teachers have lost much of their "sacrosanct status."

The issue of violence in the public schools has assumed dimensions unheard of a decade ago. Historically, violence in high schools or elementary schools has been a matter of local concern exclusively, and seldom involved more than sporadic vandalism, isolated fist fights, and occasional group melees after supercharged football or basketball games.

Now, violent disruptive behavior has become a national issue, with a swelling tide of felonious violence, widespread vandalism, and planned disruption aimed at the school as an institution and teachers as its representatives, rather than emotional, unpremeditated outbreaks.

Serious educational conflict is manifested countrywide in many forms. In New York City, a junior-high-school principal is beaten in his office by three men *(5)* and an elementary-school principal is threatened with the rape of his daughter *(12)*. A St. Louis elementary-school teacher is stabbed by a 14-year-old girl, causing other teachers to flee from the building in terror *(18)*. In staid Boston, a junior-high-school principal resigns after six weeks because of inability to control pupil disorderliness which erupts into mini-riots *(9)*; while San Francisco hosted 180 pupil assaults in elementary schools during the first three months of the 1968 school year *(17)*.

The trend in violence and vandalism is sharply upward. School

From the Spring 1969 issue of *Changing Education,* American Federation of Teachers, AFL-CIO. Reprinted by permission of the American Federation of Teachers. The numbers in parentheses refer to sources listed at the end of the essay.

arson and vandalism cost New York City $1.95 million in 1967, compared to $1.5 million in 1966, a rise of almost one-third *(6)*. The Riot Data Clearinghouse of the Lemberg Center for the Study of Violence reported that 17 percent of incidents in 1967 involved schools, while in the first four months of 1968, this rose to 44 percent *(7)*. The report noted that this trend was strong even after allowing for the violence following the Martin Luther King assassination. In New York City, there were 271 assaults on teachers in 1964 *(17)*, compared to 60 assaults in 1962 *(2)*. A Chicago board of education attorney noted a rise of 1,000 percent in assaults on teachers from 1962 to 1964 *(1)*. This lends a note of unwholesome reality to teacher perceptions which leads to claims that 415 teachers rejected teaching posts in Philadelphia in 1965 due to fear of pupil attacks *(3)*, while 317 Los Angeles teachers asked for transfers to other schools because of fear of driving through troubled areas *(4)*.

A study of the New York Times Index for the years from 1940 to 1968 validates the accelerated tempo and importance of school unrest and violence. Before 1960, the "student activities" section had very few items and these were generally about ongoing programs or inventories of student beliefs. From 1960, there were increasing signs of interest in student activities with six to 12 items a year involving problems of fraternity hazing, student-publication censorship, and violations of school-dress and appearance rules.

The year 1964 heralded the current emphasis on teacher assaults with elements of racial unrest. The major change in the student activities section occurred in 1967, which listed 56 items, compared to nine in 1966. This trend continued with the first six months of 1968 listing 42 reports. The 1967 and 1968 incidents were particularly notable because of a large incidence of group actions as opposed to previous individual activities, and almost all items had racial overtones, either explicitly or implicitly *(16)*.

Although the trend of school violence is clear enough that documentation of it runs the risk of elaboration of the obvious, the possible reasons for this violence are much less clear.

One reason is that the schools may be an all-too-faithful mirror of society and are not insulated from it. Why should school violence decline while violent crime, nationwide, is up 21 percent from the first nine months of 1967 to a similar period in 1968, with rates in urban "transition" areas, such as Newark, N.J., having double the national-rate increase *(13)*? Why should the lower educational echelons have less disruption while the first six months of 1968 resound to 221 major demonstrations at 101 colleges and universities *(8)*? How can a school expect to be exempt when even the monastic sanctuary of a library is violated enough to close it *(14)*?

There is also the development of a power vacuum in many educational relationships. The simple certainty no longer holds that pupils are in school to learn what is taught, teachers are to teach, and administrators are to administer, while parents make happy, encouraging noises to their offspring.

Now, the roles are much less-defined and tensions are generated by the various groups scrambling for a bigger piece of the action. This is particularly true of the urban areas in the Northeast, Midwest, and Far West. Role change is less advanced in the South, where tradition is stronger and dissident elements have migrated out to climates more responsive to their aspirations. This helps explain the comparative lack of turmoil in Southern schools.

The civil-rights movement is undoubtedly a major element in the present series of school crises. It was highly visible in almost all secondary-school incidents while, in colleges, issues of race relationships were the major reasons for 97 student demonstrations compared to 50 demonstrations for "student power" and 26 protesting the Vietnam War *(8)*.

The worldwide demand for self-determinism among previously subjugated people in underdeveloped areas finds a sympathetic echo from American minorities which have never been granted equal opportunity in any aspect of American life. This demand for equal opportunity inevitably must focus on the schools as a major source of friction because economic and social advancement has been traditionally linked to schools as the escalator to success in American life, while technological advances reinforce this avenue as the *sine qua non* for advancement in American civilization.

There is no doubt that American schools have been notably

unsuccessful in helping some minority groups, such as blacks, Puerto Ricans, and Indians, attain the knowledge and skills necessary for success. In the past, the reasons for this failure were believed to mainly hinge upon social and environmental weaknesses in the social structure of these groups, and many people within these groups concurred in this belief.

New currents of thought, gaining wide credence among minority people themselves, hold that the basic reason for lack of success was the unresponsiveness of the educational structure to the needs, aspirations, and learning styles of ethnic minorities which were culturally different from the majority of the American school population. A portion of the current unrest and disorderliness stems from a combination of rancor at these past wrongs combined with frustration with the slowness with which change is occurring to remedy these wrongs.

The self-deterministic aspect of this struggle is readily seen in the demands of the black students for more black teachers, greater voice in the hiring and firing of the teachers, and a share in the decision-making policies regarding what is to be taught.

Another element in school disruption is the lack of administrative foresight in recognizing potential problems, no clear pattern of successful strategy to follow to disarm this time bomb, and Hamlet-like vacillation when the situation explodes. Lacking the framework of clearcut guidelines, the students feel free to explore the nebulous limits of their powers and responsibilities while school administrators either compromise, give in, or become punitive, with few principles except momentary expedience to guide their actions. The result is a scenario calling for future outbursts, since the basis for grievances, real or imaginary, is seldom fully investigated, while future administrative reaction to further violence is neither established nor credible.

The teachers are pawns in a struggle in which they have little power to affect meaningful change. They bear the brunt of discontent they haven't caused and often don't understand. Not knowing for certain which of their actions or attitudes will irritate students and the community, and being equally uncertain of the backing they will receive from administrative echelons, they tend to exhibit the fear and uncertainty which itself becomes an invitation to student aggression.

Teachers and schools have certainly lost much of their sacrosanct status, due, in part, to conflicts with the community. There is reason to believe that some community members not only sanction aggressive pupil behavior against teachers and schools but actually encourage it. It is easily seen that the recent wave of teacher strikes further encourages erosion of the teachers' former "above-the-battle" status.

Prospects for the immediate future are not optimistic. College strife is likely to continue until a clear pattern for successfully handling grievances emerges. We can look forward to increasing dislocation at the high-school level. This is heralded by the following remark of the interorganizational secretary at the 1968 meeting of the Students for a Democratic Society: "Our high schools will be the new thrust. They are used as babysitting jails. They are used to trap people into stupid colleges to train them for jobs they don't want. They are oppressive *(15)*."

It does not take the gift of prophecy to expect accelerated problems in the junior high schools and elementary schools. The actions of an 11-year-old New York City pupil circulating a petition to oust the principal of his school may well presage a further breakdown of school authority with a concomitant rise in school violence *(11)*.

What can teachers and teachers' organizations do to counter school disruptions and their concomitant regressive educational and social consequences? Must the classroom teacher be the battered shuttlecock in power plays between the school administration and the community? Can teachers play a meaningful role in redirecting unguided social forces into educationally constructive channels?

These questions can have hopeful, encouraging answers only if teachers are willing to do five things.

First, they must build up their own personal "power base" in the community. This can be done by involving the parents in class activities via newsletters, personal get-together invitations, letters to parents that are sent on a personal rather than official basis, greater use of parents in class functions, and visitations to students' homes as an interested friend and not in the teacher role. All of this takes time and energy, both of which are in short supply after a full day's teaching, but it is a necessity in order to build up community rapport.

Second, administrators must be assured of complete teacher-organization support for any actions that must be taken to assure the safety of school personnel and property, while being told precisely what measures of self-defense will be undertaken by the teachers themselves if administrative support is not forthcoming.

Third, teachers must take the lead in demanding curricular adjustments relevant to the particular environment of the student body. This should be done before the demand arises and not in grudging response to a confrontation.

Fourth, students should not only be given a meaningful voice in school affairs, but should also be held responsible for the execution of decisions they help formulate. A step in this direction might be placing student officers on a salary basis as junior members of the school administration.

Fifth, and last, teachers should demand that community leaders be brought into the schools as paid aides and consultants and help to share the responsibility for school stability and other educational decisions.

A peaceful, learning environment will return to the schools when teachers stop being reactors to revolt and become initiators of action.

REFERENCES

(1) *New York Times,* March 5, 1964, p. 27; (2) *Ibid.,* March 6, 1964, p. 1; (3) *Ibid.,* Feb. 25, 1966, p. 15; (4) *Ibid.,* May 26, 1966, p. 41; (5) *Ibid.,* Jan. 25, 1968, p. 22; (6) *Ibid.,* April 8, 1968, p. 49; (7) *Ibid.,* Aug. 25, 1968, p. E 11; (8) *Ibid.,* Aug. 27, 1968, p. 33; (9) *Ibid.,* Dec. 7, 1968, p. 50; (10) *Ibid.,* Dec. 8, 1968, p. 52; (11) *Ibid.,* Dec. 10, 1968, p. 1; (12) *Ibid.,* Dec. 16, 1968, p. 43; (13) *Ibid.,* Dec. 17, 1968, p. 1; (14) *Ibid.,* Dec. 21, 1968, p. 30; (15) *Ibid.,* Dec. 30, 1968, p. 29; (16) *New York Times Index,* 1940–1968; (17) *U.S. News & World Report,* Dec. 2, 1968, p. 33; (18) *Ibid.,* p. 30.

ROBERT S. POWELL, JR.

Participation Is Learning

STUDY QUESTIONS FOR COMPREHENSION

1. Explain in your own words the distinction Robert Powell makes between the ultimate goal of education as school officials see it and as the dissenting students see it.
2. What is the comparison Powell makes between grades and useful evaluation?
3. Do you agree with Powell's view that student participation is necessary in all parts of the educational decision-making process?

Like it or not, the university campus is a piece of turf, the control of which is a competitive matter both in and out of the university community. In the past, the combatants were few: the ivory tower professors fighting the government and industry to keep the university's resources from being devoted to war and business research. The academics argued then that such a step would have a corrosive effect on the institution's commitments to the students, but they lost.

The competition has been renewed, but now there are new combatants, Black and other minority students, who make up barely 3 per cent of the nation's college students outside of Southern black colleges, want a piece of the turf. Denying the potential benefits of college to them is denying potential power to their people; so they have joined the battle, and for them the stakes are unmistakably high. White activists want a piece of that turf, too. They are concerned about how future generations of Americans are going to learn how to use power and resources in this world, and they know that what and how students learn in college could make a difference.

In a fundamental sense, this competition is over the issue of who shall govern the university; who shall decide what goes on within it; who decides who shall have access to its potential benefits; and who decides the terms on which those benefits shall be offered.

The current governing standard of universities—oligarchy, with decisions made by the trustees and senior faculty—has had a predictable effect on the goals of those institutions. With regard to their students, our universities today seem aimed at the goal of job accreditation. Tests, grades, honors, degrees—these tangible signs of approval and success—form the basis for what takes place in the classroom, and the students are taught that securing these things indicates that one is "accredited" and ready to take a job reserved in the society for those with such credentials.

To succeed, the student needs an enormous memory, the ability to take rapid notes, and an intensely competitive spirit (where you sit on the normal curve is generally more important than what you have learned). If a course in any way has helped to sort out some of the important questions facing young people today, that's fine, but it is secondary to getting the course over with and on the transcript as completed satisfactorily.

In so organizing the student's college experience, the institution seldom has any hidden, pernicious motives. To the contrary, the university views itself much in the role of the consummate welfare state, deciding for the students the important questions of mind as well as of body (required courses and rules governing social and personal behavior imply the same view of the student's capacities), but always *deciding for the student,* with his best interests in mind.

Student power, on the other hand, implies a more democratic standard of governance, a standard that encourages people to make their own decisions and choices, a standard that aims at developing young people who are capable of thinking for themselves, of using freedom and power wisely.

Student power is thus a critique of the university's educational assumptions, because it suggests a much different goal for the institution, the goal of freeing people by teaching them how to do *their own* learning. In this regard, learning must become a highly personal process in which the emphasis is no longer the assimilation of a body of facts and knowledge, but rather the encouragement of individual growth and self-development. Education first and foremost should teach you to know yourself.

Currently, our universities are not especially democratic, and that is not surprising. A democratic process is not needed if the object is to decide whether the student has passed enough credit hours of lectures to receive the institutional stamp of approval and get the degree. If, on the other hand, we are serious about the self-development of students and their capacities to take responsibility for their own learning, their own decisions, and their own work, then I believe we must move toward a more democratic university.

To do this we must first move to abolish the current grading system. No step could be more central to basic reform. Grades are now the central instrument of coercion employed by the university against the students, and if students are to be allowed to participate and decide matters relating to their own academic plans, this instrument must be removed from the hands of the faculty.

Grades destroy the very educational goal they purport to serve, namely, useful evaluation of learning. By testing the student's ability to memorize facts and notes, the professor discovers only the most superficial aspects of what the student has received (or not received) from a course. By giving the student a letter grade or a percentage score, he informs the student quite inadequately about his strengths, weaknesses, and future directions.

Beyond this, however, the grading system sets the context and ground rules for student-faculty relations. The student performs, and the professor judges, and the relationship is strictly one-way. Seldom is there any thought that the student and the teacher are somehow partners in the learning process; seldom any thought that perhaps the student might be competent to evaluate himself, *for the record,* and that such an experience in itself might be educative when done cooperatively with the professor.

Grades and useful evaluation are not necessarily the same things. Getting rid of the current grading system won't be easy. Schools have been using it for so long that, like a narcotic, it has become an addiction, to the point that educators are quite fearful of facing the world without grades. Often, reformers go halfway, replacing grades with pass-fail, for example. While this alternative exerts less coercion on the student to compete mindlessly for a better place on the normal curve, it still leaves the student without any substantive and useful evaluation of his work, which, after all, should be the goal.

A better direction would be to encourage the student and the professor jointly to evaluate the student's work *and* the professor's contribution to that work, with the evaluation being written up (or taped for the sake of time) and filed with other such evaluations in a personal dossier that the student builds during his stay at the university. The point is that a student ought to have a way of knowing what his skills and weaknesses are, but the grade-point average is not the most sensible way, humanely or educationally, and new ways should be developed and tried at each campus.

A second step that should be taken if we are to build a more democratic university is the restraining of faculty power. Currently, the faculty exercises a virtual monopoly over the key academic decisions of the university—course offerings, degree requirements, programs of study, and all the other facets of educational policy. I oppose such a grant of power, for two reasons.

First, most faculties make educational decisions with a particular perspective, which certainly cannot be taken as complete. This perspective might be described as "faculty elitism" and defined as the assumption that what is taught in the classroom by a professor has an inherent worth, far beyond any effect it has on the students. Such a perspective tends to be visible in the curricula that often come out of faculty deliberations. They appear designed to produce more faculty members rather than people with skills and capacities somewhat different from those possessed by professors.

Few university professors know much at all about what comprises good teaching and effective learning. Their competence within their subject discipline cannot be argued; however, their competence to make educational decisions closely tied to learning theory and teaching effectiveness is debatable. The fact that there are so many bad teachers and boring classes on a given campus is partial testament to the point. One has only to read through the published course and teacher evaluations being put out by student governments around the country to get the clear impression that students aren't terribly engaged by the majority of courses and professors with whom they come in contact. Moreover, the hundreds of student-oriented free universities and experimental colleges that have sprung up around the country indicate that large numbers of students feel their learning experience can be organized in a much more effective and exciting way.

If college professors understood as much about teaching and learning as doctors do about medicine and disease, perhaps we students would accept the professorial monopoly over the curriculum, but because the faculty is producing an experience for students that is too often dull, useless for their needs, and unworthy of what higher learning in America should be, students cannot accept the unregulated use of power.

The monopoly must be broken, by making students equal partners in building the curriculum and in making all the related decisions about the institution's academic affairs—grading, requirements, new courses, the academic calendar, admissions, degrees.

Breaking the monopoly also means including the students in decisions about faculty hiring and promotions. The present closed process has produced an incentive system for academics that is vicious, as well as destructive of the goal of undergraduate teaching and development. Few institutions really reward a man for his teaching. Virtually all reward him for his research and publications, by hiring and promoting him if he does those things, and by holding him back if he doesn't. Only the student can add a third incentive to the mix—the incentive to be a good teacher, and to become skilled at helping people learn. If universities continue to exclude students from this area, they will continue to affirm very clearly that teaching and student development are low priorities.

There are other steps to basic reform that will follow, once students begin to make their voices and votes heard in policy-making. Required courses should be eliminated, largely because they isolate and protect bad teaching and bad classes. If a professor thinks he has something important to teach, he shouldn't feel it necessary to force students to come hear him.

Students should be free to initiate their own courses, for credit. Many universities provide a simple mechanism for accrediting a student course proposal, a mechanism that functions quickly, in a supportive manner, and without endless committee red tape. Moreover, students not only should be free to plan *de novo* their personal academic agenda in collaboration with the faculty, they should be *encouraged* to do so. We might find that John Dewey was right when he spoke of the strong relationship between effort and involvement.

These examples of change are merely suggestive of a direction. From the overview, the combination of reforms is meant to underline a basic principle: if there is to be reform within the existing institutional framework, it must be radical. I have offered my suggestions not only because I think they are essential, but because I also believe they are practicable. Nonetheless, I offer them with considerable pessimism, because there is presently little evidence of sufficient energy and leadership in the American university for it to be reformed from within. It is ironic—and to students, enraging—that the university is one of the last of our institutions to reflect our national passion for the democratic process. Fundamentally, that's what student power is all about.

JESSAMYN WEST

Sixteen

STUDY QUESTIONS FOR COMPREHENSION

1. Describe Cress's personality before she rubs ointment on her grandfather's neck.
2. When Cress tells Edwin she isn't going home to her grandfather, why does Edwin tell her that going home might do her some good? Why is he cold and disapproving?
3. What does Cress mean when she says, "Edwin knew"?
4. Why is this story included in the education section of this book?

The steam from the kettle had condensed on the cold window and was running down the glass in tear-like trickles. Outside in the orchard the man from the smudge company was refilling the pots with oil. The greasy smell from last night's burning was still in the air. Mr. Delahanty gazed out at the bleak darkening orange grove; Mrs. Delahanty watched her husband eat, nibbling up to the edges of the toast, then stacking the crusts about his tea cup in a neat fence-like arrangement.

"We'll have to call Cress," Mr. Delahanty said, finally. "Your father's likely not to last out the night. She's his only grandchild. She ought to be here."

Mrs. Delahanty pressed her hands to the bones above her eyes. "Cress isn't going to like being called away from college," she said.

"We'll have to call her anyway. It's the only thing to do." Mr. Delahanty swirled the last of his tea around in his cup so as not to miss any sugar.

"Father's liable to lapse into unconsciousness any time," Mrs. Delahanty argued. "Cress'll hate coming and Father won't know whether she's here or not. Why not let her stay at Woolman?"

Neither wanted, in the midst of their sorrow for the good man whose life was ending, to enter into any discussion of Cress. What was the matter with Cress? What had happened to her since she went away to college? She, who had been open and loving? And who now lived inside a world so absolutely fitted to her own size and shape that she felt any intrusion, even that of the death of her own grandfather, to be an unmerited invasion of her privacy. Black magic could not have changed her more quickly and unpleasantly and nothing except magic, it seemed, would give them back their lost daughter.

Mr. Delahanty pushed back his cup and saucer. "Her place is here, Gertrude. I'm going to call her long distance now. She's a bright girl and it's not going to hurt her to miss a few days from classes. What's the dormitory number?"

"I know it as well as our number," Mrs. Delahanty said. "But at the minute it's gone. It's a sign of my reluctance, I suppose. Wait a minute and I'll look it up."

Mr. Delahanty squeezed out from behind the table. "Don't bother. I can get it."

Mrs. Delahanty watched her husband, his usually square shoulders sagging with weariness, wipe a clear place on the steamy windowpane with his napkin. Some of the green twilight appeared to seep into the warm dingy little kitchen. "I can't ever remember having to smudge before in February. I expect you're right," he added as he went toward the phone. "Cress isn't going to like it."

Cress didn't like it. It was February, the rains had been late and the world was burning with a green fire; a green smoke rolled down the hills and burst shoulder-high in the cover crops that filled the spaces between the trees in the orange orchards. There had been rain earlier in the day and drops still hung from the grass blades, sickle-shaped with their weight. Cress, walking across the campus with Edwin, squatted to look into one of these crystal globes.

"Green from the grass and red from the sun," she told him. "The whole world right there in one raindrop."

"As Blake observed earlier about a grain of sand," said Edwin.

"O.K., show off," Cress told him. "You know it—but I saw it."

She took his hand and he pulled her up, swinging her in a semi-circle in front of him. "Down there in the grass the world winked at me."

"Don't be precious, Cress," Edwin said.

"I will," Cress said, "just to tease you. I love to tease you, Edwin."

"Why?" Edwin asked.

"Because you love to have me," Cress said confidently, taking his hand. Being older suited Edwin. She remembered when she had liked him in spite of his looks; but now spindly had became spare, and the dark shadow of his beard—Edwin had to shave every day while other boys were still just fuzzy—lay under his pale skin; and the opinions, which had once been so embarrassingly unlike any-one else's, were now celebrated at Woolman as being "Edwinian." Yes, Edwin had changed since that day when she had knocked his tooth out trying to rescue him from the mush pot. And had she changed? Did she also look better to Edwin, almost slender now and the freckles not noticeable except at the height of summer? And with her new-found ability for light talk? They were passing beneath the eucalyptus trees and the silver drops, falling as the wind shook the leaves, stung her face, feeling at once both cool and burning. Meadow larks in the fields which edged the campus sang in the quiet way they have after the rain has stopped.

"Oh, Edwin," Cress said, "no one in the world loves the meadow lark's song the way I do!"

"It's not a competition," Edwin said, "you against the world in an 'I-love-meadow-larks' contest. Take it easy, kid. Love 'em as much as in you lieth, and let it go at that."

"No," she said. "I'm determined to overdo it. Listen," she exclaimed, as two birds sang together. "Not grieving, nor amorous, nor lost. Nothing to read into it. Simply music. Like Mozart. Complete. Finished. Oh, it is rain to listening ears." She glanced at Edwin to see how he took this rhetoric. He took it calmly. She let go his hand and capered amidst the fallen eucalyptus leaves.

"The gardener thinks you've got St. Vitus' dance," Edwin said.

Old Boat Swain, the college gardener whose name was really

Swain, was leaning on his hoe, watching her hopping and strutting. She didn't give a hoot about him or what he thought.

"He's old," she told Edwin. "He doesn't exist." She felt less akin to him than to a bird or toad.

There were lights already burning in the dorm windows. Cress could see Ardis and Nina still at their tables, finishing their *Ovid* or looking up a final logarithm. But between five and six most of the girls stopped trying to remember which form of the sonnet Milton had used or when the Congress of Vienna had met, and dressed for dinner. They got out of their sweaters and jackets and into their soft bright dresses. She knew just what she was going to wear when she came downstairs at six to meet Edwin—green silk like the merman's wife. They were going to the Poinsettia for dinner, escaping salmon-wiggle night in the college dining room.

"At six," she told him, "I'll fly down the stairs to meet you like a green wave."

"See you in thirty minutes," Edwin said, leaving her at the dorm steps.

The minute she opened the door, she began to hear the dorm sounds and smell the dorm smells—the hiss and rush of the showers, the thud of the iron, a voice singing, "Dear old Woolman we love so well," the slap of bare feet down the hall, the telephone ringing.

And the smells! Elizabeth Arden and Cashmere Bouquet frothing in the showers; talcum powder falling like snow; *Intoxication* and *Love Me* and *Devon Violet;* rubber-soled sneakers, too, and gym T-shirts still wet with sweat after basketball practice, and the smell of the hot iron on damp wool.

But while she was still listening and smelling, Edith shouted from the top of the stairs, "Long distance for you, Cress. Make it snappy."

Cress took the stairs three at a time, picked up the dangling receiver, pressed it to her ear.

"Tenant calling Crescent Delahanty," the operator said. It was her father: "Grandfather is dying, Cress. Catch the 7:30 home. I'll meet you at the depot."

"What's the matter—Cressie?" Edith asked.

"I have to catch the 7:30 Pacific Electric. Grandfather's dying."

"Oh, poor Cress," Edith cried and pressed her arm about her.

Cress scarcely heard her. Why were they calling her home to watch Grandpa die, she thought, angrily and rebelliously. An old man, past eighty. He'd never been truly alive for her, never more than a rough, hot hand, a scraggly mustache that repelled her when he kissed her, an old fellow who gathered what he called "likely-looking" stones and kept them washed and polished, to turn over and admire. It was silly and unfair to make so much of his dying.

But before she could say a word, Edith was telling the girls. They were crowding about her. "Don't cry," they said. "We'll pack for you. Be brave, darling Cress. Remember your grandfather has had a long happy life. He wouldn't want you to cry."

"Brave Cress—brave Cress," they said. "Just frozen."

She wasn't frozen. She was determined. She was not going to go. It did not make sense. She went downstairs to meet Edwin as she had planned, in her green silk, ready for dinner at the Poinsettia. The girls had told him.

"Are you wearing that home?" he asked.

"I'm not going home," she said. "It's silly and useless. I can't help Grandfather. It's just a convention. What *good* can I do him, sitting there at home?"

"He might do you some good," Edwin said. "Had you thought about that?"

"Why, Edwin!" Cress said. "Why, Edwin!" She had the girls tamed, eating out of her hand, and here was Edwin who loved her —he said so, anyway—cold and disapproving. Looking at herself through Edwin's eyes, she hesitated.

"Go on," Edwin said. "Get what you need and I'll drive you to the station."

She packed her overnight bag and went with him; there didn't seem—once she'd had Edwin's view of herself—anything else to do. But once on the train her resentment returned. The Pacific Electric was hot and smelled of metal and dusty plush. It clicked past a rickety Mexican settlement, through La Habra and Brea, where the pool hall signs swung in the night wind off the ocean. An old man in a spotted corduroy jacket, and his wife, with her hair straggling through the holes in her broken net, sat in front of her.

Neat, thought Cress, anyone can be neat, if he wants to.

Her father, bareheaded, but in his big sheepskin jacket, met her at the depot. It was after nine, cold and raw.

"This is a sorry time, Cress," he said. He put her suitcase in the back of the car and climbed into the driver's seat without opening the door for her.

Cress got in, wrapped her coat tightly about herself. The sky was clear, the wind had died down.

"I don't see any sense in my having to come home," she said at last. "What good can I do Grandpa? If he's dying, how can I help?"

"I was afraid that was the way you might feel about it. So was your mother."

"Oh, Mother," Cress burst out. "Recently she's always trying to put me . . ."

Her father cut her off. "That'll be about enough, Cress. Your place is at home and you're coming home and keeping your mouth shut, whatever you think. I don't know what's happened to you recently. If college does this to you, you'd better stay home permanently."

There was nothing more said until they turned up the palm-lined driveway that led to the house. "Here we are," Mr. Delahanty told her.

Mrs. Delahanty met them at the door, tired and haggard in her Indian design bathrobe.

"Cress," she said, "Grandfather's conscious now. I told him you were coming and he's anxious to see you. You'd better go in right away—this might be the last time he'd know you."

Cress was standing by the fireplace holding first one foot then the other toward the fire. "Oh, Mother, what am I to say?" she asked. "What can I say? Or does Grandfather just want to see me?"

Her father shook his head as if with pain. "Aren't you sorry your grandfather's dying, Cress? Haven't you any pity in your heart? Don't you understand what death means?"

"He's an old man," Cress said obstinately. "It's what we must expect when we grow old," though she, of course, would never grow old.

"Warm your hands, Cress," her mother said. "Grandfather's throat bothers him and it eases him to have it rubbed. I'll give you the ointment and you can rub it in. You won't need to say anything."

Cress slid out of her coat and went across the hall with her mother to visit her grandfather's room. His thin old body was hardly visible beneath the covers; his head, with its gray skin and sunken eyes, lay upon the pillow as if bodiless. The night light frosted his white hair but made black caverns of his closed eyes.

"Father," Mrs. Delahanty said. "Father." But the old man didn't move. There was nothing except the occasional hoarse rasp of an indrawn breath to show that he was alive.

Mrs. Delahanty pulled the cane-bottomed chair a little closer to the bed. "Sit here," she said to Cress, "and rub this into his throat and chest." She opened her father's nightshirt so that an inch or two of bony grizzled chest was bared. "He says that this rubbing relieves him, even if he's asleep or too tired to speak. Rub it in with a slow steady movement." She went out to the living room leaving the door a little ajar.

Cress sat down on the chair and put two squeamish fingers into the jar of gray ointment; but she could see far more sense to this than to any talking or being talked to. If they had brought her home from school because she was needed in helping to care for Grandpa, that she could understand—but not simply to be present at his death. What had death to do with her?

She leaned over him, rubbing, but with eyes shut, dipping her fingers often into the gray grease. The rhythm of the rubbing, the warmth and closeness of the room, after the cold drive, had almost put her to sleep when the old man startled her by lifting a shaking hand to the bunch of yellow violets Edith had pinned to the shoulder of her dress before she left Woolman. She opened her eyes suddenly at his touch, but the old man said nothing, only stroked the violets awkwardly with a trembling forefinger.

Cress unpinned the violets and put them in his hand. "There, Grandpa," she said, "there. They're for you."

The old man's voice was a harsh and faltering whisper and to hear what he said Cress had to lean very close.

"I used to—pick them—on Reservoir Hill. I was always sorry to —plow them up. Still—so sweet. Thanks," he said, "to bring them. To remember. You're like her. Your grandmother," he added after a pause. He closed his eyes, holding the bouquet against his face, letting the wilting blossoms spray across one cheek like a pulled-up sheet of flowering earth. He said one more word, not her name but her grandmother's.

The dikes about Cress's heart broke. "Oh, Grandpa, I love you," she said. He heard her. He knew what she said, his fingers returned the pressure of her hand. "You were always so good to me. You were young and you loved flowers." Then she said what was her great discovery. "And you still do. You still love yellow violets, Grandpa, just like me."

At the sound of her uncontrolled crying, Mr. and Mrs. Delahanty came to the door. "What's the matter, Cress?"

Cress turned, lifted a hand toward them. "Why didn't you tell me?" she demanded. And when they didn't answer, she said, "Edwin knew."

Then she dropped her head on to her grandfather's outstretched hand and said something, evidently to him, which neither her father nor her mother understood.

"It's just the same."

Writing Assignments for Part One

1. Respond to the cartoon at the beginning of this section.
2. In an essay, take a position on Russell's views of the functions of a teacher.
3. In an essay, take a position on the responsibilities of the student.
4. In most cases, the schools control large amounts of the students' time for a minimum of twelve years. In an essay, discuss whether you think it is possible for the educational system to eliminate deep-seated racism and bigotry in those students. If not, why not? If so, suggest specific methods.
5. If you could reconstruct the educational system, what would you include and/or eliminate?
6. Describe a teacher whom you liked or disliked. Try to explain your reactions.
7. Using any form (poetry, short story, description, personal narrative), record your response to something significant in your educational experience.
8. Write your own pledge of allegiance.

PART TWO / *Words and Their Effect*

I speak with a thousand tongues.
Hindu Proverb

PEANUTS
I GUESS I WON'T BE SEEING YOU UNTIL MONDAY, CHARLIE BROWN...
...SO HAVE A HAPPY WEEK-END..
THANK YOU
Tm. Reg. U. S. Pat Off.—All rights reserved
Copr. 1960 by United Feature Syndicate, Inc.
6-4
INCIDENTALLY, WHAT **IS** HAPPINESS?
SCHULZ

H. ALAN WYCHERLEY

Slurvian: Supplemental Notes

In order for this selection to be appreciated, it must be read aloud.

STUDY QUESTIONS FOR COMPREHENSION

1. Be sure to pronounce each word aloud, just as it is written. Check the dictionary for any words with which you are not familiar.
2. As you read this selection, formulate a definition for "Slurvian."
3. Can you think of additional examples of "Slurvian"?

In a 1949 *New Yorker* article, John Davenport identified and defined the sublanguage to which he assigned the superbly appropriate name "Slurvian." Much of the honor due him for this contribution to our knowledge arises from his distinguishing between the pure and the impure forms of this language. Mr. Davenport made it clear that the impure form consisted of nonsense words. Although the following are not his examples, they will suffice for illustration: *goan* for *going, flar* for *flower, bahl* for *bottle*. Pure Slurvian, however, consists of English words mispronounced into other English words, to the enlightenment of us all. Thus *rune* for *ruin, winner* for *winter, rye dear* (or *ride ear*) for *right here* exemplify the higher form.

My own modest contributions to this growing body of knowledge have so far gone widely unrecognized, but in view of the nature of the subject, I can only regard this as a fitting and healthy reaction. Nevertheless a collector must collect, however small the number of those who really know what he is up to. And some of those, equally beguiled by the elasticities of our language, will wish to add to the slowly evolving corpus of Slurvian. If so, perhaps they will submit their offerings to *Word Study* or at least to their local newspapers. In the end, Slurvophiles may establish a well of English so thoroughly "defyled" that it will be a source of inexhaustible, if negative, help to teachers of speech whose unhappy duty it is to insist upon clear enunciation. It is to them, rather than to lexicographers, that I offer the following contributions to Slurvian.

Consider the romantic overtones of setting a *far* in the *far place,* or the maritime character of the Southernism *yawl.* How easy it is to sense the defeat of a woman who looks at herself in the *mere!* Or the vexation of a motorist whose car has a flat *tar.* What of the woman who has to wriggle and twist to get her *girl* off, or the man who *barred* money from a loan company, or the traveler who occupied a *lore* berth on a train?

Much more attractive to the collector, however, are Slurvianisms of two or more syllables; they are naturally more difficult to discover. Two illustrations of this more sophisticated type occur to me at this juncture, and I am glad to pass them on. The first concerns the motorist who averaged forty *molls* per *are* (*molls* per *air* is a variant). This is not, of course, really good Slurvian: it exemplifies, but it is neither profound nor memorable. Here is a much better one: I mowed the lawn with my new *paramour.* This bright little locution combines the bucolic and the erotic in a way that might well have pleased the Marlowe of "The Passionate Shepherd to His Love."

It is my earnest hope that devotees of Slurvian will discover in this last illustration the beginnings of a new poetry. We could use one.

ANNE NICHOLS

Don't Sell Slang Short

STUDY QUESTIONS FOR COMPREHENSION

1. Compare your own knowledge of and attitudes toward slang with the author's.
2. Why does the author say that slang is language in capsule form?
3. Why do "the young communicate in code"?

In the 1920's women wore sequins, feather boas, fringed dresses, and skirts above the knee. They again do. Many a woman has found that her pack rat instincts or her mother's castoffs have yielded her a first or an "in" in her particular fashion circle. Similarly, in the 18th Century men wore brocaded waistcoats and either wigs or long hair. They do again today. Fashions tend to repeat themselves, and what we considered ten years ago fit only for the Salvation Army may today be the latest Paris or London innovation. What does not repeat itself, however, is the language that accompanied the fashions. The young man of 1971 may wear a brocaded waistcoat and let his hair grow, but he hardly says, "God wot," or "'Tweren't that I had not considered on't"; and the young woman wearing a sequined dress that ends four inches above the knee is unlikely to say, "Oh, you kid!"

The fact that language changes is demonstrable. It is revealed in Chaucer: "Whan that Aprille with his shoures soote," and in Shakespeare: "Now, fair Hippolyta, our nuptial hour / Draws on apace." Our language, while preserving continuity, is a different organism today than it was even 75 years ago, when Henry James was writing. Sometimes, however, the change is so gradual that the person who reads only current literature is hardly aware that his native tongue has changed and is constantly moving toward new forms. Forces of convention, such as the printed word and the schools, counteract the dynamic flow of spoken language, which is just as well, since if language were allowed to change too rapidly the literature of even 100 years ago might need translation. Where speech escapes the inhibiting force of convention, and yet does no damage to the continuity of society, is in that area usually thought of as the stepchild of language: slang.

For most people slang carries disagreeable connotations of the uneducated, the underworld denizen, or the drug addict, but it is wrongfully maligned. Slang is in its own right a fascinating manifestation of the human imagination. At the same time it exhibits in capsule form the characteristics of more formal language. Since slang is unrestricted by rules or proscriptions, it is free floating language. But it is still language. Like all language, slang changes, but incredibly rapidly. Like formal and poetic language, slang employs metaphor. Like all language, slang is capable of great variety in shades of meaning. Most significantly, slang, again like all language, reflects the changing attitudes of man toward his world and what concerns him in it.

The definition of slang is vague. The 1957 edition of *The Standard College Dictionary* defines slang in part as "Language, words, or phrases of a vigorous, colorful, facetious, or taboo nature, invented for specific occasions or uses, or derived from the unconventional use of the standard vocabulary." A good deal of modern poetry can be described by the same terms. *The Standard College Dictionary* adds a second definition: "The special vocabulary" of a certain class, group, or profession: college *slang*. "The special vocabulary of certain professions" can obviously include the jargon that accompanies most politicians, sociologists, and educators. The lack of preciseness in the dictionary definition does not indicate a weakness in either the dictionary or in slang. Rather, the definition suggests the breadth of slang, a breadth not always acknowledged or understood. A comprehensive definition of slang is further made difficult by the fact that often what used to be slang no longer is. Many people think they know instinctively when they encounter slang, and their response is usually negative. These same people may be surprised, however, to discover what slang *has* been. *Nice* started out as a slang word, and it now occupies a front position in a long and respected list of *nice* but meaningless words. A number of other words, as H. L. Mencken points out in his famous discussion of slang, start out as slang and end up filling vacuums in our existing vocabulary. Among others, Mencken mentions *rodeo, racketeer, to hold up.*

Just as a number of theories are advanced to explain the origin of language, so a number of theories are advanced to explain the origin of slang. One theory attempts to take into account a mystery of man's nature, the poetic imagination. This theory suggests that slang is the creative imagination of the uneducated put into words. Since the poetic impulse is not restricted to the educated, the man with a small vocabulary but a feeling for language must create his own metaphors. If, like any poet, such a man sees a similarity, sometimes an unusual or bizarre one, between two things, and if he lacks the conventional method of expressing this similarity or lacks the vocabulary to construct a formal metaphor, he coins words or joins words to convey his imaginative insight. Consider, for instance, the metaphors implicit in these expressions: *tightwad, cold fish, goon squad, creep, plugged in, fathead, clip joint,* and *head shrinker.* An enormous number of expressions fit this category. Many we find so vivid and so useful that we often fail to see the metaphor implicit in the terms. According to this theory, then, the same kind of genius is at work when a literate poet creates a metaphor and when a semiliterate poet creates an expression like *wet blanket.*

Another theory finds man's hesitancy to call a spade a spade the source of a large body of slang. Slang words in this group are essentially euphemisms for what men fear, such as death, or what men think is improper to allude to directly, such as organs of the body or bodily functions like sexuality, excretion, or pregnancy. *Kick the bucket* is a good example of man's inclination to make light of a dreaded eventuality. Similarly, depending upon the century and the society, perfectly normal physical functions sometimes cannot be described for what they are. In the last century, for instance, it was quite acceptable to have children, but the process of doing so seems to have been considered deplorable. The word *pregnant* was rejected (and in some circles still is) as being somehow indelicate, and expressions like *in the family way, that way,* or *expecting* replaced it. One rather strange result of rejecting the specific terms in favor of euphemisms is that the specific terms begin to take on connotations of being more vulgar than the slang terms which replace them. In some circles, for example, *knocked up* is thought to be more polite than *pregnant.* Words which refer to parts of the body have undergone similar changes in status. Women rarely have *breasts;* euphemistically, they have *measurements* or occasionally *busts.* In the 19th Century women had *limbs,* not *legs.* And an incredible amount of verbal imagination has gone into the avoidance of the word *penis.*

It should be remembered, however, that not all words referring to bodily organs or functions are slang innovations. Many of the so-called Anglo-Saxon words are indeed Anglo-Saxon words, and part of our linguistic heritage. But many of them have been relegated to the bull session and the dirty joke, while at the same time the Latin or Greek equivalents have also been outlawed. If, for instance, a group considers *breasts* improper, it would certainly not employ the slang replacements. As a result, there is sometimes no vocabulary considered proper to refer to parts of the body or to perfectly normal physical functions. Some words, in fact, generally considered slang are not slang at all, but simply excluded from polite speech because of contemporary social conventions. Fortunately, the generation of the 1960's appears to be less afraid of calling the various organs and bodily functions by their appropriate names than are their elders, so perhaps their children will find that communication is possible where in some instances it is not now.

Two interesting theories explaining the origin of slang are those which see slang as a special language of an "in" group and as a special language of a group existing outside of the law. Although the two theories differ slightly, the net result is essentially the same. The common denominator is secrecy. The "in" group uses a vocabulary to distinguish it from outsiders. If others do not use the same language, or if they do not understand the language used, obviously they are not part of the group. The same rationale operates whether the group consists of junior high school students or well-known celebrities. If a twelve-year-old says *keen* and is ridiculed because he should have said *cool* or *groovy,* he is no different from the international beauty who does not understand the meaning of *camp.* Neither one is "in."

The "in" group is secret to the extent that it wishes to wield psychological power over outsiders. Secrecy is a means in this case, not an end. The desired result is actually envy. To some extent, of course, every group which organizes itself to be separate from the rest of society is secret—even the PTA has a special language. Some groups, however, are secret out of necessity. Those who live on or beyond the periphery of the law use slang as a means of communicating on forbidden subjects. The narcotics user, the criminal, even the homosexual all have reasons for special vocabularies. This theory attempts to account for the often rapid change in vocabulary. By the time the general public learns that *pot* is marijuana, the word *pot* has outlived its usefulness as a secret signal. When, therefore, the general public learns that *grass* is also marijuana, a much more current term is probably being used. As long as the activities are against the law, or severely frowned upon by the mass of society, the vocabulary will change as the general public becomes aware of it.

Unfortunately, like all theories about the origin of slang, these theories have fuzzy margins. Often the distinction between an "in" group and an outlaw group is difficult to make. Jazz musicians, for instance, are the source of an incredibly large number of terms in our slang vocabulary. And as their language becomes assimilated into the slang vocabulary of the general public, almost certainly their own vocabulary is changing. If your ten-year-old son or brother is saying *cool,* the chances are that jazz musicians are by now saying something else, and probably have been for about five years. Many terms which we have inherited from jazz musicians obviously do not refer to illegal activities. *Swinging, groovy* and *in the groove, blow up a storm, jazzy,* and *cool* all have their origins in the activity of producing jazz, a clearly "in" activity. What complicates the matter, however, is that jazz musicians, in the past at any rate, have had associations with narcotics, and that vocabulary, stemming from a need for secrecy, becomes associated with the vocabulary which originally referred only to the kind of music produced.

Ethnic groups are still another source of slang terms, two of the most borrowed from groups being Negroes and Jews. Jazz slang, for instance, in addition to being formed by terms associated with the production of music and those associated with narcotics, reveals the influence of Negro speech. Here again the lines are fuzzy, since it is not entirely clear what "Negro speech" is, but that such an entity exists seems fairly certain. Lyrics to many of the classic jazz songs show this influence: *it must be jelly 'cause jam don't shake like that, jelly roll, your wig's too tight, rock me, baby.* Many expressions of this kind are obviously sexual in nature and perhaps arise from a need for euphemisms to refer to taboo subjects. Or they may simply be examples of "in" group language. A number of other words generally considered slang come to us from Yiddish through the language of theater people and television and night club entertainers. Such words as *nudnik, spiel, schlemiel, weh's mir* and many others occur in general use. Clearly, no one theory can explain the origins of slang. The best course probably is to accept all those that appear reasonable, while realizing that no one theory or combination of theories can fully explain a mysterious process like language.

Other factors complicate any attempt to "explain" slang or even to categorize it. Slang vocabulary differs according to the geographical location, the age, the cultural background, the occupation, and the private life of the speaker. There is not only a "language" of the underworld, of the narcotics user, of the homosexual, but also a "language" of the theater, of the southeastern Texas high school student, of the northern Oregon college student. However, the lines between these or any other groups cannot be clearly drawn. There is often an overlapping or sharing of certain terms, although sometimes the shared terms may change meanings according to the groups using them. To understand slang properly, one must be aware of the changes in meaning that have taken place simply through the passage of time and of the nuances of meaning attached to the terms by a particular group. Among *hippy* college students, for instance, *straight* generally refers to someone who does not use drugs, a *square,* in other words. In homosexual circles *straight* has the implication of the outsider, in this case a non-homosexual. However, it has an opposite connotation in the expression *straight answer,* just as it has in Negro groups, where a *straight* white is considered to be an o.k. white. (In the same sense, *square* changes its meaning in expressions like *square deal.*) In addition to all these meanings, *straight* is sometimes used to refer to a marijuana cigarette. Oddly enough, large numbers of college students seem to have a native ability to keep track of several vocabularies, even though they claim to have no ability or interest in language under formal conditions.

One of the most fascinating aspects of slang is that it reflects what is going on in the contemporary social scene. Nowadays, in 1971, the subject of importance for a large and influential segment of the college campus population is narcotics, and one cannot understand the current college generation unless he takes this fact into account. The large number of slang words with connotations of drug use reveals this preoccupation. Further, some of the terms reflect the current attitude toward drugs. The *user* is thought of as freed, unbound by conventions and willing to explore the uncharted areas of the mind. The very great dangers attendant upon drug use are ignored, and instead the liberating effect is eulogized. For example, *hang loose,* the opposite of *hung up,* signifies approval and suggests the freedom discovered through the use of drugs, particularly through the use of the so-called "mind-expanders." *Trip,* borrowed from the conventional vocabulary, also suggests a "free" journey through hitherto unexplored regions. In fact, since LSD appeared on the scene, *trip* has been appropriated so totally that it may be lost from the general vocabulary, just as several decades ago we lost the expressive word *queer,* which now cannot be used without connotations of homosexuality. The *trip* is the LSD experience, expressable in several ways: *good trip, bad trip, bum trip, trip out, on a trip.* Other words are borrowed from the conventional vocabulary or from earlier slang use, another indication of the preoccupation. *Head* refers now to a *user. Groovy* went out of style but has been revitalized with drug, rather than jazz, connotations. The same is true of *hip,* which has returned as *hippy.* It is useless to conjecture where this current trend will go. If the use of narcotics becomes either commonplace or "out," then unquestionably the language will reflect the change.

In spite of the richness of slang and in spite of its ability to communicate a vast range of subtleties, some people, unfortunately, ignore its richness and instead rely on only a few words as a kind of shorthand, thus actually preventing communication. Just as the word *nice* has been used to describe everything from girls to frying pans and is therefore completely useless for conveying information, so expressions like *crazy* and *groovy* can become substitutions for meaningful language. If the answer to all questions, from "Do you like *Hamlet*?" to "Would you like a cup of coffee?" is "Crazy, man!" then the language is not serving its purpose, for communication has broken down. Similarly, the pursuit of ideas can be prevented by ready-made responses. If someone is asked why so-and-so is unhappy, the answer that he's *hung up* may be the introduction to an actual discussion of how and why he is *hung up,* but if it is considered sufficiently meaningful as is, again communication has ended. Many who disapprove of slang do so on these grounds, that it ends meaningful communication, and sometimes the criticism is just. It should be remembered, however, that users of slang are not the only ones guilty of shorthand answers or ready-made responses. Mental lethargy appears everywhere, and one could just as easily, as many do, create a set of stock responses out of psychological, sociological, or educational vocabularies. To say that someone is *hung up* is not significantly different from saying that someone is not realizing his potential, or that he is caught in a socioeconomic construct, or that he has not been able to implement his resources. Obviously, any language that fails to communicate has failed to achieve its purpose.

Reactions to slang are often hostile, yet its chief weakness, which it shares with all language, is the one just mentioned. Although many people point to an overreliance on slang as their reason for disapproval, the real reason, in most cases, lies deeper. For many, slang carries connotations of the pool room, the "opium den," the jail. Hopefully, these connotations will change. If, in fact, the older generation really wants communication with the younger, the older and more "proper" people will have to make an effort to understand why slang is important and what is actually being said when it is used. Traditionally, the young communicate in code, and it is up to the elders to learn it. Otherwise, the pious protests about lack of communication between the generations remain empty. Indeed, the general public, which usually considers slang beneath it, could learn a great deal from an awareness of slang. Slang reveals the fluidity of language and the richness in metaphor and nuance. Perhaps even more importantly, slang reveals quickly and dynamically the connection between language and man's preoccupations and his changing attitudes toward these preoccupations.

LAWRENCE FERLINGHETTI

Sometime During Eternity

STUDY QUESTIONS FOR COMPREHENSION

1. Who is "Dad"?
2. Does Ferlinghetti's use of slang suggest disrespect?
3. At the end of the poem Ferlinghetti makes an important point about today's world. Can you express his comment in your own words?

Sometime during eternity
some guys show up
and one of them
who shows up real late
is a kind of carpenter
from some square-type place
like Galilee
and he starts wailing
and claiming he is hep
to who made heaven
and earth
and that the cat
who really laid it on us
is his Dad

And moreover
he adds
It's all writ down
on some scroll-type parchments

which some henchmen
leave lying around the Dead Sea somewheres
a long time ago
and which you won't even find
for a coupla thousand years or so
or at least for
nineteen hundred and fortyseven
of them
to be exact
and even then
nobody really believes them
or me
for that matter

You're hot
they tell him

And they cool him

They stretch him on the Tree to cool

And everybody after that
is always making models
of this Tree
with Him hung up
and always crooning His name
and calling Him to come down
and sit in
on their combo
as if he is the king cat
who's got to blow
or they can't quite make it

Only he don't come down
from His Tree

Him just hang there

on His Tree
looking real Petered out
and real cool
and also
according to a roundup
of late world news
from the usual unreliable sources
real dead

CLAUDE BROWN

The Language of Soul

STUDY QUESTIONS FOR COMPREHENSION

1. What distinction does Brown make between the users of soul language and other "Americans of African ancestry"?
2. What, in Brown's view, is one of the origins of soul language?
3. Does Brown suggest that all Negroes speak the same kind of language?
4. How does Brown view the future of soul?

Perhaps the most soulful word in the world is "nigger." Despite its very definite fundamental meaning (the Negro man), and disregarding the deprecatory connotation of the term, "nigger" has a multiplicity of nuances when used by soul people. Dictionaries define the term as being synonymous with Negro, and they generally point out that it is regarded as a vulgar expression. Nevertheless, to those of chitlins-and-neck-bones background the word nigger is neither a synonym for Negro nor an obscene expression.

"Nigger" has virtually as many shades of meaning in Colored English as the demonstrative pronoun "that," prior to application to a noun. To some Americans of African ancestry (I avoid using the term Negro whenever feasible, for fear of offending the Brothers X, a pressure group to be reckoned with), nigger seems preferable to Negro and has a unique kind of sentiment attached to it. This is exemplified in the frequent—and perhaps even excessive—usage of the term to denote either fondness or hostility.

It is probable that numerous transitional niggers and even established ex-soul brothers can—with pangs of nostalgia—reflect upon a day in the lollipop epoch of lives when an adorable lady named Mama bemoaned her spouse's fastidiousness with the strictly secular utterance: "Lord, how can one nigger be so hard to please?" Others are likely to recall a time when that drastically lovable colored woman, who was forever wiping our noses and darning our clothing, bellowed in a moment of exasperation: "Nigger, you gonna be the death o' me." And some of the brethren who have had the precarious fortune to be raised up, wised up, thrown up or simply left alone to get up as best they could, on one of the nation's South Streets or Lenox Avenues, might remember having affectionately referred to a best friend as "My nigger."

The vast majority of "back-door Americans" are apt to agree with Webster—a nigger is simply a Negro or black man. But the really profound contemporary thinkers of this distinguished ethnic group—Dick Gregory, Redd Foxx, Moms Mabley, Slappy White, etc. —are likely to differ with Mr. Webster and define nigger as "something else"—a soulful "something else." The major difference between the nigger and the Negro, who have many traits in common, is that the nigger is the more soulful.

Certain foods, customs and artistic expressions are associated almost solely with the nigger: collard greens, neck bones, hog maws, black-eyed peas, pigs' feet, etc. A nigger has no desire to conceal or disavow any of these favorite dishes or restrain other behavioral practices such as bobbing his head, patting his feet to funky jazz, and shouting and jumping in church. This is not to be construed that all niggers eat chitlins and shout in church, nor that only niggers eat the aforementioned dishes and exhibit this type of behavior. It is to say, however, that the soulful usage of the term nigger implies all of the foregoing and considerably more.

The Language of Soul—or, as it might also be called, Spoken Soul or Colored English—is simply an honest vocal portrayal of black America. The roots of it are more than three hundred years old.

Before the Civil War there were numerous restrictions placed on the speech of slaves. The newly arrived Africans had the problem of learning to speak a new language, but also there were inhibitions placed on the topics of the slaves' conversation by slave masters and overseers. The slaves made up songs to inform one another of, say, the underground railroad's activity. When they sang *Steal Away* they were planning to steal away to the North, not to heaven. Slaves who dared to speak of rebellion or even freedom usually were severely punished. Consequently, Negro slaves were compelled to create a semi-clandestine vernacular in the way that the criminal underworld has historically created words to confound law-enforcement agents. It is said that numerous Negro spirituals were inspired by the hardships of slavery, and that what later became songs were initially moanings and coded cotton-field lyrics. To hear these songs sung today by a talented soul brother or sister or by a group is to be reminded of an historical spiritual bond that cannot be satisfactorily described by the mere spoken word.

The American Negro, for virtually all of his history, has constituted a vastly disproportionate number of the country's illiterates. Illiteracy has a way of showing itself in all attempts at vocal expression by the uneducated. With the aid of colloquialisms, malapropisms, battered and fractured grammar, and a considerable amount of creativity, Colored English, the sound of soul, evolved.

The progress has been cyclical. Often terms that have been discarded from the soul people's vocabulary for one reason or another are reaccepted years later, but usually with completely different meaning. In the Thirties and Forties "stuff" was used to mean vagina. In the middle Fifties it was revived and used to refer to heroin. Why certain expressions are thus reactivated is practically an indeterminable question. But it is not difficult to see why certain terms are dropped from the soul language. Whenever a soul term becomes popular with whites it is common practice for the soul folks to relinquish it. The reasoning is that "if white people can use it, it isn't hip enough for me." To many soul brothers there is just no such creature as a genuinely hip white person. And there is nothing more detrimental to anything hip than to have it fall into the square hands of the hopelessly unhip.

White Americans wrecked the expression "something else." It was bad enough that they couldn't say "sump'n else," but they weren't even able to get out "somethin' else." They had to go around saying *something else* with perfect or nearly perfect enunciation. The white folks invariably fail to perceive the soul sound in soulful terms. They get hung up in diction and grammar, and when they vocalize the expression it's no longer a soulful thing. In fact, it can be asserted that spoken soul is more of a sound than a language. It generally possesses a pronounced lyrical quality which is frequently incompatible to any music other than that ceaseless and relentlessly driving rhythm that flows from poignantly spent lives. Spoken soul has a way of coming out metered without the intention of the speaker to invoke it. There are specific phonetic traits. To the soulless ear the vast majority of these sounds are dismissed as incorrect usage of the English language and, not infrequently, as speech impediments. To those so blessed as to have had bestowed upon them at birth the lifetime gift of soul, these are the most communicative and meaningful sounds ever to fall upon human ears: the familiar "mah" instead of "my," "gonno" for "going to," "yo" for "your." "Ain't" is pronounced "ain' "; "bread" and "bed," "bray-ud" and "bay-ud"; "baby" is never "bay-bee" but "bay-buh"; Sammy Davis Jr. is not "Sammee" but a kind of "Sam-eh"; the same goes for "Ed-deh" Jefferson. No matter how many "man's" you put into your talk, it isn't soulful unless the word has the proper plaintive, nasal "maee-yun."

Spoken soul is distinguished from slang primarily by the fact that the former lends itself easily to conventional English, and the latter is diametrically opposed to adaptations within the realm of conventional English. Police (pronounced po' lice) is a soul term, whereas "The Man" is merely slang for the same thing. Negroes seldom adopt slang terms from the white world and when they do the terms are usually given a different meaning. Such was the case with the term "bag." White racketeers used it in the Thirties to refer to the graft that was paid to the police. For the past five years soul people have used it when referring to a person's vocation, hobby, fancy, etc. And once the appropriate term is given the treatment (soul vocalization) it becomes soulful.

However, borrowings from spoken soul by white men's slang—particularly teen-age slang—are plentiful. Perhaps because soul is probably the most graphic language of modern times, everybody who is excluded from Soulville wants to usurp it, ignoring the formidable fettering to the soul folks that has brought the language about. Consider "uptight," "strung-out," "cop," "boss," "kill 'em," all now widely used outside Soulville. Soul people never question the origin of a slang term; they either dig it and make it a part of their vocabulary or don't and forget it. The expression "uptight," which meant being in financial straits, appeared on the soul scene in the general vicinity of 1953. Junkies were very fond of the word and used it literally to describe what was a perpetual condition with them. The word was pictorial and pointed; therefore it caught on quickly in Soulville across the country. In the early Sixties when "uptight" was on the move, a younger generation of soul people in the black urban communities along the Eastern Seaboard regenerated it with a new meaning: "everything is cool, under control, going my way." At present the term has the former meaning for the older generation and the latter construction for those under thirty years of age.

It is difficult to ascertain if the term "strung-out" was coined by junkies or just applied to them and accepted without protest. Like the term "uptight" in its initial interpretation, "strung-out" aptly described the constant plight of the junkie. "Strung-out" had a connotation of hopeless finality about it. "Uptight" implied a temporary situation and lacked the overwhelming despair of "strung-out."

The term "cop" (meaning "to get"), is an abbreviation of the word "copulation." "Cop," as originally used by soulful teen-agers in the early Fifties, was deciphered to mean sexual coition, nothing more. By 1955 "cop" was being uttered throughout national Soulville as a synonym for the verb "to get," especially in reference to illegal purchases, drugs, pot, hot goods, pistols, etc. ("Man, where can I cop now?") But by 1955 the meaning was all-encompassing. Anything that could be obtained could be "copped."

The word "boss," denoting something extraordinarily good or great, was a redefined term that had been popular in Soulville during the Forties and Fifties as a complimentary remark from one soul brother to another. Later it was replaced by several terms such as "groovy," "tough," "beautiful" and, most recently, "out of sight." This last expression is an outgrowth of the former term "way out," the meaning of which was equivocal. "Way out" had an ad hoc hickish ring to it which made it intolerably unsoulful and consequently it was soon replaced by "out of sight," which is also likely to experience a relatively brief period of popular usage. "Out of sight" is better than "way out," but it has some of the same negative, childish taint of its predecessor.

The expression, "kill 'em," has neither a violent nor a malicious interpretation. It means "good luck," "give 'em hell," or "I'm pulling for you," and originated in Harlem from six to nine years ago.

There are certain classic soul terms which, no matter how often borrowed, remain in the canon and are reactivated every so often, just as standard jazz tunes are continuously experiencing renaissances. Among the classical expressions are: "solid," "cool," "jive" (generally as a noun), "stuff," "thing," "swing" (or "swinging"), "pimp," "dirt," "freak," "heat," "larceny," "busted," "okee doke," "piece," "sheet" (a jail record), "squat," "square," "stash," "lay," "sting," "mire," "gone," "smooth," "joint," "blow," "play," "shot," and there are many more.

Soul language can be heard in practically all communities throughout the country, but for pure, undiluted spoken soul one must go to Soul Street. There are several. Soul is located at Seventh and "T" in Washington, D.C.; on One Two Five Street in New York City; on Springfield Avenue in Newark; on South Street in Philadelphia; on Tremont Street in Boston; on Forty-seventh Street in Chicago; on Fillmore in San Francisco, and dozens of similar locations in dozens of other cities.

As increasingly more Negroes desert Soulville for honorary membership in the Establishment clique, they experience a metamorphosis, the repercussions of which have a marked influence on the young and impressionable citizens of Soulville. The expatriates of Soulville are often greatly admired by the youth of Soulville, who emulate the behavior of such expatriates as Nancy Wilson, Ella Fitzgerald, Eartha Kitt, Lena Horne, Diahann Carroll, Billy Daniels, or Leslie Uggams. The result—more often than not—is a trend away from spoken soul among the young soul folks. This abandonment of the soul language is facilitated by the fact that more Negro youngsters than ever are acquiring college educations (which, incidentally, is not the best treatment for the continued good health and growth of soul); integration and television, too, are contributing significantly to the gradual demise of spoken soul.

Perhaps colleges in America should commence to teach a course in spoken soul. It could be entitled the Vocal History of Black America, or simply Spoken Soul. Undoubtedly there would be no difficulty finding teachers. There are literally thousands of these experts throughout the country whose talents lie idle while they await the call to duty.

Meanwhile the picture looks dark for soul. The two extremities in the Negro spectrum—the conservative and the militant—are both trying diligently to relinquish and repudiate whatever vestige they may still possess of soul. The semi-Negro—the soul brother intent on gaining admission to the Establishment even on an honorary basis—is anxiously embracing and assuming conventional English. The other extremity, the Ultra-Blacks, are frantically adopting everything from a Western version of Islam that would shock the Caliph right out of his snugly fitting shintiyan to anything that vaguely hints of that big, beautiful, bountiful black bitch lying in the arms of the Indian and Atlantic Oceans and crowned by the majestic Mediterranean Sea. Whatever the Ultra-Black is after, it's anything but soulful.

LEO ROSTEN

From *The Joys of Yiddish*

THE INFLUENCE OF YIDDISH ON ENGLISH

It is a remarkable fact that never in its history has Yiddish been so influential—among Gentiles. (Among Jews, alas, the tongue is running dry). We are clearly witnessing a revolution in values when a Pentagon officer, describing the air-bombardment pattern used around Haiphong, informs the press: "You might call it the bagel strategy." Or when a Christmas (1966) issue of *Better Homes and Gardens* features: "The Season's Delightful Jewish Traditions and Foods." Or when the London *Economist* captions a fuss over mortgage rates: HOME LOAN HOO-HA. Or when the *Wall Street Journal* headlines a feature on student movements: "REVOLUTION, SHMEVOLUTION." Or when a wall in New York bears this eloquent legend, chalked there, I suppose, by some derisive English major:

MARCEL PROUST
IS A
YENTA[1]

Or when England's illustrious *Times Literary Supplement*, discussing the modern novel, interjects this startling sentence: "Should, schmould, shouldn't, schmouldn't." Or when a musical play about the Jews in the Polish *shtetl* of fifty years ago, *Fiddler on the Roof*, scores so phenomenal a success.

[1] A gossipy shrew.

Yiddish phrasing and overtones are found in, say, the way an Irish whiskey advertises itself:

> "Scotch is a fine beverage and deserves its popularity.
> But enough is enough already."

Or in an advertisement for a satirical English movie, *Agent 8¾*:

> By Papa he's a spy,
> By Mama he's a spy,
> But from spies he's no spy!

I can cite dozens of similar uses of Yinglish idiom.

YIDDISH WORDS AND PHRASES IN ENGLISH

Every so often I run across the statement that *Webster's Unabridged Dictionary* contains 500 Yiddish words. I do not know if this is true, and I certainly doubt that anyone actually counted them. For my part, I am surprised by the number of Yiddish words, thriving beautifully in everyday English, that are *not* in *Webster's*, nor in other dictionaries of the English language—including the incomparable thirteen-volume *Oxford English Dictionary*. You will find many of these lamentably unrecognized words in the volume you now hold in your hands.

Many a scholar has commented on the growing number of Yiddish words and idioms that "invade" English. But English, far from being a supine language, has zestfully borrowed a marvelous gallimaufry of foreign locutions, including many from Yiddish; and who will deny that such brigandage has vastly enriched our cherished tongue.

Take the popular usage of the suffix, *-nik,* to convert a word into a label for an ardent practitioner or devotee of something: How could we manage without such priceless coinages as *beatnik* and *peacenik? The New York Times* recently dubbed Johann Sebastian's acolytes "Bachniks"; some homosexuals dismiss non-homosexuals as *straightniks;* the comic strip *Mary Worth* has employed *no-goodnik;* and a newspaper advertisement even employed Yiddish-in-tandem to get: "NOSHNIKS OF THE WORLD, UNITE!"

Many a student of contemporary mores has discovered the degree to which novelists, playwrights, joke writers, comedians, have poured Jewish wit and humor into the great, flowing river of English. This is also an indication of the extraordinary role of Jewish intellectuals, and their remarkable increase during the past forty years, in the United States and England.

Who has not heard or used phrases such as the following, which, whatever their origin, probably owe their presence in English to Jewish influence?

Get lost.
You should live so long.
My son, the physicist.
I need it like a hole in the head.
Who *needs* it?
So why do you?
Al*right* already.
It shouldn't happen to a dog.
O.K. by me.
He knows from nothing.
From that he makes a *liv*ing?
How come only five?
Do him something.
This I need yet?
A person could bust.
He's a regular genius.
Go hit your head against the wall.
You want it should sing, too?
Plain talk: He's crazy.
Excuse the expression.
With sense, he's loaded.
Go fight City Hall.
I should have such luck.
It's a nothing of a dress.
You should live to a hundred and twenty.
On him it looks good.
It's time, it's time.
Wear it in good health.
Listen, *bubele* . . .?

What other language is fraught with such exuberant fraughtage?

COLLOQUIAL USES IN ENGLISH OF YIDDISH LINGUISTIC DEVICES

But words and phrases are not the chief "invasionary" forces Yiddish has sent into the hallowed terrain of English. Much more significant, I think, is the adoption by English of linguistic *devices,* Yiddish in origin, to convey nuances of affection, compassion, displeasure, emphasis, disbelief, skepticism, ridicule, sarcasm, scorn. Examples abound:

1. Blithe dismissal via repetition with an *sh* play-on-the-first-sound: "Fat-shmat, as long as she's happy."
2. Mordant syntax: "Smart, he isn't."
3. Sarcasm via innocuous diction: "He only tried to shoot himself."
4. Scorn through reversed word order: "Already you're discouraged?"
5. Contempt via affirmation: "My *son*-in-law he wants to be."
6. Fearful curses sanctioned by nominal cancellation: "A fire should burn in his heart, God forbid!"
7. Politeness expedited by truncated verbs and eliminated prepositions: "You want a cup coffee?"
8. Derisive dismissal disguised as innocent interrogation: "I should pay him for such devoted service?"
9. The use of a question to answer a question to which the answer is so self-evident that the use of the first question (by you) constitutes an affront (to me) best erased either by (a) repeating the original question or (b) retorting with a question of comparably asinine self-answeringness. Thus:

Q. "Did you write your mother?"
A. "Did I write my mother!" (Scornful, for "Of course I did!")

Q. "Have you visited your father in the hospital?"
A. "Have I visited my father in the *hospital?*" (Indignant, for "What kind of a monster do you think I am?")

Q. "Would you like some chicken soup?"
A. "Would I like some *chicken* soup?" (Emphatically concurring, for "What a stupid thing to ask.")

Q. "Will a hundred dollars be enough?"
A. "Will a hundred dollars be enough?" (Incredulously offended, for "Do you think I'm crazy to accept so ridiculous a sum?")

Q. "Will a thousand dollars be enough?"
A. "Will a *thousand* dollars be enough?" (Incredulously delighted, for "Man, will it!")

Q. "Will you marry me?"
A. "Will I *marry* you?" (On a note of overdue triumph, for "Yes, yes, right away!")

Or consider the growing effect on English of those exquisite shadings of meaning, and those priceless nuances of contempt, that are achieved in Yiddish simply by shifting the stress in a sentence from one word to another. "Him you *trust?*" is entirely different, and worlds removed, from "*Him* you trust?" The first merely questions your judgment; the second vilipends the character of the scoundrel anyone must be an idiot to repose faith in.

Or consider the Ashkenazic panoply in which insult and innuendo may be arrayed. Problem: Whether to attend a concert to be given by a neighbor, niece, or friend of your wife. The same sentence may be put through maneuvers of matchless versatility:

1. "*Two* tickets for her concert I should buy?" (Meaning: "I'm having enough trouble deciding if it's worth one.")
2. "Two *tickets* for her concert I should buy?" ("You mean to say she isn't distributing free passes? The hall will be empty!")
3. "Two tickets for *her* concert I should buy?" ("Did she buy tickets to *my* daughter's recital?")
4. "Two tickets for her *concert* I should buy?" ("You mean to say they call what she does a 'concert'?!")
5. "Two tickets for her concert *I* should buy?" ("After what she did to me?")
6. "Two tickets for her concert I *should* buy?" ("Are you giving me lessons in ethics?")
7. "Two tickets for her concert I should *buy?*" ("I wouldn't go even if she gave me a complimentary!")

Each of the above formulations suggests a different prior history, offers the speaker a different catharsis, and lets fly different arrows of contumely. And if all emphasis is removed from the sentence, which is then uttered with mock neutrality, the very unstressedness becomes sardonic, and—if accompanied by a sigh, snort, cluck, or frown—lethal. . . .

[The following are a few examples of Yiddish words, as defined by Leo Rosten, that are frequently heard in English mass media.]

MAZEL TOV!

Pronounced MOZ-*z'l,* to rhyme with "schnozzle"; *tov* is pronounced TUV, TUFF, or TAWF. Hebrew: *mazel:* "luck"; *tov:* "good."

"Congratulations!" or "Thank God!" rather than its literal meaning: "Good luck." The distinction is as important as it is subtle. Don't *"mazel tov!"* a man going into the hospital; say *"mazel tov!"* when he comes out.

Do not say *"mazel tov!"* to a fighter entering a ring (it suggests you are congratulating him for having made it to the arena), or a girl about to have her nose bobbed (which would mean "and about time, too!").

Say *"mazel tov!"* to an Israeli ship captain when he first takes command: this congratulates him on his promotion; don't say *"mazel tov!"* when the ship reaches port: this suggests you're surprised he got you there. . . .

> Mournfully, Mr. Lefkowitz entered the offices of his burial society. "I've come to make the funeral arrangements for my dear wife."
>
> "Your wife?" asked the astonished secretary. "But we buried her last year!"
>
> "That was my first wife," sighed lugubrious Lefkowitz. "I'm talking about my second."
>
> "Second? I didn't know you remarried. *Mazel tov!"*

> "How am I doing?" the writer answered his friend. "You have no idea how popular my writing has become. Why, since I last saw you, my readers have doubled!"
>
> "Well, *mazel tov!* I didn't know you got married."

CHUTZPA
(noun)
CHUTSPA

CHUTZPADIK
(adjective)

Pronounced KHOOTS-*pah;* rattle the *kh* around with fervor; rhymes with "Foot spa." Do *not* pronounce the *ch* as in "choo-choo" or "Chippewa," but as the German *ch* as in *Ach!* or the Scottish in *loch*. Hebrew: "insolence," "audacity."

Gall, brazen nerve, effrontery, incredible "guts"; presumption-plus-arrogance such as no other word, and no other language, can do justice to.

The classic definition of *chutzpa* is, of course, this: *Chutzpa* is that quality enshrined in a man who, having killed his mother and father, throws himself on the mercy of the court because he is an orphan.

A *chutzpa* may be defined as the man who shouts "Help! Help!" while beating you up.

NEBECH
NEBBECH
NEBISH
NEBBISH

Pronounced NEB-*ekh* or NEB-*ikh,* with the *ch* as sounded by Scots or Germans, not the *ch* of "choo-choo." From Czech: *neboky*.

In recent years, no doubt to help the laryngeally unagile, the pronunciation NEB-*bish* (note the *sh*) has gained currency. The word is even spelled *nebbish,* notably in a collection of cartoons on cocktail napkins, matchbooks, ashtrays and, for all I know, Cape Cod lighters. My feeling is that *nebbish* should be used only by people unable to clear their throats.

As an interjection, *nebech* means:

1. Alas, too bad, unfortunately, "the poor thing." "He went to the doctor, *nebech.*" "She, *nebech,* didn't have a dime." In this usage, *nebech* expresses:

(a) Sympathy. "He lost his job, *nebech*."
(b) Regret. "They asked me, *nebech*, to break the sad news."
(c) Dismay. "He looked, *nebech*, like a ghost!"
(d) "Poor thing." "His wife, *nebech*, has to put up with him."

Never say *nebech* about something you welcome, enjoy, are happy to report, or are glad happened. Hence the irony of this: "What would make me the happiest man in the world? To be sitting on a park bench in the sun, saying to my best friend, 'Look! There, *nebech*, goes Hitler.' "

As a noun, *nebech* means:

2. An innocuous, ineffectual, weak, helpless or hapless unfortunate. A Sad Sack. A "loser." First cousin to a *shlemiel*. "He's a *nebech*." "Once a *nebech*, always a *nebech*." "Whom did she marry? A real *nebech*!"

3. A nonentity; "a nothing of a person."

To define a *nebech* simply as an unlucky man is to miss the many nuances, from pity to contempt, the word affords.

Nebech is one of the most distinctive Yiddish words; it describes a universal character type.

A *nebech* is sometimes defined as the kind of person who always picks up—what a *shlemiel* knocks over.

A *nebech* is more to be pitied than a *shlemiel*. You feel sorry for a *nebech*; you *can* dislike a *shlemiel*.

There is a well-known wisecrack: "When a *nebech* leaves the room, you feel as if someone came in."

Stories, jokes, and wisecracks about the *nebech* are, by careful count, countless.

As the apothegm has it: "A man is, *nebech*, only a man." . . .

"Better ten enemies than one *nebech*."—Proverb

A *nebech* pulled into a parking place on a busy street in Tel Aviv. Along came a policeman.

"Is it all right to park here?" asked the *nebech*.

"No," said the cop.

"*No*? But look at all those other parked cars! How come?"

"They didn't ask."

A seventh-grader was so late coming home from his suburban school that his mother was frantic.

"What happened to you?" she cried.

"I was made traffic guard today, Mamma, and all the kids have to wait for my signal, after I stop a car, before they cross the street."

"But you were due home two *hours* ago!"

"Mamma, you'd be surprised how long I had to wait before a car came along I could stop!"

He had the makings of a *nebech*—maybe even a *shlemiel*. . . .

SHLEMIEL
SCHLEMIEL
SHLEMIEHL
SHLEMIHL

Pronounced *shleh*-MEAL, to rhyme with "reveal." (Note: *Shlemiel* is often spelled *schlemiel,* or even *schlemiehl,* but I sternly oppose such complications. In Hebrew and Yiddish, the single letter, *shin,* represents the *sh* sound. And in English, to begin a word with *sch* is to call for the *sk* sound, as in "school," "scheme," "schizophrenic." Anyway, I think a *shlemiel* is plagued by enough burdens without our adding orthographic *tsuris* to them.)

1. A foolish person; a simpleton. "He has the brains of a *shlemiel.*"

2. A consistently unlucky or unfortunate person; a "fall guy"; a hard-luck type; a born loser; a submissive and uncomplaining victim. "That poor *schlemiel* always gets the short end of the stick." A Yiddish proverb goes: "The *shlemiel* falls on his back and breaks his nose."

3. A clumsy, butterfingered, all-thumbs, gauche type. "Why does a *shlemiel* like that ever try to fix anything?"

4. A social misfit, congenitally maladjusted. "Don't invite that *shlemiel* to the party."

5. A pipsqueak, a Caspar Milquetoast. "He throws as much weight as a *shlemiel.*" "No one pays attention to that *shlemiel.*"

6. A naive, trusting, gullible customer. This usage is common

among furniture dealers, especially those who sell the gaudy, gimcrack stuff called "borax."

7. Anyone who makes a foolish bargain, or wagers a foolish bet. This usage is wide in Europe; it probably comes from Chamisso's tale, *Peter Schlemihl's Wunderbare Geschichte*, a fable in which the protagonist sold his shadow and, like Faust, sold his soul to Satan.

It is important to observe that *shlemiel*, like *nebech*, carries a distinctive note of pity. In fact, a *shlemiel* is often the *nebech*'s twin brother. The classic definition goes: "A *shlemiel* is always knocking things off a table; the *nebech* always picks them up."

Shlemiel is said to come from the name Shlumiel, the son of a leader of the tribe of Simeon (Numbers, 2). Whereas the other generals in Zion often triumphed on the field of war, poor Shlumiel was always losing. . . .

"A *shlemiel* takes a bath, and forgets to wash his face." . . .

A man came home from the steam baths—minus his shirt.

"Shlemiel!" cried his wife. "Where's your shirt?"

"My shirt? That's right. Where can it be? Aha! Someone at the baths must have taken my shirt by mistake, instead of his."

"So where is *his* shirt?"

The *shlemiel* scratched his head. "The fellow who took my shirt —he forgot to leave his."

Two *shlemiels* were drinking tea. In time, one looked up and announced portentously: "Life! What is it? Life—is like a fountain!"

The other pondered for a few minutes, then asked, "Why?"

The first thought and thought, then sighed, "So O.K.: Life *isn't* like a fountain."

SAMUEL ALLEN

A Moment Please

AID FOR COMPREHENSION

1. Read the entire poem.
2. Read only the italicized words.
3. Read only the *non*italicized words.
4. Now read the entire poem again.

When I gaze at the sun
I walked to the subway booth
for change for a dime.
and know that this great earth
Two adolescent girls stood there
alive with eagerness to know
is but a fragment from it thrown
all in their new found world
there was for them to know
in heat and flame a billion years ago,
they looked at me and brightly asked
"Are you Arabian?"
that then this world was lifeless
I smiled and cautiously
—for one grows cautious—
shook my head.
as, a billion hence,
"Egyptian?"
it shall again be,
Again I smiled and shook my head
and walked away.
what moment is it that I am betrayed,
I've gone but seven paces now
oppressed, cast down,
and from behind comes swift the sneer

or warm with love or triumph?
    "Or Nigger?"

    A moment, please
What is it that to fury I am roused?
    for still it takes a moment
What meaning for me
    and now
in this homeless clan
    I'll turn
the dupe of space
    and smile
the toy of time?
    and nod my head.

The following two poems are by children. "This Is a Poem" was written by a five-year-old; "Poems," by an eleven-year-old. Note the differences in language.

HILARY-ANNE FARLEY, age 5

This Is a Poem

This is a poem about god looks after things:
He looks after lions, mooses and reindeer and tigers,
Anything that dies,
and mans and little girls when they get to be old,
and mothers he can look after,
and god can look after many old things.
That's why I do this.

PETER KELSO, age 11

Poems

In poems, our earth's wonders
Are windowed through
Words

A good poem must haunt the heart
And be heeded by the head of the
Hearer

With a wave of words, a poet can
Change his feelings into cool, magical, mysterious
Mirages

Without poetry our world would be
Locked within itself—no longer enchanted by the poet's
Spell.

CHRISTOPHER MARLOWE

The Passionate Shepherd to His Love

This poem was written in the sixteenth century and therefore sounds different from modern English. Note, however, that the same theme appears in twentieth-century love poems and songs.

Come live with me and be my love,
And we will all the pleasures prove
That valleys, groves, hills, and fields,
Woods, or steepy mountains yields.

And we will sit upon the rocks,
Seeing the shepherds feed their flocks,
By shallow rivers, to whose falls
Melodious birds sing madrigals.

And I will make thee beds of roses
And a thousand fragrant posies,
A cap of flowers, and a kirtle
Embroidered all with leaves of myrtle;

A gown made of the finest wool,
Which from our pretty lambs we pull;
Fair linëd slippers for the cold,
With buckles of the purest gold;

A belt of straw and ivy-buds
With coral clasps and amber studs.

And if these pleasures may thee move,
Come live with me and be my love.

The shepherd swains shall dance and sing
For thy delight each May morning.
If these delights thy mind may move,
Then live with me and be my love.

MELL LAZARUS

Miss Peach

Courtesy of Publishers-Hall Syndicate

WARNER BLOOMBERG

Obscenity?? Sticks and Stones May Break My Bones but Words Only Clarify Our Experience

STUDY QUESTIONS FOR COMPREHENSION

1. How does Bloomberg, a high-school student, define obscenity?
2. What does the author see as the essential purpose of language?
3. Why does Bloomberg call war and killing obscene?

Obscenity, according to Webster's New World Dictionary of the American Language, is something which is: 1) offensive to modesty or decency; lewd; 2) disgusting; repulsive. While these adjectives are descriptive enough, they do little to adequately show what really is "an obscenity."

Most teachers, adults, and kids seem to think that whenever they or someone else starts throwing around words that have been categorized as "swearing" that something big is happening. They either gasp with horror as if they were witnessing some great crime or add to the conversation with their own choices of supposed grossness as if it were something to brag about. Neither of these examples, of course, is the correct response to language.

"Language," writes Richard Carrington in his book, *A Million Years of Man,* "has evolved to a coherent system of sound symbolism, enabling experience and culture to be transmitted from one individual

From *How Old Will You Be in 1984?* edited by Diane Divoky. Reprinted by permission of Avon Books.

to another." The purpose of language then is communication—whether it is an explanation of a person's emotion or information as to where to meet for the next game of poker. "Swearing," more often than not, is either used to express a sudden hate or feeling of disgust, or awe or beauty, or as part of one's daily language—without any connotation of the "immorality" a lot of people would associate them with. Obscenity, then, like beauty, occurs in the mind of the beholders. What makes me mad is when people say that a word is obscene. How can something which is such a necessary part of this society (i.e. language, for meaningful communication) be "disgusting"?

What also angers me is when people become apathetic to things that *are* obscene. War and killing is certainly one of the most "repulsive" things that man has invented. Yet how many people flinch or cry anymore when scenes from Vietnam or Biafra are flashed across the TV screen every night? The shape and smell of the Milwaukee River is certainly "offensive." Where is the public hue and cry over what man has done to this natural resource? I happen to think that any photograph of a nuclear bomb is about the most "obscene" picture there could be, for it represents the final destruction of humanity. Where is the massive campaign to stop the stockpiling of the bombs and the start of the elimination of all nuclear arms in the world?

Like why pick on language when there are so many other obviously obscene things around? From now on, when you hear someone deriding the use of four-letter words (and others), ask yourself whether this person isn't really missing the point about the purpose of words and what actually constitutes an obscenity. It wouldn't hurt too much if the greater part of society would throw away the arbitrary standards of propriety it now holds as "truth" and get to work on some of the more pressing problems that face it. A little bit of ——ing can't destroy the world—but hate and war just might.

The Open Door
Milwaukee, Wisconsin

"Your honor, this woman gave birth to a naked child!"

Cartoon by Robert Minor, from *The Masses* (1915). From *A History of American Graphic Humor,* by William Murrell (New York: The Macmillan Company, published for the Whitney Museum of American Art, 1938).

PAUL ROBERTS

How to Say Nothing in Five Hundred Words

STUDY QUESTIONS FOR COMPREHENSION

1. Explain, using specific references, why the essay, "Why College Football Should Be Abolished," is poor.
2. Summarize the suggestions Roberts makes about the ways a student can improve his writing.
3. Explain the following: euphemism, the pat expression, colored words.

It's Friday afternoon, and you have almost survived another week of classes. You are just looking forward dreamily to the week end when the English instructor says: "For Monday you will turn in a five-hundred word composition on college football."

Well, that puts a good big hole in the week end. You don't have any strong views on college football one way or the other. You get rather excited during the season and go to all the home games and find it rather more fun than not. On the other hand, the class has been reading Robert Hutchins in the anthology and perhaps Shaw's "Eighty-Yard Run," and from the class discussion you have got the idea that the instructor thinks college football is for the birds. You are no fool, you. You can figure out what side to take.

After dinner you get out the portable typewriter that you got for high school graduation. You might as well get it over with and enjoy Saturday and Sunday. Five hundred words is about two double-spaced pages with normal margins. You put in a sheet of paper, think up a title, and you're off:

Why College Football Should Be Abolished

College football should be abolished because it's bad for the school

> and also bad for the players. The players are so busy practicing that they don't have time for their studies.

This, you feel, is a mighty good start. The only trouble is that it's only thirty-two words. You still have four hundred and sixty-eight to go, and you've pretty well exhausted the subject. It comes to you that you do your best thinking in the morning, so you put away the typewriter and go to the movies. But the next morning you have to do your washing and some math problems, and in the afternoon you go to the game. The English instructor turns up too, and you wonder if you've taken the right side after all. Saturday night you have a date, and Sunday morning you have to go to church. (You shouldn't let English assignments interfere with your religion.) What with one thing and another, it's ten o'clock Sunday night before you get out the typewriter again. You make a pot of coffee and start to fill out your views on college football. Put a little meat on the bones.

> *Why College Football Should Be Abolished*
>
> In my opinion, it seems to me that college football should be abolished. The reason why I think this to be true is because I feel that football is bad for the colleges in nearly every respect. As Robert Hutchins says in his article in our anthology in which he discusses college football, it would be better if the colleges had race horses and had races with one another, because then the horses would not have to attend classes. I firmly agree with Mr. Hutchins on this point, and I am sure that many other students would agree too.
>
> One reason why it seems to me that college football is bad is that it has become too commercial. In the olden times when people played football just for the fun of it, maybe college football was all right, but they do not play football just for the fun of it now as they used to in the old days. Nowadays college football is what you might call a big business. Maybe this is not true at all schools, and I don't think it is especially true here at State, but certainly this is the case at most colleges and universities in America nowadays, as Mr. Hutchins points out in his very interesting article. Actually the coaches and alumni go around to the high schools and offer the high school stars large salaries to come to their colleges and play football for them. There was one case where a high school star was offered a convertible if he would play football for a certain college.
>
> Another reason for abolishing college football is that it is bad for the players. They do not have time to get a college education, because they are so busy playing football. A football player has to practice every afternoon from three to six, and then he is so tired that he can't

> concentrate on his studies. He just feels like dropping off to sleep after dinner, and then the next day he goes to his classes without having studied and maybe he fails the test.

(Good ripe stuff so far, but you're still a hundred and fifty-one words from home. One more push.)

> Also I think college football is bad for the colleges and the universities because not very many students get to participate in it. Out of a college of ten thousand students only seventy-five or a hundred play football, if that many. Football is what you might call a spectator sport. That means that most people go to watch it but do not play it themselves.

(Four hundred and fifteen. Well, you still have the conclusion, and when you retype it, you can make the margins a little wider.)

> These are the reasons why I agree with Mr. Hutchins that college football should be abolished in American colleges and universities.

On Monday you turn it in, moderately hopeful, and on Friday it comes back marked "weak in content" and sporting a big "D."

This essay is exaggerated a little, not much. The English instructor will recognize it as reasonably typical of what an assignment on college football will bring in. He knows that nearly half of the class will contrive in five hundred words to say that college football is too commercial and bad for the players. Most of the other half will inform him that college football builds character and prepares one for life and brings prestige to the school. As he reads paper after paper all saying the same thing in almost the same words, all bloodless, five hundred words dripping out of nothing, he wonders how he allowed himself to get trapped into teaching English when he might have had a happy and interesting life as an electrician or a confidence man.

Well, you may ask, what can you do about it? The subject is one on which you have few convictions and little information. Can you be expected to make a dull subject interesting? As a matter of fact, this is precisely what you are expected to do. This is the writer's essenital task. All subjects, except sex, are dull until somebody makes them interesting. The writer's job is to find the argument, the approach, the angle, the wording that will take the reader with him. This is seldom easy, and it is particularly hard in subjects that have been much discussed: College Football, Fraternities, Popular Music, Is Chivalry Dead?, and the like. You will feel that there is nothing you can do with such subjects except repeat the old bromides. But there are some things you can do which will make your papers, if not throbbingly alive, at least less insufferably tedious than they might otherwise be.

Say the assignment is college football. Say that you've decided to be against it. Begin by putting down the arguments that come to your mind: it is too commercial, it takes the students' minds off their studies, it is hard on the players, it makes the university a kind of circus instead of an intellectual center, for most schools it is financially ruinous. Can you think of any more arguments just off hand? All right. Now when you write your paper, *make sure that you don't use any of the material on this list.* If these are the points that leap to your mind, they will leap to everyone else's too, and whether you get a "C" or a "D" may depend on whether the instructor reads your paper early when he is fresh and tolerant or late, when the sentence "In my opinion, college football has become too commercial," inexorably repeated, has brought him to the brink of lunacy.

Be against college football for some reason or reasons of your own. If they are keen and perceptive ones, that's splendid. But even if they are trivial or foolish or indefensible, you are still ahead so long as they are not everybody else's reasons too. Be against it because the colleges don't spend enough money on it to make it worth while, because it is bad for the characters of the spectators, because the players are forced to attend classes, because the football stars hog all the beautiful women, because it competes with baseball and is therefore un-American and possibly Communist inspired. There are lots of more or less unused reasons for being against college football.

Sometimes it is a good idea to sum up and dispose of the trite and conventional points before going on to your own. This has the advantage of indicating to the reader that you are going to be neither trite nor conventional. Something like this:

> We are often told that college football should be abolished because it has become too commercial or because it is bad for the players. These arguments are no doubt very cogent, but they don't really go to the heart of the matter.

Then you go to the heart of the matter.

One rather simple way of getting into your paper is to take the side of the argument that most of the citizens will want to avoid. If the assignment is an essay on dogs, you can, if you choose, explain that dogs are faithful and lovable companions, intelligent, useful as guardians of the house and protectors of children, indispensable in police work—in short, when all is said and done, man's best friends. Or you can suggest that those big brown eyes conceal, more often than not, a vacuity of mind and an inconstancy of purpose; that the dogs you have known most intimately have been mangy, ill-tempered brutes, incapable of instruction; and that only your nobility of mind and fear of arrest prevent you from kicking the flea-ridden animals when you pass them on the street.

Naturally, personal convictions will sometimes dictate your approach. If the assigned subject is "Is Methodism Rewarding to the Individual?" and you are a pious Methodist, you have really no choice. But few assigned subjects, if any, will fall in this category. Most of them will lie in broad areas of discussion with much to be said on both sides. They are intellectual exercises, and it is legitimate to argue now one way and now another, as debaters do in similar circumstances. Always take the side that looks to you hardest, least defensible. It will almost always turn out to be easier to write interestingly on that side.

This general advice applies where you have a choice of subjects. If you are to choose among "The Value of Fraternities" and "My Favorite High School Teacher" and "What I Think About Beetles," by all means plump for the beetles. By the time the instructor gets to your paper, he will be up to his ears in tedious tales about the French teacher at Bloombury High and assertions about how fraternities build character and prepare one for life. Your views on beetles, whatever they are, are bound to be a refreshing change.

Don't worry too much about figuring out what the instructor thinks about the subject so that you can cuddle up with him. Chances are his views are no stronger than yours. If he does have convictions and you oppose them, his problem is to keep from grading you higher than you deserve in order to show he is not biased. This doesn't mean that you should always cantankerously dissent from what the instructor says; that gets tiresome too. And if the subject assigned is

"My Pet Peeve," do not begin, "My pet peeve is the English instructor who assigns papers on 'my pet peeve.' " This was still funny during the War of 1812, but it has sort of lost its edge since then. It is in general good manners to avoid personalities.

If you will study the essay on college football [near the beginning of this essay], you will perceive that one reason for its appalling dullness is that it never gets down to particulars. It is just a series of not very glittering generalities: "football is bad for the colleges," "it has become too commercial," "football is a big business," "it is bad for the players," and so on. Such round phrases thudding against the reader's brain are unlikely to convince him, though they may well render him unconscious.

If you want the reader to believe that college football is bad for the players, you have to do more than say so. You have to display the evil. Take your roommate, Alfred Simkins, the second-string center. Picture poor old Alfy coming home from football practice every evening, bruised and aching, agonizingly tired, scarcely able to shovel the mashed potatoes into his mouth. Let us see him staggering up to the room, getting out his econ textbook, peering desperately at it with his good eye, falling asleep and failing the test in the morning. Let us share his unbearable tension as Saturday draws near. Will he fail, be demoted, lose his monthly allowance, be forced to return to the coal mines? And if he succeeds, what will be his reward? Perhaps a slight ripple of applause when the third-string center replaces him, a moment of elation in the locker room if the team wins, of despair if it loses. What will he look back on when he graduates from college? Toil and torn ligaments. And what will be his future? He is not good enough for pro football, and he is too obscure and weak in econ to succeed in stock and bonds. College football is tearing the heart from Alfy Simkins and, when it finishes with him, will callously toss aside the shattered hulk.

This is no doubt a weak enough argument for the abolition of college football, but it is a sight better than saying, in three or four variations, that college football (in your opinion) is bad for the players.

Look at the work of any professional writer and notice how constantly he is moving from the generality, the abstract statement, to the concrete example, the facts and figures, the illustration. If he is writing on juvenile delinquency, he does not just tell you that juveniles are (it seems to him) delinquent and that (in his opinion) something should be done about it. He shows you juveniles being delinquent, tearing up movie theatres in Buffalo, stabbing high school principals in Dallas, smoking marijuana in Palo Alto. And more than likely he is moving toward some specific remedy, not just a general wringing of the hands.

It is no doubt possible to be *too* concrete, too illustrative or anecdotal, but few inexperienced writers err this way. For most the soundest advice is to be seeking always for the picture, to be always turning general remarks into seeable examples. Don't say, "Sororities teach girls the social graces." Say, "Sorority life teaches a girl how to carry on a conversation while pouring tea, without sloshing the tea in the saucer." Don't say, "I like certain kinds of popular music very much." Say, "Whenever I hear Gerber Sprinklittle play 'Mississippi Man' on the trombone, my socks creep up my ankles."

The student toiling away at his weekly English theme is too often tormented by a figure: five hundred words. How, he asks himself, is he to achieve this staggering total? Obviously by never using one word when he can somehow work in ten.

He is therefore seldom content with a plain statement like "Fast driving is dangerous." This has only four words in it. He takes thought, and the sentence becomes:

> In my opinion, fast driving is dangerous.

Better, but he can do better still:

> In my opinion, fast driving would seem to be rather dangerous.

If he is really adept, it may come out:

> In my humble opinion, though I do not claim to be an expert on this complicated subject, fast driving, in most circumstances, would seem to be rather dangerous in many respects, or at least so it would seem to me.

Thus four words have been turned into forty, and not an iota of content has been added.

Now this is a way to go about reaching five hundred words, and if you are content with a "D" grade, it is as good a way as any. But if you aim higher, you must work differently. Instead of stuffing your sentences with straw, you must try steadily to get rid of the padding, to make your sentences lean and tough. If you are really working at it, your first draft will greatly exceed the required total, and then you will work it down, thus:

> It is thought in some quarters that fraternities do not contribute as much as might be expected to campus life.
> Some people think that fraternities contribute little to campus life.
>
> The average doctor who practices in small towns or in the country must toil night and day to heal the sick.
> Most country doctors work long hours.
>
> When I was a little girl, I suffered from shyness and embarrassment in the presence of others.
> I was a shy little girl.
>
> It is absolutely necessary for the person employed as a marine fireman to give the matter of steam pressure his undivided attention at all times.
> The fireman has to keep his eye on the steam gauge.

You may ask how you can arrive at five hundred words at this rate. Simply. You dig up more real content. Instead of taking a couple of obvious points off the surface of the topic and then circling warily around them for six paragraphs, you work in and explore, figure out the details. You illustrate. You say that fast driving is dangerous, and then you prove it. How long does it take to stop a car at forty and at eighty? How far can you see at night? What happens when a tire blows? What happens in a head-on collison at fifty miles an hour? Pretty soon your paper will be full of broken glass and blood and headless torsos, and reaching five hundred words will not really be a problem.

Some of the padding in freshman themes is to be blamed not on anxiety about the word minimum but on excessive timidity. The student writes, "In my opinion, the principal of my high school acted in ways that I believe every unbiased person would have to call foolish." This isn't exactly what he means. What he means is, "My high school principal was a fool." If he was a fool, call him a fool. Hedging the thing about with "in-my-opinion's" and "it-seems-to-me's" and "as-I-see-it's" and "at-least-from-my-point-of-view's" gains you nothing. Delete these phrases whenever they creep into your paper.

The student's tendency to hedge stems from a modesty that in other circumstances would be commendable. He is, he realizes, young and inexperienced, and he half suspects that he is dopey and fuzzy-minded beyond the average. Probably only too true. But it doesn't help to announce your incompetence six times in every paragraph. Decide what you want to say and say it as vigorously as possible, without apology and in plain words.

Linguistic diffidence can take various forms. One is what we call *euphemism*. This is the tendency to call a spade "a certain garden implement" or women's underwear "unmentionables." It is stronger in some eras than others and in some people than others but it always operates more or less in subjects that are touchy or taboo: death, sex, madness, and so on. Thus we shrink from saying "He died last night" but say instead "passed away," "left us," "joined his Maker," "went to his reward." Or we try to take off the tension with a lighter cliché: "kicked the bucket," "cashed in his chips," "handed in his dinner pail." We have found all sorts of ways to avoid saying *mad*: "mentally ill," "touched," "not quite right upstairs," "feeble-minded," "innocent," "simple," "off his trolley," "not in his right mind." Even such a now plain word as *insane* began as a euphemism with the meaning "not healthy."

Modern science, particularly psychology, contributes many polysyllables in which we can wrap our thoughts and blunt their force. To many writers there is no such thing as a bad schoolboy. Schoolboys are maladjusted or unoriented or misunderstood or in need of guidance or lacking in continued success toward satisfactory integration of the personality as a social unit, but they are never bad. Psychology no doubt makes us better men or women, more sympathetic and tolerant, but it doesn't make writing any easier. Had Shakespeare been confronted with psychology, "To be or not to be" might have come out, "To continue as a social unit or not to do so.

That is the personality problem. Whether 'tis a better sign of integration at the conscious level to display a psychic tolerance toward the maladjustments and repressions induced by one's lack of orientation in one's environment or—" But Hamlet would never have finished the soliloquy.

Writing in the modern world, you cannot altogether avoid modern jargon. Nor, in an effort to get away from euphemism, should you salt your paper with four-letter words. But you can do much if you will mount guard against those roundabout phrases, those echoing polysyllables that tend to slip into your writing to rob it of its crispness and force.

Other things being equal, avoid phrases like "other things being equal." Those sentences that come to you whole, or in two or three doughy lumps, are sure to be bad sentences. They are no creation of yours but pieces of common thought floating in the community soup.

Pat expressions are hard, often impossible, to avoid, because they come too easily to be noticed and seem too necessary to be dispensed with. No writer avoids them altogether, but good writers avoid them more often than poor writers.

By "pat expressions" we mean such tags as "to all practical intents and purposes," "the pure and simple truth," "from where I sit," "the time of his life," "to the ends of the earth," "in the twinkling of an eye," "as sure as you're born," "over my dead body," "under cover of darkness," "took the easy way out," "when all is said and done," "told him time and time again," "parted the best of friends," "stand up and be counted," "gave him the best years of her life," "worked her fingers to the bone." Like other clichés, these expressions were once forceful. Now we should use them only when we can't possibly think of anything else.

Some pat expressions stand like a wall between the writer and thought. Such a one is "the American way of life." Many student writers feel that when they have said that something accords with the American way of life or does not they have exhausted the subject. Actually, they have stopped at the highest level of abstraction. The American way of life is the complicated set of bonds between a hundred and eighty million ways. All of us know this when we think about it, but the tag phrase too often keeps us from thinking about it.

So with many another phrase dear to the politician: "this great land of ours," "the man in the street," "our national heritage." These may prove our patriotism or give a clue to our political beliefs, but otherwise they add nothing to the paper except words.

The writer builds with words, and no builder uses a raw material more slippery and elusive and treacherous. A writer's work is a constant struggle to get the right word in the right place, to find that particular word that will convey his meaning exactly, that will persuade the reader or soothe him or startle or amuse him. He never succeeds altogether—sometimes he feels that he scarcely succeeds at all—but such successes as he has are what make the thing worth doing.

There is no book of rules for this game. One progresses through everlasting experiment on the basis of ever-widening experience. There are few useful generalizations that one can make about words as words, but there are perhaps a few.

Some words are what we call "colorful." By this we mean that they are calculated to produce a picture or induce an emotion. They are dressy instead of plain, specific instead of general, loud instead of soft. Thus, in place of "Her heart beat," we may write "Her heart *pounded, throbbed, fluttered, danced.*" Instead of "He sat in his chair," we may say, "He *lounged, sprawled, coiled.*" Instead of "It was hot," we may say "It was *blistering, sultry, muggy, suffocating, steamy, wilting.*"

However, it should not be supposed that the fancy word is always better. Often it is as well to write "Her heart beat" or "It was hot" if that is all it did or all it was. Ages differ in how they like their prose. The nineteenth century liked it rich and smoky. The twentieth has usually preferred it lean and cool. The twentieth century writer, like all writers, is forever seeking the exact word, but he is wary of sounding feverish. He tends to pitch it low, to understate it, to throw it away. He knows that if he gets too colorful, the audience is likely to giggle.

See how this strikes you: "As the rich, golden glow of the sunset died away along the eternal western hills, Angela's limpid blue eyes looked softly and trustingly into Montague's flashing brown ones, and her heart pounded like a drum in time with the joyous song surging in her soul." Some people like that sort of thing, but most modern readers would say, "Good grief," and turn on the televis on.

Some words we would call not so much colorful as colored—that is, loaded with associations, good or bad. All words—except perhaps structure words—have associations of some sort. We have said that the meaning of a word is the sum of the contexts in which it occurs. When we hear a word, we hear with it an echo of all the situations in which we have heard it before.

In some words, these echoes are obvious and discussable. The word *mother,* for example, has, for most people, agreeable associations. When you hear *mother* you probably think of home, safety, love, food, and various other pleasant things. If one writes, "She was like a mother to me," he gets an effect which he would not get in "She was like an aunt to me." The advertiser makes use of the associations of *mother* by working it in when he talks about his product. The politician works it in when he talks about himself.

So also with such words as *home, liberty, fireside, contentment, patriot, tenderness, sacrifice, childlike, manly, bluff, limpid.* All of these words are loaded with favorable associations that would be rather hard to indicate in a straightforward definition. There is more than a literal difference between "They sat around the fireside" and "They sat around the stove." They might have been equally warm and happy around the stove, but *fireside* suggests leisure, grace, quiet tradition, congenial company, and *stove* does not.

Conversely, some words have bad associations. *Mother* suggests pleasant things, but *mother-in-law* does not. Many mothers-in-law are heroically lovable and some mothers drink gin all day and beat their children insensible, but these facts of life are beside the point. The thing is that *mother* sounds good and *mother-in-law* does not.

Or consider the word *intellectual.* This would seem to be a complimentary term, but in point of fact it is not, for it has picked up associations of impracticality and ineffectuality and general dopiness. So also with such words as *liberal, reactionary, Communist, socialist, capitalist, radical, schoolteacher, truck driver, undertaker, operator, salesman, huckster, speculator.* These convey meanings on the literal level, but beyond that—sometimes, in some places—they convey contempt on the part of the speaker.

The question of whether to use loaded words or not depends on what is being written. The scientist, the scholar, try to avoid them; for the poet, the advertising writer, the public speaker, they are standard equipment. But every writer should take care that they do not substitute for thought. If you write, "Anyone who thinks that is nothing but a Socialist (or Communist or capitalist)" you have said nothing except that you don't like people who think that, and such remarks are effective only with the most naïve readers. It is always a bad mistake to think your readers more naïve than they really are.

But probably most student writers come to grief not with words that are colorful or those that are colored but with those that have no color at all. A pet example is *nice,* a word we would find it hard to dispense with in casual conversation but which is no longer capable of adding much to a description. Colorless words are those of such general meaning that in a particular sentence they mean nothing. Slang adjectives, like *cool* ("That's real cool") tend to explode all over the language. They are applied to everything, lose their original force, and quickly die.

Beware also of nouns of very general meaning, like *circumstances, cases, instances, aspects, factors, relationships, attitudes, eventualities, etc.* In most circumstances you will find that those cases of writing which contain too many instances of words like these will in this and other aspects have factors leading to unsatisfactory relationships with the reader resulting in unfavorable attitudes on his part and perhaps other eventualities, like a grade of "D." Notice also what "etc." means. It means "I'd like to make this list longer, but I can't think of any more examples."

Writing Assignments for Part Two

1. Write a brief informational report on the development of the English language.
2. Make a list of slang words or phrases and their counterparts that would be used in formal writing, for example,

   flipped his lid   went berserk
3. Write a short dictionary of the language used by your particular peer group.
4. Many students have a negative attitude toward expressing themselves in writing. Write an essay in which you discuss probable reasons for this attitude. Incorporate in your essay suggestions for preventing or changing this negative reaction.
5. What do you think Claude Brown means by "soul"? Support your statements by references to the selection.
6. Write an essay in which you define *obscenity*.
7. Using your own language, idiom, dialect, put Marlowe's poem, p. 189, into your own words. Do not worry about rhyming.
8. In any form you wish (poem, short story, description, personal narration) respond to one or more selections in this section.

PART THREE / *Conscience in Conflict with Authority*

All concord's born of contraries.
Ben Jonson, *Cynthia's Revels,* Act 5, scene 2

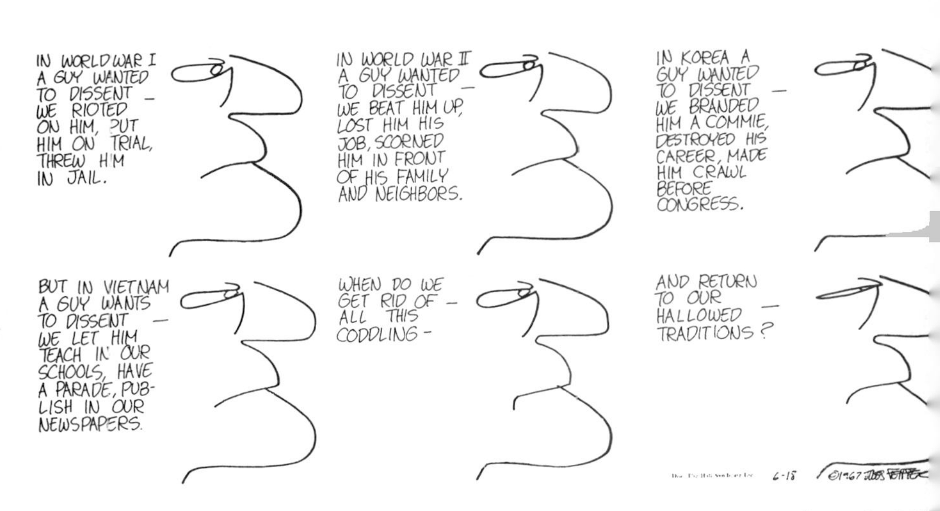
IN WORLD WAR I A GUY WANTED TO DISSENT – WE RIOTED ON HIM, PUT HIM ON TRIAL, THREW HIM IN JAIL.
IN WORLD WAR II A GUY WANTED TO DISSENT – WE BEAT HIM UP, LOST HIM HIS JOB, SCORNED HIM IN FRONT OF HIS FAMILY AND NEIGHBORS.
IN KOREA A GUY WANTED TO DISSENT – WE BRANDED HIM A COMMIE, DESTROYED HIS CAREER, MADE HIM CRAWL BEFORE CONGRESS.
BUT IN VIETNAM A GUY WANTS TO DISSENT – WE LET HIM TEACH IN OUR SCHOOLS, HAVE A PARADE, PUBLISH IN OUR NEWSPAPERS.
WHEN DO WE GET RID OF – ALL THIS CODDLING –
AND RETURN TO OUR – HALLOWED TRADITIONS?
6-18

HENRY STEELE COMMAGER

The Problem of Dissent

STUDY QUESTIONS FOR COMPREHENSION

1. Define dissent.
2. According to Commager, have students and others the right to demonstrate against government policies?
3. What is the purpose of Commager's inclusion of examples of the many who, in the past, were dissenters?
4. What does the author claim to be the purpose of free speech?
5. How does Commager answer the charge that criticism of government policy gives aid to the enemy?

It is barely two months now since Pope Paul VI made his historic plea to the United Nations and to the peoples of the world for an end to war and a restoration of brotherhood. "No more war. War never again," he said, and the whole nation applauded his noble plea. But when young men and women from our colleges and universities take the papal plea in good faith, and demonstrate against the war in Vietnam, they are overwhelmed with a torrent of recrimination and obloquy that is almost hysterical. Even students catch the contagion. "We're sick and tired of peaceniks" shriek the students of the Catholic Manhattan College. Are they sick and tired of Pope Paul, who said, "It is peace that must guide the destinies of mankind"?

Surely it is time to bring a little clarity and common sense to the discussion of this matter of student protests and demonstrations.

First, as Attorney General Katzenbach has reminded us, there is no question about the right of students, or of others, to agitate, to demonstrate, to protest, in any nonviolent manner, against policies they consider misguided. That is, after all, not only a right but a necessity if our democracy is to function. People who ought to know better—Senator Dodd of Connecticut, for example—have loosely identified agitation with "treason." Treason is the one crime defined in the Constitution, and the Senator would do well to read that

From *Saturday Review*, December 18, 1965. Reprinted by permission of the author.

document before he flings those charges of treason about. Students have the same right to agitate and demonstrate against what they think unsound policies—even military policies—as have businessmen to agitate against the TVA or doctors against Medicare. When, back in New Deal days, distinguished lawyers publicly advised corporations to disregard the Wagner Act and the Social Security Act on the ground that they were unconstitutional, when distinguished medical men called for the sabotage of Medicare, no one called them traitors. Businessmen and doctors and lawyers, to be sure, funnel their protests through respectable organizations like chambers of commerce, or the American Medical Association, or the American, and state, bar associations, or resort to well-paid lobbyists to express their discontent; students have no such effective organizations nor can they support lobbying. To penalize them for their weakness and their poverty is to repeat the error of the Cleveland administration in arresting Coxey's army for walking on the grass, or of the Hoover administration in sending soldiers to destroy the pitiful Bonus Army. The rich and respectable have always had their ways of making their discontent heard; the poor and the unorganized must resort to protests and marches and demonstrations. Such methods have not customarily been considered un-American.

Second, we are not yet legally at war with Vietnam, though what is going on there has, to be sure, the character of war. Nor are we acting in Vietnam under the authority of the auspices of the United Nations, as we did in the Korean crisis. We are in Vietnam as a result of executive decision and executive action, and it is not yet traitorous or unpatriotic to criticize executive action. In so far as they were consulted on the matter, the American people voted, in 1964, for the candidate who appeared to promise them peace in Vietnam, and against the candidate who advocated war. It was not thought unpatriotic for President Johnson to demonstrate against war in Vietnam in 1964; what has changed in the past year is not the law or the principle, but Presidential policy, and it is not unpatriotic to fail to change when the President changes his policy.

But, it is said, whatever the legal situation, war is a fact. We do have 165,000 men in Vietnam; we do send our bombers out every day to rain destruction on our "enemies" there. The time for discussion, therefore, has passed; we must close ranks behind our government.

What is the principle behind this line of reasoning? What but that it is right and proper to protest an error—or what seemed even to President Johnson to be an error, as long as it was a modest one, but that it is unpatriotic to protest an error when it is immense. If this is sound logic, the moral for men in high position is clear. If any policy upon which you are embarked excites criticism, expand it, enlarge it, pledge all of your resources to it; then criticism will be unpatriotic and critics will be silenced. A little error is fair game for critics, but a gigantic error, an error that might plunge us into a world war, is exempt from criticism.

Is this the principle Senators Dodd and Lausche, Kuchel and Stennis, wish to adopt?

Third, there is the now popular argument that whatever the logic of protests, they are intolerable because they might give comfort to the enemy. Whatever may be said for the sentiment behind this argument, it can be said with certainty that it runs counter not only to logic but to history and tradition as well. When George III resolved on war against rebellious colonies, nineteen lords signed a solemn protest against the war, the commander-in-chief of the Army, Lord Jeffery Amherst, refused to serve; the highest commanding naval officer, Admiral Keppel, refused to serve; Lieutenant General Frederick Cavendish resigned his commission. We do not think poorly of them today for refusing to fight in what they thought an unjust war, and Amherst College is not about to change its name to Lord North.

Nor do we think poorly of preachers and men of letters who denounced the war with Mexico as unjust and counseled civil disobedience. President Polk, who at the last minute found a dubious justification for the war, is remembered, a century later, as "Polk the Mendacious" while Abraham Lincoln, who called upon him to indicate the "spot" where American blood had been shed, does not suffer in our esteem for his contumaciousness. Henry David Thoreau, who went to jail rather than pay taxes to support a war he thought iniquitous, is one of the glories of our literature and his essay celebrating civil disobedience is read in every high school and college in the land. Does Senator Dodd think it ought to be banned? James Russell Lowell wrote of the warmongers in his day (it is Hosea Biglow who is speaking):

> They may talk of Freedom's array,
> 'Tell they're pupple in the face;
> It's a gran' great cemetery
> Fer the barthrights of our race.

And he charged that

> Ez fer war, I call it murder;
> There you hev it plain and flat;
> I don't want to go no furder
> Then my testyment fer that.

And he concluded with words that are as apt today as they were in 1846:

> Call me coward, call me traitor,
> Jest ez suits your mean idees;
> Here I stand a tyrant-hater
> An' the friend o' God an' Peace.

A grateful government later sent Lowell as Minister to the Court of St. James's. And while the war was on, Lincoln's favorite clergyman, Theodore Parker, denounced it from the most eloquent pulpit in America, Sunday after Sunday. He is remembered today as The Great American Preacher.

In 1899 we fought a war that has interesting parallels with that which we are fighting today—a war which we now have almost wholly forgotten, perhaps for reasons that psychologists can understand better than politicians. That was the war to put down the Filipino "insurrection." For the Filipinos—like the Cubans—thought that they were to be liberated, but Admiral Dewey cabled that the Filipino Republic represented only a fraction of the Filipino people and that independence was not to be thought of, and the United States threw her military might into the task of defeating what they called an insurrection. Soon the presses were filled with stories of concentration camps and tortures; soon American soldiers were singing

> Damn, damn, damn the Filipinos
> Slant-eye'd Kakiack Ladrones
> And beneath the starry flag
> Civilize them with a Krag
> And return us to our own beloved Homes!

The Filipino war excited a wave of outrage and protest among intellectuals, reformers, and idealists as vociferous as that which we now witness. Mark Twain addressed a powerful letter, "To a Person Sitting in Darkness," which asserted that the Stars and Stripes should have the white stripes painted black and the stars replaced by skull and crossbones. The philosopher William James charged that "we are now engaged in crushing out the sacredest thing in this great human world. . . . Why do we go on? First, the war fever, and then the pride which always refuses to back down when under fire." And from the poet William Vaughn Moody came a memorable "Ode in Time of Hesitation":

> Alas, what sounds are these that come
> Sullenly over the Pacific seas. . . .
> Sounds of ignoble battle, striking dumb
> The season's half awakened ecstacies. . . .
>
> Was it for this our fathers kept the law?
> Are we the eagle nation Milton saw
> Mewing its mighty youth,
> Soon to possess the mountain winds of truth
> And be a swift familiar of the sun. . . .
> Or have we but the talons and the maw?

And "To a Soldier Fallen in the Philippines" he wrote just such an ode as might be written for a soldier fallen in Vietnam:

> A flag for the soldier's bier
> Who dies that his land may live;
> O banners, banners, here
> That he doubt not, nor misgive . . .
> Let him never dream that his bullet's scream
> Went wide of its island mark
> Home to the heart of his darling land
> Where she stumbled and sinned in the dark.

Nor were these men of letters alone in their passionate outcry against what they thought an unjust war. They had the support of a brilliant galaxy of public leaders: Carl Schurz and Samuel Gompers, E. L. Godkin of the *Nation* and Felix Adler of the Ethical Culture Society, Jane Addams of Hull House and President Jordan of Stanford University, and Andrew Carnegie and scores of others. And when the defenders of the war raised the cry, "Don't haul down the flag," it was no other than William Jennings Bryan, titular head of the Democratic party, who asked, "Who will haul down the President?"

We need not decide now whether those who protested this war were right or wrong. It is sufficient to remember that we honor Mark Twain and William James, regard Jane Addams as one of the greatest of American women, and still read Godkin, and that Bryan is somewhat better remembered than William McKinley. Those infatuated patriots who now assert that it is somewhat treasonable to criticize any policy that involves Americans in fighting overseas would do well to ponder the lessons of the Philippine War.

But, it will be said, as it is always said, this war is different. Whether history will judge this war to be different or not, we cannot say. But this we can say with certainty: a government and a society that silences those who dissent is one that has lost its way. This we can say: that what is essential in a free society is that there should be an atmosphere where those who wish to dissent and even to demonstrate can do so without fear of recrimination or vilification.

What is the alternative? What is implicit in the demand, now, that agitation be silenced, that demonstrators be punished? What is implicit in the insistence that we "pull up by the roots and rend to pieces" the protests from students—it is Senator Stennis we are quoting here. What is implicit in the charge that those who demonstrate against the war are somehow guilty of treason?

It is, of course, this: that once our government has embarked upon a policy there is to be no more criticism, protest, or dissent. All must close ranks and unite behind the government.

Now we have had a good idea of experience, first and last, with this view of the duty of the citizen to his government and it behooves us to recall that experience before we go too far astray.

We ourselves had experience with this philosophy in the antebellum South. The dominant forces of Southern life were, by the 1840's, convinced that slavery was a positive good, a blessing alike for slaves and for masters; they were just as sure of the righteousness of the "peculiar institution" as is Senator Dodd of the righteousness of the war in Vietnam. And they adopted a policy that so many Senators now want to impose upon us: that of silencing criticism and intimidating critics. Teachers who attacked slavery were deprived of their posts—just what Mr. Nixon now advises as the sovereign cure for what ails our universities! Editors who raised their voices in criticism of slavery lost their papers. Clergymen who did not realize that slavery was enjoined by the Bible were forced out of their pulpits. Books that criticized slavery were burned. In the end the dominant forces of the South got their way: critics were silenced. The South closed its ranks against critics, and closed its mind; it closed, too, every avenue of solution to the slavery problem except that of violence.

Nazi Germany provides us with an even more sobering spectacle. There, too, under Hitler, opposition to government was equated with treason. Those who dared question the inferiority of Jews, or the justice of the conquest of inferior peoples like the Poles, were effectually silenced, by exile or by the gas chamber. With criticism and dissent eliminated, Hitler and his followers were able to lead their nation, and the world, down the path to destruction.

There is, alas, a tragic example of this attitude toward criticism before our eyes, and in a people who inherit, if they do not cherish, our traditions of law and liberty. Like the slaveocracy of the Old South, the dominant leaders of South Africa today are convinced that whites are superior to Negroes, and that Negroes must not be allowed to enjoy the freedoms available to whites. To maintain this policy and to silence criticism—criticism coming from the academic community and from the press—they have dispensed with the traditions of due process and of fair trial, violated academic freedom, and are in process of destroying centuries of constitutional guarantees. And with criticism silenced, they are able to delude themselves that what they do is just and right.

Now, it would be absurd and iniquitous to equate our current policies toward Vietnam with the defense of slavery, or with Nazi or Afrikaner policies. But the point is not whether these policies have anything in common. The point is that when a nation silences criticism and dissent, it deprives itself of the power to correct its errors. The process of silencing need not be as savage as in Nazi Germany or in South Africa today; it is enough that an atmosphere be created where men prefer silence to protest. As has been observed of book-burning, it is not necessary to burn books, it is enough to discourage men from writing them.

It cannot be too often repeated that the justification and the purpose of freedom of speech is not to indulge those who want to speak their minds. It is to prevent error and discover truth. There may be other ways of detecting error and discovering truth than that of free discussion, but so far we have not found them.

There is one final argument for silencing criticism that is reasonable and even persuasive. It is this: that critics of our Vietnam policy are in fact defeating their own ends. For by protesting and agitating, they may persuade the Vietcong, or the North Vietnamese, or the Chinese, that the American people are really deeply divided, and that if they but hold out long enough the Americans will tire of the war and throw in the sponge. As there is in fact no likelihood of this, the critics are merely prolonging the agony of war.

These predictions about the effect of criticism in other countries are of course purely speculative. One thing that is not mere speculation is that American opinion is, in fact, divided; that's what all the excitement is about. We do not know how the Vietcong or the Chinese will react to the sounds of argument coming across the waters. Perhaps they will interpret criticism as a sign of American weakness. But perhaps they will interpret it as an indication or our reasonableness. And assuredly they will, if they have any understanding of these matters at all, interpret it as a sign of the strength of our democracy—that it can tolerate differences of opinion.

But there are two considerations here that invite our attention. First, if critics of our Vietnamese war are right, then some modification of our policy is clearly desirable, and those who call for such modification serve a necessary purpose. We do not know whether they are right or not. We will not find out by silencing them. Second, if government, or those in positions of power and authority, can silence criticism by the argument that such criticism might be misunderstood somewhere, then there is an end to all criticism, and perhaps an end to our kind of political system. For men in authority will always think that criticism of their policies is dangerous. They will always equate their policies with patriotism, and find criticism subversive. The Federalists found criticism of President Adams so subversive that they legislated to expel critics from the country. Southerners found criticism of slavery so subversive that they drove critics out of the South. Attorney General Palmer thought criticism of our Siberian misadventure—now remembered only with embarrassment—so subversive that he hounded the critics into prison for twenty-year terms. McCarthy found almost all teachers and writers so subversive that he was ready to burn down the libraries and close the universities. Experience should harden us against the argument that dissent and criticism are so dangerous that they must always give way to consensus.

And as for the argument that criticism may give aid and comfort to some enemy, that is a form of blackmail unworthy of those who profess it. If it is to be accepted, we have an end to genuine discussion of foreign policies, for it will inevitably be invoked to stop debate and criticism whenever that debate gets acrimonious or the criticism cuts too close to the bone. And to the fevered mind of the FBI, the CIA, and some Senators, criticism always gives aid and comfort to the enemy or cuts too close to the bone.

"The only thing we have to fear," said Franklin Roosevelt, "is fear itself." That is as true in the intellectual and the moral realm as in the political and the economic. We do not need to fear ideas, but the censorship of ideas. We do not need to fear criticism, but the silencing of criticism. We do not need to fear excitement or agitation in the academic community, but timidity and apathy. We do not need to fear resistance to political leaders, but unquestioning acquiescence in whatever policies those leaders adopt. We do not even need to fear those who take too literally the anguished pleas of a Pope Paul VI or the moral lessons of the Sermon on the Mount, but those who reject the notion that morality has any place in politics. For that, indeed, is to stumble and sin in the dark.

ART FINLEY

Art's Gallery

Courtesy of Chronicle Features Syndicate

"Inform him of his rights, THEN beat hell out of him!"

MALVINA REYNOLDS

Little Boxes

STUDY QUESTIONS FOR COMPREHENSION

1. Restate the main idea of the song in your own words.
2. Do you agree with Malvina Reynolds' point of view?
3. If you agree, are there other examples of conformity you can add from your own experiences?
4. Do you think uniform, ugly housing has an effect on the inhabitants' lives and attitudes?

Little boxes on the hillside, little boxes made of ticky tacky,
Little boxes on the hillside, little boxes all the same.
There's a green one and a pink one and a blue one and a yellow one,
And they're all made out of ticky tacky,
And they all look just the same.

And the people in the houses all went to the university,
Where they all were put in boxes, little boxes all the same,
And there's doctors, and there's lawyers and business executives,
And they're all made out of ticky tacky and they all look just the same.

And they all play on the golf course and drink their martinis dry,
And they all have pretty children and the children go to school,
And the children go to summer camp and then to the university,
And they all get put in boxes and they all come out the same.

And the boys go into business and marry and raise a family,
And they all get put in boxes, little boxes all the same,
There's a green one and a pink one and a blue one and a yellow one,
And they're all made out of ticky tacky, and they all look just the same.

CHARLES E. ROTKIN

New Housing on the Outskirts of Scottsdale

Courtesy of Rotkin, P.F.I.

HENRY DAVID THOREAU

From *Civil Disobedience*

"Civil Disobedience" was written shortly after Thoreau was jailed for refusing to pay the poll tax. He was, in effect, challenging the constitutionality of slavery, to which he was strongly opposed. He also opposed, equally strongly, the Mexican-American War (1846–48).

STUDY QUESTIONS FOR COMPREHENSION

1. What does Thoreau mean when he says that "It is not desirable to cultivate a respect for the law, so much as for the right"?
2. Thoreau mentions three choices open to men who live under unjust laws. What are they?
3. What is the condition that Thoreau sees as a reason for responsible men to break the law?

Can there not be a government in which majorities do not virtually decide right and wrong, but conscience?—in which majorities decide only those questions to which the rule of expediency is applicable? Must the citizen ever for a moment, or in the least degree, resign his conscience to the legislator? Why has every man a conscience, then? I think that we should be men first, and subjects afterward. It is not desirable to cultivate a respect for the law, so much as for the right. The only obligation which I have a right to assume, is to do at any time what I think right. It is truly enough said, that a corporation has no conscience; but a corporation of conscientious men is a corporation *with* a conscience. Law never made men a whit more just; and, by means of their respect for it, even the well-disposed are daily made the agents of injustice. A common and natural result of an undue respect for law is, that you may see a file of soldiers, colonel, captain, corporal, privates, powder-monkeys and all, marching in ad-

From Henry David Thoreau, *Civil Disobedience*, published in 1849.

mirable order over hill and dale to the wars, against their wills, aye, against their common sense and consciences, which makes it very steep marching indeed, and produces a palpitation of the heart. They have no doubt that it is a damnable business in which they are concerned; they are all peaceably inclined. . . .

The mass of men serve the State thus, not as men mainly, but as machines, with their bodies. They are the standing army, and the militia, jailers, constables, . . . etc. In most cases there is no free exercise whatever of the judgment or of the moral sense; but they put themselves on a level with wood and earth and stones; and wooden men can perhaps be manufactured that will serve the purpose as well. Such command no more respect than men of straw, or a lump of dirt. . . .

How does it become a man to behave toward this American Government today? I answer that he cannot without disgrace be associated with it. I cannot for an instant recognize that political organization as *my* government which is the *slave's* government also. . . .

If the injustice is part of the necessary friction of the machine of government, let it go, let it go; perchance it will wear smooth,—certainly the machine will wear out. If the injustice has a spring, or a pulley, or a rope, or a crank, exclusively for itself, then perhaps you may consider whether the remedy will not be worse than the evil; but if it is of such a nature that it requires you to be the agent of injustice to another, then, I say, break the law. Let your life be a counterfriction to stop the machine. What I have to do is to see, at any rate, that I do not lend myself to the wrong which I condemn. . . .

The authority of government, even such as I am willing to submit to—for I will cheerfully obey those who know and can do better than I, and in many things even those who neither know nor can do so well—is still an impure one: to be strictly just, it must have the sanction and consent of the governed. It can have no pure right over my person and property but what I concede to it. The progress from an absolute to a limited monarchy, from a limited monarchy to a democracy, is a progress toward a true respect for the individual. Is a democracy, such as we know it, the last improvement possible in government? Is it not possible to take a step further towards recognizing and organizing the rights of man? There will never be a really free and enlightened State, until the State comes to recognize the individual as a higher and independent power, from which all its own power and authority are derived, and treats him accordingly. I please myself with imagining a State at last which can afford to be just to all men, and to treat the individual with respect as a neighbor; which even would not think it inconsistent with its own repose, if a few were to live aloof from it, not meddling with it, nor embraced by it, who fulfilled all the duties of neighbors and fellow men. A State which bore this kind of fruit, and suffered it to drop off as fast as it ripened, would prepare the way for a still more perfect and glorious State, which also I have imagined, but not yet anywhere seen.

CY OLSON

Office Hours

"He's the only man on my staff independent enough to tell me what he thinks of my ideas. Fire him."

MAHATMA GANDHI

Civil Disobedience

STUDY QUESTIONS FOR COMPREHENSION

1. Some people think that civil disobedience is as reprehensible as the use of violence. What is your opinion?
2. Does Gandhi state that civil disobedience precludes a respect for the law?
3. What does Gandhi mean by his sentence, "For when tyranny is rampant, much rage is generated among the victims"?

A little reflection will show that Civil Disobedience is a necessary part of noncooperation. You assist an administration most effectively by obeying its orders and decrees. An evil administration never deserves such allegiance. Allegiance to it means partaking of the evil. A good man will therefore resist an evil system or administration with his whole soul. Disobedience of the laws of an evil State is therefore a duty. Violent disobedience deals with men, who can be replaced. It leaves the evil itself untouched and often accentuates it. Nonviolent, or civil, disobedience is the only and most successful remedy and is obligatory upon him who would dissociate himself from evil.

There is danger in Civil Disobedience, only because it is still just a partially tried remedy and has always to be tried in an atmosphere surcharged with violence. For when tyranny is rampant, much rage is generated among the victims. It remains latent because of their weakness and bursts in all its fury on the lightest pretext. Civil Disobedience is a sovereign method of transmuting this undisciplined, life-destroying, latent energy into disciplined, life-saving energy whose use ensures absolute success. The attendant risk is nothing compared to the result promised. When the world has become familiar with its use and when it has had a series of demonstrations of its success, there will be less risk in Civil Disobedience than there is in aviation.

My error in trying to let Civil Disobedience take the people by storm appears to me to be Himalayan, because of the discovery I have made that he only is able, and attains the right, to offer Civil Disobedience who has known how to offer voluntary and deliberate obedience to the laws of the State in which he is living. It is only after one has voluntarily obeyed such laws a thousand times that an occasion comes to him civilly to disobey certain laws.

CHARLES M. SCHULZ

Peanuts

THOMAS PAINE

Profession of Faith

STUDY QUESTIONS FOR COMPREHENSION

1. What is Paine's profession of faith?
2. Even though Paine obviously feels that his views of religion are the correct ones, does he condemn those who think differently from him? Support your answer.
3. What are the reasons Paine advances for his rejection of organized religion?

As several of my colleagues, and others of my fellow-citizens of France, have given me the example of making their voluntary and individual profession of faith, I also will make mine; and I do this with all that sincerity and frankness with which the mind of man communicates with itself.

I believe in one God, and no more; and I hope for happiness beyond this life.

I believe in the equality of man, and I believe that religious duties consist of doing justice, loving mercy, and endeavoring to make our fellow-creatures happy.

But lest it should be supposed that I believe many other things in addition to these, I shall, in the progress of this work, declare the things I do not believe, and my reasons for not believing them.

I do not believe in the creed professed by the Jewish Church, by the Roman Church, by the Greek Church, by the Turkish Church, by the Protestant Church, nor by any church that I know of. My own mind is my own church.

All national institutions of churches, whether Jewish, Christian, or Turkish, appear to me no other than human inventions set up to terrify and enslave mankind, and monopolize power and profit.

I do not mean by this declaration to condemn those who believe otherwise. They have the same right to their belief as I have to mine.

From *The Age of Reason, Being an Investigation of True and Fabulous Theology* by Thomas Paine (Paris, Barrois edition, 1794).

But it is necessary to the happiness of man, that he be mentally faithful to himself. Infidelity does not consist in believing, or in disbelieving: it consists in professing to believe what he does not believe.

It is impossible to calculate the moral mischief, if I may so express it, that mental lying has produced in society. When a man has so far corrupted and prostituted the chastity of his mind, as to subscribe his professional belief to things he does not believe, he has prepared himself for the commission of every other crime. He takes up the trade of a priest for the sake of gain, and in order to *qualify* himself for that trade, he begins with a perjury. Can we conceive any thing more destructive to morality than this?

Soon after I had published the pamphlet *Common Sense* in America, I saw the exceeding probability that a revolution in the System of Government would be followed by a revolution in the System of Religion. The adulterous connection of church and state, wherever it has taken place, whether Jewish, Christian, or Turkish, has so effectually prohibited, by pains and penalties, every discussion upon established creeds, and upon first principles of religion, that until the system of government should be changed, those subjects could not be brought fairly and openly before the world: but that whenever this should be done, a revolution in the system of religion would follow. Human inventions and priest-craft would be detected: and man would return to the pure, unmixed, and unadulterated belief of one God, and no more.

SAKI (H. H. MUNRO)

The Story-Teller

STUDY QUESTIONS FOR COMPREHENSION

1. Why was this story included with the readings on dissent?
2. Do you agree with the bachelor that it is possible to be *too* good?
3. Why is the bachelor's story so much more intriguing than the aunt's?

It was a hot afternoon, and the railway carriage was correspondingly sultry, and the next stop was at Templecombe, nearly an hour ahead. The occupants of the carriage were a small girl, and a smaller girl, and a small boy. An aunt belonging to the children occupied one corner seat, and the further corner seat on the opposite side was occupied by a bachelor who was a stranger to their party, but the small girls and the small boy emphatically occupied the compartment. Both the aunt and the children were conversational in a limited, persistent way, reminding one of the attentions of a housefly that refused to be discouraged. Most of the aunt's remarks seemed to begin with "Don't," and nearly all of the children's remarks began with "Why?" The bachelor said nothing out loud.

"Don't, Cyril, don't," exclaimed the aunt, as the small boy began smacking the cushions of the seat, producing a cloud of dust at each blow.

"Come and look out of the window," she added.

The child moved reluctantly to the window. "Why are those sheep being driven out of that field?" he asked.

"I expect they are being driven to another field where there is more grass," said the aunt weakly.

"But there is lots of grass in that field," protested the boy;

"there's nothing else but grass there. Aunt, there's lots of grass in that field."

"Perhaps the grass in the other field is better," suggested the aunt fatuously.

"Why is it better?" came the swift, inevitable question.

"Oh, look at those cows!" exclaimed the aunt. Nearly every field along the line had contained cows or bullocks, but she spoke as though she were drawing attention to a rarity.

"Why is the grass in the other field better?" persisted Cyril.

The frown on the bachelor's face was deepening to a scowl. He was a hard, unsympathetic man, the aunt decided in her mind. She was utterly unable to come to any satisfactory decision about the grass in the other field.

The smaller girl created a diversion by beginning to recite "On the Road to Mandalay." She only knew the first line, but she put her limited knowledge to the fullest possible use. She repeated the line over and over again in a dreamy but resolute and very audible voice; it seemed to the bachelor as though some one had had a bet with her that she could not repeat the line aloud two thousand times without stopping. Whoever it was who had made the wager was likely to lose his bet.

"Come over here and listen to a story," said the aunt, when the bachelor had looked twice at her and once at the communication cord.

The children moved listlessly towards the aunt's end of the carriage. Evidently her reputation as a story-teller did not rank high in their estimation.

In a low, confidential voice, interrupted at frequent intervals by loud, petulant questions from her listeners, she began an unenterprising and deplorably uninteresting story about a little girl who was good, and made friends with every one on account of her goodness, and was finally saved from a mad bull by a number of rescuers who admired her moral character.

"Wouldn't they have saved her if she hadn't been good?" demanded the bigger of the small girls. It was exactly the question that the bachelor had wanted to ask.

"Well, yes," admitted the aunt lamely, "but I don't think they would have run quite so fast to her help if they had not liked her so much."

"It's the stupidest story I've ever heard," said the bigger of the small girls, with immense conviction.

"I didn't listen after the first bit, it was so stupid," said Cyril.

The smaller girl made no actual comment on the story, but she had long ago recommenced a murmured repetition of her favourite line.

"You don't seem to be a success as a story-teller," said the bachelor suddenly from his corner.

The aunt bristled in instant defence at this unexpected attack.

"It's a very difficult thing to tell stories that children can both understand and appreciate," she said stiffly.

"I don't agree with you," said the bachelor.

"Perhaps *you* would like to tell them a story," was the aunt's retort.

"Tell us a story," demanded the bigger of the small girls.

"Once upon a time," began the bachelor, "there was a little girl called Bertha, who was extraordinarily good."

The children's momentarily-aroused interest began at once to flicker; all stories seemed dreadfully alike, no matter who told them.

"She did all that she was told, she was always truthful, she kept her clothes clean, ate milk puddings as though they were jam tarts, learned her lessons perfectly, and was polite in her manners."

"Was she pretty?" asked the bigger of the small girls.

"Not as pretty as any of you," said the bachelor, "but she was horribly good."

There was a wave of reaction in favour of the story; the word *horrible* in connection with goodness was a novelty that commended itself. It seemed to introduce a ring of truth that was absent from the aunt's tales of infant life.

"She was so good," continued the bachelor, "that she won several medals for goodness, which she always wore, pinned to her dress. There was a medal for obedience, another medal for punctuality, and a third for good behaviour. They were large metal medals and they clicked against one another as she walked. No other child in the town where she lived had as many as three medals, so everybody knew that she must be an extra good child."

"Horribly good," quoted Cyril.

"Everybody talked about her goodness, and the Prince of the country got to hear about it, and he said that as she was so very good she might be allowed once a week to walk in his park, which was just outside the town. It was a beautiful park, and no children were ever allowed in it, so it was a great honour for Bertha to be allowed to go there."

"Were there any sheep in the park?" demanded Cyril.

"No," said the bachelor, "there were no sheep."

"Why weren't there any sheep?" came the inevitable question arising out of that answer.

The aunt permitted herself a smile, which might almost have been described as a grin.

"There were no sheep in the park," said the bachelor, "because the Prince's mother had once had a dream that her son would either be killed by a sheep or else by a clock falling on him. For that reason the Prince never kept a sheep in his park or a clock in his palace."

The aunt suppressed a gasp of admiration.

"Was the Prince killed by a sheep or by a clock?" asked Cyril.

"He is still alive so we can't tell whether the dream will come true," said the bachelor unconcernedly; "anyway, there were no sheep in the park, but there were lots of little pigs running all over the place."

"What colour were they?"

"Black with white faces, white with black spots, black all over, grey with white patches, and some were white all over."

The story-teller paused to let a full idea of the park's treasures sink into the children's imaginations; then he resumed:

"Bertha was rather sorry to find that there were no flowers in the park. She had promised her aunts, with tears in her eyes, that she would not pick any of the kind Prince's flowers, and she had meant to keep her promise, so of course it made her feel silly to find that there were no flowers to pick."

"Why weren't there any flowers?"

"Because the pigs had eaten them all," said the bachelor promptly. "The gardeners had told the Prince that you couldn't have pigs and flowers, so he decided to have pigs and no flowers."

There was a murmur of approval at the excellence of the Prince's decision; so many people would have decided the other way.

"There were lots of other delightful things in the park. There were ponds with gold and blue and green fish in them, and trees with beautiful parrots that said clever things at a moment's notice, and humming birds that hummed all the popular tunes of the day. Bertha walked up and down and enjoyed herself immensely, and thought to herself: 'If I were not so extraordinarily good I should not have been allowed to come into this beautiful park and enjoy all that there is to be seen in it,' and her three medals clinked against one another as she walked and helped to remind her how very good she really was. Just then an enormous wolf came prowling into the park to see if it could catch a fat little pig for its supper."

"What colour was it?" asked the children, amid an immediate quickening of interest.

"Mud-colour all over, with a black tongue and pale grey eyes that gleamed with unspeakable ferocity. The first thing that it saw in the park was Bertha; her pinafore was so spotlessly white and clean that it could be seen from a great distance. Bertha saw the wolf and saw that it was stealing towards her, and she began to wish that she had never been allowed to come into the park. She ran as hard as she could, and the wolf came after her with huge leaps and bounds. She managed to reach a shrubbery of myrtle bushes and she hid herself in one of the thickest of the bushes. The wolf came sniffing among the branches, its black tongue lolling out of its mouth and its pale grey eyes glaring with rage. Bertha was terribly frightened, and thought to herself: 'If I had not been so extraordinarily good I should have been safe in the town at this moment.' However, the scent of the myrtle was so strong that the wolf could not sniff out where Bertha was hiding, and the bushes were so thick that he might have hunted about in them for a long time without catching sight of her, so he thought he might as well go off and catch a little pig instead. Bertha was trembling very much at having the wolf prowling and sniffing so near her, and as she trembled the medal for obedience clinked against the medals for good conduct and punctuality. The wolf was just moving away when he heard the sound of the medals clinking and stopped to listen; they clinked again in a bush quite near him. He dashed into the brush, his pale grey eyes gleaming with ferocity and triumph, and dragged Bertha out and devoured her to the last morsel. All that were left of her were her shoes, bits of clothing, and the three medals for goodness."

"Were any of the little pigs killed?"

"No, they all escaped."

"The story began badly," said the smaller of the small girls, "but it had a beautiful ending."

"It is the most beautiful story I ever heard," said the bigger of the small girls, with immense decision.

"It is the *only* beautiful story I have ever heard," said Cyril.

A dissentient opinion came from the aunt.

"A most improper story to tell to young children! You have undermined the effect of years of careful teaching."

"At any rate," said the bachelor, collecting his belongings preparatory to leaving the carriage, "I kept them quiet for ten minutes, which was more than you were able to do."

"Unhappy woman!" he observed to himself as he walked down the platform of Templecombe station; "for the next six months or so those children will assail her in public with demands for an improper story!"

NEWTON JOSEPH

The Great Hair Hassle

STUDY QUESTIONS FOR COMPREHENSION

1. Examine the statement: ". . . when we become a member of an organization or a team, there are certain things we must all give up."
2. Can you give reasons why athletic directors, school officials, and law enforcement officers frequently seem to be opposed to long hair on males?
3. What are some of the reasons given by Joseph for dislike of long hair on males?

Because Mayor Daley of Chicago has had more than his share of troubles with hippies, many people were shocked recently when he defended the right of young people to wear beards and long hair. "You look at pictures of Christ, Abraham Lincoln," said Mayor Daley. "You see them with wigs and beards."

The hassle over hair, however, is far from over. On the basis of a recent survey, the Bureau of National Affairs says, "It would appear to be a wise decision for young men to clip their whiskers when seeking employment." In fact there is evidence that the militant polarity in the Great Hair Hassle is hardening.

Many authorities—educators, psychologists, physicians, sociologists—suspect that hair has become a symbol of a youthful disillusionment deeper and more profound than the so-called "generation gaps" of earlier times. Says Dr. Stuart Wilson, a Newport Beach, California, clinical psychologist who deals with a good many disaffected young people and their parents: "The people who get up tight to an incredible degree about long hair are the people who value change-

From the March 1970 issue of *Today's Health*, published by the American Medical Association. Reprinted by permission of *Today's Health*.

lessness, who find it difficult to cope with change in their lives or anybody else's life. They want the 'good old days' to go on as always. They don't know it, but that's been done away with in this country. There are people here who value change, who live by the credo of change. That's where the real war is—between the belief that we should have change and that we shouldn't."

The battlefields of this war have been many and varied and the rhetoric and performance of the protagonists have sometimes bordered on the hysterical. Nowhere has this been more apparent than in the confrontations between the athletic establishment and the long-haired athletes.

Last year's official entry card of the Pacific Southwest National Open Tennis Tournament, for example, included a paragraph that read: "All boys are required to be clean-shaven and have short haircuts." Questioned about this, the tournament director explained: "We're trying to keep this game fine. We don't want boys coming in here looking like hippies. We want them to have a nice trim, and we're not ashamed of it. I think it's time people took a stand on this."

In Marin County last February, the four Redwood High trackmen who had been ordered by school authorities to lop their locks went to court. Their appeal was denied by Federal District Judge George B. Harris.

Thus they lost their opportunity to compete in the Redwood-Tamalpais track meet, which they subsequently picketed.

But the outcome of the meet provided vindication for the long-hairs. Without their shaggy runners, Redwood High lost.

Such an enlightened bastion of liberalism as Stanford University kicked a record-breaking sprinter off the track team because he wouldn't cut his hair. (He was from Britain and had worn it long all his life.) Two Purdue runners were dropped from the track team when they refused to shave off moustaches. (They were later reinstated by an athletic affairs committee that overruled the coaches.) When Oregon State football coach Dee Andros ordered one of his players to shave off a Van Dyke beard and moustache last spring, nearly two-thirds of the black students enrolled there—including 17 athletes—threatened to leave the campus.

Andros defended his action vigorously. "It is essential for team morale and unity," he told the *Los Angeles Times,* "for each individual player to conform to the rules and regulations set up for the rest of his teammates. I guess I'm the old-fashioned sort; I've always liked the Jack Armstrong, all-American boy type of athlete. Although I believe in human rights and in individual rights, when we become a member of an organization or a team, there are certain things we must all give up. No individual can be put before the team."

When the *Times* polled other coaches for reaction, Notre Dame's Ara Parseghian put it even more vehemently. "Wearing a beard or moustache," he said, "doesn't make anyone like the scum that populates Haight-Ashbury. But it *does* give an empathy or sympathy for a movement that is certainly the direct opposite of what we strive for in college football, which is goal-oriented."

Added USC coach John McKay: "We don't really keep our players from growing their hair long. If they do, all that happens is we make them play without helmets. I like a little conformity on our team. If we permit our players to grow long hair, what is the next step? What else do we permit? . . . I like long hair. My wife has it. I don't want people with long hair to get angry with me. But you have to have certain standards to have a country, to do anything."

Not all coaches share these views. Pete Newell, former athletic director at the University of California and now general manager of the San Diego Rockets, took a different tack. "A coach," he said, "now has to be more aware of social changes and adjust to them. What was true three or four years ago is not necessarily true now. Sure, it's a voluntary act when an athlete goes out for a team. It's something he has chosen to do. He is responsible for the rules of the scholarship and the coach's rules. If he doesn't like them he has the choice to say, 'thanks but no thanks.' But it's a two-way response. Coaches are vulnerable if they put rules on a team that are contrary to accepted, normal modes of dress. Times change. What wasn't acceptable before is acceptable now—meaning long sideburns, beards, and long hair. It is mandatory that a coach recognize these changes."

The same challenge might be extended to other segments of

American society. Consider these random samples of the Great Hair Hassle, taken from across the nation within the last year.

In a small Oregon town, a 20-year-old hitchhiker was forced to submit to a haircut under orders of the sheriff. The boy had been arrested for illegal possession of alcohol and hitchhiking and fined $20 on both offenses. After sentencing, the judge said, "I suggest you do something about your hair," and a sergeant in the sheriff's department apparently took this as a mandate to act. According to a quoted statement of the sergeant, "Two of us held him while the third put handcuffs on. We didn't use any more force than necessary."

In Reno, a judge told police to give haircuts to nine hippies who were arrested on charges of littering a park. The American Civil Liberties Union protested, calling the decision "an arbitrary extra-judicial punishment that violates the cruel-and-unusual-punishment clause of the Eighth Amendment and the due-process clause of the Fourteenth Amendment."

A 17-year-old youth was arrested in the Chicago suburb of Rolling Meadows for allegedly swearing at police. Forcibly shorn while handcuffed, he complained to the state's attorney. Subsequent investigation disclosed that it had been routine practice in that police department for two years to barber long-haired miscreants—"ever since a judge reprimanded one of our men for bringing a dirty-haired kid into court."

In Hampton, Virginia, a 16-year-old youth brought into court on a drunk charge was offered his freedom if he would cut his hair. He declined and went to jail.

In spite of a California Court of Appeals ruling holding that school restrictions on hair styles are unconstitutional, 17-year-old Doran Howitt was suspended at a Fullerton high school after a running argument triggered by the youth's long hair. Although school officials insist the suspension was caused by insubordination rather than hair length, the boy was readmitted after he cut his hair. About the same time, in Garden Grove, California, a near straight-A student and vice president of the student body was suspended for refusing to shave off "muttonchop" sideburns. The student, who works part-time and paid his own attorney bills, took the case to court, where

Superior Court Judge Claude Owens agreed with school officials that the boy's sideburns were indeed a "disruption in educational processes." The boy—already accepted by several colleges whether or not he got his high school diploma—wondered aloud "why my sideburns are disruptive to the educational process and my counselor's are not?"

Even Disneyland—which doesn't hesitate to employ long-haired musicians when it helps build the box-office—has felt the need to exercise restraint on the hair length of its customers. Hundreds of young people are turned away at the gates of Disneyland each year because the moonlighting physical education teachers who serve as security guards—particularly during the summer—don't approve of their appearance. Youthful author James Simon Kunen (*The Strawberry Statement*), for example, was recently refused entrance to Disneyland because of his hair. (He was also turned away at the Mexican border by a guard who said to him: "Are you a senorita? Go back."

An almost endless list of other examples of the hysteria over hair—distinguished only by their geographical location—might be cited. In Norwalk, Connecticut, the principal of a high school visited all of his classrooms one day, pulled 53 students out of class, and suspended them until they had their hair cut. The head of a Roman Catholic high school in Concord, New Hampshire, followed up a warning by piling 18 long-haired students on a bus and dispatching them to a barber. A Fallbrook, California, high school teacher wound up with an assault-and-battery suit when he allegedly cut the hair of a 16-year-old student with sheep shears.

Not every over-30 old-timer is against long hair, however. For example, columnist Sidney J. Harris noted recently: "Much of the adult rancor against the manners and dress of today's youth springs from an unexpressed resentment that they have a freedom we didn't have—or didn't take—when we were younger." And Justice William O. Douglas, filing a sharp dissent from a Supreme Court refusal to hear the complaint of three Dallas high school students expelled because of the length of their hair, insisted that the Declaration of Independence intended to allow "idiosyncrasies to flourish, especially when they concern the image of one's personality and his philosophy toward government and his fellow man."

But legal interpretations notwithstanding, long hair on youth has been a frequently indigestible idiosyncracy. As John Barron Mays, professor of social science at the University of Liverpool, pointed out recently: "In contemporary U.S.A. . . . youth is being pushed further and further into the margins of social life, being given an increasingly frivolous and protracted waiting role to perform, with the result that young people there have sought to create their own specific youth culture out of sheer desperation."

In the process—as tends to happen in the United States—the Hair Hassle has managed to turn a buck or two. According to a recent consumer study by *Supermarketing Magazine,* the trend to long hair on men has rocketed the sale of hair conditioning products to record heights. Meanwhile, a musical happening called *Hair* continues to do capacity business in New York, Chicago, and other major cities.

These may well be indicators that the opponents in the hair war are beginning to pull back from the battlefield. Said the *New York Times* at the beginning of the last school year: "After several years of excoriating pop singers, arty types whom they rightly or wrongly suspected of being homosexual, and their own teen-age sons of hirsuteness, city men of middle-age are letting their hair grow. Such traditional squares as stockbrokers, physicians and corporation executives are relinquishing the crew cuts to which they have clung since they returned from service in World War II."

Evidence seems to indicate that members of the older generation have finally decided if they can't lick the longhairs, they'll have to join them. There's a pervading impression to be found in the current rhetoric about hair that slowly—painfully slowly—it is becoming less of an issue between generations. Certainly one symptom of this movement is the growing number of public schools that are now moderating their rules on male hair styles.

James G. March, dean of the social sciences at the nearby University of California, Irvine, sees a deeper significance in youthful long hair and challenges the older generation to probe that significance.

"By wearing long hair," says Dean March, "these kids are saying something. The problem is that a lot of us are misunderstanding their message. The message depends on the kid's subgroup; if most of his immediate peers have long hair, he's saying simply, 'I like this group.' But he also may be saying: 'I'm growing up, I'm changing, so give me some more rope.' We hold on to our children too long. When they finally go off on their own, when they move out, the break is often sudden. It would be better if they went gradually, and correct parental understanding of the real meaning of a kid's actions would make this possible.

"Instead, parents are perpetually competing with one another through their children, though many don't realize it and few would admit it if they did. To these parents, long hair on their boy is like failure in school. Instead of sitting down with the boy and suggesting 'Let's talk about what you're saying,' they tend to ask themselves 'Where have we failed?' "

Stuart Wilson, a clinical psychologist in the same community, feels the young people's message *is* getting through—if grudgingly. "The whole hair trend," he says, "is over the hill. Most parents are more tolerant of their kid's long hair now—even sometimes to the point of secretly championing it. Long hair has lost its hippie image. The fact that most schools have come around is the hallmark of the change in attitude about hair. There are still some schools in the dark ages, probably because they see themselves as the guardians of faith and morals, as parental substitutes. But my own feeling is that as long as the kid is in school to do something productive, the school should not be concerned with the length of his hair.

"Kids feel social pressure in the hair sphere just as they do in the drug sphere. But there is a more basic reason for their emphasis on hair, an intrinsic factor pretty deeply imbedded. Where the kid's sense of identity may be in the hair realm, it is also his sense of self, an area where he can exert his independent thinking and his independent planning. Kids with short hair are asserting they're on the side of the establishment; they've identified very closely with their parents' wishes and made them their own. The whole athlete image now is an interesting phenomenon of the split within the peer group.

But you also have to look at the *kind* of long hair that someone is wearing. The difference within the group of longhairs is like night and day—hippie types versus movie stars. The fact that fashion and Hollywood have picked up on the hair thing—that highly respected and even idolized people have taken on this mantle—has lent a credibility and a respectability to long hair.

"People generally don't realize what a revolution we have been through in the last five years. Kids aren't afraid to rock the boat, and there will always be a means for them to assert their individuality and uniqueness. In 10 years, it might be something different; right now, it's hair. And long hair is going to be in for a very long time."

Conformity and Nonconformity

STUDY QUESTIONS FOR COMPREHENSION

1. The gentleman on the left was a conformist. The boy on the right is a nonconformist. Do you find either of them humorous? Why?
2. Since men have worn their hair long for more centuries than they have worn it short, why do you suppose that long hair on men causes so much criticism today?
3. Do you believe that hair and clothing styles reflect attitudes in society? How?

FIG. 374. *Steinkirk, 1690's. Redrawn from N. Bonnart, Louis, Marquis de Bade. (Metropolitan Musenm of Art, Dick Fund)*

"Sorry, I can't make it tonight. I just washed my hair."

Drawing on left by Elizabeth Curtis of "Steinkirk, 1690's" in *History of Costume* by Blanche Payne (Harper & Row, 1965). Reprinted by permission of Harper & Row, Publishers. Drawing on right by Herbert Goldberg, reproduced from *Saturday Review* (September 25, 1965) with permission of the artist and publisher.

Writing Assignments for Part Three

1. Use the library to obtain information about a great dissenter, past or present, in one of the following areas: religion, politics, science. Write either a report or an essay based on the information you obtained.
2. Write an essay in which you discuss whether conformity or nonconformity is predominant in the U.S. Be sure to use specific examples to support your point.
3. Write an essay in which you explain why the right to dissent is protected in a democracy but outlawed in a totalitarian state.
4. If you were a high-school principal, would you impose a hair or dress code? Write an essay explaining the reasons for the position you take.
5. Do you consider long hair on males a form of dissent? Support your answer in essay form.
6. Write an essay evaluating the various means used to dissent from the "Establishment," the schools, the government (whatever you wish). Be sure to have a clear point in mind.
7. Narrate an incident in which you or someone close to you was mistreated because of nonconformity.
8. Describe the conditions under which conformity would be more desirable than nonconformity.
9. Describe an incident in which you or someone close to you was forced to make a decision against conscience because of obedience to authority. Or describe the reverse situation, in which you or someone close to you acted against authority *because* of conscience.
10. In any form you choose, write your own profession of faith.
11. Respond in any form you choose (poem, short story, description, personal narrative) to any one or more of the selections in this section.

PART FOUR / *The Emerging Majority: Women*

April 13, 1645: Mr. Hopkins, the governor of Hartford upon Connecticut, came to Boston, and brought his wife with him, (a godly young woman, and of special parts,) who was fallen into a sad infirmity, the loss of her understanding and reason, which had been growing upon her divers years, by occasion of her giving herself wholly to reading and writing, and had written many books. Her husband being very loving and tender of her, was loath to grieve her; but he saw his error, when it was too late. For if she had attended her household affairs, and such things as belong to women, and not gone out of her way and calling to meddle in such things as are proper for men, whose minds are stronger, etc., she had kept her wits, and might have improved them usefully and honorably in the place God set her.

John Winthrop, first governor of the Massachusetts Bay Colony

SARA DAVIDSON

An Oppressed Majority Demands Its Rights

STUDY QUESTIONS FOR COMPREHENSION

1. How do you react to Sara Davidson's comment that "women are the most depressed and underprivileged class in any society"?
2. What are some of the points of view expressed about sexuality and fidelity?
3. Do you agree with Miss Davidson's statement that "Almost every woman, even if she is happy in her role, has buried within her rankling resentment"?

To demonstrate against the Miss America pageant was a glorious idea! "Protest the mindless boob girlie symbol of American womanhood. Help crown a live sheep Miss America. Burn bras, fashion magazines and cosmetic goop in a freedom trash can." The handbills were signed, "Women's Liberation." It was September 1968 and my immediate reaction was "Beautiful." After a fling at modeling as a teen-ager, I had long resented the plastic (buy-me!) images of the fashion press, and beauty contests where women are paraded like prize cattle. If I had had free time, I would have wandered out to Atlantic City. Women's liberation was a grand joke, the supreme, anarchist zap to the system.

Three weeks later, I was at Columbia University for a political meeting when a member of women's liberation asked to speak. She was a pretty, soft-featured brunette who wore a loose gray sweater and no bra, and she was dead earnest. She said women are the most oppressed and underprivileged class in any society. The audience laughed and hooted. One man drew vulgar pictures on the blackboard, S.D.S. members yelled obscenities, and the girl walked out near tears. I remember laughing and feeling, inexplicably, embarrassed.

Today women's liberation has become a serious national movement. In less than two years, it has grown in numbers and militancy, embracing a wide spectrum of women: housewives, professionals, students, women who are married, single, divorced, with children or childless. Fifty years after American women were granted the right to vote, a new feminist movement, predominantly middle-class and centered around universities and the cities, has begun at the grass roots level. The movement, which some say is 10,000 strong, has no national organization, no formal title, but "women's liberation" is the collective name most often used to describe it. The groups vary in every community, but all raise common themes: women are denied opportunity to fulfill their talents; traditional sex roles and family structure must be changed; women must relate in new ways to one another and to men.

Members of women's liberation point to civil rights, radical activism and the black liberation struggle as having inspired them. The birth control pill, which gave women more options, was also a factor. But perhaps most important, women in the last few decades were allowed small measures of equality, which aroused greater expectations. In colleges, women received the same education as men, only to find they could not use it upon graduation.

As I read more about the movement, I felt certain chords in my own experience were being hit. Almost every woman, even if she is happy in her role, has buried within her rankling resentment. From our earliest years, we were taught our lives would be determined not by ourselves but by the men we married. We sang rhymes about whom we would marry: "Rich man, poor man, beggar man, thief; doctor, lawyer, Indian chief." Little boys do not sing, "Actress, heiress, social worker, nurse." If our mothers pursued careers on top of being housewives, our situation was more ambiguous. We were encouraged to become self-sufficient, but to stay flexible enough so that we could adapt our life work, or give it up, for the right man. We worried ceaselessly about getting married and if we did not do so by our early 20s, we were pressured and insulted. "What's wrong with you? How come you're not married?" When we did marry, our husbands usually determined where and how we lived.

Early this fall I set out to contact women's liberation in New York, not an easy task, because the groups are not listed in the phone book. You have to find someone who knows the number of someone, or learn about a demonstration and attend it. The first group I was able to locate was the Feminists, who appeared one afternoon at the Marriage License Bureau to protest the marriage contract. Ti-Grace Atkinson, a tall blonde from Louisiana who is a doctoral candidate in philosophy and a longtime radical feminist, told the women reporters, who stifled smiles, that husbands should pay wives for all labor in the house. She grimaced. "Tony Bennett sings these songs of propaganda: get married and everything will be all right. Marriage means rape and lifelong slavery." A reporter asked, "What about pregnancy?" Ti-Grace (her name is Cajun for petite, or little, Grace) constricted her face, as if suffering. "It's very painful. It's so immature to grow babies in people's bodies. If we had test-tube babies, there would be less chance of deformed fetuses."

Five of the Feminists, who ranged from 25 to 30, met with me later in the one-room, one-windowed apartment of Pamela Kearon in a Greenwich Village tenement. They said they joined forces a year ago to annihilate sex roles. The group is highly regimented; all tasks are assigned by lot, members cannot miss meetings or disagree with the Feminists' line, and no more than a third of the group can be married or living with a man. "The purpose of our quota is to show that we mean what we say," Ti-Grace said. "We reject marriage both in theory and in practice." I began to feel self-conscious about the wedding ring on my finger. "Aren't there any positive differences between the sexes?" I asked. Linda Feldman, a heavy-set office worker, said, "I don't know if there are any differences between men and women. What differences could there be except genitals?" I said men are physically stronger. She said, "I don't think that would be true if women exercised more strenuously while growing up."

On to love. Ti-Grace said, "Love has to be destroyed. It's an illusion that people care for each other. Friendship is reciprocal, love isn't." And sex? "In the good society, we can't tell what will happen to sexual attraction. It may be that sex is a neurotic manifestation of oppression. It's like a mass psychosis."

"The more I understand what's going on with men," Ti-Grace said, "the less I miss male companionship and sex. Men *brag* about domination, conquest, trickery, exploitation. It gets so I can't even respond. Male chauvinism comes out in waves—every gesture, every word."

After three hours on this subject, I was depressed. What had led these women to the point where they could coldly dismiss feeling and touching, sex and love? Some of them are quite beautiful, which creates political contradictions. Women's liberation rejects the glossy magazines' vision of the liberated girl, who wears see-through clothes, smokes Virginia Slims and gives free love. The feminists say this fake liberated girl is a sex object, a bigger and better prostitute, not a human being. Women's liberation members avoid makeup, fancy hair styles and seductive clothes. If they go without bras, it is to be natural, not erotic. A girl in Chicago described the progression of giving up short skirts, then makeup, and recently, shaving her legs. "I still look at my legs and think, oh my God, I cannot go through with this. I'll die for the revolution, but don't ask me not to shave my legs! I have to keep reminding myself that there's nothing wrong with body hair, and no reason for one sex to scrape a razor over their legs."

Even the most radical feminists, however, retain many female character traits: soft-spokenness; talkiness (interviews and phone calls are difficult to terminate); and a proclivity for handwork. There was hardly a meeting I attended where someone was not knitting. While they condemn seductiveness, many want to look attractive. Pam Kearon of the Feminists said, "People like to look nice for other people. It's a statement of respect. It's just not true that we want to look like ugly freaks."

Some of the Feminists were active in the National Organization for Women (NOW), which they left in 1968 because they felt it was not radical enough. NOW was founded by Betty Friedan, whose book, *The Feminine Mystique,* was the signal flare of the new feminism in 1963. NOW members are, for the most part, professional women who want to end sex discrimination in hiring, promotions and salaries;

repeal abortion laws; establish comprehensive child care; and place women in policy-making posts. NOW has been called "the NAACP of the women's movement," but in the past year it has moved left, influenced by the younger activists.

In an apartment on the Lower East Side, Redstockings, a group which takes its name from "Blue Stockings," a term used in the past for intellectual women, meets each Sunday. A poster on the wall reads: "Speak pains to recall pains—the Chinese Revolution. Tell it like it is—the black revolution. Bitch, sisters, bitch!—the final revolution." The group employs consciousness-raising, or the bitch session, to gain political insights from shared feelings. More than 30 young women sit crowded on the floor of the small, stuffy room for five to six hours. A question is posed, such as, "Did you choose to stay single or marry?" Each girl relates specific incidents in her life, and at the end, the "testimony" is analyzed. They find that problems they thought were their own private sorrows are shared by everyone in the group. "If all women share the same problem, how can it be personal? Women's pain is not personal, it's political."

In the past month Redstockings has been considering, "How do you feel about sexual commitment and fidelity? Have you ever wanted to have more than one sex relationship at a time?" Several said their boyfriends or husbands felt women should be faithful while men could be free. One said she'd mind less if her husband had affairs with people he didn't care about than if he were emotionally involved. Another disagreed: "Since I've been in women's liberation, I object to my husband using other women like that."

One girl said, "I would like to be able to be tolerant and understanding if I learned my husband was having an affair, but I don't think I would be." Another said, "We say we'd like to be that way, but no one in this room would not feel hurt and angry. Maybe infidelity is a bad thing, and our feelings are right." The point struck me. Why should women not listen to their feelings; why should they feel guilty about them? The group was split on the desire for sexual commitment. Some felt it was imprisonment; others saw it as true freedom. At length they hit on the idea that women might write up their own marriage contract that would spell out commitment to fidelity or lack of it, priorities in life, and what division of labor there would be in the home.

Members of Redstockings have spent much time analyzing why women feel competitive and suspicious of one another, why so many like to say, "I'm a man's woman," and place little value on female friendships. Those who succeed in careers often feel they are special and look down on other women. Redstockings members say they identify with all women, and will always take the woman's side. "In fighting for our liberation . . . we will not ask what is 'revolutionary' or 'reformist,' only what is good for women."

About the time of the Redstockings meeting, I began to encounter hostility, fear and a distressing contrariness in some of the women's groups. I called a member of WITCH (Women's International Terrorist Conspiracy from Hell), a feminist revolutionary group which, in its manifesto, sees witches as the first guerrilla fighters against women's oppression: "Witches have always been women who dared to be groovy, courageous, aggressive, intelligent, nonconformist, sexually liberated, revolutionary." We spoke for an hour with what I felt was warmth and rapport, and arranged to meet the next week. When I called later to set the time, the woman hung up. I thought it was a mistake; I called back, and she said, "I've decided I don't want to be used as an object by *Life* magazine." In the background, a woman was screaming, "Don't apologize, just hang up."

Members of another group said they would vote at their meeting on whether to talk with me. I was informed the decision had been affirmative. When I appeared at the appointed hour, one of the women said she had changed her mind. "We've been ridiculed by so many journalists. I don't think we should cooperate." The group flipped over like a row of cards.

In Boston, a girl active in a new group, Bread and Roses, invited me to stay at her home. I declined, but asked to meet her. When I arrived, she said nervously that a mistake had been made. She had spoken with others, who urged her not to talk to me. I made further calls. Several people cursed and hung up. One girl said she was torn between wanting to communicate about women's liberation and fear of the American public's reaction. "We've been attacked as lesbians, or sick, frustrated bitches." Others ranted at me as a member of the "corrupt, bourgeois press," asked for money, and insisted they be allowed to censor anything I would write.

These experiences unnerved me, despite reminders that I should not take it personally and an understanding of what lay behind the fear and hostility. The negative reactions toward me expressed a great deal of what women's liberation is about: women's long-suppressed anger at being used; women's sense of vulnerability and defenselessness; women's suspicion and mistrust of other women; women's insecurity, lack of confidence in their judgments, the "secret fear," as one girl put it, "that maybe we are inferior."

I had dinner with Diana Gerrity, a staff editor at the *Atlantic,* who sympathized with my frustration. She said people in women's liberation are just getting in touch with the anger pent up inside them. "It takes a long time for any girl to realize she can register her outrage." Diana, tall and willowy, with long chestnut hair, was a fashion model while doing graduate work at the University of Chicago. She is 25, has been married two years, and joined a liberation group last May. "We've gotten to know each other very well. I don't think I ever trusted women before or really thought they were valuable people to be with. Friendships were based on competing for men."

As Diana spoke she would interrupt herself and say, "I don't know if I'm making sense." There is not a woman I know who doesn't feel, at some points, that she is rambling, not being rational. This must stem from expectations that women will be imprecise and fuzzy in their logic. In universities, a compliment paid to bright women is, "You think like a man." Women who are successful in professions come to think they have male attributes. A girl who was telling me about the difficulties of her job made an interesting slip: "I'm harassed by all the other men."

Diana is studying Tae Kwon Do, the Korean form of karate, two nights a week. "I've always felt great fear whenever I had to go out alone. Several friends of mine have been raped. Karate is as much psychological as it is physical training. It gives you the confidence to be able to judge a situation, or maybe fight your way out, instead of just collapsing."

The karate class is taught by Jayne West, a member of Boston Female Liberation, formerly called Cell 16. Female Liberation is a tight-knit, fiercely committed and clannish group which includes Abby Rockefeller, daughter of David Rockefeller, chairman of the Chase Manhattan Bank, and Roxanne Dunbar, who grew up on a poor white farm in the South and has been writing and lecturing on women's liberation for more than six years.

There were 12 women in the class, three of them teen-agers, and one 7-year-old who said she wanted to be able to beat up the 16-year-old bully on her block. Wearing coarse white uniforms, the women worked in precise, military rows, punching, jabbing and kicking, biting their lips and yelling "Kee-up!" Jayne West, a blue belt, who wears a headband Indian style over her long dark hair, rammed the floor with a board as she called out instructions. She kicked at the girls' legs and shoved them from behind. "You've got to be very steady. Your punch has to be accurate. You want to hit the person's solar plexus." I was watching from the back of the room when suddenly Jayne said, "Bricks!" The women wheeled and stampeded toward me. My blood froze. Bricks? I found I was sitting next to a pile of bricks; each woman grabbed one, tore back to line and began pounding it with her fists.

In their journal, *No More Fun and Games,* Female Liberation members urged women to leave their husbands and children and to avoid pregnancy. Women should dress plainly, chop their hair short, and begin to "reclaim themselves" by dropping their husbands' or fathers' names. They should live alone and abstain from sexual relationships.

Women's liberation has flowered in Boston to the point where it is impossible to attend a social gathering without hearing the subject discussed. There are probably more than 1,000 women in the area engaged in feminist study groups, theater, groups of secretaries and clerical workers, groups to legalize abortion, child care groups, encounter groups and women's communes.

A longtime friend of mine, Jane Harriman, joined a women's

liberation group last May, and we stayed up through the night talking about the movement. Jane is 29, an expressive, blue-eyed, affection-giving woman who likes to play sad sack and be humorous at her own expense. She is not married and supports herself and her 2-year-old son by working as a writer for a social research firm. Members of her group, which meets once a week, have been examining their personal lives to see where options were narrowed, restrictions imposed because of sex. When Jane was 14, she decided she wanted to be a doctor. "I began working in a hospital and studied science like mad. Gradually I got the idea I should be a nurse instead. My father told me I was bright, so I would be an exceptional nurse, but as a woman I would be only a fair doctor." After high school, she was urged to go to college, primarily, she thinks, to meet college men. Then when she had been at Bennington College two years, her father began sending her brochures for secretarial schools.

Along with the pressure to pursue a womanly career, Jane remembers the pressure to get a man. "As a teen-ager, your whole personality had to change to be popular with boys. You had to be empty-headed and amusing. You wore falsies and a girdle, and bleached your hair. I remember the horror of thinking, what if boys see me without makeup?"

Since women's liberation, Jane believes sex roles should be redefined. "Why shouldn't men share the responsibility for raising children and keeping house? I used to laugh about that, but I don't now. Why shouldn't a woman, if she's attracted to a man, be able to call and invite him to a movie? Why aren't there Playboy Clubs for women where we could go after work and have a very attractive man serve us drinks and say, 'Hi, I'm your bull, Mike'?"

Jane feels women's liberation is not anti-male. "Because you believe women are human beings, not objects, doesn't mean you don't like men. It's terrible to need a man for your identity. You want a man as an enrichment to your life."

The next morning, I drove from Boston to Windham College in Putney, Vt., where women's liberation members had been invited to speak. The college of 840 students is an arresting sight: white double-decker buildings with domed skylights set in a wooded field. About 100 people were waiting in the science auditorium. Janet Murray, a social worker who was wearing an orange blouse with the sleeves rolled up, a tweed skirt and oxford shoes, said: "The most painful and the greatest cause of women's oppression is the nuclear family. We think it should be broken up or radically changed, so that men and women share the economic responsibility, the child-care and the drudgery. As it is now, women get all the drudgery. It's a bad division of labor." Marya Levenson, a young graduate student and member of Bread and Roses, said people are experimenting with communal child-raising and cooperative play groups, where the fathers put in equal time. "The men begin to see taking care of children is boring and it's not all groovy being mother earth."

When they asked for questions, only male hands went up. Marya smiled. "You can see that in a mixed group the men tend to dominate and the women don't talk. That's why women's liberation groups have to be all women." After a pause, a fair-skinned girl rose and said, "I'm married, I have two children, and I'm happy as a clam. Some people naturally enjoy the passive role. I'd hate to see a society where there was no choice of being a housewife." Marya said, "There's no choice under the present society. If women resent being a housewife, or don't want to get married, they're told to see a psychiatrist." About 25 women, many faculty wives, stayed afterward to talk about forming a women's liberation group.

We slept that night on cots in the farmhouse of a political science professor. Next morning, as we drove back to Boston, Janet Murray, who is married and has a 3-year-old daughter, said: "I miss my nuclear family."

The first feminist movement in America took 50 years to gain mass support. Toward the end, the struggle for women's suffrage, won in 1920, eclipsed the deeper social changes the suffragettes had been calling for. Since 1920, the social and economic position of women has advanced little. Women's liberation has already revived national interest in feminism. Some of the groups, which grew out of the New Left, believe socialism is a prerequisite for women's liberation, and that women must confront racism and imperialism as well as their own oppression. Other groups do not feel associated with the left, and see male chauvinism, not capitalism, as the main enemy.

All the groups have more members than they know what to do with. "We don't have money to even distribute literature," a member of Redstockings said. "It's enough at this point for people to just start thinking and talking about women's liberation." Several groups are publishing feminist journals—*Aphra* in New York and *Women: A Journal of Liberation* in Baltimore. The Caravan Theater in Boston performs *How to Make a Woman* every weekend, followed by audience discussions. The New Feminist Repertory Theater in New York, directed by Anselma dell'Olio, is preparing a revue to tour the country. One sketch shows a man's reaction when he finds an impregnated uterus has been placed in his body.

Those who have been in women's liberation for many months are trying to incorporate their politics in their personal lives. Some have formed communes—all women, or mixed, with work divided equally. Many are restructuring their nuclear families. Robin Morgan, a member of WITCH, who is a poet, editor and former child actress (she played Dagmar in the television series *Mama*), has been married seven years and has a 5-month-old son. Robin and her husband, poet Kenneth Pitchford, have consciously worked to share all roles. Both have part-time jobs, he in the mornings, she afternoons; while one works, the other takes care of the baby. "We're both mothers," Robin says. "He bottle feeds, I breast feed." Before the baby was born, they chose a name they felt was genderless—Blake, after the English romantic poet, William Blake, who, Robin says, was an early feminist. If the baby had been a girl, she would have taken her mother's last name instead of her father's. Robin hopes they will be living in a commune before Blake grows up. "Our arrangement is one attempt at an interim solution. But no personal solution will work until we have a complete social and economic revolution which stresses the liberation of 51% of the people."

Overexposure to women's liberation leads, I found, to headaches, depression and a fierce case of the shakes. A friend of mine retreated to her kitchen after a weekend of meetings to lose herself in an orgy of baking pies. I stayed home for three days and stopped answering the phone. But women's liberation was accelerating each day.

In New York court suits were filed to have the state abortion laws declared unconstitutional.

Women's liberation in San Francisco learned a group of radical men were publishing a pornographic magazine to raise money for politics. They confronted the editor, convinced him he could not advance his cause at the expense of women, and burned the magazine layouts.

A WITCH coven, carrying pails and brooms, performed guerrilla skits on Wall Street to shocked and amused crowds.

NOW picketed the headquarters of the three candidates for mayor of New York for failing to take a stand on women's rights. At John Lindsay's headquarters on Fifth Avenue, Nancy Seifer, who works for Lindsay, brought out a statement of partial support. Nancy told me, "I agree with their ideas, but some of their demands are unrealistic." We began arguing, casually, about what women should demand, when a young salesman, tall and beanpole thin, with crew-cut blond hair, interrupted us: "Women aren't discriminated against! Women aren't capable of certain types of work, just like men aren't capable of raising children. A woman will fold under pressure more easily than a man. A woman can't make decisions or quick judgments."

Nancy and I both got mad. The salesman, Hugh Wessell, said, "Women aren't open about sex."

Nancy cried, "What has that got to do with making decisions?"

I asked Wessell, "Would you say the same things about black people?" He grew sober. "I have nothing against black people."

"But you wouldn't make jokes about their abilities," I said. "Why do you joke about women?"

Wessell grinned. "Well, most of the women I know are not that sensitive about it."

I smiled back at him. "Not for long."

MELL LAZARUS

Miss Peach

Courtesy of Publishers-Hall Syndicate

JUANITA M. KREPS

Six Clichés in Search of a Woman

STUDY QUESTIONS FOR COMPREHENSION

1. What differences does Juanita Kreps claim exist between men's and women's expectations in marriage?
2. Do you think that the three sets of clichés mentioned are actually believed by men and women?
3. How does Juanita Kreps answer the charge that career women are neurotic?
4. What reasons does she give for her insistence that education and career plans are important for women?

Once upon a time in a far away land a princess was born. In the midst of the celebration a wicked godmother appeared and decreed that on her sixteenth birthday the princess would prick her finger on a spinning wheel and fall dead. Only through the power of a good godmother could this dreadful sentence be reduced from death to a hundred years of sleep. And so it happened that the princess did find the tragic spinning wheel, she did prick her finger, and she did fall into a deep sleep. But after her century-long nap a handsome prince kissed her lips and she awakened. Whereupon they married and lived happily ever after.

This concludes the story. And let no one suggest that it be in any way edited, for it has for centuries been a story of pure enchantment for little girls. To bigger girls, however, particularly those of us who have been asked to read the story over and over till the pages fell from the book, certain questions surely have arisen.

An address delivered before the North Carolina Association of Women Deans and Counselors, Wilmington, North Carolina, October 22, 1964. Printed in *Vital Speeches* (December 15, 1964).

Have you ever wondered what actually happened to the prince and particularly to the princess after they were married? For example, did they go to live in his father's castle? If so, how did she get on with the queen who was, incidentally, her mother-in-law? How many children did she have? Were they well adjusted or did she have to seek "professional help" for them? How did she handle the problem of sibling rivalry, which in this case may have been over no smaller a goal than the throne itself?

How much did she see of her husband? Did wars, affairs of state, and commuting time ruin his family life? How could she possibly keep house without detergents? What did she do with herself when the children were all in school? She couldn't very well spend her time cleaning out the closets, as is sometimes the refuge of non-princesses. Did she grow old gracefully? Did she outlive her husband and, if so, by how many years? What kind of pension could she claim in an era that preceded the advent of Social Security? In short, what was it like to live happily ever after?

These unromantic queries, you may protest, do violence to the "happily ever after" theme. The essence of the fairy tale was of course to show that the young lovers had overcome all the obstacles by the time of the marriage; no new problems could possibly be on the horizon, once the vows were spoken. All the dragons were slain, all the witches' spells broken.

In the days when life's problems could be so easily traced to the powers of the traditional witch, perhaps the solution was in fact as simple as the stories relate. But, alas, the modern world brings with it a prevalence of new witches, and today's breed have the disquieting capacity to haunt after as well as before the wedding. Evidence that the married princess is not immune to evil spirits is on every hand: in the "Dear Abby" columns, on the psychiatrist's couch, in the divorce courts. The evidence is so unmistakable, in fact, that one may well wonder why those of us who influence the thinking of young princesses permit the myth to be perpetuated.

We have done so, of course, either deliberately or by default, and we have been greatly abetted by advertisers eager to sell household goods, by parents eager to see their children "married and settled down," by writers who portray, over and over, the romantic story that begins with calculated pursuit and ends with legalized surrender. In this modern version of the pursuit it is sometimes difficult to tell which sex plays which role. Apparently the reversal of roles is permitted—even applauded—as long as the man is not allowed to suspect that he is the pursued and not the pursuer.

Because we have done such a thorough job of persuading young girls that they must, above all (and on schedule) marry and have a family, we have made them terribly afraid that they will fail to find a husband. It is perfectly understandable, then, that young ladies begin to feel that something is wrong if they aren't engaged by the time they are seniors and married shortly thereafter. Increasingly, such pressures have apparently been felt even among high school students. In her concentration on this major objective, the college girl finds it difficult to conceive of herself ten years hence, when she is likely to have a husband who works, children who are in school, and a home that requires something less than her complete intellectual attention. And she finds it impossible to imagine herself at middle-age (that nice, vague term that to the young denotes not an age, but a state of vegetation), when her time is very largely her own. Since middle-age is incomprehensible, the prospect of old age, and particularly the probable years of widowhood, may well be postponed for later consideration.

We have placed marriage above all else. That is where it properly belongs for most women. But we have failed to emphasize certain related data. First, we have somehow not convinced college girls that husbands really aren't that hard to find. Chances are not very good, in fact, that the coeds could escape marriage even if they tried. Every minute of every day women are getting married—tall women, short ones, skinny, fat, rich and poor—to an equally wide assortment of men. Some women aren't getting married because they choose to remain single, a status which many of their hastily-married sisters may come to envy. There is a great deal of freedom of choice in the matter of getting married.

In addition to making the capture of a husband seem unnecessarily difficult, we have failed to direct the coed's attention to the evolutionary nature of her life after marriage. The first year or so, yes—she has to work till her husband finishes school, or till they can buy a home. We may hint at the drudgery of housework, particularly when she has small children. But almost never do we ask the coed how she imagines her life will be in a later period in her life. And never do we ask her, when she says she is getting married at graduation: "And what do you plan to do with your mind?"

Yet isn't it our responsibility to ask her that question? We are the faculty and staff of institutions of higher learning; we are not, after all, merely the window dressing for a marriage bureau. An exciting by-product of the pursuit of knowledge may indeed be the pursuit of the opposite sex. Universities erect very few roadblocks in either case. But our attitude toward the relative value of the two pursuits seems to depend to a great extent on whether the student is male or female. The man is expected to develop intellectual interests that will spark a lifetime; the woman, if she marries, not so.

We are not pushing the coed hard enough on this point. If she is led to think of the lifetime ahead of her, instead of just her first year of marriage, her attitude will reflect this long-run view. She will be much more interested in developing some minimum preparation for future explorations in the discipline she finds most appealing. She will give time and thought to ways of "keeping up" with a subject that intrigues her, knowing that in later years she can pick up where she left off. If she seriously wants a career, she will realize that there will be ample time for one, even if she has a family.

The tide is surely turning toward a greater insistence that college women consider themselves permanent participants in intellectual matters, and moreover, that they view their long-run professional prospects as delayed, but not necessarily terminated, by marriage and a family. But though many professors and counselors may be forcing the coed to look ahead, we seem to be victims of a number of half-truths. Some of these clichés are found primarily in industry and the professions. Others are implicit in current fiction. They are voiced by men who have little to gain and by women who ought to know better. Until we lay these ghosts to rest, young women will continue to minimize the long-run importance of their intellectual development, and will continue actually to avoid preparation for a lifetime of learning.

Two of the most familiar of these clichés have to do with the role of marriage in a woman's life: one, *a successful marriage fulfills a woman,* and two, *homemaking is a fulltime job.* In reality, a woman who goes through four years of college these days runs the risk of becoming interested in *something* that she feels obliged to study further. To insist that she forego her own particular interests altogether, either because she isn't supposed to want anything but a happy family, or because her family needs her full time, is pretty absurd. Nobody *will* insist, probably, but all the same mothers of the postwar generation were made to feel guilty when they went back to school, and there is still some hangover of this notion.

The question of fulfillment is an elusive one. Since no one has ever suggested that marriage is supposed to fulfill a man, we must conclude that the woman is supposed to be very much more dependent on marriage for gratification and that she receives much more satisfaction from marriage than her husband. Herein may lie the source of some of our bitterest disappointments. If a woman expects marriage to satisfy her completely and then finds it doesn't, she is very likely to reason that it is a poor marriage. Actually, she has been led to expect of marriage something that marriage *per se* cannot provide, that is, growth of her own personality and intellect.

The question of whether homemaking is a fulltime job is not elusive; it is merely controversial. When there are small children to care for, it takes as many hours a day as one can stand on her feet for as many years as the children remain small. But then, one day these demands are greatly reduced. Many women say that they continue to be frantically busy running the home. I'm sure they are. And this confirms what I have long suspected, which is that I am a very poor housekeeper. Because I can't for the life of me find much to do after the children leave for school.

The second set of clichés has to do with women's intellects, or lack thereof. The first is that *woman's forte is intuition, not intellect,* and the second: *it's unfeminine to be intelligent.* Well. Whoever it was that introduced the notion that sex appeal and I.Q. were inversely related did bright girls a great disservice. But to see women *accept* it as gospel and deliberately try to mask their intellects behind a vacant, simpering approach to men is the surprising thing. The final blow is, of course, to see how often it works.

In the classroom this doesn't happen very often. A girl may be very quiet for a while, but it's impossible for her not to come alive often enough to give herself away. The interesting thing is, though, that the coeds won't *argue* as vehemently as the men. Is this from fear of being found unattractive? The undergraduate men would probably find it challenging—at least this would be true of those men the bright girls find interesting. As for intuition, women of all ages use it for winning arguments when they are in a hurry and don't have time to marshall the facts. It is understood that, given time for research, the gal could win fair and square.

The more serious complaints against women turn on their alleged use of tears instead of logic, their insistence that their sex gives them certain prerogatives as to changing their minds, failing to observe schedules, etc. How can women answer these charges except by disproving them? How many dedicated, hardworking professional women does it take to undo the damage inflicted by one cry-baby?

The third set of clichés is related to women in careers. First, *career women are neurotic,* and, second, *women can't get along* (professionally) *with other women.* A woman with a career is supposed to be neurotic because she went into the career in the first place because she was frustrated in her love life because she was probably a cold, unfeeling kind of woman and thus her career is a substitute for the kind of life a normal woman leads. She gets along poorly with other women in her profession because she envies them, and she persecutes the poor women who work for her because they are generally younger and more successful with men. Ergo, women never like to work for other women.

Whether career women have more neuroses than nonworking women can be answered only by psychiatrists. But you can pretty well explode the myth by one test: What career woman do you know who has time for a respectable neurosis? Moreover, the unhappy woman in a career would probably be equally unhappy at home, only in the latter case her husband and children would bear the discomfort she now heaps on her colleagues. The important point is that a woman with a keen intellect plus the willingness to work at a job outside the home is likely to find life interesting, and an interest in her work is probably the best insurance against neuroses.

Often the term "neurotic career woman" is applied to a particular type of woman, generally one who is both extremely ambitious and somewhat unsure of her ability to achieve. The combination may lead her to fall back upon the complaint that she is being discriminated against because she is a woman. Discrimination against women in the job market is of course not a new phenomenon, nor is it a pleasant fact of life. But the woman who really wants to go for the big job needs to remind herself that work, not complaints, may be more effective. She has to be willing to play the game like a pro, and nurse her disappointments in private. Moreover, it may reduce her frustrations somewhat to remember the comment that Irene Tauber, the noted demographer, made when she was on the Duke campus a year or so ago. "When a job I would have liked to do is assigned to a man, I always entertain the possibility—just entertain it, mind you—that he was better equipped to do that particular job."

It's hard to be objective about one's own capabilities. In fact, Irene is one of the women whose ability has been so clearly demonstrated that she can afford to raise the question without any qualms; most of us are still in the process of proving ourselves. But it's one thing to warn young women that they may not "arrive" on schedule in a demanding profession, and quite another to let them leave the halls of learning with the notion that the rigorous pursuit of a career is somehow "unnatural." And we would make a glorious contribution to the welfare of mankind (womankind?) if we could, once and for all, dispel the idea that certain disciplines and certain professions are not open to women. It seems to me unnecessary to demonstrate further the capabilities of women in the natural sciences, in law and medicine. Yet young women enter these fields with great misgivings, as though they are doomed to failure.

We have been confusing ability to master these disciplines, which the coeds certainly have, with motivation to do so, which, alas, the girls do not have. For though they plan to work after graduation, they have no plans to do so beyond the usual couple of years. And though they have keen interest and demonstrated abilities in say, drama or music, they often have no long-run plans for developing their talents either for fun or for the marketplace. Yet at age thirty-five the woman college graduate will have worked two years, had three children two years apart, sent the youngest one off to school, and begun to look for new outlets for her energies.

A vast array of community service projects stands ready and waiting. The woman who devotes herself to this form of public service often works harder than the rest of us, and she receives little praise and no money. But even so, if these activities satisfy her and actually utilize her talents, there can be no complaint. The fact that by the time they are age forty-five half of the women will be in the labor force indicates, however, that jobs are increasingly the outlet for middle-aged women. The woman who takes a job at thirty-five will have thirty years to work before retirement.

This makes the question of the *kind* of job very important. No longer can the coed dismiss her brief pre-baby bout in the labor force as a temporary expedient. She is compelled to give some attention to the work that is to occupy her for thirty years. Her preparation needs to be aimed at the development of skills and interests that will serve her well in this longer-run context. Given the much longer length of her working life, today's coed is well advised to lay the groundwork very carefully.

In many cases it isn't necessary for her to stop school with an A.B. She can often get a fellowship (that will pay almost as much as typing pays) and continue in school, with or without a husband. Having an M.A. or a teacher's certificate or some experience with the kind of work she likes to do makes it very much easier to pick this work up again.

In conclusion, we have three major challenges before us. We have first, to disprove the clichés that persist in discouraging young women from using their intellects; we need second, to focus the coed's attention on her long-run marriage-family-work pattern, rather than allowing her to assume that love conquers all; and finally, for the sake of the nation, if not the women themselves, we have somehow to lift the level of aspirations of our brighter women students, and thereby help to meet today's vast shortage of highly trained personnel.

Three Nursery Rhymes

STUDY QUESTIONS FOR COMPREHENSION

1. What cultural attitudes do these three nursery rhymes reveal?
2. How do you account for the differences in stereotyping between young girls and married women?
3. To what extent do these cultural attitudes exist today?
4. What practical effects in daily life result from these cultural attitudes?

1/

What are little boys made of?
What are little boys made of?
  Frogs and snails
  And puppy-dogs' tails,
That's what little boys are made of.

What are little girls made of?
What are little girls made of?
  Sugar and spice
  And all that's nice,
That's what little girls are made of.

What are young men made of?
What are young men made of?
  Sighs and leers
  And crocodile tears,
That's what young men are made of.

What are young women made of?
What are young women made of?
  Ribbons and laces,
  And sweet pretty faces,
That's what young women are made of.

2/

Mother, may I go out to swim?
   Yes, my darling daughter,
Hang your clothes on a hickory limb
   And don't go near the water.

3/

I married a wife on Sunday,
She began to scold on Monday,
Bad was she on Tuesday,
Middling was she on Wednesday,
Worse she was on Thursday,
Dead was she on Friday;
Glad was I on Saturday night,
To bury my wife on Sunday.

EDWARD J. BLOUSTEIN

Man's Work Goes from Sun to Sun but Woman's Work Is Never Done

STUDY QUESTIONS FOR COMPREHENSION

1. Explain Bloustein's comment that the woman's role in a marriage is "submissive and inferior even though the couple intended their marriage to be a relation of equals."
2. What areas of discrimination against women does Bloustein mention?
3. What does Bloustein have to say about the sexual revolution?

A cruel hoax is being perpetrated by our society on the middle-class American woman. This is not intentional, but it is very real. The young woman is assured that she can combine marriage and family successfully with a meaningful career. But if this is what she wants and tries, she finds formidable—sometimes impossible—obstacles in her path. Perhaps a searching examination of the very institution of marriage may be necessary to make reality of the hope that too often now precedes frustration and even heartbreak.

Besides the waste of women's capacity, the other catastrophic consequence of the present marriage-career hoax is that women who might otherwise lead rich, fulfilling lives in the home—in the leisure that our affluent society provides—are being deprived of this opportunity by the American compulsion to achieve and to produce, something women are told they can and should do.

There are two obvious solutions to this dilemma. We could tell women: Your place is in the home. Stay there. Don't aspire to anything else. This is an understandable position that women might have accepted without terrible frustration or unhappiness a hundred years ago. It will not work today.

On the other hand, we could say: Go out into the world, seek careers, find independent sources of sustenance and satisfaction. Saying this, we would at the same time provide the altered social institutions to make such a solution possible.

Our society has taken neither of these realistic alternatives.

If a woman seeks satisfaction solely in the housewife's role, she often is torn with guilt because she is not "doing something" with her education. But if she responds to society's invitation to enter the wider world and to build a career, she finds the avenues to success virtually closed. She encounters at every turn obstacles of prejudice and discrimination and lack of institutional supports. Soon the early blush of optimism and enthusiasm gives way to frustration and grinding anxiety.

In other words, society holds out opportunities that are not really there. It promises women the chance to build a career but it does not make the adjustments in our social institutions necessary for career fulfillment for women. That is the hoax—the promise unfulfilled.

What are some of the difficulties that a career-bound woman is likely to encounter? These usually arise in the latter stages of her education. She can attain an undergraduate education comfortably, but she cannot fit her graduate education into the socially established pattern of marriage and child-rearing without severe strain.

The woman's dilemma is compounded by two intersecting social trends. Women tend to marry at an earlier and earlier age, but the education they require to qualify for a desirable career takes longer and longer. Women often marry before they are equipped adequately to do what they want to do professionally, and marriage often prevents continuation of their career.

For many women, even a second-class education becomes impossible after marriage. This happens when the cupboard is bare, and the wife drops out of school to take an ordinary job. More and more women today are working to put their husbands through graduate school and by doing so deprive themselves of the career satisfactions which our society promises them.

Even when man and wife both finish the necessary schooling, the wife almost invariably is obliged to take leftovers in career openings. This happens even when she has been able to complete the required graduate training for her profession. Her status requires her to go wherever her husband's work takes him—sometimes through several moves—and then to look around for something to do with her own training.

I think of a typical example, a Bennington student, who decided as an undergraduate that she wanted to become a teacher of philosophy. During her senior year, she married a young man who was headed toward a promising career in anthropology.

The young couple agreed not to have children until both had completed their graduate degrees. Helen, the bride, was not to be deprived of her career, but when her husband got a fellowship to do his graduate work at a university with a superior anthropology department, Helen naturally had to go with him, even though the university's philosophy department left something to be desired.

The couple postponed their family. They intended their marriage to be a relation of equals, yet the very submissive and inferior status of Helen meant that her education took second place to his.

I do not suggest that early marriage is necessarily wrong, nor that women's search for a career should be of paramount importance. I urge only that we should not lure women with the promise of an independent and equal career opportunity, when the pattern of early marriage—even without children—makes it a pledge impossible to fulfill. And, as is obvious, the woman who marries and has children before completing her education carries a far greater burden.

The very institutional form of marriage is, in a sense, an impediment to the promise of a career, a promise which our society holds open to women. One of the more radical suggestions for coping with this dilemma is to revise the basic marriage pattern. As far as I can see, this could happen only if young people felt free to have deep, fulfilling love relationships outside marriage. This "solution" obviously would have side ramifications for our society and is not something one can recommend casually.

The fact is, however, that growing numbers of young people *do* find love at an early age, but at the same time realize that early marriage represents an impediment to their careers. Therefore they are working out forms of love relationships which enable them to postpone marriage while fulfilling their career interests. Neither the man nor the woman sacrifices his interest to the other.

Even without a revision in the basic marriage pattern, there are other things society could do to enable women to undertake a career on equal terms with men. One thing would be to eliminate the widespread discrimination that exists in most occupations and professions. Men are the ones who determine the conditions of employment for both men and women, and they simply are discriminatory in the crudest sense of the word.

We all know that women traditionally are paid less than men. Moreover, there are patterns of discrimination in the educational process itself. The very men who complain that women never fulfill the careers they set out upon are the same men who make it extraordinarily difficult for them to do so. They set up what are, in effect, if not in form, different requirements for entry into graduate school, and different regulations for gaining fellowships and financial aid. And they make no effort to create new educational forms suited to the special needs of young married women. Many a graduate school department refuses women students, for instance, on the rationale that they are a waste of time because women will leave their fields to raise their children.

If we were truly serious about making it possible for women to marry and have children and still attend graduate school, we would begin to make radical changes in curricula, and we would establish nursery schools in university settings—a widespread practice in Denmark and in the Soviet Union. Child-care centers especially are needed because the "extended family" virtually has disappeared from our society. The situation is complicated by the fact that middle-class women in America now feel very guilty about hiring domestic help.

These are both recent developments. A generation or so ago, my mother-in-law decided to go to medical school. She was in her late 30's at the time and her youngest child was five. She invited an aunt to come live with the family, and she also was able to hire a maid. But today live-in aunts and grandmothers are in short supply, and to many women, employing a maid somehow seems immoral.

Another adjustment our society should make is to experiment with job forms that are somewhere between the professions and the blue-collar and low white-collar work women usually are shunted into when they lack full professional training. There are many opportunities in our society for quasi-professional people. If we gave these opportunities some status and turned them into satisfying and identifiable roles, women could fulfill them with dignity and without meeting precisely the same requirements as men.

An example that comes to mind is the person who is not a professionally trained social worker but who could do a good job in social work without fulfilling professional training requirements. Another might be the job of a medical assistant at a level beyond that of laboratory bottlewasher or routine tester. One could go on to suggest dozens of similar opportunities.

An advantage of the quasi-professional role is that it allows the woman to work part-time. Part-time employment might be very fulfilling for a large number of women, giving them the best of two worlds.

But even if these educational and vocational changes were made, there would remain another important obstacle to the woman's career. When a husband goes to work he leaves the home behind, but a wife never does. She has to worry about meals, about adequate preparations for the children, about giving the housekeeper instructions, about entertaining. She must always have a dual responsibility.

If women are ever to be free to pursue careers on approximately the same terms as men, their husbands must be willing to assume some of the concerns which traditionally have been regarded as "women's work." A husband and wife should strive for some kind of compromise where each gives a little to help further the other's career.

For the man who is ready to make this compromise, a whole new world of satisfactions becomes possible. When my children were born I was finishing my doctorate, writing most of it at home, and my wife was busy setting up a practice as a pediatrician. I spent more time with our daughters than she did. I fed them, bathed them, did many of the things that only a woman usually gets the chance to do. And I enjoyed every moment that I was a "mother" to my children.

I think most men are deprived—they lose an extraordinarily valuable part of human life not to feel what it is like to be a mother. Thus the compromise works both ways: Not only does the man give up some of his career opportunities for his wife, but he gains some of her satisfactions.

Our culture is too hung-up about what is male and what is female, too quick to assert that there is a man's function and a woman's function and never the twain shall meet. There are functions which men and women easily can share and which they *should* share. We need to recognize that each of us has within himself the capacity for some male and some female satisfactions. Women can revel in commercial maneuvering, and men can find joy in cooking, in furnishing a home, in feeding and cuddling a baby.

The major compensation for the man who is willing to make this kind of adjustment is the satisfaction of having at his side a great, vibrant, alive woman. This satisfaction spreads throughout the marriage, and one of its most potent effects is on the sexual relationship. Far from becoming "masculinized," the woman who has a sense of her identity as an independent person rather than as a mere appendage of her husband, is a more fulfilling sexual partner. At the same time she is a partner in every other aspect of marriage.

Unfortunately, the pressures against the man who is willing to upset the male-female applecart are great indeed. The male who sacrifices anything to the female is regarded as less than a man. He is looked down upon.

When I was in graduate school, my wife was already a practicing physician. She used her maiden name in practice, and for several years I was known as "Mr. Steinman." Her patients and colleagues never knew me in any role other than that of her husband. Some of my friends used to take this as a mark of indignity, and wondered how it was possible that I could suffer it. I not only "suffered it," but reveled in it. It delighted me that my wife had her own identity fixed and that I was, for a while, an appendage to her rather than she an appendage to me. But the pressure was constantly on me to reject such a role in favor of asserting my "manhood."

Too many men are unable to counter this pressure because they fear the loss of their masculinity. For this reason the woman's problem in our society today is essentially a man's problem. For a man to be able to make the appropriate compromises, he must be strong enough as a male figure not to feel threatened by his wife's independence and self-assertion.

At the heart of this problem is the traditional pattern of male dominance in the sexual act. The man who believes that the only satisfactory sexual relationship is one in which a woman is submissive to him is also the man who would be challenged if his wife had a career. He is also the man who determines the social mechanisms which make it virtually impossible for women to undertake careers. He is the man who would find himself threatened as a male if his wife assumed an independent, or on occasion, a dominant role either in their sexual relationship or in the so-called "world of work."

I sense that many women are awakening to the fact that their sexual role need not be a submissive one. And many men are becoming aware that their own sexual lives would be far more satisfactory if their wives were not submissive. They are realizing that the traditional dominance-submission pattern of sexual relations is only one narrow stratum of sexual satisfaction, one which borders, I believe, on the sadistic. Egalitarian sharing of sexual life seems to me to be a much more normal and fulfilling pattern for the male as well as for the female.

Where a man and woman share sexual life rather than attempting to dominate one another—especially one where the man can cope with the woman in a position of independence or even of occasional dominance—it is easier for the woman to go out into the world and succeed occupationally and professionally.

New contraceptive devices and altered attitudes toward premarital sexual intercourse have made remarkable changes in the pattern of male-female dominance in sexual relations—changes which ultimately will be reflected in the pattern of possible careers for women. One long-standing element in male dominance has been man's control over the most popular and convenient forms of contraception. The advent of The Pill has taken away some of woman's sense of powerlessness in the sexual act. Now she is able to avoid pregnancy without the man's knowing a thing about it, and to that degree she need no longer be submissive.

There also has been an important shift in the attitudes of both men and women toward premarital sex. It is not that more women are participating in sexual intercourse before marriage, but that they have begun to talk about it openly and to accept it as a respectable and moral phenomenon.

So, too, have men, and in this sense today's sexual revolution has taken place not in the woman but in the man. The young collegiate male no longer feels that the undergraduate girl with whom he has sexual intercourse is dirty, unmarriageable, immoral, sluttish. He now accepts her as normal, decent, and moral. The young woman no longer needs to feel the huge guilt about premarital sex that she formerly did; she can express this aspect of her life just as the man does. Again, a subtle but significant change has occurred in the traditional dominance-submission pattern between the sexes.

But it is not enough to rely on fortuitous changes. Major social remedies are needed to redefine male and female roles in a more realistic light. This means going back to the home, the nursery school, and the kindergarten, and telling parents and teachers to stop assigning completely exclusive definitions to male-female roles. We must begin to treat children at a very early age as a little bit male and a little bit female.

Mind you, I am not suggesting that we give up "maledom" or "femaledom." Nor am I saying that we all should have to be some kind of mixed, undefined sex. I am rather saying that a well-defined male still can appreciate significantly some aspects of the female role, and that a well-defined female can find satisfaction in some aspects of the traditional male role. What is needed is not to make one vague sex, but to realize that there is an in-between gray area where the male and female easily can exchange roles without abandoning their primary identification as either male or female.

One thing that our society can do right now to further this goal is to move into the centers of the male ego—men's colleges and universities—and teach men what the female is all about. The object would be to foster readjustments in the status and sexual relation of men and women in our society, readjustments which I believe are necessary before there can be any satisfactory resolution of the women's career issue.

Although the female in search of a career suffers many disadvantages, there are some important advantages which flow from her role as a woman in our society. Having achieved a career, a woman need not pursue it with the same compulsions for success as a man. Moreover, she can always "drop out" of her career and retreat into the traditional role if she so desires. These luxuries are not possible for the man, caught up as he is in the rat race of career pressures.

To cite once again from my own experience, I believe that my wife practiced more satisfying medicine because she did not have to achieve the things a man in our society is driven to achieve. Because she was not the sole "bread-winner" of the family, she did not feel obliged, as many male physicians do, to earn a munificent annual income. She could find fulfillment in her medical practice which might otherwise have been unavailable, because she did not have to look for a fee commensurate with her work in every case.

Thus, although the pressures to succeed and to achieve in our society are very strong, they impose a lesser burden on women than on men. This explains why some women's liberal arts colleges can continue to pursue the ideal of liberal education as education for a cultivated life, while men's colleges turn increasingly to education as preparation for graduate school and for specialized occupational and professional roles.

Women's special difficulty is that they are unable to pursue a career on the same terms that men do and yet they are made to feel guilty if they "stay at home" and fail to seek a career. They are allowed to enjoy neither the world of work nor their home. They should be able to choose and find fulfillment in either.

Emmy Lou®
GOLLY, MY REPORT CARD ISN'T TOO GREAT!
MINE, EITHER
'C' IN MATH IS VERY HIGH FOR THAT CLASS, REALLY
T'S A VERY HARD COURSE
YEH
MY FATHER WILL CERTAINLY GIVE ME A LECTURE ON MY REPORT CARD THIS TIME!
MY FATHER IS ALWAYS TALKING ABOUT ME AND COLLEGE
HE HAS A THING ABOUT COLLEGE
HE SAYS EVERYBODY IN THE FUTURE HAS TO HAVE AT LEAST ONE COLLEGE DEGREE
HE SAYS EVEN A BACHELOR'S DEGREE WON'T BE ENOUGH
HE SAYS COLLEGE IS AS NECESSARY AS HIGH SCHOOL ONCE WAS
ALL HE TALKS ABOUT IS ME AND COLLEGE
I REALLY DO AGREE WITH HIM
I THINK COLLEGE IS ABSOLUTELY NECESSARY, TOO!
UNLESS, OF COURSE, YOU CAN MEET THE RIGHT BOY IN HIGH SCHOOL!
5-3

NICHOLAS VON HOFFMAN

Marriage and Mankind

STUDY QUESTIONS FOR COMPREHENSION

1. What are the rewards of separation and divorce?
2. Why do many remain married even though they are not happy?
3. Is it the divorce or marriage laws that von Hoffman recommends changing?

A bunch of us were sitting around, drinking, gossiping about our friends when a youngish divorcee remarked about a couple that we all know: "Helen is miserable and Harry is morbidly unhappy, but their marriage is healthy. They're both dying, but their marriage is alive and thriving."

Everybody laughed, and then a man, also divorced, said, "I don't know a single happily married couple."

"Well," another divorced woman put in, continuing the theme, "when I look back on it, I can't believe I lived those 14 awful years with Jimmy. Not that he was awful. Jimmy was a good husband. Jimmy's my best friend now, but he wasn't a man, at least not my kind of man. I was afraid to give up that marriage. I didn't want to be divorced, and then I was afraid the kids would grow up to be fairies without a father."

"Hmmmf," the divorced man responded, "I see my children more and pay more attention to them now that I'm separated than I did when we were married. When we were married, I'd come home, mix a drink, crack open the newspaper and tell the kids, 'run along and don't bother me.' Divorce is what introduced me to my children. They come on weekends, and there's no woman around to cook and take care of them, so I have to do it. I've really gotten to know them. They're pretty nice people, my kids."

Neither the conversation nor the sentiments expressed are new or unusual. Faith in the traditional Western European marriage has been dying a long death. An increasingly large number of people just don't think they can make it in holy matrimony; the ideal of matching up with somebody in the early 20s and sticking together happily for 40 or 50 years seems unattainable.

For an unknown, but indubitably large number of people, marriage isn't a comfort, a source of companionship or a means of sexual satisfaction. But they adhere to their affliction out of concern for their children, anxiety as to what other, probably unhappily married, people may say, or perhaps out of an undifferentiated sense of fear about changing their social status.

The lucky ones continue to believe that marriage is a God-made sacrament; they, at least, can feel that the suffering of joyless domesticity has religious merit. The rest of the unhappily married mitigate the pain with alcohol or make unsatisfactory trysts in motel rooms or pay good money to shrinks and marriage counselors in hopes that these professionals can voodoo them into liking what they hate.

Such is the weight of tradition and the perversity of human beings that, as matrimony has become more onerous to more people, we haven't tried to change it, but instead have gone on tinkering with our divorce laws. Gradually, divorce has been made cheaper, less complicated and more available to more people, although it is still often out of reach of a poor man or woman.

Making divorce more obtainable is a relief for people caught in the agony of a hateful marriage, but legal farewells are difficult, unpleasant and sometimes traumatic. A better solution would be to change the institution of marriage to fit the needs and desire of husbands and wives.

Our difficulty is that we have millions of different kinds of people and only one kind of marriage, which can best be defined as monogamous perpetuity. People who, like the old Mormons, want to do it their own way are outlawed.

BLONDIE
by CHIC YOUNG

YOU BUNGLED THE FRICKLEY CONTRACT YOU FAT-HEAD!

YOU'VE CALLED ME A FAT-HEAD FOR THE LAST TIME -- I'M QUITTING AND THAT'S FINAL!

THAT FAT-HEAD ACTUALLY WALKED OUT ON ME! HE WON'T GET AWAY WITH THIS!

BLONDIE, I DID IT! I TOLD OFF THE OLD TYRANT AND QUIT MY JOB!

IT'LL MEAN STARTING AT THE BOTTOM AGAIN, BUT WITH YOU BY MY SIDE WE'LL MAKE IT, SOMEHOW

MAYBE YOU WERE TOO HASTY, DEAR -- MR. DITHERS IS REALLY A FINE MAN

REMEMBER HOW HE TOOK YOU WHEN YOU WERE NOTHING AND MADE YOU WHAT YOU ARE TODAY?
YEH

YOU'RE RIGHT, DEAR -- IF MR. DITHERS WERE HERE RIGHT NOW, I'D APOLOGIZE TO HIM

HE IS HERE -- HE'S HIDING IN THE CLOTHES CLOSET
AND I ACCEPT YOUR APOLOGY

THE TWO OF YOU PLOTTED AGAINST ME
IT WAS FOR YOUR OWN GOOD, DEAR

NOW GET BACK ON THE JOB AND STOP ACTING LIKE A FAT-HEAD!

THE NEXT TIME I QUIT MY JOB, I'M NOT GOING TO TELL ANYBODY
CHIC YOUNG 3-15

STUDY QUESTIONS FOR COMPREHENSION

The strip on the facing page is supposed to typify American suburbia. With this assumption in mind consider the following questions:

1. What is the role of the husband?
2. What is the role of the boss?
3. What is the role of the wife?

FRITZ PERLS

I Do My Thing

I do my thing, and you do your thing.
I am not in this world to live up to your expectations
And you are not in this world to live up to mine.
You are you and I am I,
And if by chance we find each other, it's beautiful.
If not, it can't be helped.

Writing Assignments for Part Four

1. In an essay, discuss why both men and women react with laughter or anger to any mention of "women's rights."
2. Discuss the positive aspects of the institution of marriage.
3. Write an essay in which you discuss whether a woman can find fulfillment in marriage only (or in a career only).
4. In an essay suggest substitutes for marriage that you think will result in happiness for the people involved and for any children who may be born because of the relationship.
5. Narrate any situation in which you felt you were discriminated against simply because you were a woman. Or, if you are a man, describe a situation you witnessed in which the person was discriminated against simply because she was a woman.
6. Discuss, in essay form, the view that women have as many rights, or even more, than men have.
7. Discuss the specific difficulties that the married couple faces when the woman attempts to combine a career and marriage.
8. Write an essay in which you discuss what the roles of men and women should be.
9. Using any form you wish (poetry, short story, personal narrative, description) try to foresee the future relations of men and women.
10. If you, as a woman, knew you would not be permitted to have children, what effect would that knowledge have on your attitudes and plans for the future?
11. Respond in any form you wish to the theme of this section.

PART FIVE / *Human Relations*

Modes and customs vary often, but human nature is always the same.
Lord Chesterfield, *Letters*, 7 February 1749

JAMES NISSEN

Sculpture on the Welfare Building of Santa Clara County, California

EDVARD MUNCH

The Cry

Courtesy of the National Gallery of Art, Washington, D.C.
Rosenwald Collection

ASHLEY MONTAGU

The Direction of Human Behavior

STUDY QUESTIONS FOR COMPREHENSION

1. How does Ashley Montagu define "love"?
2. What does Montagu mean by "man's sense of mutuality"?
3. To what is the author referring when he mentions "fusion"?

Cooperative behavior has great survival value. When social behavior is not cooperative it is diseased behavior. The dominant principle which informs all behavior which is biologically healthy is love. Love, social behavior, cooperation, and security mean very much the same thing. Without love the other three cannot exist. To love thy neighbor as thyself is not simply good text material for Sunday morning sermons, but perfectly sound biology.

Men who do not love one another are sick—sick not from any disease arising within themselves, but from a disease which has been enculturated within them by the false values of their societies. Belief in false values, in competition instead of cooperation, in narrow selfish interests instead of altruism, in atomism (especially atom- and hydrogen-bombism) instead of universalism, in the value of things and of money instead of the value of life and of man, represents man turning upon all that is innately good in him.

Man's sense of mutuality and cooperativeness may be suppressed, but so long as man continues to exist it cannot be destroyed, for these are traits which are part of his protoplasm. His combativeness and competitiveness arise from the frustration of his need to

From *The Direction of Human Development* by Ashley Montagu (New York: Hawthorn Books, 1970). Reprinted by permission of the author.

cooperate. These are important facts to bear in mind at a time when all the surface evidence seems to point in a contrary direction. The word of the moment may be "fission"—whether with respect to physics or human affairs—but "fusion" comes much closer to reflecting man's natural behavior patterns.

DAVE HEATH

Vengeful Sister

Courtesy of Dave Heath

FRANK O'CONNOR

My Oedipus Complex

STUDY QUESTIONS FOR COMPREHENSION

1. What is an Oedipus complex?
2. What different kinds of love are suggested?
3. What kinds of jealousy are suggested?
4. The story takes place in Ireland around the time of World War I. Why is it still a "modern" story?

Father was in the army all through the war—the first war, I mean—so, up to the age of five, I never saw much of him, and what I saw did not worry me. Sometimes I woke and there was a big figure in khaki peering down at me in the candlelight. Sometimes in the early morning I heard the slamming of the front door and the clatter of nailed boots down the cobbles of the lane. These were Father's entrances and exits. Like Santa Claus he came and went mysteriously.

In fact, I rather liked his visits, though it was an uncomfortable squeeze between Mother and him when I got into the big bed in the early morning. He smoked, which gave him a pleasant musty smell, and shaved, an operation of astounding interest. Each time he left a trail of souvenirs—model tanks and Gurkha knives with handles made of bullet cases, and German helmets and cap badges and button-sticks, and all sorts of military equipment—carefully stowed away in a long box on top of the wardrobe, in case they ever came in handy. There was a bit of the magpie about Father; he expected everything to come in handy. When his back was turned, Mother let me get a chair and rummage through his treasures. She didn't seem to think so highly of them as he did.

The war was the most peaceful period of my life. The window of my attic faced southeast. My mother had curtained it, but that had small effect. I always woke with the first light and, with all the responsibilities of the previous day melted, feeling myself rather like the sun, ready to illumine and rejoice. Life never seemed so simple and clear and full of possibilities as then. I put my feet out from under the clothes—I called them Mrs. Left and Mrs. Right—and invented dramatic situations for them in which they discussed the problems of the day. At least Mrs. Right did; she was very demonstrative, but I hadn't the same control of Mrs. Left, so she mostly contented herself with nodding agreement.

They discussed what Mother and I should do during the day, what Santa Claus should give a fellow for Christmas, and what steps should be taken to brighten the home. There was that little matter of the baby, for instance. Mother and I could never agree about that. Ours was the only house in the terrace without a new baby, and Mother said we couldn't afford one till Father came back from the war because they cost seventeen and six. That showed how simple she was. The Geneys up the road had a baby, and everyone knew they couldn't afford seventeen and six. It was probably a cheap baby, and Mother wanted something really good, but I felt she was too exclusive. The Geneys' baby would have done us fine.

Having settled my plans for the day, I got up, put a chair under the attic window, and lifted the frame high enough to stick out my head. The window overlooked the front gardens of the terrace behind ours, and beyond these it looked over a deep valley to the tall, red-brick houses terraced up the opposite hillside, which were all still in shadow, while those at our side of the valley were all lit up, though with long strange shadows that made them seem unfamiliar, rigid and painted.

After that I went into Mother's room and climbed into the big bed. She woke and I began to tell her of my schemes. By this time, though I never seem to have noticed it, I was petrified in my nightshirt, and I thawed as I talked until, the last frost melted, I fell asleep beside her and woke again only when I heard her below in the kitchen, making the breakfast.

After breakfast we went into town; heard Mass at St. Augustine's and said a prayer for Father, and did the shopping. If the afternoon was fine we either went for a walk in the country or a visit to Mother's great friend in the convent, Mother St. Dominic. Mother had them all praying for Father, and every night, going to bed, I asked God to send him back safe from the war to us. Little, indeed, did I know what I was praying for!

One morning, I got into the big bed, and there, sure enough, was Father in his usual Santa Claus manner, but later, instead of uniform, he put on his best blue suit, and Mother was as pleased as anything. I saw nothing to be pleased about, because, out of uniform, Father was altogether less interesting, but she only beamed, and explained that our prayers had been answered, and off we went to Mass to thank God for having brought Father safely home.

The irony of it! That very day when he came in to dinner he took off his boots and put on his slippers, donned the dirty old cap he wore about the house to save him from colds, crossed his legs, and began to talk gravely to Mother, who looked anxious. Naturally, I disliked her looking anxious, because it destroyed her good looks, so I interrupted him.

"Just a moment, Larry!" she said gently.

This was only what she said when we had boring visitors, so I attached no importance to it and went on talking.

"Do be quiet, Larry!" she said impatiently. "Don't you hear me talking to Daddy?"

This was the first time I had heard those ominous words, "talking to Daddy," and I couldn't help feeling that if this was how God answered prayers, he couldn't listen to them very attentively.

"Why are you talking to Daddy?" I asked with as great a show of indifference as I could muster.

"Because Daddy and I have business to discuss. Now, don't interrupt again!"

In the afternoon, at Mother's request, Father took me for a walk. This time we went into town instead of out in the country, and I thought at first, in my usual optimistic way, that it might be an improvement. It was nothing of the sort. Father and I had quite different notions of a walk in town. He had no proper interest in trams, ships, and horses, and the only thing that seemed to divert him was talking to fellows as old as himself. When I wanted to stop he simply went on, dragging me behind him by the hand; when he wanted to stop I had no alternative but to do the same. I noticed that it seemed to be a sign that he wanted to stop for a long time whenever he leaned against a wall. The second time I saw him do it I got wild. He seemed to be settling himself forever. I pulled him by the coat and trousers, but, unlike Mother who, if you were too persistent, got into a wax and said: "Larry, if you don't behave yourself, I'll give you a good slap," Father had an extraordinary capacity for amiable inattention. I sized him up and wondered would I cry, but he seemed to be too remote to be annoyed even by that. Really, it was like going for a walk with a mountain! He either ignored the wrenching and pummeling entirely, or else glanced down with a grin of amusement from his peak. I had never met anyone so absorbed in himself as he seemed.

At teatime, "talking to Daddy" began again, complicated this time by the fact that he had an evening paper, and every few minutes he put it down and told Mother something new out of it. I felt this was foul play. Man for man, I was prepared to compete with him any time for Mother's attention, but when he had it all made up for him by other people it left me no chance. Several times I tried to change the subject without success.

"You must be quiet while Daddy is reading, Larry," Mother said impatiently.

It was clear that she either genuinely liked talking to Father better than talking to me, or else that he had some terrible hold on her which made her afraid to admit the truth.

"Mummy," I said that night when she was tucking me up, "do you think if I prayed hard God would send Daddy back to the war?"

She seemed to think about that for a moment.

"No, dear," she said with a smile. "I don't think he would."

"Why wouldn't he, Mummy?"

"Because there isn't a war any longer, dear."

"But, Mummy, couldn't God make another war, if He liked?"

"He wouldn't like to, dear. It's not God who makes wars, but bad people."

"Oh!" I said.

I was disappointed about that. I began to think that God wasn't quite what he was cracked up to be.

Next morning I woke at my usual hour, feeling like a bottle of champagne. I put out my feet and invented a long conversation in which Mrs. Right talked of the trouble she had with her own father till she put him in the Home. I didn't quite know what the Home was but it sounded like the right place for Father. Then I got my chair and stuck my head out of the attic window. Dawn was just breaking, with a guilty air that made me feel I had caught it in the act. My head bursting with stories and schemes, I stumbled in next door, and in the half-darkness scrambled into the big bed. There was no room at Mother's side so I had to get between her and Father. For the time being I had forgotten about him, and for several minutes I sat bolt upright, racking my brains to know what I could do with him. He was taking up more than his fair share of the bed, and I couldn't get comfortable, so I gave him several kicks that made him grunt and stretch. He made room all right, though. Mother waked and felt for me. I settled back comfortably in the warmth of the bed with my thumb in my mouth.

"Mummy!" I hummed, loudly and contentedly.

"Sssh! dear," she whispered. "Don't wake Daddy!"

This was a new development, which threatened to be even more serious than "talking to Daddy." Life without my early-morning conferences was unthinkable.

"Why?" I asked severely.

"Because poor Daddy is tired."

This seemed to me a quite inadequate reason, and I was sickened by the sentimentality of her "poor Daddy." I never liked that sort of gush; it always struck me as insincere.

"Oh!" I said lightly. Then in my most winning tone: "Do you know where I want to go with you today, Mummy?"

"No, dear," she sighed.

"I want to go down the Glen and fish for thornybacks with my new net, and then I want to go out to the Fox and Hounds, and—"

"Don't-wake-Daddy!" she hissed angrily, clapping her hand across my mouth.

But it was too late. He was awake, or nearly so. He grunted and reached for the matches. Then he stared incredulously at his watch.

"Like a cup of tea, dear?" asked Mother in a meek, hushed voice I had never heard her use before. It sounded almost as though she were afraid.

"Tea?" he exclaimed indignantly. "Do you know what the time is?"

"And after that I want to go up the Rathcooney Road," I said loudly, afraid I'd forget something in all those interruptions.

"Go to sleep at once, Larry!" she said sharply.

I began to snivel. I couldn't concentrate, the way that pair went on, and smothering my early-morning schemes was like burying a family from the cradle.

Father said nothing, but lit his pipe and sucked it, looking out into the shadows without minding Mother or me. I knew he was mad. Every time I made a remark Mother hushed me irritably. I was mortified. I felt it wasn't fair; there was even something sinister in it. Every time I had pointed out to her the waste of making two beds when we could both sleep in one, she had told me it was healthier like that, and now here was this man, this stranger sleeping with her without the least regard for her health!

He got up early and made tea but though he brought Mother a cup he brought none for me.

"Mummy," I shouted, "I want a cup of tea, too."

"Yes, dear," she said patiently. "You can drink from Mummy's saucer."

That settled it. Either Father or I would have to leave the house. I didn't want to drink from Mother's saucer; I wanted to be treated as an equal in my own home, so, just to spite her, I drank it all and left none for her. She took that quietly, too.

But that night when she was putting me to bed she said gently:

"Larry, I want you to promise me something."

"What is it?" I asked.

"Not to come in and disturb poor Daddy in the morning. Promise?"

"Poor Daddy" again! I was becoming suspicious of everything involving that quite impossible man.

STUDY QUESTIONS FOR COMPREHENSION

1. Study the paintings on the next two pages. Which painting do you react to more strongly? Can you explain why?
2. Do you think you can determine from these two paintings the artists' attitudes toward mothers?
3. Remembering that there is no "right" answer, attempt to explore the symbolism in the two paintings.

MARC CHAGALL

Maternity

Courtesy of Stedelijk Museum

JOAN MIRÓ

Maternity

Courtesy of Thames and Hudson Ltd.

"Why?" I asked.

"Because poor Daddy is worried and tired and he doesn't sleep well."

"Why doesn't he, Mummy?"

"Well, you know, don't you, that while he was at the war Mummy got the pennies from the Post Office?"

"From Miss MacCarthy?"

"That's right. But now, you see, Miss MacCarthy hasn't any more pennies, so Daddy must go out and find us some. You know what would happen if he couldn't?"

"No," I said, "tell us."

"Well, I think we might have to go out and beg for them like the poor old woman on Fridays. We wouldn't like that, would we?"

"No," I agreed. "We wouldn't."

"So you'll promise not to come in and wake him?"

"Promise."

Mind you, I meant that. I knew pennies were a serious matter, and I was all against having to go out and beg like the old woman on Fridays. Mother laid out all my toys in a complete ring round the bed so that, whatever way I got out, I was bound to fall over one of them.

When I woke I remembered my promise all right. I got up and sat on the floor and played—for hours, it seemed to me. Then I got my chair and looked out the attic window for more hours. I wished it was time for Father to wake; I wished someone would make me a cup of tea. I didn't feel in the least like the sun; instead, I was bored and so very, very cold! I simply longed for the warmth and depth of the big featherbed.

At last I could stand it no longer. I went into the next room. As there was still no room at Mother's side I climbed over her and she woke with a start.

"Larry," she whispered, gripping my arm very tightly, "what did you promise?"

"But I did, Mummy," I wailed, caught in the very act. "I was quiet for ever so long."

"Oh, dear, and you're perished!" she said sadly, feeling me all over. "Now, if I let you stay will you promise not to talk?"

"But I want to talk, Mummy," I wailed.

"That has nothing to do with it," she said with a firmness that was new to me. "Daddy wants to sleep. Now, do you understand that?"

I understood it only too well. I wanted to talk, he wanted to sleep—whose house was it, anyway?

"Mummy," I said with equal firmness, "I think it would be healthier for Daddy to sleep in his own bed."

That seemed to stagger her, because she said nothing for a while.

"Now, once for all," she went on, "you're to be perfectly quiet or go back to your own bed. Which is it to be?"

The injustice of it got me down. I had convicted her out of her own mouth of inconsistency and unreasonableness, and she hadn't even attempted to reply. Full of spite, I gave Father a kick, which she didn't notice but which made him grunt and open his eyes in alarm.

"What time is it?" he asked in a panic-stricken voice, not looking at Mother but at the door, as if he saw someone there.

"It's early yet," she replied soothingly. "It's only the child. Go to sleep again. . . . Now, Larry," she added, getting out of bed, "you've wakened Daddy and you must go back."

This time, for all her quiet air, I knew she meant it, and knew that my principal rights and privileges were as good as lost unless I asserted them at once. As she lifted me, I gave a screech, enough to wake the dead, not to mind Father. He groaned.

"That damn child! Doesn't he ever sleep?"

"It's only a habit, dear," she said quietly, though I could see she was vexed.

"Well, it's time he got out of it," shouted Father, beginning to heave in the bed. He suddenly gathered all the bedclothes about him, turned to the wall, and then looked back over his shoulder with nothing showing only two small, spiteful, dark eyes. The man looked very wicked.

To open the bedroom door, Mother had to let me down, and I broke free and dashed for the farthest corner, screeching. Father sat bolt upright in bed.

"Shut up, you little puppy!" he said in a choking voice.

I was so astonished that I stopped screeching. Never, never had anyone spoken to me in that tone before. I looked at him incredulously and saw his face convulsed with rage. It was only then that I fully realized how God had coddled me, listening to my prayers for the safe return of this monster.

"Shut up, you!" I bawled, beside myself.

"What's that you said?" shouted Father, making a wild leap out of the bed.

"Mick, Mick!" cried Mother. "Don't you see the child isn't used to you?'

"I see he's better fed than taught," snarled Father, waving his arms wildly. "He wants his bottom smacked."

All his previous shouting was as nothing to these obscene words referring to my person. They really made my blood boil.

"Smack your own!" I screamed hysterically. "Smack your own! Shut up! Shut up!"

At this he lost his patience and let fly at me. He did it with the lack of conviction you'd expect of a man under Mother's horrified eyes, and it ended up as a mere tap, but the sheer indignity of being struck at all by a stranger, a total stranger who had cajoled his way back from the war into our big bed as a result of my innocent intercession, made me completely dotty. I shrieked and shrieked, and danced in my bare feet, and Father, looking awkward and hairy in nothing but a short grey army shirt, glared down at me like a mountain out for murder. I think it must have been then that I realized he was jealous too. And there stood Mother in her nightdress, looking as if her heart was broken between us. I hoped she felt as she looked. It seemed to me that she deserved it all.

From that morning out my life was a hell. Father and I were enemies, open and avowed. We conducted a series of skirmishes against one another, he trying to steal my time with Mother and I his. When she was sitting on my bed, telling me a story, he took to looking for some pair of old boots which he alleged he had left behind him at the beginning of the war. While he talked to Mother I played loudly with my toys to show my total lack of concern. He created a terrible scene one evening when he came in from work and found me at his box, playing with his regimental badges, Gurkha knives and button-sticks. Mother got up and took the box from me.

"You mustn't play with Daddy's toys unless he lets you, Larry," she said severely. "Daddy doesn't play with yours."

For some reason Father looked at her as if she had struck him and then turned away with a scowl.

"Those are not toys," he growled, taking down the box again to see had I lifted anything. "Some of those curios are very rare and valuable."

But as time went on I saw more and more how he managed to alienate Mother and me. What made it worse was that I couldn't grasp his method or see what attraction he had for Mother. In every possible way he was less winning than I. He had a common accent and made noises at his tea. I thought for a while that it might be the newspapers she was interested in, so I made up bits of news of my own to read to her. Then I thought it might be the smoking, which I personally thought attractive, and took his pipes and went round the house dribbling into them till he caught me. I even made noises at my tea, but Mother only told me I was disgusting. It all seemed to hinge round that unhealthy habit of sleeping together, so I made a point of dropping into their bedroom and nosing round, talking to myself, so that they wouldn't know I was watching them, but they were never up to anything that I could see. In the end it beat me. It seemed to depend on being grown-up and giving people rings, and I realized I'd have to wait.

But at the same time I wanted him to see that I was only waiting, not giving up the fight. One evening when he was being particularly obnoxious, chattering away well above my head, I let him have it.

"Mummy," I said, "do you know what I'm going to do when I grow up?"

"No, dear," she replied. "What?"

"I'm going to marry you," I said quietly.

Father gave a great guffaw out of him, but he didn't take me in. I knew it must only be pretence. And Mother, in spite of everything, was pleased. I felt she was probably relieved to know that one day Father's hold on her would be broken.

"Won't that be nice?" she said with a smile.

"It'll be very nice," I said confidently. "Because we're going to have lots and lots of babies."

"That's right, dear," she said placidly. "I think we'll have one soon, and then you'll have plenty of company."

I was no end pleased about that because it showed that in spite of the way she gave in to Father she still considered my wishes. Besides, it would put the Geneys in their place.

It didn't turn out like that, though. To begin with, she was very preoccupied—I suppose about where she would get the seventeen and six—and though Father took to staying out late in the evenings it did me no particular good. She stopped taking me for walks, became as touchy as blazes, and smacked me for nothing at all. Sometimes I wished I'd never mentioned the confounded baby—I seemed to have a genius for bringing calamity on myself.

And calamity it was! Sonny arrived in the most appalling hullabaloo—even that much he couldn't do without a fuss—and from the first moment I disliked him. He was a difficult child—so far as I was concerned he was always difficult—and demanded far too much attention. Mother was simply silly about him, and couldn't see when he was only showing off. As company he was worse than useless. He slept all day, and I had to go round the house on tiptoe to avoid waking him. It wasn't any longer a question of not waking Father. The slogan now was "Don't-wake-Sonny!" I couldn't understand why the child wouldn't sleep at the proper time, so whenever Mother's back was turned I woke him. Sometimes to keep him awake I pinched him as well. Mother caught me at it one day and gave me a most unmerciful flaking.

One evening, when Father was coming in from work, I was playing trains in the front garden. I let on not to notice him; instead, I pretended to be talking to myself, and said in a loud voice: "If another bloody baby comes into this house, I'm going out."

Father stopped dead and looked at me over his shoulder.

"What's that you said" he asked sternly.

"I was only talking to myself," I replied, trying to conceal my panic. "It's private."

He turned and went in without a word. Mind you, I intended it as a solemn warning, but its effect was quite different. Father started being quite nice to me. I could understand that, of course. Mother was quite sickening about Sonny. Even at mealtimes she'd get up and gawk at him in the cradle with an idiotic smile, and tell Father to do the same. He was always polite about it, but he looked so puzzled you could see he didn't know what she was talking about. He complained of the way Sonny cried at night but she only got cross and said that Sonny never cried except when there was something up with him—which was a flaming lie, because Sonny never had anything up with him, and only cried for attention. It was really painful to see how simple-minded she was. Father wasn't attractive, but he had a fine intelligence. He saw through Sonny, and now he knew that I saw through him as well.

One night I woke with a start. There was someone beside me in the bed. For one wild moment I felt sure it must be Mother, having come to her senses and left Father for good, but then I heard Sonny in convulsions in the next room, and Mother saying: "There! There! There!" and I knew it wasn't she. It was Father. He was lying beside me, wide awake, breathing hard and apparently as mad as hell.

After a while it came to me what he was mad about. It was his turn now. After turning me out of the big bed, he had been turned out himself. Mother had no consideration now for anyone but that poisonous pup, Sonny. I couldn't help feeling sorry for Father. I had been through it all myself, and even at that age I was magnanimous. I began to stroke him down and say: "There! There!" He wasn't exactly responsive.

"Aren't you asleep either?" he snarled.

"Ah, come on and put your arm around us, can't you?" I said, and he did, in a sort of way. Gingerly, I suppose, is how you'd describe it. He was very bony but better than nothing.

At Christmas he went out of his way to buy me a really nice model railway.

JAMES THURBER

Unicorn in the Garden

STUDY QUESTIONS FOR COMPREHENSION

1. What is a unicorn?
2. Why does the husband trick his wife in this fashion?
3. What are the implications of the line, "The husband lived happily ever after"?

Once upon a sunny morning a man who sat in a breakfast nook looked up from his scrambled eggs to see a white unicorn with a gold horn quietly cropping the roses in the garden. The man went up to the bedroom where his wife was still asleep and woke her. "There's a unicorn in the garden," he said. "Eating roses." She opened one unfriendly eye and looked at him. "The unicorn is a mythical beast," she said, and turned her back on him. The man walked slowly downstairs and out into the garden. The unicorn was still there; he was now browsing among the tulips. "Here, unicorn," said the man, and he pulled up a lily and gave it to him. The unicorn ate it gravely. With a high heart, because there was a unicorn in his garden, the man went upstairs and roused his wife again. "The unicorn," he said, "ate a lily." His wife sat up in bed and looked at him, coldly. "You are a booby," she said, "and I am going to have you put in the booby-hatch." The man, who had never liked the words "booby" and "booby-hatch," and who liked them even less on a shining morning when there was a unicorn in the garden, thought for a moment. "We'll see about that," he said. He walked over to the door. "He has a golden horn in the middle of his forehead," he told her. Then he went back to the garden to watch the unicorn; but the unicorn had gone away. The man sat down among the roses and went to sleep.

As soon as the husband had gone out of the house, the wife got

up and dressed as fast as she could. She was very excited and there was a gloat in her eye. She telephoned the police and she telephoned a psychiatrist; she told them to hurry to her house and bring a strait-jacket. When the police and the psychiatrist arrived they sat down in chairs and looked at her, with great interest. "My husband," she said, "saw a unicorn this morning." The police looked at the psychiatrist and the psychiatrist looked at the police. "He told me it ate a lily," she said. The psychiatrist looked at the police and the police looked at the psychiatrist. "He told me it had a golden horn in the middle of its forehead," she said. At a solemn signal from the psychiatrist, the police leaped from their chairs and seized the wife. They had a hard time subduing her, for she put up a terrific struggle, but they finally subdued her. Just as they got her into the strait-jacket, the husband came back into the house.

"Did you tell your wife you saw a unicorn?" asked the police. "Of course not," said the husband. "The unicorn is a mythical beast." "That's all I wanted to know," said the psychiatrist. "Take her away. I'm sorry, sir, but your wife is as crazy as a jay bird." So they took her away, cursing and screaming, and shut her up in an institution. The husband lived happily ever after.

Moral: Don't count your boobies until they are hatched.

JAMES THURBER

Home

RAY BRADBURY

The Veldt

STUDY QUESTIONS FOR COMPREHENSION

1. What is the sequence of events in this story?
2. Does Bradbury account for the children's hostility toward their parents? Explain by specific reference to the story.
3. How and why does the "house" affect the life of the family?

"George, I wish you'd look at the nursery."

"What's wrong with it?"

"I don't know."

"Well, then."

"I just want you to look at it, is all, or call a psychologist in to look at it."

"What would a psychologist want with a nursery?"

"You know very well what he'd want." His wife paused in the middle of the kitchen and watched the stove busy humming to itself, making supper for four.

"It's just that the nursery is different now than it was."

"All right, let's have a look."

They walked down the hall of their soundproofed, Happy-life Home, which had cost them thirty thousand dollars installed, this house which clothed and fed and rocked them to sleep and played and sang and was good to them. Their approach sensitized a switch somewhere and the nursery light flicked on when they came within ten feet of it. Similarly, behind them, in the halls, lights went on and off as they left them behind, with a soft automaticity.

"Well," said George Hadley.

They stood on the thatched floor of the nursery. It was forty feet across by forty feet long and thirty feet high; it had cost half again as much as the rest of the house. "But nothing's too good for our children," George had said.

The nursery was silent. It was empty as a jungle glade at hot high noon. The walls were blank and two dimensional. Now, as George and Lydia Hadley stood in the center of the room, the walls began to purr and recede into crystalline distance, it seemed, and presently an African veldt appeared, in three dimensions; on all sides, in colors reproduced to the final pebble and a bit of straw. The ceiling above them became a deep sky with a hot yellow sun.

George Hadley felt the perspiration start on his brow.

"Let's get out of the sun," he said. "This is a little too real. But I don't see anything wrong."

"Wait a moment, you'll see," said this wife.

Now the hidden odorophonics were beginning to blow a wind of odor at the two people in the middle of the baked veldtland. The hot straw smell of lion grass, the cool green smell of the hidden water hole, the great rusty smell of animals, the smell of dust like a red paprika in the hot air. And now the sounds: the thump of distant antelope feet on grassy sod, the papery rustling of vultures. A shadow passed through the sky. The shadow flickered on George Hadley's upturned, sweating face.

"Filthy creatures," he heard his wife say.

"The vultures."

"You see, there are the lions, far over, that way. Now they're on their way to the water hole. They've just been eating," said Lydia. "I don't know what."

"Some animal." George Hadley put his hand up to shield off the burning light from his squinted eyes. "A zebra or a baby giraffe, maybe."

"Are you sure?" his wife sounded peculiarly tense.

"No, it's a little late to be sure," he said, amused. "Nothing over there that I can see but cleaned bone, and the vultures dropping for what's left."

"Did you hear that scream?" she asked.

"No."

"About a minute ago?"

"Sorry, no."

The lions were coming. And again George Hadley was filled with admiration for the mechanical genius who had conceived this room. A miracle of efficiency selling for an absurdly low price. Every home should have one. Oh, occasionally they frightened you, with their clinical accuracy, they startled you, gave you a twinge, but most of the time what fun for everyone, not only your own son and daughter, but for yourself when you felt like a quick jaunt to a foreign land, a quick change of scenery. Well, here it was.

And here were the lions now, fifteen feet away, so real, so feverishly and startlingly real that you could feel the prickling fur on your hand, and your mouth was stuffed with the dusty upholstery smell of their heated pelts, and the yellow of them was in your eyes like the yellow of an exquisite French tapestry, the yellows of lions and summer grass, and the sound of the matted lion lungs exhaling on the silent noontide, and the smell of meat from the panting, dripping mouths.

The lions stood looking at George and Lydia Hadley with terrible green-yellow eyes.

"Watch out!" screamed Lydia.

The lions came running at them.

Lydia bolted and ran. Instinctively, George sprang after her. Outside, in the hall, with the door slammed, he was laughing and she was crying, and they both stood appalled at the other's reaction.

"George!"

"Lydia! Oh, my dear poor sweet Lydia!"

"They almost got us!"

"Walls, Lydia, remember; crystal walls that's all they are. Oh, they look real, I must admit—Africa in your parlor—but it's all dimensional superreactionary, supersensitive color film and mental tape film behind glass screens. It's all odorophonics and sonics, Lydia. Here's my handkerchief."

"I'm afraid." She came to him and put her body against him and cried steadily. "Did you see? Did you feel? It's too real."

"Now, Lydia . . ."

"You've got to tell Wendy and Peter not to read any more on Africa."

"Of course—of course." He patted her.

"Promise."

"Sure."

"And lock the nursery for a few days until I get my nerves settled."

"You know how difficult Peter is about that. When I punished him a month ago by locking the nursery for even a few hours—the tantrum he threw! And Wendy too. They live for that nursery."

"It's got to be locked, that's all there is to it."

"All right." Reluctantly he locked the huge door. "You've been working too hard. You need a rest."

"I don't know—I don't know," she said, blowing her nose, sitting down in a chair that immediately began to rock and comfort her. "Maybe I don't have enough to do. Maybe I have time to think too much. Why don't we shut the whole house off for a few days and take a vacation?"

"You mean you want to fry my eggs for me?"

"Yes." She nodded.

"And darn my socks?"

"Yes." A frantic, watery-eyed nodding.

"And sweep the house?"

"Yes, yes—oh, yes!"

"But I thought that's why we bought this house, so we wouldn't have to do anything?"

"That's just it. I feel like I don't belong here. The house is wife and mother and nursemaid. Can I compete with an African veldt? Can I give a bath and scrub the children as efficiently or quickly as the automatic scrub bath can? I can not. And it isn't just me. It's you. You've been awfully nervous lately."

"I suppose I have been smoking too much."

"You look as if you didn't know what to do with yourself in this house, either. You smoke a little more every morning and drink a little more every afternoon and need a little more sedative every night. You're beginning to feel unnecessary too."

"Am I?" He paused and tried to feel into himself to see what was really there.

"Oh, George!" She looked beyond him, at the nursery door. "Those lions can't get out of there, can they?"

He looked at the door and saw it tremble as if something had jumped against it from the other side.

"Of course not," he said.

At dinner they ate alone, for Wendy and Peter were at a special plastic carnival across town and had televised home to say they'd be late, to go ahead eating. So George Hadley, bemused, sat watching the dining-room table produce warm dishes of food from its mechanical interior.

"We forgot the ketchup," he said.

"Sorry," said a small voice within the table, and ketchup appeared.

As for the nursery, thought George Hadley, it won't hurt for the children to be locked out of it for awhile. Too much of anything isn't good for anyone. And it was clearly indicated that the children had been spending a little too much time on Africa. That sun. He could feel it on his neck, still, like a hot paw. And the lions. And the smell of blood. Remarkable how the nursery caught the telepathic emanations of the children's minds and created life to fill their every desire. The children thought zebras, and there were zebras. Sun—sun. Giraffes—giraffes. Death and death.

That last. He chewed tastelessly on the meat that the table had cut for him. Death thoughts. They were awfully young, Wendy and Peter, for death thoughts. Or, no, you were never too young, really. Long before you knew what death was you were wishing it on someone else. When you were two years old you were shooting people with cap pistols.

But this—the long, hot African veldt—the awful death in the jaws of a lion. And repeated again and again.

"Where are you going?"

He didn't answer Lydia. Preoccupied, he let the lights glow softly on ahead of him, extinguish behind him as he padded to the nursery door. He listened against it. Far away, a lion roared.

He unlocked the door and opened it. Just before he stepped inside, he heard a faraway scream. And then another roar from the lions, which subsided quickly.

He stepped into Africa. How many times in the last year had he opened this door and found Wonderland, Alice, the Mock Turtle, or Aladdin and his Magical Lamp, or Jack Pumpkinhead of Oz, or Dr. Doolittle, or the cow jumping over a very real-appearing moon—all the delightful contraptions of a make-believe world. How often had he seen Pegasus flying in the sky ceiling or seen fountains of red fireworks, or heard angel voices singing. But now, this yellow hot Africa, this bake oven with murder in the heat. Perhaps Lydia was right. Perhaps they needed a little vacation from the fantasy which was growing a bit too real for ten-year-old children. It was all right to exercise one's mind with gymnastic fantasies, but when the lively child mind settled on one pattern . . . ? It seemed that, at a distance, for the past month, he had heard lions roaring, and smelled their strong odor seeping as far away as his study door. But, being busy, he had paid it no attention.

George Hadley stood on the African grassland alone. The lions looked up from their feeding, watching him. The only flaw to the illusion was the open door through which he could see his wife, far down the dark hall, like a framed picture, eating her dinner abstractedly.

"Go away," he said to the lions.

They did not go.

He knew the principle of the room exactly. You sent out your thoughts. Whatever you thought would appear.

"Let's have Aladdin and his lamp," he snapped.

The veldtland remained; the lions remained.

"Come on, room! I demand Aladdin!" he said.

Nothing happened. The lions mumbled in their baked pelts.

"Aladdin!"

He went back to dinner. "The fool room's out of order," he said. "It won't respond."

"Or —"

"Or what?"

"Or it can't respond," said Lydia, "because the children have thought about Africa and lions and killing so many days that the room's in a rut."

"Could be."

"Or Peter's set it to remain that way."

"Set it?"

"He may have got into the machinery and fixed something."

"Peter doesn't know machinery."

"He's a wise one for ten. That I.Q. of his —"

"Nevertheless —"

"Hello, Mom. Hello, Dad."

The Hadleys turned. Wendy and Peter were coming in the front door, cheeks like peppermint candy, eyes like bright blue agate marbles, a smell of ozone on their jumpers from their trip in the helicopter.

"You're just in time for supper," said both parents.

"We're full of strawberry ice cream and hot dogs," said the children, holding hands. "But we'll sit and watch."

"Yes, come tell us about the nursery," said George Hadley.

The brother and sister blinked at him and then at each other. "Nursery?"

"All about Africa and everything," said the father with false joviality.

"I don't understand," said Peter.

"Your mother and I were just traveling through Africa with rod and reel; Tom Swift and his Electric Lion," said George Hadley.

"There's no Africa in the nursery," said Peter simply.

"Oh, come now, Peter. We know better."

"I don't remember any Africa," said Peter to Wendy. "Do you?"

"No."

"Run see and come tell."

She obeyed.

"Wendy, come back here!" said George Hadley, but she was gone. The house lights followed her like a flock of fireflies. Too late, he realized he had forgotten to lock the nursery door after his last inspection.

"Wendy'll look and come tell us," said Peter.

"She doesn't have to tell me, I've seen it."

"I'm sure you're mistaken, Father."

"I'm not, Peter. Come along now."

But Wendy was back. "It's not Africa," she said breathlessly.

"We'll see about this," said George Hadley, and they all walked down the hall together and opened the nursery door.

There was a green, lovely forest, a lovely river, a purple mountain, high voices singing, and Rima, lovely and mysterious, lurking in the trees with colorful flights of butterflies, like animated bouquets, lingering in her long hair. The African veldtland was gone. The lions were gone. Only Rima was here now, singing a song so beautiful that it brought tears to your eyes.

George Hadley looked in at the changed scene. "Go to bed," he said to the children.

They opened their mouths.

"You heard me," he said.

They went off to the air closet, where a wind sucked them like brown leaves up the flue to their slumber rooms.

George Hadley walked through the singing glade and picked up something that lay in the corner near where the lions had been. He walked slowly back to his wife.

"What is that?" she asked.

"An old wallet of mine," he said.

He showed it to her. The smell of hot grass was on it and the smell of a lion. There were drops of saliva on it, it had been chewed, and there were blood smears on both sides.

He closed the nursery door and locked it, tight.

In the middle of the night he was still awake and he knew his wife was awake. "Do you think Wendy changed it?" she said at last, in the dark room.

"Of course."

"Made it from a veldt into a forest and put Rima there instead of lions?"

"Yes."

"Why?"

"I don't know. But it's staying locked until I find out."

"How did your wallet get there?"

"I don't know anything," he said, "except that I'm beginning to be sorry we bought that room for the children. If children are neurotic at all, a room like that —"

"It's supposed to help them work off their neuroses in a healthful way."

"I'm starting to wonder." He stared at the ceiling.

"We've given the children everything they ever wanted. Is this our reward—secrecy, disobedience?"

"Who was it said, 'Children are carpets, they should be stepped on occasionally'? We've never lifted a hand. They're insufferable—let's admit it. They come and go when they like; they treat us as if we were offspring. They're spoiled and we're spoiled."

"They've been acting funny ever since you forbade them to take the rocket to New York a few months ago."

"They're not old enough to do that alone, I explained."

"Nevertheless, I've noticed they've been decidedly cool toward us since."

"I think I'll have David McClean come tomorrow morning to have a look at Africa."

"But it's not Africa now, it's Green Mansions country and Rima."

"I have a feeling it'll be Africa before then."

A moment later they heard the screams.

Two screams. Two people screaming from downstairs. And then a roar of lions.

"Wendy and Peter aren't in their rooms," said his wife.

He lay in his bed with his beating heart. "No," he said. "They've broken into the nursery."

"Those screams—they sound familiar."

"Do they?"

"Yes, awfully."

And although their beds tried very hard, the two adults couldn't be rocked to sleep for another hour. A smell of cats was in the night air.

"Father?" said Peter.

"Yes."

Peter looked at his shoes. He never looked at his father any more, nor at his mother. "You aren't going to lock up the nursery for good, are you?"

"That all depends."

"On what?" snapped Peter.

"On you and your sister. If you intersperse this Africa with a little variety—oh, Sweden perhaps, or Denmark or China—"

"I thought we were free to play as we wished."

"You are, within reasonable bounds."

"What's wrong with Africa, Father?"

"Oh, so now you admit you have been conjuring up Africa, do you?"

"I wouldn't want the nursery locked up," said Peter coldly. "Ever."

"Matter of fact, we're thinking of turning the whole house off for about a month. Live sort of a carefree one-for-all existence."

"That sounds dreadful! Would I have to tie my own shoes instead of letting the shoe tier do it? And brush my own teeth and comb my own hair and give myself a bath?"

"It would be fun for a change, don't you think?"

"No, it would be horrid. I didn't like it when you took out the picture painter last month."

"That's because I wanted you to learn to paint all by yourself, son."

"I don't want to do anything but look and listen and smell; what else is there to do?"

"All right, go play in Africa."

"Will you shut off the house sometime soon?"

"We're considering it."

"I don't think you'd better consider it any more, Father."

"I won't have any threats from my son!"

"Very well." And Peter strolled off to the nursery.

"Am I on time?" said David McClean.

"Breakfast?" asked George Hadley.

"Thanks, had some. What's the trouble?"

"David, you're a psychologist."

"I should hope so."

"Well, then, have a look at our nursery. You saw it a year ago when you dropped by; did you notice anything peculiar about it then?"

"Can't say I did; the usual violences, a tendency toward a slight paranoia here or there, usual in children because they feel persecuted by parents constantly, but, oh, really nothing."

They walked down the hall. "I locked the nursery up," explained the father, "and the children broke back into it during the night. I let them stay so they could form the patterns for you to see."

There was a terrible screaming from the nursery.

"There it is," said George Hadley. "See what you make of it."

They walked in on the children without rapping.

The screams had faded. The lions were feeding.

"Run outside a moment, children," said George Hadley. "No, don't change the mental combination. Leave the walls as they are. Get."

With the children gone, the two men stood studying the lions clustered at a distance, eating with great relish whatever it was they had caught.

"I wish I knew what it was," said George Hadley. "Sometimes I can almost see. Do you think if I brought high-powered binoculars here and —"

David McClean laughed dryly. "Hardly." He turned to study all four walls. "How long has this been going on?"

"A little over a month."

"It certainly doesn't feel good."

"I want facts, not feelings."

"My dear George, a psychologist never saw a fact in his life. He only hears about feelings; vague things. This doesn't feel good, I tell you. Trust my hunches and my instincts. I have a nose for something bad. This is very bad. My advice to you is to have the whole damn room torn down and your children brought to me every day during the next year for treatment."

"Is it that bad?"

"I'm afraid so. One of the original uses of these nurseries was so that we could study the patterns left on the walls by the child's mind, study at our leisure, and help the child. In this case, however, the room has become a channel toward—destructive thoughts, instead of a release away from them."

"Didn't you sense this before?"

"I sensed only that you had spoiled your children more than most. And now you're letting them down in some way. What way?"

"I wouldn't let them go to New York."

"What else?"

"I've taken a few machines from the house and threatened them, a month ago, with closing up the nursery unless they did their homework. I did close it for a few days to show I meant business."

"Ah, ha!"

"Does that mean anything?"

"Everything. Where before they had a Santa Claus now they have a Scrooge. Children prefer Santas. You've let this room and this house replace you and your wife in your children's affections. This room is their mother and father, far more important in their lives than their real parents. And now you come along and want to shut it off. No wonder there's hatred here. You can feel it coming out of the sky. Feel that sun. George, you'll have to change your life. Like too many others, you've built it around creature comforts. Why, you'd starve tomorrow if something went wrong in your kitchen. You wouldn't know how to tap an egg. Nevertheless, turn everything off. Start new. It'll take time. But we'll make good children out of bad in a year, wait and see."

"But won't the shock be too much for the children, shutting the room up abruptly, for good?"

"I don't want them going any deeper into this, that's all."

The lions were finished with their red feast.

The lions were standing on the edge of the clearing watching the two men.

"Now I'm feeling persecuted," said McClean. "Let's get out of here. I never have cared for these damned rooms. Make me nervous."

"The lions look real, don't they?" said George Hadley. "I don't suppose there's any way —"

"What?"

"— that they could become real?"

"Not that I know."

"Some flaw in the machinery, a tampering or something?"

"No."

They went to the door.

"I don't imagine the room will like being turned off," said the father.

"Nothing ever likes to die—even a room."

"I wonder if it hates me for wanting to switch it off?"

"Paranoia is thick around here today," said David McClean. "You can follow it like a spoor. Hello." He bent and picked up a bloody scarf. "This yours?"

"No." George Hadley's face was rigid. "It belongs to Lydia."

They went to the fuse box together and threw the switch that killed the nursery.

The two children were in hysterics. They screamed and pranced and threw things. They yelled and sobbed and swore and jumped at the furniture.

"You can't do that to the nursery, you can't!"

"Now, children."

The children flung themselves onto a couch, weeping.

"George," said Lydia Hadley, "turn on the nursery, just for a few moments. You can't be so abrupt."

"No."

"You can't be so cruel."

"Lydia, it's off, and it stays off. And the whole damn house dies as of here and now. The more I see of the mess we've put ourselves in, the more it sickens me. We've been contemplating our mechanical, electronic navels for too long. My God, how we need a breath of honest air."

And he marched about the house turning off the voice clocks, the stoves, the heaters, the shoe shiners, the shoe lacers, the body scrubbers and swabbers and massagers, and every other machine he could put his hand to.

The house was full of dead bodies, it seemed. It felt like a mechanical cemetery. So silent. None of the humming hidden energy of machines waiting to function at the tap of a button.

"Don't let them do it!" wailed Peter at the ceiling, as if he was talking to the house, his nursery. "Don't let Father kill everything." He turned to his father. "Oh, I hate you!"

"Insults won't get you anywhere."

"I wish you were dead!"

"We were, for a long while. Now we're going to really start living. Instead of being handled and massaged, we're going to live."

Wendy was still crying and Peter joined her again. "Just a moment, just one moment, just another moment of nursery," they wailed.

"Oh, George," said the wife, "it can't hurt."

"All right—all right, if they'll only just shut up. One minute, mind you, and then off forever."

"Daddy, Daddy, Daddy!" sang the children, smiling with wet faces.

"And then we're going on a vacation. David McClean is coming back in half an hour to help us move out and get to the airport. I'm going to dress. You turn the nursery on for a minute, Lydia, just a minute, mind you."

And the three of them went babbling off while he let himself be vacuumed upstairs through the air flue and set about dressing himself. A minute later Lydia appeared.

"I'll be glad when we get away," she sighed.

"Did you leave them in the nursery?"

"I wanted to dress too. Oh, that horrid Africa. What can they see in it?"

"Well, in five minutes we'll be on our way to Iowa. Lord, how did we ever get in this house? What prompted us to buy a nightmare?"

"Pride, money, foolishness."

"I think we'd better get downstairs before those kids get engrossed with those damned beasts again."

Just then they heard the children calling, "Daddy, Mommy, come quick—quick!"

They went downstairs in the air flue and ran down the hall. The children were nowhere in sight. "Wendy? Peter!"

They ran into the nursery. The veldtland was empty save for the lions waiting, looking at them. "Peter, Wendy?"

The door slammed.

"Wendy, Peter!"

George Hadley and his wife whirled and ran back to the door.

"Open the door!" cried George Hadley, trying the knob. "Why, they've locked it from the outside! Peter!" He beat at the door. "Open up!"

He heard Peter's voice outside, against the door.

"Don't let them switch off the nursery and the house," he was saying.

Mr. and Mrs. George Hadley beat at the door. "Now, don't be ridiculous, children. It's time to go. Mr. McClean'll be here in a minute and . . ."

And then they heard the sounds.

The lions, on three sides of them, in the yellow veldt grass, padding through the dry straw, rumbling and roaring in their throats.

The lions.

Mr. Hadley looked at his wife and they turned and looked back at the beasts edging slowly forward, crouching, tails stiff.

Mr. and Mrs. Hadley screamed.

And suddenly they realized why those other screams had sounded familiar.

"Well, here I am," said David McClean in the nursery doorway. "Oh, hello." He stared at the children seated in the center of the open glade eating a little picnic lunch. Beyond them was the water hole and the yellow veldtland; above was the hot sun. He began to perspire. "Where are your father and mother?"

The children looked up and smiled. "Oh, they'll be here directly."

"Good, we must get going." At a distance Mr. McClean saw the lions fighting and clawing and then quieting down to feed in silence under the shady trees.

He squinted at the lions with his hand up to his eyes.

Now the lions were done feeding. They moved to the water hole to drink.

A shadow flickered over Mr. McClean's hot face. Many shadows flickered. The vultures were dropping down the blazing sky.

"A cup of tea?" asked Wendy in the silence.

EDWARD SHUSTER

Two Photographs

Courtesy of Edward Shuster

STUDY QUESTIONS FOR COMPREHENSION

1. What mood or moods are suggested by these photographs? Do you find any differences between them?
2. Do you find the presence of doorways significant? Why? Why not?
3. What relationship, if any, do you find between these photographs and the youth of today?

HENRY MOORE

Family Group

Collection, The Museum of Modern Art, New York

STUDY QUESTIONS FOR COMPREHENSION

1. Could the child in the Moore sculpture grow up to be one of the young people in the Shuster photographs?
2. What is your reaction to the "Family Group"? Can you explain why you react as you do?
3. Do you find that the sculpture suggests protection or overprotection?
4. What similarities or differences do you find between this sculpture and the family group on p. 292.

Japanese Poems and American Negro Blues

Japanese poems of the ninth century may seem a far cry from traditional American Negro blues. However, emotions, such as those which stem from disappointment in love, are timeless.

STUDY QUESTIONS FOR COMPREHENSION

1. What mood do the two poems and the song have in common?
2. Do you feel a sense of identification with the poets even though they are totally different from you in culture and time? Why?
3. If you were to add a fourth song or poem to this group, what would it be?

The weeds grow so thick
You cannot even see the path
That leads to my house:
It happened while I waited
For someone who would not come.

Sojo Henjo (815–890)

Although I am sure
That he will not be coming,
In the evening light
When the locusts shrilly call
I go to the door and wait.

Anonymous, 9th c.

GOOD MORNIN' BLUES

Good mornin', blues,
Blues, how do you do?
Good mornin', blues,
Blues how do you do?
Good mornin', how are you?

I laid down last night,
Turnin' from side to side;
Yes, I was turnin' from side to side,
I was not sick,
I was just dissatisfied.

When I got up this mornin',
Blues walkin' round my bed;
Yes, the blues walkin' round my bed,
I went to eat my breakfast,
The blues was all in my bread.

I sent for you yesterday baby,
Here you come a walkin' today;
Yes, here you come a walkin' today,

Got your mouth wide open,
You don't know what to say.

Good mornin', blues,
Blues, how do you do?
Yes, blues, how do you do?
I'm doin' all right,
Good mornin', how are you?

Traditional Negro Blues

e. e. cummings

it may not always be so

STUDY QUESTIONS FOR COMPREHENSION

1. About what circumstances is cummings writing?
2. What does the poet mean by "if this should be"?
3. Do you respond emotionally to the last two lines of the poem? What words in the lines carry the emotional impact?

it may not always be so; and i say
that if your lips, which i have loved, should touch
another's, and your dear strong fingers clutch
his heart, as mine in time not far away;
if on another's face your sweet hair lay
in such a silence as i know, or such
great writhing words as, uttering overmuch,
stand helplessly before the spirit at bay;

if this should be, i say if this should be—
you of my heart, send me a little word;
that i may go unto him, and take his hands,
saying, Accept all happiness from me.
Then shall i turn my face, and hear one bird
sing terribly afar in the lost lands.

WILLIAM SHAKESPEARE

Sonnet 29

STUDY QUESTIONS FOR COMPREHENSION

1. Read the poem twice. Explain its point in one or two sentences.
2. At which line does the poem change its mood?
3. Compare Shakespeare's imagery of the bird with cummings's.

When in disgrace with fortune and men's eyes,
I all alone beweep my outcast state,
And trouble deaf heaven with my bootless cries,
And look upon myself and curse my fate,
Wishing me like to one more rich in hope,
Featured like him, like him with friends possessed,
Desiring this man's art and that man's scope,
With what I most enjoy contented least;
Yet in these thoughts myself almost despising,
Haply I think on thee, and then my state,
Like to the lark at break of day arising
From sullen earth, sings hymns at heaven's gate;
For thy sweet love remembered such wealth brings
That then I scorn to change my state with kings.

Writing Assignments for Part Five

1. Many claim that today's young people are alienated from their culture and their parents. Write an essay in which you discuss this subject.

2. Using one or more selections from this section, write an essay about a specific human relationship (for example, parent–child, man–woman, brother–sister, student–student).

3. Write an essay in which you take a position on the relationships of people to people. Try to use some specific examples for whatever point of view you take.

4. React in any form you choose (short story, poem, description, personal narrative) to any one or more selections in this section. You might, for instance, consider pairs of opposites: the sculpture of the families (pp. 292, 330) and "The Cry" (p. 293) or "Vengeful Sister" (p. 296), or the two representations of maternity (following p. 302).

PART SIX / *Man's Inhumanity to Man*

When they came for the Communists, I did not speak up, for I was not a Communist. When they came for the Jews, I did not speak up, for I was not a Jew. When they came for the trade unionists, I did not speak up, for I was not a trade unionist. When they came for the Catholics, I did not speak up, for I was a Protestant. When they came for me, there was no one left to speak up.

Pastor Martin Niemoller

RALPH LINTON

One Hundred Percent American

There can be no question about the average American's Americanism or his desire to preserve this precious heritage at all costs. Nevertheless, some insidious foreign ideas have already wormed their way into his civilization without his realizing what was going on. Thus dawn finds the unsuspecting patriot garbed in pajamas, a garment of East Indian origin; and lying in a bed built on a pattern which originated in either Persia or Asia Minor. He is muffled to the ears in un-American materials: cotton, first domesticated in India; linen, domesticated in the Near East; wool from an animal native to Asia Minor; or silk whose uses were first discovered by the Chinese. All these substances have been transformed into cloth by methods invented in Southwestern Asia. If the weather is cold enough he may even be sleeping under an eiderdown quilt invented in Scandinavia.

On awakening he glances at the clock, a medieval European invention, uses one potent Latin word in abbreviated form, rises in haste, and goes to the bathroom. Here, if he stops to think about it, he must feel himself in the presence of a great American institution; he will have heard stories of both the quality and frequency of foreign plumbing and will know that in no other country does the average man perform his ablutions in the midst of such splendor. But the insidious foreign influence pursues him even here. Glass was invented by the ancient Egyptians, the use of glazed tiles for floors and walls in the Near East, porcelain in China, and the art of enameling on metal by Mediterranean artisans of the Bronze Age. Even his bathtub and toilet are but slightly modified copies of Roman originals. The only purely American contribution to the ensemble is the steam radiator, against which our patriot very briefly and unintentionally places his posterior.

In this bathroom the American washes with soap invented by the ancient Gauls. Next he cleans his teeth, a subversive European practice which did not invade America until the latter part of the eighteenth century. He then shaves, a masochistic rite first developed by the heathen priests of ancient Egypt and Sumer. The process is made less of a penance by the fact that his razor is of steel, an iron-carbon alloy discovered in either India or Turkestan. Lastly, he dries himself on a Turkish towel.

Returning to the bedroom, the unconscious victim of un-American practices removes his clothes from a chair, invented in the Near East, and proceeds to dress. He puts on close-fitting tailored garments whose form derives from the skin clothing of the ancient nomads of the Asiatic steppes and fastens them with buttons whose prototypes appeared in Europe at the close of the Stone Age. This costume is appropriate enough for outdoor exercise in a cold climate, but is quite unsuited to American summers, steam-heated houses, and Pullmans. Nevertheless, foreign ideas and habits hold the unfortunate man in thrall even when common sense tells him that the authentically American costume of gee string and moccasins would be far more comfortable. He puts on his feet stiff coverings made from hide prepared by a process invented in ancient Egypt and cut to a pattern which can be traced back to ancient Greece, and makes sure that they are properly polished, also a Greek idea. Lastly, he ties about his neck a strip of bright-colored cloth which is a vestigial survival of the shoulder shawls worn by seventeenth-century Croats. He gives himself a final appraisal in the mirror, an old Mediterranean invention, and goes downstairs to breakfast.

Here a whole new series of foreign things confronts him. His food and drink are placed before him in pottery vessels, the popular name of which—china—is sufficient evidence of their origin. His fork is a medieval Italian invention and his spoon a copy of a Roman original. He will usually begin the meal with coffee, an Abyssinian plant first discovered by the Arabs. The American is quite likely to need it to dispel the morning-after effects of over-indulgence in fermented drinks, invented in the Near East; or distilled ones, invented by the alchemists of medieval Europe. Whereas the Arabs took their coffee straight, he will probably sweeten it with sugar, discovered in India; and dilute it with cream, both the domestication of cattle and the technique of milking having originated in Asia Minor.

If our patriot is old-fashioned enough to adhere to the so-called American breakfast, his coffee will be accompanied by an orange, domesticated in the Mediterranean region, a cantaloupe domesticated in Persia, or grapes domesticated in Asia Minor. He will follow this with a bowl of cereal made from grain domesticated in the Near East and prepared by methods also invented there. From this he will go on to waffles, a Scandinavian invention, with plenty of butter, originally a Near-Eastern cosmetic. As a side dish he may have the egg of a bird domesticated in Southeastern Asia or strips of the flesh of an animal domesticated in the same region, which have been salted and smoked by a process invented in Northern Europe.

Breakfast over, he places upon his head a molded piece of felt, invented by the nomads of Eastern Asia, and, if it looks like rain, puts on outer shoes of rubber, discovered by the ancient Mexicans, and takes an umbrella, invented in India. He then sprints for his train—the train, not the sprinting, being an English invention. At the station he pauses for a moment to buy a newspaper, paying for it with coins invented in ancient Lydia. Once on board he settles back to inhale the fumes of a cigarette invented in Mexico, or a cigar invented in Brazil. Meanwhile, he reads the news of the day, imprinted in characters invented by the ancient Semites by a process invented in Germany upon a material invented in China. As he scans the latest editorial pointing out the dire results to our institutions of accepting foreign ideas, he will not fail to thank a Hebrew God in an Indo-European language that he is a one hundred percent (decimal system invented by the Greeks) American (from Americus Vespucci, Italian geographer).

ADOLF HITLER

From *Mein Kampf*

Adolf Hitler was the most infamous proponent of racial purity the world has known. In the following selection from Mein Kampf *he equates national and religious groups with breeds of dogs. His solution to the "Jewish question" resulted in the deaths of six million Jews. He was also responsible for the deaths of hundreds of thousands of gypsies, Catholics, and political dissenters.*

STUDY QUESTIONS FOR COMPREHENSION

1. What are the two basic points Hitler makes about race?
2. Do Hitler's views of race conform to scientific knowledge?

All great questions of the times are questions of the moment, and they represent only consequences of certain causes. Only one of them is of causal importance, that is, the question of the racial preservation of the nationality. In the blood alone there rests the strength as well as the weakness of man. As long as the people do not recognize and pay attention to the importance of their racial foundation, they resemble people who would like to teach the greyhound's qualities to poodles, without realizing that the greyhound's speed and the poodle's docility are qualities which are not taught, but are peculiar to the race. Peoples who renounce the preservation of their racial purity renounce also the unity of their soul in all its expressions. The torn condition of their nature is the natural, necessary consequence of the torn condition of their blood, and the change in

From *Mein Kampf* by Adolph Hitler, trans. Ralph Manheim, pp. 469-470. Reprinted by permission of the publisher, Houghton Mifflin Company.

their spiritual and creative force is only the effect of the change in their racial foundations.

He who wants to redeem the German people from the qualities and the vices which are alien to its original nature will have to redeem it first from the alien originators of these expressions.

Without the clearest recognition of the race problem and, with it, of the Jewish question, there will be no rise of the German nation.

WHITNEY R. HARRIS

From *Tyranny on Trial*

This selection, which follows Hitler's theory of racial purity, is only one example of the "solution" in action, a supreme example of one group's hatred of another. The excerpt is an eyewitness account from the Nuremberg trials; the speaker has just been asked if she could describe the selection of prisoners who were to be gassed as they arrived at Auschwitz in convoys. As horrifying as this account is, it is mild compared to the photographs, films, and other eyewitness accounts which document Hitler's attempt to achieve "racial purity."

STUDY QUESTION FOR COMPREHENSION

Most people when confronted with stories of atrocity tend to say, "That's too horrible. I don't want to think about it." Do you think that a responsible human being can afford to turn his back upon "man's inhumanity to man"?

Madame Vaillant-Couturier was asked whether she could describe the selection of victims for gassing at the time of the arrival of the convoys.

Yes, because when we worked at the sewing block in 1944, the block where we lived directly faced the stopping place of the trains. The system had been improved. Instead of making the selection at the place where they arrived, a side line now took the train practically right up to the gas chamber; and the stopping place about 100 meters from the gas chamber, was right opposite our block though, of course,

From *Tyranny on Trial* by Whitney R. Harris, Southern Methodist University Press, Dallas, 1954. Reprinted by permission of Southern Methodist University Press and the author.

separated from us by two rows of barbed wire. Consequently, we saw the unsealing of the cars and the soldiers letting men, women, and children out of them. We then witnessed heartrending scenes; old couples forced to part from each other, mothers made to abandon their young daughters, since the latter were sent to the camp, whereas mothers and children were sent to the gas chambers. All these people were unaware of the fate awaiting them. They were merely upset at being separated, but they did not know that they were going to their death. To render their welcome more pleasant at this time—June–July 1944—an orchestra composed of internees, all young and pretty girls dressed in little white blouses and navy blue skirts, played during the selection, at the arrival of the trains, gay tunes such as "The Merry Widow," the "Barcarolle" from *The Tales of Hoffman,* and so forth. They were then informed that this was a labor camp and since they were not brought into the camp they saw only the small platform surrounded by flowering plants. Naturally, they could not realize what was in store for them. Those selected for the gas chamber, that is, the old people, mothers, and children, were escorted to a red-brick building . . . which bore the letters "Baden," that is to say "Baths." There, to begin with, they were made to undress and given a towel before they went into the so-called shower room. Later on, at the time of the large convoys from Hungary, they had no more time left to play-act or to pretend; they were brutally undressed, and I know these details as I knew a little Jewess from France who lived with her family at the "Republique" district. . . .

She was called "little Marie" and she was the only one, the sole survivor of a family of nine. Her mother and her seven brothers and sisters had been gassed on arrival. When I met her she was employed to undress the babies before they were taken into the gas chamber. Once the people were undressed they took them into a room which was somewhat like a shower room, and gas capsules were thrown through an opening in the ceiling. An SS man would watch the effect produced through a porthole. At the end of 5 or 7 minutes, when the gas had completed its work, he gave the signal to open the doors: and men with gas masks—they too were internees—went into the room and removed the corpses. They told us that the internees must have suffered before dying, because they were closely clinging to one another and it was very difficult to separate them.

After that a special squad would come to pull out gold teeth and dentures; and again, when the bodies had been reduced to ashes they would sift them in an attempt to recover the gold.

At Auschwitz there were eight crematories, but, as from 1944, these proved insufficient. The SS had large pits dug by the internees, where they put branches, sprinkled with gasoline, which they set on fire. Then they threw the corpses into the pits. From our block we could see after about three-quarters of an hour or an hour after the arrival of a convoy, large flames coming from the crematory, and the sky was lighted up by the burning pits.

RUTH ANGRESS

The Horizontal Line

This story takes place at the time of Hitler's rise to power. Vienna was Hitler's birthplace. All Jews at that time were required to wear the yellow Star of David, ostensibly for the purpose of identification, but in reality for the purpose of humiliation and abuse.

STUDY QUESTIONS FOR COMPREHENSION

1. How would you describe the young girl in the story?
2. How would you describe von Reiner?
3. What is your reaction to the treatment the child receives?
4. Why is the cat and parrot incident so significant?

There is a line that runs through the past. It is not neat, it has curves and edges (it is these that I should like to tell you about), but still it is a line, a roughly horizontal one, the kind that divides a "before" from an "after," and not the kind that runs vertically down to deepest childhood, connecting. We have been taught to be suspicious of such dividing lines, circumscribed as they are by haphazard events, pressed on us by outsiders, sometimes violently, and we have been told to think of their effects, even their reality, as superficial, if not illusory. I know therefore that my memory may play me a trick. I am speaking of my own past, of course, and if I am stating my reservations at the outset, it is simply because I have them and not, as you may think, because I want to disclaim responsibility for the fact that the remembered details that follow insist that they are related to one another. In fact, I could probably say to you with impunity, "As an Austrian Jew, my childhood came to an end with the German invasion." I suspect that such a blatant pomposity would

Reprinted by permission of the author.

be greeted with the respectful silence which intelligent Americans accord to History and those whose lives were directly affected by it. Meanwhile my memory persists in drawing that line. If anything, it gets sharper as the years go by.

There is at first a slightly unhappy vagueness around a little girl whom I recognize as myself, but of whom I cannot really say "I." So I shan't say I, I shall give it to you as I recall it, the first of the tricks of which memory has a bagful.

"You rotten . . . you . . ." A volley of jubilant obscenities landed like a ball on her side of the fence. It seemed well-aimed, but was not meant for her. The boys on the other side were shouting the still fresh-tasting words for the sheer pleasure of knowing them. She stood, a well-protected listener, on the other side, in her garden, wearing a sweater she did not want, but that her aunt insisted on. She thought of the generous wide open gestures that the boys used when they played ball, and that she had often and vainly tried to approximate. Longing to have a part in their kind of camaraderie, she wished she could shout something in return, something like the unrepeatable obscurities they were so carefree with. Only a moment's thought, and shocked, shy and rapidly she walked to the house. "It would not be wise," she said aloud, relishing the odd sound of the last word.

In the cool hallway she sniffed a smell moistly reminding her of wooden beach cabins where one changed clothes. "Oh corridor," she said and listened to the indistinct echo. (Only in books did the echo ever repeat a whole word.) "Oh corridor," she repeated and explained to herself, "I like O's."———

No more than that. And do we think on strips of celluloid that become torn with time and warped with the soft and hard liquids and liquors that are spilled on them, while here a soundtrack gets lost, there a tape remains without picture? Then a clear shred in a hopelessly lonely corner of the mind.

But of course you are asking for circumstances. My parents were dead and I lived with an aunt in a suburban part of Vienna in a house that my grandfather had left. There was an uncle to go with the aunt, but he does not enter the picture. They had a grownup son in Linz, and I gather that my aunt was not immoderately fond of me, a feeling that I reciprocated. The war was to separate us, and when I saw her again many years later, she had become a tough and humorous old lady who frankly admitted that she preferred me as an adult to the child that she had had to take care of.

Life was full of things that children were not supposed to know, and so we knew remarkably little, more shadows and hints than shapes and substances. In fact, considering the pathetic efforts that were made to shelter us, who were soon to be the most unsheltered generation of children the world has known, I wonder how they managed to teach us anything, even in school. History for instance. We were heirs to a truncated little country that had until recently been a monstrosity among empires; an unexplained circumstance, since politics was out of the question, though I gathered that it was made in Germany, as salami was made in Hungary, and that its import, unlike that of salami, was undesirable.

So I learned to look backward to an undifferentiated past with the flavor of empire. I remembered my dead grandfather's whiskers and how he used to take the paper curlers out of them in the morning. They were called Franz Joseph whiskers, after the Kaiser who wore them on his aged baby face. And the memory of my grandfather's whiskers remained as a memento of the same past as the crescent-shaped breakfast rolls that are to be had in no other city and are said to date from the siege of Vienna by the Turks in the 17th century. The imagination stubbornly refused to make an essential difference between the two, even after I knew the dates.

Vienna was a disgruntled city, rather squalid, a piece of old furniture with the polish gone, successfully posing as an antique to strangers. Dust collected everywhere, in the corners and under the doilies, and if you looked closely, all the exquisite, useless china statuettes in the better homes had tiny, and not so tiny, cracks. The dust bred germs, vermin, coughs and worse. And the city grumbled and scratched herself and closed her eyes and sealed those of her children. Yes, of course she also had her medicine man, her great exorciser; I know that right around the corner as it were, the biggest of the soul-searchers was blowing the dust of the world sky-high. Only in Vienna it immediately settled again. He was not a son of whom the city was proud. And I never heard his name; it was carefully kept out of the earshot of children.

I was sulky and read quantities of poetry.

My aunt believed not only that children in general and girls in particular should grow up in a state of ignorance (whether blissful or anxious was none of her concern), but also that the worst thing you could do to them was ask their opinion. I was given the food, clothes, toys that she considered proper and was expected to think likewise. I resented dolls, but I was a girl and had to have them. In a standing battle over woolen sweaters and a shorter haircut, I invariably lost out. The sweaters itched and the hair was unmanageable and my requests in this respect were aimed at comfort, not vanity. I was perennially uncomfortable. I wore ill-fitting shoes, because my aunt believed the salesman who said they fitted and not me who said they hurt. God knows what I would have had to read if they hadn't let me rummage through my grandfather's library at will, on the assumption that any book more than fifty years old must be innocuous. So I came to take it for granted that books with gaudy dust-jackets were for grownups and that somber-looking uniformly bound sets of "collected works" were for minors, an idea that I have since vainly tried to instill in other children.

The rest of the household consisted of an elderly maid, an enormous tomcat named Billy, and a parrot who survived from my grandfather's days and whose name, like that of most German-speaking parrots, was Laura. It was assumed that this bird was a great favorite of mine. I was never asked, presumably because I was too young to know the state of my feelings even in the matter of a pet. Actually I was only curious about Laura, tried to teach her a few additional words (without success) and was mildly flattered by her greeting me with shouts of "Gretel" and peals of laughter when I entered the room. (My name has never been Gretel.) She was old and crabby and would not let anyone come too close. The door of her large cage which stood on a small, imitation marble-topped table of its own, was always open, but Laura never ventured further than the edge of the table and that only rarely. Perhaps she was afraid of her arch-enemy, Billy the cat, who every now and then tried an attack. And yet she once sat on my grandfather's shoulder and they marched through the house, singing together, to the horror of my grandmother who fancied herself musical.

I suffered from insomnia. My aunt used to get me out of the way as early as she could, and she did not change my bedtime as I grew older, so that on the long light summer evenings I lay on my back and stared at the ceiling, incapable of falling asleep and trying to catch snatches of the adult conversation in the drawing room, the "salon," as it was called. Never more than snatches. But adult conversation in the thirties was not pleasant, and what I heard were uncertainties that became nightmares in the uncertain dusk. And sometimes loneliness was sickening and I called for my aunt under a variety of excuses. The excuses were as thin as those of most children; when I got too old for the glass of water, I thought of the spiders.

There were plenty of spiders, especially in the summer; they came in from the garden, and I could usually spot one in a corner of my room. Frequently two, three or four. I really did not like them, but of course I did not mind them as much as I pretended when I implored my aunt to take them away. She did for a long time, with a sigh, but good-naturedly enough, until one day she decreed that I was old enough to stop pestering her in the evenings with trifles. That is when mild annoyance changed into panic and the insomnia started. The spiders were bearable enough as long as it was in my power to have them removed, but now I was Andromeda chained to her rock waiting for death and destruction. Only my open eyes could ward off the danger. So I lay staring at the ceiling, my eyeballs burning with tiredness, unable, unwilling to fall asleep, straining to listen to the conversation next door.

But I had von Reiner. A frequent visitor at our house and a former admirer of my mother's (maybe her lover, I don't know), I remember him as a short, stubby, bespectacled middle-aged man, with thin remnants of blond hair, my friend of friends . . .

Where his title, the "von," came from, nobody knew exactly. My aunt claimed that he had lived for a number of years in Hungary and that a title could be purchased there for a reasonable sum. (You see the sort of things I *was* allowed to hear.) He had a private income of some kind, and his only regular occupation that I know of was to invent crossword puzzles and chess problems for local newspapers.

He had a bachelor's overestimation of a child's capacities, a tendency which was in refreshing contrast to my aunt. He taught me chess and he took me on long walks, too long really, and he talked science and philosophy to me, nine tenths of which was over my head. But there was always a tenth that antennae of comprehension could touch and that changed my world. There was something about him that has always made me think that Plato must have looked like him. Very likely this is simply because he told me the story of the trial and death of Socrates. He told it very dramatically, as if he had been there, had supported Crito in his arguments for flight and been moved by the jailer's tears. Years later, when I read the *Dialogues,* it struck me that he must have known large portions of them by heart. I tried to forget him later, to minimize the importance he had for me, tried to think of him as a pompous stuffed shirt and as a failure and as a coward. But today, with much of my old spite siphoned off by the years, I add and stress that he was also my teacher and that, for better or for worse, wherever he lives or lies buried, he can claim his own in me. I might as well say it now, von Reiner joined the Nazi party, late and undoubtedly under pressure (though how great could the pressure have been, since he did not depend on a job for his living?); and once when I met him on the street, he in the company of a tall and forbidding woman who marched alongside of him as if she was on parade, and I with the yellow star of David that I was required to wear, I opened my mouth to greet him, and he turned the other way and began to talk and walk faster, and I closed my mouth and walked faster myself and held my head very high and didn't even feel hurt, only contemptuous, because by then he didn't matter anymore. But I am getting ahead of my story.

One evening I was in bed and von Reiner was in the house as a dinner guest. His presence encouraged me to make a last effort on behalf of a medium-sized black spider which was peacefully spinning its web in a corner near the ceiling. I called. They ignored me. I called again. Nothing. The third time I called, I heard a chair being moved and a minute later von Reiner appeared, a broom in his hand. The broom was considerably longer than he, and he looked as if he had never held one, but I was too relieved to be amused. I pointed and said, "There it is."

He sat down on my bed and said with mild reproach, "But spiders are harmless, Kitty."

Didn't I know, and hadn't I heard this often enough from my aunt. I felt foolish for being so irrational, and resentful that he should have nothing better to say to me. "In America they have a spider that's poisonous," I informed him triumphantly, "and it's black, like the one over there, and it's got a red mark like an hourglass on its belly, and you can't see the belly of this one."

"You mean the black widow," he said even more mildly, "but surely you know that we haven't got those in Austria?"

"How do you know?" I replied hotly. "It could have been imported or something. Like the potato, for instance."

He knew that I knew I was being silly, and ignoring my last remark sat thinking for a while. "You are lucky tonight, Kitty," he finally said. "Most of the time we haven't got much of a choice, any of us. I mean we get up in the morning, tie our shoelaces and go to work or to school. And eat our lunches and go to bed at night. We've got to do these things, more or less, and that's the way it goes all the time or almost. Very little choice, if you come to consider. But every now and then we get a hold of a chance for a bit of freedom, and it tends to be no bigger than one end of an average size horseshoe and no thicker than the leaf of a four-leaved clover. You are lucky tonight, Kitty. You decide whether I should take the spider away or not."

He took it for granted that I would understand perfectly and waited. And I understood only too well that I was supposed to send him out again, broom and all, and turn on my side and go to sleep with a good conscience and forget all about spiders. But so far I lay on my back, and my spider had started to crawl along the ceiling and was approaching, so that in a minute it would be straight over my face; and then I knew that what he had said was nonsense, that there was no alternative, since I could never go to sleep with that creature in my room. "Take it away, please, please take it away!"

He was as good as his word. He got up with a slight shrug and looked a little smaller than usual and a bit ridiculous to boot, handling that broom. I remember that he did not kill the animal, but shook it gently out of the window. And he said "Good night, Kitty," kindly and only with a trace of disappointment in his voice. I was ashamed of myself, but not so ashamed that I did not go to sleep with relief.

And now, was it the next day, or was it weeks, months later? The incident follows in memory and there is nothing between the two. I used to play a game with myself, in which I pretended that somebody was following me from school and that I had to run for my life. I always reached the "fort" in the nick of time. Perhaps on that particular day I was really being followed; I had seen enough oddly behaved characters lounging about the school and the parks. Or perhaps my imagination was unusually lively. In any case, the game was no game that day, and I see myself dashing down the street in a frenzy of fear. Myself? A child with a mess of black hair and a satchel on her back, whose experience has been recorded, through a biochemical quirk, in my mind, the mind of a stranger, not even a friend. And so she runs down the streets of recollection, and reaching the hall slams the gate.

Safe, for a moment at least, clinging to safety, trying to prolong the delicious closed-in feeling, three seconds, two seconds, and now no longer. Tumbling, violent reproaches. Coward, coward, coward, what did you run away from anyhow, nobody followed you, coward. I am not a coward, she said, I know I am not a coward. Prove it. Yes, it had to be proved, that was fair enough, it had to be proved now and for good. She looked around and saw, next to her, halfway up the wall and crawling higher, a hideous, repulsive, black long-legged spider. Now, before it is out of reach, pick it up, look at it, spiders are harmless. Spiders are harmless, are harmless, harmless. She could hardly lift her hand, heavy with sweat, blood, flesh, bone. She felt the white mask of disgust on her face and her flesh crawled as if with hundreds of spiders. Then, for a second, decision leaped and with fingers in which she could have counted the nerves one by one, she grasped the animal hard and seemed to feel a sting at the same time red dots danced before her eyes and were red marks on the spider's body, and she dropped it and screamed and screamed and screamed, and thought she was merely gasping for air. Faintly she heard the sound of footsteps. But louder, much louder, houses and hallways and arches collapsed, and she in the center of crumbling edifices, crouching and panting, while blocks and bricks piled higher and buried her in their darkness.

It was simple enough. I had fainted. A hysterical fit of some sort, due to an overwrought imagination, and the family doctor claimed that an oncoming cold and my not having eaten my lunch had something to do with it too. They kept me in bed for a few days, and when I got up again, I learned that the name of our little country had changed from *Oesterreich* to *Ostmark,* and that we had a new currency, not Groschen and Schillings anymore, but Pfennige and Mark. Also, but that inadvertently, that my aunt's son (the one who lived in Linz) had been arrested on unknown charges.

Von Reiner came with a bouquet of roses. The maid (who left us two weeks later), opened the door and showed him in, while I ran into the kitchen to tell my aunt. She took off her apron, dried her hands and said vindictively, "Wants to clear his conscience with a batch of flowers."

"Why, what has he done?" I asked in surprise.

"How should I know?"

"But you just said. . . ."

"Well, he is one of them, isn't he?" she asked rhetorically.

"One of whom?" I insisted.

"Why people like him!" she exclaimed in exasperation at my stubbornness or stupidity and walked off. I stood, trying to understand many things fast, as I had to, and my grownup cousin in jail at Linz occurred to me. Then without even wondering whether it was mannerly to do so or not, I walked into the oversized salon, where my aunt and her visitor were. On the walls a reproduction of Murillo's grape-eaters and a still-life with a lobster in the center. From the ceiling a large candelabra. At the right of the door where I entered the parrot. On the left a piano. They were at the opposite end of the room, and I stood still near the piano, so that they did not notice me. My aunt sat at the table, fingering the roses with the fixed smile she put on when she wished to indicate that she was clearly superior to whatever confronted her. At this point it was not entirely clear whether the enemy was von Reiner or the Nazis. It struck me that he must have been trying to impress her with his good will for some minutes and that she was not convinced. Or perhaps, I analyzed quickly, she believes him and doesn't show it, so that he'll feel humiliated. (Oh, these were the days when I learned in a hurry.) But for my own part, I did not doubt him an instant. He stood at the window, his back turned to her, and I could see that his shoulders were literally shaking. He turned around and quoted with heavy emphasis,

> "When the mobs of every kind
> Dance around the golden calf . . ."

My aunt continued her fixed, hard smile. Incomprehension or does she think him silly? I wanted to show that I at least appreciated him, and on an impulse I finished the verse as fiercely as I could:

> "Think that in the end you have
> No one but yourself to mind."

He glanced at me in more astonishment than was warranted by my presence or by my knowledge of the verse, which is heavily anthologized. Perhaps he gathered from my tone that I, like him, had found in it more than a generous platitude. He walked quickly over to me and took my hand, and for a moment I was afraid that he would kiss it. But he merely stood holding it and looked at me with a smile, then said to my aunt, "Gracious lady" (I have never known anyone who used the address *"gnaedige Frau"* so frequently and with such relish), "will you permit me to take Kitty for a walk?"

I ran for my coat. On the street it turned out that we were not going to the outskirts of the city today. We went by subway to its center, where the invader had been received with cheers and flowers a few days earlier. "You might as well see it," von Reiner said. "After all, you'll have to live with it, who more than you?"

After that he said very little. We walked along several of the largest and most fashionable avenues in town, the Kaertnerstrasse, the Ring. He held my hand and we looked around us. We looked at brown shirts and black shirts and a profusion of white knee stockings. The first time we saw the broken windowpanes of a large coffee house, I looked up at him inquiringly, and he nodded and said undramatically, "Yes, the owner is a Jew." He did not repeat the information the other times. And we looked at the signs that read "Jewish shop" and "Aryan shop" and "Jews and dogs are not permitted to enter," and at that point I started to laugh, and for the first time in my life I was struck by the absurdity of all the seven deadly sins. He was displeased and must have thought that I was not aware of the seriousness of it all, which was partially true; and yet I knew that the joke depended on the gravity of the sin.

Then we passed a man. He stared at us so intently that I looked back at him. He had turned too, our glances met, and that may have decided him. In any case, he came quickly after us and began to speak to von Reiner. I recall the peculiar, frozen feeling of almost-guilt in his approach. But I do not recall his face; while he was there I looked at my companion and nowhere else. My memory gives me a faceless man, in black, with live swastikas crawling all over him. So he must have belonged to the SS. He spoke with an accent I had never heard before, difficult to understand, perhaps Saxon, though I had no way of even guessing then. And what did he say? The scene is so vivid and yet blurred, drenched and dredged in the salt of the years. Was von Reiner an Aryan? That was the first question, and I remember it clearly, because shortly before my friend had explained to me in a humorous and authoritative manner that the term was, anthropologically speaking, meaningless. It was partly for that reason, partly because of the tone of the answer that I was so startled by the prompt, clipped "Jawohl" that came in reply. But the dark-haired child was surely not? Von Reiner admitted it. Was I his child? This question puzzled me, in view of the preceding ones, as did von Reiner's fervent no, no, no, oh no. What could the gentleman be thinking of? And I continued to look up at my friend and so missed the grin on the face of the German, but heard it in his voice when he told my mentor, my teacher, that just as a piece of friendly advice he would counsel a fellow Aryan not to be seen anymore in the company of Jews, regardless of their sex, age, or other qualifications, as they were the destroyers and leeches of the people. Von Reiner choked over his answer: I could not hear it.

We went on walking, silently both of us, and I thought at first he was embarrassed and sorry for me and trying to think of something good to say. I kept looking into his bewildered, frightened face and pressed his hand and skipped a little (for which I was quite too old) to show him that it didn't matter. But still he said nothing. Perhaps he was tactfully ignoring the whole scene and planned to continue our walk as if nothing had happened. Until we reached the subway and he took me unceremoniously down the stairs. When I asked where we were going, he said "Home," and I realized that it was I who had ceased to matter. . . .

That night, after von Reiner had taken me home for the last time, I found it harder than ever to fall asleep. Patterns of conduct emerged and disintegrated, mocked by the twilight, denied by my day. I sensed that the effort to understand was all that was left, the only way out of humiliation, disappointment. And I had a little fantasy about a road map with a labyrinth of crooked lines which I would study for years, if necessary. I would make them yield their meaning, regardless how complex, if I could only get a hold of the road map in the first place. I closed my eyes and immediately had the impression that the window was miles away and the door as far, and that I lay, three inches long, in the middle of nowhere. I opened my eyes angrily and the familiar dimensions returned, but the anger remained, boiling anger. Then I thought of the spiders and the swastikas, and the sign about the Jews and the dogs, and the stranger's phrase about leeches. And I wondered where I fitted into this menagerie, and suddenly I started to laugh again.

I must have dozed off after all, for I was awakened by a piercing screech that made me sit upright, my hands clammy, my back covered with goosepimples. It was high, agonized, inhuman. I had seen puppet plays in which the devil carried a box with the souls of the damned in the shapes of moths and butterflies, and occasionally a thin, helpless sound would come from the box. Once down in hell they would screech like this, I thought, and I actually wrung my hands in fear and impotence. For the horror did not stop. It started again, having caught its breath, only half smothered now, and still I had not the least idea what was happening, and jumped out of bed and ran into the hall and began to scream, not out of necessity but in order to cover the hideous noise. My aunt, my uncle and the maid came running out of the drawing room, and my uncle said to my aunt, "Take her to bed or she'll faint again." "Oh what is it, what is it?" I asked sobbing. "Never mind what it is, go to bed now," my aunt said. But through the open door I saw the empty cage of the parrot, and I calmed down immediately once I understood, the explanation being so simple.

I walked past the adults into the room and looked underneath the furniture, until I saw Billy's two eyes glowing in the dark under the sofa. I realized with a sentimental nostalgia that the bird who used to call me "Gretel" was being torn to pieces, and that in consequence I would never be called "Gretel" again. I cannot explain how this prospectively reminiscent mood managed to co-exist with the clear sense of emergency which was uppermost. I started to crawl under the sofa. "Come on out of there, he'll scratch your eyes," the maid said anxiously. But it was inconceivable that I should stand by and watch and wait. I took Billy by the scruff of his neck, dragged him into the light, forced him to relinquish the bird and threw him out. Then I returned to look at the mess. Feathers and gore. But there was satisfaction in surveying the spectacle I had brought under control. To be sure, saving the parrot's life would have been better, but this was a good second best. I even cleaned up the worst of it and wondered whether they'd ever get the bloodstains out of the oriental patterns of the rug. Then I washed my hands and went back to bed. My aunt came and for the first time offered me a sleeping pill. I was flattered, but I refused it.

And I went to sleep. I had seen what there was to be seen. I had been up at night instead of trying to fall asleep in the dusk. It was like swimming for the first time without a safety belt: now one could really drown, but that was part of the joy of being able to keep afloat. In all the years and all the strangeness that followed, I never spent a sleepless night again.

Status of the American Indian

The following is an excerpt from the report of the United States Civil Rights Commission. The report in its entirety attempts to analyze the civil rights status of the almost forgotten but second largest "racial" minority group in the United States, the American Indian. The entire report covers all areas that involve civil rights—housing, for instance, and voting rights. The following excerpt concerns the American Indian and his right to free public education. Note the careful use, characteristic of report writing, of "some" and "reportedly."

STUDY QUESTIONS FOR COMPREHENSION

1. What is the Indian's position in the American culture?
2. How does the education of the Indian differ from the education of the Caucasian?
3. Relate this report to the general problem of segregation.

The 1960 census reported on five racial minorities. In order of population size, they were as follows: Negroes, 18,871,831; American Indians, 523,591; Japanese, 464,332; Chinese, 237,292; and Filipinos, 176,310. Indians are thus the second largest "racial" minority in the United States. As a minority, Indians fall into three categories—reservation, nonreservation, and off reservation. The civil rights of the latter, sometimes referred to as "relocated" Indians, are not specially treated in this study. There is little reason to doubt however that this group suffers many of the denials inflicted on other Indians. . . .

From *Justice*, Book 5 of *1961 Commission on Civil Rights Report*, Supt. of Documents, Washington, D.C. (1961), pp. 135–53 (Part VIII, "The American Indian," Chapter 3, "Status as a Minority"). Printed in *Law in American Society*, ed. Sara Toll East (New York: H. W. Wilson Co., 1963).

In the recent past, signs, such as "Indians Not Allowed," were commonplaces in many small communities near reservations. Most of these have disappeared, but the prejudice they expressed remains. For example, the city commission of Chamberlain, a small community in South Dakota sixty miles from a reservation, passed a resolution in 1954 stating that its citizens were "opposed to the city being made an Indian town and are opposed to having Indians in our schools or living in unsanitary conditions about the city. . . ."

Hostility is sometimes found in bordering towns even where the Indian population is large and potentially holds the balance of political power, as in South Dakota where thousands of destitute Indians reside off reservations. . . .

As complex as community life has now become, the uneducated man has little chance to make his way through the labyrinth. If, in addition to being uneducated, he is Indian (or Negro, or Mexican, for that matter), his chances are less than slim. For the Indian child whose education the Federal Government provides through Federal schools, the problem is the adequacy and availability of the education. Where civil rights problems have arisen is with respect to the states. Although reservation Indians enrolling in public schools have encountered hostility, the Federal policy of paying grants or subsidies to public schools for admitting reservation Indians helped to break down policies of exclusion. . . . Hence, apart from the South, the exclusion of reservation Indians from public schools is rare. However, the Federal government does not compel states to admit Indian children to public schools, let alone admit them on a nonsegregated basis. Its position is that eligibility for reservation Indian enrollment in public schools is a matter of state determination. Thus discrimination can and does occur in some areas.

As for reservation Indians the Bureau of Indian Affairs reported to the Commission in 1958 it had some difficulty enrolling children on a nondiscriminatory basis in Louisiana, Mississippi, and North Carolina.

An Oklahoma Choctaw, engaged in missionary work among the Mississippi Choctaws, recently complained to the Bureau of Indian Affairs that he was not allowed to enroll his daughter in the public elementary school in Philadelphia, Mississippi, because of her race. He accused the Bureau of acquiescing in racial discrimination. In its reply the Bureau stated that there was nothing it could do. While there are some Choctaws in white schools in Mississippi, the bulk of Choctaw children suffer from the exclusionary policy of local public schools. This is true also of the Cherokee Indians in North Carolina. In 1960 only 91 of 992 Choctaw children in Mississippi and only 136 of 1053 Cherokee children of school age were in white public schools. The remainder were in Federal Indian schools. . . .

Some Indian tribes are not considered a Federal responsibility and hence the states wherein they reside have the primary duty of providing schooling. It is often provided on a segregated basis in southern states. In nine North Carolina counties, for example, there are three separate sets of public schools—for whites, Negroes, and Indians. One of the nine, Robeson, reportedly has a fourth school reserved for mixed bloods. Another, Parson, takes some Indian students from Virginia. In the nine counties there are 19 separate schools for Indians, 100 for whites, and 70 for Negroes, serving 10,771 Indians, 32,895 Negroes and 46,465 whites. All of the Indian schools are public schools operated with state aid and state-paid teachers under county boards of education. In 1959, Indian students of Harnett County sought admission to the all-white high school in the county. Harnett County has an Indian elementary school (78 students in 1960), but no high school. Its high school students must travel seventy miles daily round trip by bus to East Carolina Indian School near Clinton in Sampson County. They were refused admission by the Harnett County board. . . .

As a result of refusals to admit Indian children to white public schools, and the general indisposition of states to spend money on the education of Indians residing on tax-exempt lands, the Indian Bureau has had to build schools on reservations in southern states at a time when its policy favored assimilation of Indian children into local public school systems. In some cases it has had to send Indian students long distances because of state policies. For example, Bureau schools in Mississippi go only to the tenth grade and Choctaw Indian students wishing to complete high school must transfer to Bureau schools over a thousand miles away. Local exclusion policies, therefore, work a considerable hardship on Indian teenagers and their parents.

Segregation may crop up elsewhere than in the South. Until 1958 there was a segregated school system in Round Valley, California, with Indian children attending one public school and white children another. A forceful school superintendent consolidated both and reportedly lost his job as a result. . . .

In summary, state public schools have accepted a fair proportion of reservation Indian children on a nondiscriminatory basis—not always without special money inducement from the Federal Government in Federal schools. Some "Federal-Indian" children are admitted by some states only to segregated schools and, in some cases, they are not admitted to local public schools at all. Most nonreservation Indian children in southern states attend separate public schools.

It is therefore apparent that, with respect to non-Federal schooling, Indians in some states are denied equal protection of the laws.

ESTELLE FUCHS

Time to Redeem an Old Promise

STUDY QUESTIONS FOR COMPREHENSION

1. What is the BIA?
2. Are all Indians alike?
3. Summarize some of the educational problems Indians face.
4. What is meant by "termination" in this essay?
5. What does Estelle Fuchs suggest others can learn from the Indians?

The complexity of the issues raised by Indian education and the passion that pervades discussion of them can be understood only as part of the long and tortured history of Indian-white relations in this country. The Indian cannot easily forget the white man's attempts to exterminate his people, their forcible removal from ancestral lands, the efforts to convert them from their ancient religions, and the guarantees of rights to traditional homelands that were so often broken in practice. The record is varied; no one tribe's story is an exact duplicate of another's. But all share a history of subjugation and deliberate attempts to destroy their diverse cultures—sometimes by force, at other times by missionary zeal. And always their very identity and diversity (as Navahos, Pimas, Cherokees, Pawnees, etc.) were obscured by the common misnomer "Indian."

Concern for the education of American Indians appeared early in the history of the English colonies in the New World. Dartmouth was founded for the education of "youth of Indian tribes . . . and also of English youth and others." Harvard was established for the schooling of English and Indian youth, and the campus of William and Mary still treasures an early building erected for Indians. But the issues raised by the white man's efforts to extend the benefits of his educational tradition to the natives of the New World were clearly defined at an early date—and still endure. Benjamin Franklin told of the response by Indian leaders to an offer of education for Indian youth:

> You who are wise must know that different nations have different conceptions of things and will therefore not take it amiss if our ideas of this kind of education happen not to be the same as yours. We have had some experience with it. Several of our young people were formerly brought up at the colleges of the northern provinces; but when they came back to us, they were bad runners, ignorant of every means of living in the woods . . . totally good for nothing. We are, however . . . obliged by your kind offer . . . and to show our grateful sense of it, if the gentlemen of Virginia will send up a dozen of their sons, we will take great care of their educations; instruct them in all we know and make men of them.

Today, nearly a quarter of a million Indian children are in American schools. About half of them are the educational responsibility of the Bureau of Indian Affairs (BIA), which is an agency in the Department of the Interior. But the problems of education and cultural differences remain. After two years of exhaustive hearings on Indian education, a recent Senate subcommittee report was entitled "Indian Education: A National Tragedy—A National Challenge."

The dimensions of the problem are indicated by the record of absenteeism, retardation, and dropout rates in Indian schools. Yet, despite the dreary statistics, more Indian children are coming to school, and they are remaining in school longer. Thus, the issues in Indian education today cut to the core of the problems facing all American education—the quality of the educational environment, its responsiveness to the rich diversity of American life, the roles of federal and state governments in supporting the educational enterprise, and, perhaps most important of all, the degree to which the local community shall share in educational decision making.

The position of the Indian differs from that of other minorities, because Congress, as it extended its rule across the continent, recognized the Indian tribes as sovereign nations, and concluded some 400 separate treaties with them. Many of these agreements promised education as one of the federal services that would be provided in exchange for Indian lands.

From the beginning the federal government was uneasy about running schools itself and sought to turn over responsibility to other agencies. During the late nineteenth century, funds were distributed to various religious denominations to maintain mission schools. But public protest against federal aid to sectarian schools led the government to discontinue the practice. As a result, a system of federally operated schools was developed. (The government chose to close down two successful nineteenth century Indian school systems organized by the Cherokee and the Choctaw.)

Paying little attention to the multitude of linguistic and other cultural differences among the tribes, and the varied traditions of child rearing in preparation for adulthood in the tribal communities, the government entered the school business with a vigor that caused consternation among the Indians. The package deal that accompanied literacy included continuing efforts to "civilize the natives." Old abandoned Army forts were converted into boarding schools, children were removed—sometimes forcibly—long distances from their homes, the use of Indian languages by children was forbidden under threat of corporal punishment, students were boarded out to white families during vacation times, and native religions were suppressed. These practices were rationalized by the notion that the removal from the influence of home and tribe was the most effective means of preparing the Indian child to become an American.

The Carlisle Indian School in Pennsylvania, perhaps best known for its famous alumnus, the athlete Jim Thorpe, helped to usher in this ignominious period in the history of education for Indians. The policy might even have succeeded in obliterating Indian cultures and destroying Indian children, if it had not been for two factors. First, the facilities available were totally inadequate, leaving enormous numbers of children untouched by the policy's influence, and second, children resisted the system by running away, and lower echelon BIA personnel sometimes conspired with Indian families to keep the children at home.

Attempts to force Indians into the white man's mold extended to economic policy as well. The Dawes Act of 1887, ignoring the fact that the Indian had no tradition of private ownership of land, and that some tribes did no farming, distributed tracts of reservation lands, called allotments, in parcels of forty to 160 acres. The result was disastrous for the Indians, because the land left over after the allotments were made was declared surplus by the government, and some unsuccessful Indians lost even their allotments. But the result was extremely profitable for those who, by 1934, had managed to grab ninety million acres of former Indian lands.

Both the educational and the economic policies of this period led to the impoverishment of the Indians and to the shattering of their morale. The bitterness of that era remains in the living memory of many older Indians today.

The general pattern of corruption and intolerance of cultural differences that was characteristic of American society in the 1920s pervaded the Indian Service as well, and led to a Senate investigation that produced the best critical survey of federal Indian programs conducted to that date. The Meriam Report of 1928 called for a reversal of former policy in order to strengthen the Indian family and social structure rather than destroy it, to expand day schools and to humanize the boarding schools, to stimulate community participation, and to relate schooling more closely to the postschool needs of Indian youth.

The ensuing years ushered in a more humane and creative period in Indian affairs. It was the era of the New Deal and generally progressive legislation. John Collier, commissioner of Indian Affairs, was empathetic to Indian problems and a strong proponent of the value of cultural diversity and the rights of Indian peoples. The Indian Reorganization Act, passed in 1934, put a stop to land allotments. Tribal governments were formed, funds were pooled for the purchase of lost lands, and community schools were built. Although problems of poverty and economic development remained to be solved fully, it was a generally exciting and hopeful period.

World War II brought a cutback in federal spending for the New

Deal Indian programs, and before they could be vigorously renewed another radical reversal in policy took place that today leaves its mark in anger, suspicion, and fear that will not be easily erased.

The new policy, known as "termination," was instituted in the 1950s and aimed to sever reservations from the services of the Bureau of Indian Affairs. Although different in form, it smacked of the allotment era and other previous attempts by the government to escape its obligations to Indians by forcing them into the general population. Even when they received large sums of money for their lands, the Indians enjoyed little lasting benefit, and many former reservation residents became city dwellers—too often lower-class, with their income from tribal resources gone. The experience of the Klamath of Oregon, who lost their timberland income, has served as a warning to all reservation Indians. They are wary of any program leading in the direction of hated termination.

Although the termination policy has been currently halted, all contemporary issues in Indian affairs—including Indian education—are interpreted in the light of possible relationship to the ending of federal services to Indians.

Within this shifting pattern of government policy, the federal school system for Indians has grown tremendously in size and complexity from its small beginnings at the turn of the century. At present, the BIA operates 226 schools located in Alaska, Arizona, New Mexico, North Dakota, and South Dakota—states where the greatest concentrations of Indians are to be found. There are schools also in California, Florida, Iowa, Kansas, Louisiana, Mississippi, Montana, Nevada, North Carolina, Oklahoma, Oregon, and Utah.

Most of the schools located off reservations are secondary schools with boarding facilities. The majority of elementary schools, both day and boarding, are located on reservations. Attending this far-flung school system are almost 35,000 Indian children in boarding schools, more than 15,000 in day schools, and nearly 4,000 who are housed in dormitories close to reservations, while attending local public schools. The BIA also administers federal funds under the Johnson-O'Malley Act for some 63,000 Indian youngsters attending public schools on or near reservations, runs programs for some 30,000 adults, and offers a modest scholarship program for 4,000 college undergraduates.

Like other growing school systems, enrollment in the BIA schools doubled from 1959 to 1967. The present rate of growth of the Indian population on reservations is 3.3 per cent per year, three times the rate of increase for the national population at large. More than 200,000 Indians out of a total estimated population of fewer than a million are of school age, and the bureau is responsible for educating nearly half of them.

This natural population increase is compounded by the rather recent acceptance of universal schooling on the part of the Indians generally, and the growing expectation that it extend through secondary school and into college. At present, grades eight and ten have the highest dropout rates, but the numbers remaining in school longer appear to be growing yearly. A generation ago, for example, only one child out of four school-age Navahos was in school. Today, more than 90 per cent of the children are, and dropout rates are no greater than the national levels. The Hopi too are making extraordinary progress. But in some tribes the picture is far less bright.

To keep pace with growing enrollment, the BIA has sought to provide classroom space by a crash program of building schools both on and off the reservations. And because the federal government has not instituted the kind of road building program that would have made school attendance more feasible in remote areas, an extensive pattern of boarding schools has been maintained, and transfers to public schools have been encouraged.

Like schools all over the country, those for Indians are a mixed lot. While older buildings with unattractive barracks-like dormitories remain, the newer BIA schools are modern structures that could sit comfortably in any of the more affluent suburbs of the nation. Complete with inviting cafeterias, spacious dormitories with semiprivate sleeping quarters, large social halls, and auditorium-gymnasiums, they include modern classrooms with the latest textbooks and equipment. If these new school plants are to be subjected to any criticism, it is that they are too conventional, too much like schools that might be anywhere. They have not been imaginatively styled for the communities they serve. While conditions vary depending upon the administration, often the interiors of these suburban-type school buildings offer no indication that the children within them are Indian. There are, of course, notable exceptions, among them the Indian Arts and Crafts School at Santa Fe, which, although in an older building, clearly honors the Indian heritage of its students.

It is characteristic, too, that the usual federal school sits apart from the Indian community it serves. Located on or off reservation, in a compound surrounded by a fence, it is an enclave of federal property. On reservation, the life of the staff tends to be quite separate from that of the local people. The schools are characterized by what has come to be called "compound culture," in which staff members generally socialize with one another rather than with the Indians. There is little visiting back and forth in the community.

The BIA system has its share of concerned professionals as well as those who find safety within the protective confines of a tenured civil service system. And staff turnover is high; the isolation and the compound culture do not appeal to many.

With rare exceptions, employment in the schools of the BIA is subject to the rules and regulations of the federal civil service system. Consequently, teachers in Indian schools meet national standards. The civil service requires at least a B.A. degree from an accredited university and training in education or relatively high scores on national teaching tests. Salaries have also risen to national levels, ranging at present from $7,649 to $12,119. These standards represent a vast improvement over the past, and there are generally few differences between BIA teachers and public school teachers in regard to educational background, sex, experience, and age.

However, the establishment of rigid requirements for certification within the system seems to be operating to keep Indians from easily entering the teaching ranks. Efforts to improve this situation by the employment of paraprofessionals are being made, but these do not solve the problem of moving increasing numbers of Indian professionals into decision-making positions within the schools themselves.

At present, 16 per cent of the teachers in BIA schools are Indians. But fewer Indians are entering teaching now, compared with twenty years ago, and most Indian teachers are not assigned to teach in their home communities.

Controversy over goals for Indian education becomes evident in the area of curriculum. Inhumane, forced assimilationist practices are largely a thing of the past. Today, some would like to see the schools emphasize traditional Indian life. Others see the schools serving the function of teaching "Anglo" culture. Growing among Indians and educators alike is the desire to develop curricula that are pluralistic in emphases—retaining respect for the various Indian traditions and for Indian identity while teaching skills needed for life in urban, industrial America as well as on the reservations, where new economic and political developments are taking place.

The complexity of the curriculum problem is indicated by the fact that even today two-thirds of all Indian children entering BIA schools have little or no skill in English. There are nearly 300 Indian languages in use today; more than one-half of the Indian youth between the ages of six and eighteen use their native tongue. All Indians express a concern that the schools teach English, and experience indicates that programs in Teaching English as a Second Language (TESL) provide a more valid and humane way to teach English than to depend upon exposure. TESL programs have been developed and instituted, but funding language programs in both BIA and public schools is a perennial problem. Of the $7.5-million appropriated for the National Bilingual Education Act, only $300,000 is being spent on Indian programs benefiting 773 children.

Aside from the TESL program, curriculum and methodology for Indian children are little different from those employed in schools throughout America. Minimum or no attention is given to the Indian heritage, or to contemporary issues in Indian life. On the whole, attention to the pedagogical complexities of cross-cultural education has been neglected by educators despite their clear relationship to school success or failure, and very few social scientists have concerned themselves with Indian children and the preparation of teachers to work especially in this setting. It is usual for the schools to ignore the cultural heritage of the children as if it didn't exist—or worse, as if it required eradication.

An exciting departure in Indian education is provided by the program of the DINE (Demonstration in Navaho Education) experimental school at Rough Rock, Arizona. Instruction in Navaho language and culture is part of the curriculum, and the school itself is supervised by an all-Navaho school board. The newly organized first Indian college, the Navaho Junior College at Many Farms, is also gearing its curriculum to the special needs of Indian students. These are among the first tribal-run schools since the Choctaw and the Cherokee ran their own school systems during the last century.

Critics of the BIA and its schools are responding to conditions that are sometimes peculiar to the BIA, but in other cases are not unlike those found throughout American education: the discontinuity between teacher education institutions and the schools in which their graduates will be teaching; the inadequate number of Indians recruited into teaching; the lack of understanding and empathy for the culturally different and the poor; unsuitable instructional materials; inadequate professional leadership; and the lack of involvement of the communities being served.

Aside from its inheritance of distrust and suspicion stemming from an earlier era, the BIA is also beset with all the usual problems faced by an entrenched bureaucratic system. Official policy from above is often frustrated by inadequate execution in the field. Indeed, the educational staff in the field is responsible to BIA area offices concerned with many matters other than education, rather than to the director of educational programs.

Also, the system tends to encourage the maintenance of the traditional structure and methods; advancement into administration is through the ranks and encourages the promotion of those defensive of the system rather than those who are innovative or experimentally inclined. Most important, responsibility and accountability, at all levels, are to the bureau rather than to the Indian communities.

Part of the BIA's difficulty is due to the fact that, while it maintains an educational system of its own, it has been committed to the principle that, whenever possible, Indian children should be placed in public schools. This policy is in keeping with assimilationist goals, the general reluctance of the federal government to run a school system, and the unwillingness, except on a small experimental basis, to allow Indians to run their own schools. This ambivalent position of presiding over a school system dedicated to its own demise is not conducive to adequate Congressional funding, support, and planning.

States and local communities generally have been unwilling to assume educational responsibility for Indians living on reservations because the land is tax-free. Therefore, the federal government has provided subsidies to reimburse public schools for the education of Indian students.

But the transfer of Indians to public schools is a two-edged sword. On the one hand, it seems reasonable that public education allows the Indian child access to common schooling along with others. It appears to encourage integration, and it supports the rights of states to oversee education. It appeals to liberals as a means of rescuing Indians from the custodianship of the BIA, which smacks of a colonial service.

On the other hand, attendance at public schools has frequently placed the Indian child in the position of a minority group within a largely white institution. It often puts him in a position of economic and social disadvantage, especially in areas with long histories of antipathy toward the Indian population. Sometimes the public schools are a greater distance from home than the bureau day schools, and in some instances the federally supervised BIA school is superior to the local public school in facilities and staff, as well as in attention to the special needs of Indian children.

In addition, Indians have rarely been in a strong political position in their local communities, and thus have had little say over the design of programs and the allocation of funds received for their people by the local school districts. And again, in the light of the long history of Indian-white relations, transfer to public schools without approval of the local Indian community is suspected as a policy of reneging on the federal obligations to provide education.

Growing Indian political consciousness has led several Rio

Grande pueblos to institute court actions charging misappropriations of federal funds by local public school boards; Indians are exercising their vote to elect school board members; and demands are being made that no school transfers take place without community approval.

Increasingly, nevertheless, the problems of Indian education are likely to be found in the public schools. Since World War II, growing numbers of American Indians, together with other rural Americans, have moved to the cities. Some have gone on their own, searching for jobs, others in urban relocation programs designed by the federal government to assist young Indians to move from the reservations to urban employment. One-third of the Indian population now lives in cities, although for many reservation ties remain strong and there is much moving back and forth.

For those Indian children who are recent migrants to the city, school generally means attendance at a large, inner-city slum school, where they are submerged among the rest of the "disadvantaged" children of the city. The absence of special programs to meet their particular needs, plus the high transiency rate typical of many, is not conducive to successful completion of school programs, and dropout rates are high. As members of the urban poor, they lose out in the competition with other larger and more powerful minorities as recipients of federal programs.

Virtually every critic of American Indian education has pointed to the urgent need to elevate the BIA, which is now a relatively low-level bureau within the Department of the Interior. Some, such as Alvin M. Josephy reporting to President Kennedy, have argued for transferring the BIA to the executive office of the President where it would be more visible and have a mandate for change. Others have urged that it be transferred to the Department of Health, Education, and Welfare, kept intact, and be placed under an Assistant Secretary or Administrator for Indian Affairs. Still others have proposed that the educational functions of the BIA be transferred to the Office of Education in HEW. A proposal for a more fundamental change was made in a Carnegie Corporation report that called for the creation of a federal commission to assume control of Indian education, with an explicit mandate to transfer this control to Indian communities within five years. The report was careful to state that it was not calling for termination, but rather the continuation of federal responsibility except with Indian control.

The recent Senate subcommittee report elected to retain the BIA in an elevated position within the Department of the Interior. Taking a strong stand in favor of fulfilling federal responsibilities to Indians, it urged that the federal Indian school system be developed into an exemplary system that can play an important role in improving education for Indian children. In addition, it recommended increased and extended funding to public schools, calling for the involvement of Indians in the planning, execution, and evaluation of the use to which the funds are put. Over and above the strengthening of existing schools, it urged policies that permit tribal governments and Indian communities to run their own schools.

In calling for the government to commit itself to a national policy of educational excellence for Indian children, the report emphasized the need for maximum participation and control by Indian adults and communities, more demonstration and experimental programs, and a substantial increase in appropriations to achieve these goals.

The 1960s was a period of intense search and evaluation concerning American Indian education. It began with great hope for change with President Kennedy's proposed task force to examine the problems, and ended with a call for a national commitment to excellence. In the interim, while termination practices have halted, little has happened to change the Indians' basic position of powerlessness, and Indian affairs have continued to take a back seat in Department of the Interior programs.

It is too soon to judge the policies of the 1970s, but certain aspects are clear. The myths of the vanishing and silent Indians have been shattered. Active participation and organization by American Indians themselves are growing, whether in the National Congress of American Indian Tribes, meetings such as the National Indian Education Conference, or the proliferating groups of organized college students and "Red Power" advocates.

Despite the pessimistic past there is still time and great promise for America. The heterogeneity of the Indian populations matches that of the nation. If we can be responsive to the education needs of culturally different groups, many of whose members resist loss of identity in a common, bland "melting pot," if we can provide flexible programs with massive federal funding that allows people themselves to engage in the educational enterprise and to develop the programs best suited for their children, we will have gone a long way in tackling the needs of all American education.

The old chiefs are gone; the young men are to be found in school rather than in the woods, but the lesson is clear. It is not just the Indian who has to learn from us, there is much to be learned from him—the values inherent in group identity; respect for nature; the right of men to participate in the institutions that affect their lives; and that no policy or program, regardless of how well intended, will succeed without his approval.

DAN O'NEILL

Odd Bodkins

Courtesy of Chronicle Features Syndicate

BILOINE W. YOUNG

The American Indian: Citizen in Captivity

STUDY QUESTIONS FOR COMPREHENSION

1. Explain why Mrs. Yazzi did not participate in the negotiations for the sale of her land.
2. What does the word "paternalism" mean? How is it used in this article?
3. What factors handicap the Indian student?

The school board of a city in the Southwest bordering an Indian reservation had been looking for a tract of land to acquire as a site for a new public high school. The acreage finally selected was owned by a Mrs. Yazzi, a Navajo (the name is fictitious, but the incident isn't). When the superintendent of schools opened negotiations to purchase the land he learned that he would not be dealing with Mrs. Yazzi, nor with her attorney, but with the realty agent for the Bureau of Indian Affairs of the Navajo Agency. This agent would do the negotiating, make all of the decisions (including whether or not to sell the land), and would stipulate the terms of the sale. If the sale is consummated, the income derived will not be given to Mrs. Yazzi but will be invested for her by the Bureau realty officer.

The federal government has intervened in the sale of the Yazzi land for one reason alone: Mrs. Yazzi is an American Indian. Although she is an adult, mentally competent, a citizen of the United States, a speaker of English, Mrs. Yazzi cannot, without permission from the Secretary of the Interior, enter into a contract with an attorney to sell her land for her. Nor can she sell, lease, rent, or give it away herself without authorization from the Department of the Interior. Ever since its establishment in 1824, the Bureau of Indian Affairs has op-

From *Saturday Review*, December 11, 1965. Reprinted by permission of the author.

erated under a set of paternalistic assumptions about the Indians that have resulted not in a participating citizenship for them (as they were surely designed to do) but in the perpetuation of isolation, dependence on government charity, and the illusion of self-government through a cluster of quasi-nations housed on government-granted enclaves throughout the country.

Overseeing the lives of most of the Indians in the United States is the Bureau of Indian Affairs, a vast agency under the Secretary of the Interior. The Bureau provides schooling, social services, jobs, and, through the Public Health Service, free medical and dental care for most of the 552,228 Indians living on 286 separate land units. Through the Bureau of Indian Affairs the federal government acts as a trustee "to protect the interests of minors and incompetents," to quote the expression used in the booklet *Answers to Questions About American Indians,* published by the Department of the Interior.

If the Bureau of Indian Affairs views its Indian trusts as "minors and incompetents" it is not surprising that a great many of the Indians have also come to accept this view of themselves. Many Indians now expect to be retarded in school. They expect to drink to excess (when an Indian alcoholic was asked why he drank, he replied, "Because I'm an Indian").

In their application for the Community Action Program (approved and funded March 3, 1965, by the Office of Economic Opportunity) the Navajo themselves identify these attitudes as being among their more severe problems. In their proposal they wrote, "One of the greatest needs existing today on the Navajo reservation lies in creating a feeling that the people in the isolated areas are important and that they do have an important role in determining their own future and destiny. . . . Many Navajos believe their future lies outside their control, and a dependency on either the Bureau of Indian Affairs or the Navajo Tribe has been substituted."

Although Mrs. Yazzi was present at the meeting between the Bureau officials and the school board to negotiate the sale of her land, she did not participate in the discussion. She, and everyone else, knew that she was only the figurehead owner of the land, that her presence at the meeting was only to perpetuate a fiction. She was not expected to take any part in the negotiations and so she did not.

The land owned by Mrs. Yazzi is known as "allotment land." There are currently about 4,185 allotments of 160 acres each still remaining in the Navajo country. These are similar in origin to homestead lands. Between 1907 and 1922 federal officers allotted 160 acres of land in the public domain to heads of Indian families and equal acreages for wives and each of the children. These allotments were made to protect Indians who were living on the public domain in the tenure of their land.

Although the Indians may have been under the impression that they held exclusive titles to their allotted land, they were mistaken. As the *Navajo Yearbook* explains it, "The United States Government holds, in trust for the Navajo Tribe, the title to the Reservation lands, including those areas purchased by the Tribe; and the United States government holds, in trust status for recipients of allotments or for their heirs, title to such areas of individual ownership. As trustee, the Federal Government is responsible for protection and management of property to which title is vested in Indian Tribes (or in individuals, in the case of trust allotments) and this responsibility is exercised, in part, by the Branch of Realty. The functions of this agency of the Federal Government include the sale, exchange, partition, patenting and leasing of Tribal and allotted lands. . . ."

Federal involvement with the Indians is divided into four major areas: land management, health services, education, and industrial development. The Bureau is also trying to teach the Indian how to govern himself through the establishment of various carefully controlled tribal organizations or pseudo-nations.

The paternalism of the government toward the Indians is nowhere better illustrated than in Public Law 474, passed by the Eighty-first Congress. Section 6 of the act authorizes the Navajo tribe to draw up a tribal constitution: "The constitution shall authorize the fullest possible participation of the Navajos in the administration of their affairs as approved by the Secretary of the Interior and shall become effective when approved by the Secretary. The constitution may be amended from time to time . . . and the Secretary of the Interior shall approve any amendment which in the opinion of the Secretary of the

Interior advances the development of the Navajo people. . . ." Tribal funds may be spent only upon approval of the Secretary of the Interior. The tribe is also prohibited from entering into an agreement with an attorney involving tribal lands or funds.

The tragedy of the Indian is that, although he is an adult in the world of adults, he is still going through the adolescent play-acting of governing himself—playing at making decisions when, in reality, these decisions are being made for him by agents of the federal government. This federal trusteeship has not resulted, by and large, in the development of citizens who are particularly noted for their ability to make wise choices. The Navajo tribe, the largest single group of Indians in the United States (in 1960 they totaled 80,364 and, according to the Navajos, may have passed the 100,000 mark by now), has a birth rate that is one of the highest in the world, estimated at from 4.5 to 7 per cent annually; a rate of alcoholism that runs from an estimated 10 to 20 per cent of the adult population, topping that of almost any other group in the country; and a per capita income that is among the lowest in the nation. Problem drinking has long been associated with cultural stress. Gallup, New Mexico, known as the Indian capital, averages 750 arrests per month for drinking. Ninety per cent of those arrested are Indians. In 1958, 83 per cent of all the crimes committed by Navajos involved excessive drinking.

The Bureau of Indian Affairs in 1961 estimated the average per capita income among the Navajo at about $521. If each family contains five members, then the average family income would be approximately $2,600. When the value of free goods and services is included, the average per capita rises to about $645 and the average family income to about $3,225. This is 35.6 per cent of the comparable amount received by other citizens of New Mexico and only 29.8 per cent of the comparable amount received by fellow citizens of the United States.

The Indians themselves, however, declare their income to be far below the Bureau's estimates. In their application to the Office of Economic Opportunity for funds to initiate a Community Action Program, the Navajos estimated their average family income at $600 per year. Of 16,000 families now living on the reservation, 12,800 are listed as earning less than $1,000 per year. Of a total of 15,000 housing units extant, 13,000 are listed as substandard, with an average of six persons occupying each room.

The relationship between education and social and economic development has long been observed, and it is on education that the Bureau of Indian Affairs has spent the major portion of its budget, more than $121,000,000 for the current fiscal year. Despite these expenditures, the Indians continue to be retarded educationally. Of 9,751 elementary-level Navajo children whose records were analyzed in December 1957, only 6 per cent were up to grade level, 40 per cent were retarded at least one year, and 54 per cent were retarded two or more years.

Moreover, when the records of 100 Southwest Indians enrolled at the University of New Mexico between 1954 and 1958 were studied, they showed that 70 per cent dropped out of school with low grades, 20 per cent were currently enrolled, and 10 per cent obtained degrees. Of the 30 per cent who remained in school or obtained degrees, the majority were at some time placed on probation for inadequate scholarship. Of the thirty-one Indian students enrolled at the University of New Mexico in 1958, 84 per cent did not finish the first semester with a C average.

What holds back the Indian students? A lack of knowledge of English is the single most serious cause of Indian retardation in school, according to Dr. Anne Smith, of the Museum of New Mexico. Yet neither the Bureau of Indian Affairs nor the State Department of Education of New Mexico makes any requirement that elementary teachers in either the Bureau or public schools have training in the teaching of English as a second language.

A second factor in the retardation of Indian children is the segregated schooling provided by the Bureau of Indian Affairs. In Bureau schools, attended only by Indian children, the cultural and linguistic isolation of the reservation is institutionalized and perpetuated. Although the stated policy of the Bureau is to place Indian children in public schools as rapidly as possible, Commissioner of Indian Affairs Philleo Nash, in a speech in June 1965, reported that contracts totaling more than $8,000,000 had been let for Indian school construction since the beginning of 1965—despite the fact that research indicates that Indian children perform better in public than in Bureau schools.

More than six years ago the Bureau agreed to place 1,000 Indian students in the Albuquerque school system, but to date it has placed only 339. Recently the Bureau announced plans to build a $13,000,000 boarding school in Albuquerque. The plan was temporarily dropped after an outcry from the New Mexico State Department of Education and public school superintendents in the state.

The experience of Dr. Charles Spain, late superintendent of the Albuquerque schools, is typical. Dr. Spain says, "The BIA [Bureau of Indian Affairs] has never contacted the schools to see if special classes could be arranged to better prepare more students for entering public schools. We've never been informed why the BIA isn't meeting its contractual obligations to send 1,000 students a year to the public schools." Dr. Spain adds that BIA has never approached the Albuquerque system to accept students at an earlier age, or to provide special remedial classes, to include them in planning for the Technical-Vocational Institute, or otherwise try to work out arrangements for incorporating more students in the schools. "We would be happy to work with the BIA to work out some of these problems. But they haven't asked us."

Segregated Bureau of Indian Affairs schools are continuing to be built, one within ten miles of Gallup, New Mexico.

Despite the Indian's economic and educational failures, and despite his alcoholic response to the stresses of living simultaneously in two cultures, he is showing signs of impatience with his role as a "minor and incompetent." Many are saying they want to manage their own affairs. Unfortunately, they must convince the Bureau of Indian Affairs that they are ready to do more than play at making their own decisions. The way it is now, the quiet Bureau agent who sits at the back of the Chapter House meetings can outvote the whole tribe. In subtle ways we still hold the Indian captive. Isn't it time we inaugurated a constructive program to set him free?

STINA SANTIESTEVAN

Racism Is Crazy

STUDY QUESTIONS FOR COMPREHENSION

1. What did the UNESCO scientists discover about the differences between one race and another?
2. What does the author mean by her statement that as a matter of scientific fact "All marriages everywhere can be called mixed," but that in another sense "No marriage anywhere can be called mixed"?
3. What validity do the findings of scientists give to racist theories?

Racism is nonsense.

It violates our common sense and our moral code and that's enough for most of us.

But last year a group of the world's best scientists got together to look into the matter.

After they had conscientiously listened to each other, read all the reports, surveyed all the research, and peered into the nooks and crannies of their knowledge, they issued a statement that said:

Racism is nonsense.

These scientists—22 of them from the world's major universities and centers of scholarship—together wrote a unanimous declaration on biological aspects of race. They met at the request of UNESCO—the UN's Economic and Social Council—in August 1964.

Included in the group were specialists in anthropology, genetics, biology, haematology, sociology, medicine, historical research.

They had traveled from London, Montreal, Caracas, Paris, Mexico City, Dakar, Calcutta, Oslo, Tokyo, Philadelphia, and when they had completed their meetings they said:

"All men living today belong to a single species, *Homo sapiens,* and are derived from a common stock."

They also said, emphatically and unanimously, there is no na-

From Industrial Union Department Agenda, AFL-CIO, December 1965.

tional or religious or geographic or linguistic or cultural group which properly can be called a race, and all races today are about as pure as an alleycat's kittens.

History and not biology has created any achievement differences we see in races today. The scientists put it in their own language:

"The peoples of the world today appear to possess equal biological potentialities for attaining any civilization level."

The scientists agreed you *can* classify mankind into several apparently major "stocks" (three are usually recognized by anthropologists) but you have to sharpen your focus right away if you intend to apply this classification to today's world:

> The UNESCO scientists first point to variations in human characteristics—on which are based any classification into stocks or races—and remind us that variations are common *within* a supposed race. In other words, many Negroes have straight hair and many Caucasians have dark skin.
>
> These same variations flow in and out of one another, all around the planet, without any distinct divisions. As one scientist wrote:
>
> "If one were to go on foot from the sources of the Nile to the Nile delta, then across the Arab countries of Asia, through Turkey, Bulgaria, Rumania and Ukraine to northern Russia and finally towards Mongolia via the homes of the Udmurt, Bashkir, and Kazakh peoples, no difference of physical type would be apparent between the inhabitants of any neighboring points on this route." If you take a man at the beginning and a man at the midpoint and a man at the end of your journey, they of course would be obviously different from each other.
>
> Human history—migration, conquest, war—is an egg beater which continually has blended this mish-mash called humanity.
>
> Therefore, to cubbyhole correctly any particular group of human beings living today is about impossible.

And besides, said those UNESCO sages, individual people *within* a group may differ more—one from another—than the average man of one race or population group from the average man of another. And these average men are much more like each other than they are unlike each other.

Certain human traits are universally necessary for survival. These traits turn up in *everybody*—pink, beige, golden, or fudge color. Our human *differences*—on which racial cubbyholing is based—have nothing to do with these universal survival traits, so it makes no sense to talk about the biological superiority or inferiority of this or that race.

Mental ability is one of those survival traits. Your characteristic ability to think in your brain, walk on your hind feet, grasp with your thumbs and fingers, and use your several senses is part of the equipment you have to have in order to survive. Your characteristic skin color and the texture of your hair and the shape of your nose in no way affect survival (except in certain Southern states, perhaps!) but do add pleasing variety to the human family.

Traits generally called racial are inherited independently of one another and not passed on to the next generation in unchanging combinations. Traits often lumped together—(thick lips, kinky hair, dark skin)—are not always found within a single individual (some Negroes have kinky hair and thin lips, some have thick lips and straight hair, and some Caucasians have all these traits).

Most of the obvious physical differences between people living in different parts of the world are caused by differences in the *frequency* of the hereditary characteristics which are being observed. In other words, genes bearing flared noses may be more frequently transmitted to offspring of parents living in a particular Alaskan river valley, say, or long straight-nosed babies may be more frequently born in southern Sweden, but there will be some babies in the Alaskan valley with long straight noses and some Swedish babies with flared noses.

Each person in a population is the product of a unique combination of genes which he got from his parents. Each of these combinations has been differently affected.

—by natural selection (which in man, however, has tended

toward adaptation to the environment rather than any genetic adaptation),

—by lucky mutations, and

—by accidental, random concentrations of various genes bearing characteristics which have come to be called racial.

Much more than any other animal, man has shown stubborn adaptability to all kinds of environments (and we are getting better and better at this non-genetic adaptability, too, adapting to everything from empty space to the waters under the earth and all points between—coal mines, Swiss Alps, South Seas, Harlem).

History, ancient to modern, shows that any progress we've made was made by passing along our cultural and environment-taming achievements (books, know-how to dam a river, plows, filing cabinets, micro-biology) and not by any transmission of genes bearing racial characteristics. This means that having white, Anglo-Saxon Protestant babies won't guarantee progress, but educating babies—all kinds of babies—will bring progress if we do the job properly.

Babies . . .

Sooner or later, in any discussion of races and the relationships between races, sex gets into the conversation. "Would you want your sister to marry one?"

"Why not?" say the biologists and the geneticists.

Interbreeding—"miscegenation"—has gone on for centuries, at least as far back as history can take us and probably much further. This mixing gets more and more frequent and of course the mixed offspring multiply too.

So, said UNESCO's anthropologists and biologists, apparently distinct races are at any given time involved in a process of emergence or dissolution, and as geographical and social barriers are broken or revised, the breeding population is enlarged or shifted and racial clues are further diluted.

Like coastlines and water levels, the races we think we can distinguish today were quite different in an earlier age and will be different in the future, Debetz says:

"In central Europe as in other regions, the human head has become much rounder over the last eight centuries but more recently has tended to lengthen again; the average height in certain countries has risen by ten centimeters in the last 100 years."

"Miscegenation" is neither new nor evil.

As a matter of scientific fact all marriages everywhere can be called mixed. And in another sense of course, no marriage anywhere can be called mixed. We are all specimens of that single species after all.

Before they went home to their laboratories and libraries and museums, the UNESCO scientists wrote a conclusion to their statement:

"Neither in the field of hereditary potentialities concerning the overall intelligence and the capacity for cultural development, nor in that of physical traits, is there any justification for the concept of 'inferior' and 'superior' races.

"The biological data given . . . are in open contradiction to the tenets of racism. Racist theories can in no way pretend to have any scientific foundation. . . ."

Go tell it on the mountains, over the hills, and everywhere!

NICK C. VACA

The Purchase

STUDY QUESTIONS FOR COMPREHENSION

1. Why does Doña Lupe finally embroider dish towels?
2. Could this incident happen to a member of another minority group?
3. How do you suppose a young person might react if she were subjected to the same situation?

"Ave Maria Purísima, I must make another pago hoy or else it'll be too late. Si, too late and then what would I do? Christmas is so close and if I don't hurry con los pagos I'll have nothing to give any of mis hijos. If that should happen it would weigh muy pesado on my mind. Even now, con el pensamiento that I may not be able to give them anything, I have trouble durmiendo en la noche. And, Santo Niño de Atocha, if Christmas should come and catch me sin nada I would never sleep well por el resto de mi vida."

Sitting on a large, bulky sofa, its brown cover worn and frayed at the arm rests and back, Doña Lupe was thinking over the progress she had made in her Christmas shopping. Surrounded by the wrinkles of her small, sad face, two dark eyes closed and opened intermittently as her grey head nodded in deep absorption, figuring the amount of time and money she needed to complete her shopping. Becoming agitated with pleasure and anxiety she lifted her thin body off the sofa, wrapped her faded green sweater around her waist and began shuffling from one end of the three-room apartment to the other as she tightly pursed her thin lips and placed her gathered fingers on her sunken cheeks, again losing herself in a world of calculations. As she reached the far end of her apartment she stopped at the bay window, gathered her arms about herself and dropped her head slightly to one side. Outside the sky was a cold gray with the dark clouds and fog combining to form low, dark shadows that covered

From *El Espejo–The Mirror,* ed. Octavio Ignacio Romano V. (Berkeley: Quinto Sol Publications, 1969). Reprinted by permission of the author.

Stockton as far as Doña Lupe could see. Below her apartment an elm tree with morning dew drops still fresh on its naked branches began to sway slightly as the first gush of cold morning wind disturbed its somnolent serenity, causing Doña Lupe to shiver slightly. Shuffling to the kitchen table, she sat down and pulled a grease-spotted piece of brown paper out of her apron pocket. Clearing the salt shaker, a bowl of chili salsa, and some cold tortillas that remained from last evening's dinner, Doña Lupe placed the paper on the table. As she squinted under the light of the naked light bulb that hung directly overhead, her fingers underlined names and x's on the paper. The names were those of her children and the x's indicated who had been bought a gift. The names were meaningless. That is, they meant a great deal to her but she did not know them. Doña Lupe could not read. But she had memorized them in the order that they appeared on the paper after having Antonio, her youngest son, read them over and over to her during the past two months; so now even if she didn't know how to read she knew for whom the various scrawlings stood. The list began with Gilbert, her eldest son, and ended with Gloria, her youngest daughter, and everyone but Rudy, who was in the Army, had the large, dark trembling "x" of her black grease pencil.

Had anyone told Doña Lupe three years ago when her husband died that she would be able to buy store gifts for her children she would have shaken her head in polite disagreement. Her monthly welfare allowance only covered the necessities that life imposed on her—the rent of her apartment, her food, clothing, and her weekly movie at the Mexican movie house every Saturday with Doña Pifora, another widow who met her necessities in the same manner. To even think that she would ever be able to buy store gifts for her children was very much out of the question. As Doña Lupe reasoned, either she had to come into a lot of money or she would have to buy on credit. The chances of her coming into a lot of money did not even occupy her thoughts and credit, well, that was something that only people with money could afford. So she contented herself with giving her daughters colorfully embroidered dish towels and inexpensive handkerchiefs to her sons. That's the way it had been for the past five years, ever since her husband's death when a lack of money and friends had driven her to her apartment and her daily existence. And so it would have probably continued until her death had she not sighed during one of her Saturday movie dates with Doña Pifora.

"Ay, Doña Pifora, Christmas is coming again, and I have to start making mis hijos something again. I'm getting tired of giving them the same thing year after year. I know they don't mind my presents, but I do. You know how it is, you have hijos of your own, it's not like you're ignorant of the matter."

Doña Pifora nodded in agreement.

"It's difficult to explain," continued Doña Lupe, "but when you don't give your hijos anything for Christmas you don't feel good inside. My hijos tell me that it doesn't matter, that I shouldn't even think about giving gifts to so many of them. They say its silly what I do every year, but I still feel bad if I can't give them anything for Christmas. Christmas is special, and special times shouldn't go unnoticed."

"Well," inquired Doña Pifora, "why don't you give them gifts from the store? They're right you know. It's too much what you do for them each year," added Doña Pifora cautiously.

"Why?" answered Doña Lupe. "You know that all my money, every bit of it, is used en la casa. For food, la renta, some clothing, things like that. That's why. I don't have money to go around buying store presents."

"Of course you do," countered Doña Pifora, "everybody does. Listen, it's clear you haven't heard of lay-away," Doña Pifora declared so loudly that several people in the foyer of the theater turned and looked at them.

"Lay-away, ¿qué es eso?" inquired Doña Lupe.

"It's like credit," proceeded Doña Pifora, "but not really credit. That is, it works almost the same. What you do is this. You go to a store that has lay-away and look around. If you find something you like, you just take it to the counter and tell the lady you want to buy it, but that you don't have enough money and that you would like it put on lay-away. Then you give the lady about fifty cents or whatever you have. Then every week or when you have money you give them what you can. The only thing is that you can't have the thing you want until you pay for it."

"What?" asked Doña Lupe.

"Oh, sí, until you finish the payments you can't have it," answered Doña Pifora.

"Well, that's not too bad, I guess," said Doña Lupe. "After all it's only fair that they should keep the things until you finish paying for them. It's the only right thing to do."

"Where do they have this lay-away, Doña Pifora?" inquired Doña Lupe.

"Well I always do my lay-away at Clifford's, you know, the store on the big street with the large trees across from the big hotel," answered Doña Pifora.

"Clifford's, eh?" added Doña Lupe softly, almost to herself.

Though Doña Lupe feigned a mild interest in the lay-away plan, her heart was beating furiously with excitement at the prospect that for the first time in five years she would have a chance to give her children some store-bought presents. What she had told Doña Pifora about needing all her money was true. But for store gifts she would sacrifice a little. Perhaps she didn't have to eat as well, not buy any clothes for a while, and give up her Saturday movies. That would be the most painful sacrifice, but she would do it.

It was on a cold and windy October morning when Doña Lupe set out for Clifford's, a dollar in her apron pocket and a head full of dreams. As she shuffled past children playing in the park near her house the autumn leaves swirled about her feet and the crisp morning air foretold the coming of winter. Clifford's was a variety store of the sort that sold most anything, and the anything it sold was generally of poor quality. It was to this store that most of the pensioners and mothers on welfare came to buy their clothing, ironing boards, sweets, and the other necessities that the corner grocery store could not provide. In short, it was the type of store that can be found in almost any small town in the San Joaquin Valley. Catering to the poor and aged, Clifford's reflected its attitude toward its clientele in the arrangement and treatment of its goods. Shoes were thrown in with plastic balls, orlon sweaters were placed alongside cans of paint; potted plants were surrounded by greeting cards, and the floor was unswept. The clerks were generally fresh out of high school and even if they had worked at Clifford's for years they still looked as if they were fresh out of high school. They chewed gum as they arranged items on counters and engaged in conversation with each other while they waited on customers. The boys would shoulder each other as they worked in pairs along the aisles. The young girls would constantly pat their hair to insure its perfection.

Ambling along the aisles looking cautiously at items, even daring to touch and examine them, Doña Lupe attempted to settle in her mind that the explanation Doña Pifora had made of the lay-away was both real and accurate and what she saw could be hers. Whatever doubts she had about the existence of lay-away were dispelled by the sense of exhilaration that she could own what she saw. Her eyes moved rapidly, selecting items with her eyes tightened to cover the smile that strove to break through all her restraint. For Ruth she chose a black porcelain cat with diamond eyes that sparkled nicely when they were held against the light; for Felicia she chose a bouquet of plastic flowers; for Antonio she chose a gold colored key chain; for Antonia she chose a porcelain collie dog, and so it went until all ten children had been selected presents. Cradling them in her arms she carefully placed them one by one on the counter as the clerk, a girl of about eighteen years with pimples and heavy make-up, began to examine them. Before the girl could begin totaling the items, the words "lay-away" slipped from Doña Lupe's mouth. The young girl's forehead furrowed.

"What?" she said.

"Lay-away," blurted Doña Lupe.

"Oh yea, wait a minute, huh," mumbled the girl.

Turning towards the back of the store the girl shouted, "Oh, Mr. Clifford, this Mexican woman wants this stuff on lay-away."

From behind the candy counter a tall man, with thinning hair, wire rim glasses, a large straight nose, and a pale, colorless face approached Doña Lupe.

"Want this stuff on lay-away, huh?" he asked.

"Lay-away," repeated Doña Lupe. Her English was limited, but she felt that lay-away was all the man needed to know. If such a thing existed she knew that it would be self-explanatory. If it didn't exist, it was no use trying to explain how it worked, especially if she had to refer to Doña Pifora. Because if lay-away didn't exist then how would he know about Doña Pifora.

"Yea, alright," said the tall man in a resigned tone.

The items, all of them, totalled twenty-five dollars. Writing out a receipt for the items the tall man placed them in a cardboard box, taped the receipt on the box and placed it underneath the counter, then he turned to Doña Lupe and said,

"How much you gonna put down?"

Doña Lupe reached into her apron pocket and pulled out the crumpled dollar she had saved in the last week and placed it on the counter.

"Just one dollar. That all you gonna put down?" inquired the man.

Doña Lupe nodded her head.

"Well if that's all you got that's all you got," said the tall man philosophically as he placed the dollar in the cash register.

"You know the deal," continued the tall man, "come in every week and give a dollar or whatever you got to give and when you finish paying the twenty-five dollars then you get the stuff. Okay?"

Doña Lupe nodded her head and shuffled out the door happy that the October wind was cold, the sun bright, and that winter was on its way.

That had occurred two months ago, or as Doña Lupe counted, eight payments ago. Now all she had left to pay was $6.43, and today was the ninth week of her payments. This week she planned to pay three dollars, which she had saved by . . . well modesty hoards that secret, and next week she planned to pay the remaining amount.

As she reached the kitchen table for the fifth time in her pacing, Doña Lupe stopped and noticed that the clock showed eight. She put on her heavy coat, placed a black scarf on her head, and stepped into the dull December day with the fog still hanging low and the houses and trees shivering in the damp morning. The thought that this was the second to the last payment gave her a feeling of modest satisfaction that even such a sad morning could not dispel. As was now the custom, when she made her payments she was usually the only customer in the store at such an early hour. Following her usual routine she located the tall man in the back of the store and paid her three dollars; but instead of leaving the store as was her usual fashion, she lingered along the aisles looking and holding things that caught her attention—plastic flowers, small, furry dogs that squealed when squeezed and made Doña Lupe smile, sweaters, velvet ribbons. Having satisfied her curiosity she slowly shuffled out the door. As she began crossing the street her right arm was grabbed and a nervous but firm voice said,

"All right lady, what you got?"

Doña Lupe turned to see a tall, redheaded boy wearing the familiar green smock that all Clifford's employees were made to wear. The boy could not have been over seventeen years, and his young face showed a combination of determination and confusion. Doña Lupe was dumfounded.

"Yea, don't act dumb, what you got? What's under the coat? I know it's there. You weren't walking around for so long for nothing. I had my eye on you. Come on now, what is it? We get your kind all the time. Walk around acting dumb and then pinch something like nothing happened."

Flustered from embarrassment and hurt at the thought that she should be accused of stealing, Doña Lupe simply stared at the young man. In her sixty-eight years of life she had never stolen a thing, and to be accused of such an act was the most horrible thing she could imagine. She held herself stiffly.

"All right since you're not gonna talk, then let's see what you got."

The young man flung open her coat to find that she had stolen nothing. A sheepish grin came over his face, he muttered something and quickly went inside the store.

Doña Lupe could not bear the thought of being accused of

stealing. She wept quietly all the way home. Arriving at her apartment she took off her coat, but left her scarf on, and began to pace the floor again. It was one o'clock in the morning when she finally stopped pacing, sat down on the brown sofa and began embroidering dish towels.

The Comments of a Judge

The following is part of legal proceedings that took place on September 2, 1969. The names have been omitted to protect all parties involved.

STUDY QUESTIONS FOR COMPREHENSION

1. After you have read this selection, reread the excerpts from *Mein Kampf* (p. 342) and from *Tyranny on Trial* (p. 344).
2. What is the difference in dates between Hitler's "solution" and this judge's remarks that "Maybe Hitler was right"?
3. Why, in your view, is the judge so angry?
4. What are the essential points the defending lawyer makes?

September 2, 1969
10:25 a.m.

STATEMENTS OF THE COURT

The Court: There is some indication that you more or less didn't think that it was against the law or was improper. Haven't you had any moral training? Have you and your family gone to church?

The Minor: Yes, sir.

The Court: Don't you know that things like this are terribly wrong? This is one of the worst crimes that a person can commit. I just get so disgusted that I just figure what is the use? You are just an animal. You are lower than an animal. Even animals don't do that. You are pretty low.

I don't know why your parents haven't been able to teach you anything or train you. Mexican people, after 13 years of age, it's

This transcription was reprinted in *El Grito*.

perfectly all right to go out and act like an animal. It's not even right to do that to a stranger, let alone a member of your own family. I don't have much hope for you. You will probably end up in State's Prison before you are 25, and that's where you belong, anyhow. There is nothing much you can do.

I think you haven't got any moral principles. You won't acquire anything. Your parents won't teach you what is right or wrong and won't watch out.

Apparently, your sister is pregnant; is that right?

The Minor's Father: Yes.

The Court: It's a fine situation. How old is she?

The Minor's Mother: Fifteen.

The Court: Well, probably she will have a half a dozen children and three or four marriages before she is 18.

The County will have to take care of you. You are no particular good to anybody. We ought to send you out of the country—send you back to Mexico. You belong in prison for the rest of your life for doing things of this kind. You ought to commit suicide. That's what I think of people of this kind. You are lower than animals and haven't the right to live in organized society—just miserable, lousy, rotten people.

There is nothing we can do with you. You expect the County to take care of you. Maybe Hitler was right. The animals in our society probably ought to be destroyed because they have no right to live among human beings. If you refuse to act like a human being, then, you don't belong among the society of human beings.

Attorney for the Defense: Your Honor, I don't think I can sit here and listen to that sort of thing.

The Court: You are going to have to listen to it because I consider this a very vulgar, rotten human being.

Attorney for the Defense: The Court is indicting the whole Mexican group.

The Court: When they are 10 or 12 years of age, going out and having intercourse with anybody without any moral training—they don't even understand the Ten Commandments. That's all. Apparently, they don't want to.

So if you want to act like that, the County has a system of taking care of them. They don't care about that. They have no personal self-respect.

Attorney for the Defense: The Court ought to look at this youngster and deal with this youngster's case.

The Court: All right. That's what I am going to do. The family should be able to control this boy and the young girl.

Attorney for the Defense: What appalls me is that the Court is saying that Hitler was right in genocide.

The Court: What are we going to do with the mad dogs of our society? Either we have to kill them or send them to an institution or place them out of the hands of good people because that's the theory—one of the theories of punishment is if they get to the position that they want to act like mad dogs, then, we have to separate them from our society.

Well, I will go along with the recommendation. You will learn in time or else you will have to pay for the penalty with the law because the law grinds slowly but exceedingly well. If you are going to be a law violator—you have to make up your mind whether you are going to observe the law or not. If you can't observe the law, then, you have to be put away.

State of ——————
County of —————— } ss.

I, ———, do hereby certify that the foregoing is a true and correct transcript of the STATEMENTS OF THE COURT had in the within-entitled action taken on the 2nd day of September, 1969; that I reported the same in stenotype, being the qualified and acting Official Court Reporter of the Superior Court of the State of

———————, in and for the County of ———————, appointed to said Court, and thereafter had the same transcribed into typewriting as herein appears.

Dated: This 8th day of September, 1969.

———————, C.S.R.

ALICE OGLE

The Plight of Migrant America

STUDY QUESTIONS FOR COMPREHENSION

1. What is the "world" of the migrant worker?
2. Why is the migrant situation "as out of place in modern America as a slave ship in New York harbor"?
3. How can Americans find "within their economy a place for conscience"?

"The story of the deprivation of millions of farm workers is an old and harsh one in America," says Walter P. Reuther. "Unfortunately, the desperate pleas of poverty-stricken and deprived farm labor have not reached far enough. That story must be told and retold to the American people."

Reuther is right—with perhaps one exception. The California farm-labor story has been told and retold. The *New Republic's* Andrew Kopkind claims that this State has produced almost as much literature as fruits and vegetables: "Mark Twain, Frank Norris, Steinbeck, Saroyan and a hundred offshoots grew amidst the beets and grapes and cotton and spinach. From it emerges a rough provincial epic." A great deal, too, has been written recently about the grape-pickers under Cesar Chavez.

Seen against the background provided by the many writers who have pictured California's farm-labor situation, Cesar Chavez is indeed a hero of epic size. It was he who founded and now directs the National Farm Workers Association (NFWA), which has been on strike since Sept. 8, 1965. When, however, you see him in terms of the entire American farm-labor story, the stocky, dark and mild Spanish-speaking American seems almost incredible. It is some kind of miracle that he came along, to become the first farm-worker citizen of the United States to achieve what no real student of American farm

From *America*, July 9, 1966. Reprinted by permission from *America*, The National Catholic Weekly Review, 106 W. 56th Street, New York, New York, 10019.

labor would have believed possible. And this makes Chavez more than just a California leader. It is probable that, by this time, every farm worker in the country knows this man's name and what he stands for.

It is those other farm workers who need publicity now. The farm-labor problem is not concentrated in California. It is very much alive in 36 other States—especially Texas, Michigan and New York, which employ nearly as many domestic workers as California. Dale Wright, a New York newspaper man, reported on a tour he made across the country while studying the farm labor problem: "I came away angry and sick from the tomato fields just 30 miles south of the glitter and wealth of Miami Beach. I found the same crude exploitation, the same dreadful living conditions just 30 miles south of New York City."

While the focus is on California, we forget that the yearly trek of domestic farm workers begins every spring from States other than California. Fr. John A. Wagner, executive secretary of the Bishops' Committee for the Spanish Speaking, has called this a "leaderless army" that erupts from its winter headquarters and "spreads into many States of the Union."

In a statement he submitted in 1965 to a subcommittee of the Committee on Labor and Public Welfare of the U.S. Senate, Fr. Wagner compared the many thousands of Texas migrant farm workers to "tumbleweeds that roll helter-skelter," moving around 37 States "in search of that constantly eluding hope that they will have a chance to make enough to keep their families alive."

They pack their meager belongings and drift off to "countless destinations." There isn't "much fuss" made over this vast migration. There is not much said about the children who "leave school early only to return long after school resumes in September."

Most domestic farm workers winter in the South—Texas, Florida, the Carolinas. Many are Negroes. Others are Spanish-speaking Americans. And still others are Anglos, people who have followed the crops since dust-bowl days.

Some move up the East Coast to New York and travel from spring to fall. Some go to the Central and Great Lakes States. Another group follows the ripening wheat from New Mexico to the Dakotas and Montana. Another works the Rocky Mountain States. And yet another, the West Coast.

Men, women and children invade a large part of the United States each year to pick cotton or fruit, to bunch carrots, pull corn, top onions, to fill hampers with the richest harvest this earth has ever yielded to man. Their plight is described in *The Slaves We Rent,* by Truman E. Moore (Random House. $4.95), published last year. The author, a man who grew up on a small Southern farm, writes: "They come from wherever men are desperate for work. They come by whatever means they can find. These are the migrants . . . crossing and recrossing America, scouring the countryside in a land where the season never ends."

But in spite of their mobility, they are "confined within their own world." America's migrant workers inhabit a world of side roads, farmtowns, labor camps and river banks, of fields and packing sheds. "No host community sees them as a potential source of revenue," Moore says. Rather they are considered a blight on the community's health and a "threat to the relief rolls."

As Moore notes, businessmen, tourists and dance bands making their way across the country find many comforts and services at their disposal. But the migrant hopes only for "good weather, a grassy bank and a filling station that will permit him to use the rest-room."

This book paints a distressing picture of American farm workers living under nearly unbelievable circumstances and excluded from the protection of the labor and social legislation that have benefited other workers for more than a quarter century. It tells the truth about a situation that Moore says is "as out of place in modern America as a slave ship in New York harbor."

He wants Americans to ponder the fact that without the men, women and children who work our fields every year, "the rise of American agriculture would not have been possible." Paradoxically, "while holding up our proud harvests to show the world the fruits of democracy," we go on maintaining these people in their deprivation.

On May 13, the U.S. Government authorized the importation

of 1,000 men from Mexico into California to work the Salinas Valley strawberry harvest. It is doubtful if any member of Chavez' NFWA would fail to see this as a direct result of chronic American apathy toward the American citizens who labor in our fields. In fact, it was this kind of thing that provoked the vineyard workers' strike to begin with.

It is seven years since Fr. Thomas McCullough, a thin, tired young priest, working in and around Stockton, Calif., with the Spanish-speaking, observed that Americans, generally, have few scruples where domestic farm workers are concerned. "They'll spend any amount of money to buy comforts and luxuries—but won't subscribe to the idea of paying the wages that are necessary to decent living for the people who harvest our food. We stoop, instead, to take advantage of the desperate poverty of the working men of other nations. . . .

"Remember how it was told that old-time aristocrats used to amuse themselves throwing scraps of food to beggars around the manor houses? When I go to the Mexican border and see those hordes of miserable peons from Mexico scrambling to get scraps of United States labor, I wonder whether the fundamental honor of the American character will revolt against the compromising position in which it is put."

Fr. James L. Vizzard, S.J., director of the Washington office of the National Catholic Rural Life Conference, is another priest who does not hesitate to speak frankly. Disturbed at the new flood of imported workers into the United States after termination of Public Law 78, he declared, while testifying last year at a Labor Department hearing, that since those growers who employ foreign workers show no sign of self-reform, they need to be told strongly and with finality that the "approximation of slave-labor conditions that they have perpetuated" will no longer be tolerated by this nation. They must be forced to realize, he said, that "to exploit the poverty of other nations in order to beat down and crush the poor of our own country is the grossest kind of immorality."

This century has witnessed, according to the National Advisory Committee on Farm Labor, an estimated 150 attempts to improve the conditions of farm workers through legislation and administrative action. All of them have failed. Legislative action now is desperately needed, and so are protest marches and pilgrimages, or anything else that might rouse the public out of its apathy.

Something said by former Secretary of Labor James P. Mitchell in 1964, the year of his death, underlines the really great need in this country:

"The shameful migrant problem will finally be solved when there are enough Americans with wisdom, compassion and good sense to save their final censure for those who stand by and seem unable to find within their economy a place for conscience."

The Little Strike That Grew to La Causa

STUDY QUESTIONS FOR COMPREHENSION

1. What is Chavez's goal?
2. What is the relation of the National Labor Relations Board to the agricultural worker?
3. What does Dr. Valdez mean when he says, "We are about ten years behind the Negroes"?

The table grape, *Vitis vinifera,* has become the symbol of the four-year-old strike of California's predominantly Mexican-American farm workers. For more than a year now, table grapes have been the object of a national boycott that has won the sympathy and support of many Americans—and the ire of many others. The strike is widely known as *la causa,* which has come to represent not only a protest against working conditions among California grape pickers but the wider aspirations of the nation's Mexican-American minority as well. *La causa's* magnetic champion and the country's most prominent Mexican-American leader is Cesar Estrada Chavez, 42, a onetime grape picker who combines a mystical mien with peasant earthiness. *La causa* is Chavez's whole life; for it, he has impoverished himself and endangered his health by fasting. In soft, slow speech, he urges his people—nearly 5,000,000 of them in the U.S.—to rescue themselves from society's cellar. As he sees it, the first step is to win the battle of the grapes. . . .

Like the blacks, Mexican Americans, who are known as *Chicanos,* are a varied and diverse people. Only recently have they emerged from a stereotype: the lazy, placid peasant lost in a centuries-long siesta under a sombrero. Unlike the blacks, who were brought to the U.S. involuntarily, the *Chicanos* have flocked to the U.S. over the past 30 years, legally and illegally, in an attempt to escape the poverty of their native Mexico and find a better life. Whatever their present condition may be, many obviously find it better than their former one, as evidenced by the fact that relatives have often followed families into the U.S. The *Chicanos* do not speak in one voice but many, follow no one leader or strategy. Their level of ambition and militance varies greatly from *barrio* to *barrio* between Texas and California.

No man, however, personifies the *Chicanos'* bleak past, restless present and possible future in quite the manner of Cesar Chavez. He was the unshod, unlettered child of migrant workers. He attended dozens of schools but never got to the eighth grade. He was a street-corner tough who now claims as his models Emiliano Zapata, Gandhi, Nehru and Martin Luther King. He tells his people: "We make a solemn promise: to enjoy our rightful part of the riches of this land, to throw off the yoke of being considered as agricultural implements or slaves. We are free men and we demand justice." . . .

The conditions under which farm laborers toil have improved somewhat since the squalid Depression era so well evoked by John Steinbeck in *The Grapes of Wrath* and *In Dubious Battle;* yet field work remains one of the most unpleasant of human occupations. It demands long hours of back-breaking labor, often in choking dust amid insects and under a flaming sun. The harvest-time wage for grape pickers averages $1.65 an hour, plus a 25¢ bonus for each box picked, while the current federal minimum wage is $1.60.

Despite this, the seasonal and sporadic nature of the work keeps total income far below the poverty level. Average family income is less than $1,600 a year. There is no job security, and fringe benefits are few. If they are migrants, the workers must frequently live in fetid shacks without light or plumbing (though housing, bad as it is, is frequently free or very cheap). As a result, many have moved to the cities, where even unskilled labor can find work at decent wages. . . .

Cesar Chavez came to his mission from a background of poverty and prejudice that is a paradigm of that of many *Chicanos*. Like most Mexican Americans, he is of mixed Spanish and Indian blood, with liquid brown eyes, deeply bronze skin and thick, jet-black hair. He was born on an 80-acre farm in Arizona's Gila Valley near Yuma, where his parents tried to scratch a living from the arid desert earth. Chavez met racial hostility early in daily rock fights between Anglo and *Chicano* kids at the village school.

The farm failed in the Depression, and when Chavez was ten, the family packed everything it owned into a decrepit automobile and headed across the Colorado River into California. In Oxnard, Chavez's father found work threshing lima beans; when all the beans were harvested, the family took off, looking for other jobs and often turning up just a few days after a crop was in.

ANGLOS ON THE LEFT

That first winter back in Oxnard, with the little money earned in the fields already gone, was the family's worst time. Cesar's brother Richard remembers: "There was this nice lady there, and she had a vacant lot that she let us use. So we put up a tent. It was a very small tent—I guess about 8 by 10. That's all we had. All the family stayed there. And it rained that winter. Oh, it rained. Rain, rain, rain. We had to go to school barefoot. We had no shoes. I can't forget it."

The family lived that winter on beans, tortillas and an occasional potato. Chavez's father sometimes picked peas for 50¢ a day, half of which went to the contractor who drove the workers to the fields in the back of a flatbed truck. There was nothing else to do. By the next spring, the family had learned more of the harvest schedule, and it set off for the first of many years on the circuit familiar to every migrant worker in California. Starting in the Imperial and Coachella valleys of the south, through the state's bulging middle, the San Joaquin Valley, on up north of San Francisco and into the Napa Valley, they worked each crop in its turn: asparagus, grapes, beets, potatoes, beans, plums, apricots—anything that needed picking, hoeing, thinning, leafing, tipping, girdling, digging or pruning.

In 1941, the family moved to Delano, where Chavez met his future wife, Helen Fabela. At the movies with her one night, he had a jarring brush with discrimination. He refused to stay on the right side of the theater, which was reserved for Mexicans, and sat instead with the Anglos on the left. "The assistant manager came," Chavez recalls. "The girl who sold the popcorn came. And the girl with the tickets came. Then the manager came. They tried to pull me up, and I said, 'No, you have to break my arms before I get up,' " Chavez, then 16, was hustled off to the station house for a lecture from the chief of police, but he would not promise not to do the same thing again.

Like many other teen-age Mexican Americans, Chavez became a *pachuco,* affecting a zoot suit with pegged pants, a broad flat hat and a ducktail haircut. Some sociologists now see the *pachuco* movement as the first example of militant separatism among *Chicanos,* an assertion of a distinct identity hostile to Anglo culture. The Anglos took it that way, in any case, and reacted violently: during a series of riots in the Southwest during the summer of 1943, several thousand soldiers, sailors and Marines beat up hundreds of *Chicano* youths. Police promptly arrested some of the victims. . . .

There have never been Jim Crow laws against them, like those against blacks, but overt discrimination undeniably exists. *Chicanos* still find it hard to get into the barbershops and public swimming pools of south Texas. Still, though the *Chicano* is set apart by language, assimilation is often easier for him than for the Negro. For this reason, and because most of the *Chicano* population lives in relative obscurity in the *barrios* or rural areas, the Mexican-American community has been slow to develop aggressive leadership.

Now, because they have seen that organized black action gets results, the *Chicanos* have begun to stir with a new militancy. They have formed the Brown Berets, modeled on the Black Panthers, and set up a $2,200,000 Mexican-American Legal Defense and Educational Fund, financed by the Ford Foundation. "We are about ten years behind the Negroes, and we must catch up," says Dr. Daniel Valdes, a Denver behavioral scientist. "But I think we will do it without extreme violence." Lawyer Donald Pacheco puts the plight of the Mexican American more bluntly: "We're the 'nigger' of ten years ago."

If he is a migrant farm worker, the Mexican American has a life expectancy of about 48 years *v.* 70 for the average U.S. resident. The

Chicano birth rate is double the U.S. average—but so is the rate of infant mortality. More than one-third live below the $3,000-a-year level of family income that federal statisticians define as poverty. Eighty percent of the Mexican-American population is now urban, and most live in the *barrio*.

The overwhelming majority work as unskilled or semiskilled labor in factories and packing plants, or in service jobs as maids, waitresses, yard boys and deliverymen. Particularly in Texas, Mexican Americans sometimes get less pay than others for the same work. Even the few who have some education do not escape discrimination. *Chicano* women find that jobs as public contacts at airline ticket counters are rarely open; they are welcome as switchboard operators out of the public eye. Mexican-American men who work in banks are assigned to the less fashionable branches. Promotions come slowly, responsibility hardly ever.

One major impediment to the Mexican American is his Spanish language, because it holds him back in U.S. schools. Mexican Americans average eight years of schooling, two years less than Negroes and a full four years less than whites. Often they are forced to learn English from scratch in the first grade, and the frequent result is that they become not bilingual but nearly nonlingual. In Texas, 40% of *Chicanos* are considered functionally illiterate. In Los Angeles, only an estimated 25% can speak English fluently. *Chicano* children in some rural areas are still punished for speaking Spanish in school. Only this year, *Chicano* students at Bowie High School in El Paso—in a predominantly Mexican-American section—managed to get a rule abolished that forbade the speaking of Spanish on the school grounds.

The *Chicano* is as vulnerable to mistreatment at the hands of the law as the black. Seven Mexicans were beaten by drunken policemen at a Los Angeles police station on Christmas Eve, 1952; six of the officers were eventually given jail terms. During an 18-month period ending last April, the American Civil Liberties Union received 174 complaints of police abuses from Los Angeles Mexican Americans. Two of the recent landmark Supreme Court decisions limiting police questioning of suspects involved Mexican Americans—*Escobedo* v.

Illinois and *Miranda* v. *Arizona*. Many Mexicans still look on the Texas Rangers and U.S. border patrols with terror.

PLURALISM V. THE MELTING POT

That Chavez has dramatized the problems of Mexican Americans in the city as well as on the farm seems beyond dispute. Father Bernardo Kenny, a Sacramento priest with a sizable Mexican-American congregation, believes that even if Chavez never wins his strike he will have made a "tremendous contribution." Says Kenny: "He focused attention on the problem of the farm workers, and he made the Mexican Americans proud to be Mexican Americans. Chavez must be given credit, I think, for really starting the Mexican-American civil rights movement." Ironically, mechanization hastened by unionization may eventually diminish Chavez's farm-labor base—but it will not slow the momentum of *la causa*.

The new Mexican-American militancy has turned up a mixed *piñata* of leaders, some of them significantly more strident than Chavez. In Los Angeles, 20-year-old David Sanchez is "prime minister" of the well-disciplined Brown Berets, who help keep intramural peace in the *barrio* and are setting up a free medical clinic. Some of them also carry machetes and talk tough about the Anglo. Reies Lopez Tijerina, 45, is trying to establish a "Free City State of San Joaquin" for *Chicanos* on historic Spanish land grants in New Mexico; at the moment, while his appeal on an assault conviction is being adjudicated, he is in jail for burning a sign in the Carson National Forest. Denver's Rudolfo ("Corky") Gonzales, 40, an ex-prizefighter, has started a "Crusade for Justice" to make the city's 85,000 Mexican Americans *la causa*-conscious.

As with the blacks, the question for those who lead the *Chicanos* is whether progress means separatism or assimilation. Cal State Professor Rafael Guzman, who helped carry out a four-year Ford Foundation study of Mexican Americans, warns that the *barrio* is potentially as explosive as the black ghetto. He argues for a new pluralism in the U.S. that means something other than forcing minorities into the established Anglo-Saxon mold; each group should be free to develop its own culture while contributing to the whole.

Yet there is no real consensus in the *barrio*. The forces for assimilation are powerful. A young Tucson militant, Salomon Baldenegro, contends: "Our values are just like any Manhattan executive's, but we have a ceiling on our social mobility." While federal programs for bilingual instruction in Mexican-American areas are still inadequate, that kind of approach—if made readily available to all who want it—leaves the choice between separatism and assimilation ultimately to the individual *Chicano* himself. He learns in his father's tongue, but he also learns in English well enough so that language is no longer a barrier; he retains his own culture, but he also knows enough of the majority's rules and ways to compete successfully if he chooses to.

Cesar Chavez has made the *Chicano*'s cause well enough known to make that goal possible. . . .

LANGSTON HUGHES

I Dream a World

I dream a world where man
No other will scorn,
Where love will bless the earth
And peace its paths adorn.
I dream a world where all
Will know sweet freedom's way,
Where greed no longer saps the soul
Nor avarice blights our day.
A world I dream where black or white,
Whatever race you be,
Will share the bounties of the earth
And every man is free,
Where wretchedness will hang its head,
And joy, like a pearl,
Attend the needs of all mankind.
Of such I dream—
Our world!

EDMUND JARECKI

Street Scene During the Martin Luther King Riots

LANGSTON HUGHES

From *Lenox Avenue Mural*

HARLEM

What happens to a dream deferred?
    Does it dry up
    like a raisin in the sun?
    Or fester like a sore—
    And then run?

    Does it stink like rotten meat?
    Or crust and sugar over—
    like a syrupy sweet?

    Maybe it just sags
    like a heavy load.

    Or does it explode?

"Harlem" is reprinted from *The Panther and the Lash*, copyright 1951 by Langston Hughes, by permission of Alfred A. Knopf, Inc. The photograph is reprinted by permission from the *Chicago Daily News*. "Harlem" and the photograph first appeared together in *You Can't Kill the Dream*, published by the John Knox Press.

MALCOLM X

Racism: The Cancer That Is Destroying America

STUDY QUESTIONS FOR COMPREHENSION

1. What does Malcolm X mean by his statement, "Time is running out for America"?
2. What does Malcolm X mean by "light"?
3. Explain what Malcolm X means by "human being" or "human rights"?
4. What, in your view, does Malcolm X mean by "racism"?

I am not a racist, and I do not subscribe to any of the tenets of racism. But the seed of racism has been firmly planted in the hearts of most American whites ever since the beginning of that country. This seed of racism has rooted itself so deeply in the subconsciousness of many American whites that they themselves ofttimes are not even aware of its existence, but it can be easily detected in their thoughts, their words, and in their deeds.

In the past I permitted myself to be used by Elijah Muhammad, the leader of the sect known as the Black Muslims, to make sweeping indictments of all white people, the entire white race, and these generalizations have caused injuries to some whites who perhaps did not deserve to be hurt. Because of the spiritual enlightenment which I was blessed to receive as the result of my recent pilgrimage to the Holy City of Mecca, I no longer subscribe to sweeping indictments of any one race.

My religious pilgrimage (hajj) to Mecca has given me a new insight into the true brotherhood of Islam, which encompasses all the races of mankind. The pilgrimage broadened my scope, my mind, my outlook, and made me more flexible in approaching life's many complexities and in my reactions to its paradoxes.

At Mecca I saw the spirit of unity and true brotherhood displayed by tens of thousands of people from all over the world, from blue-eyed blonds to black-skinned Africans. This served to convince me that perhaps some American whites can also be cured of the rampant racism which is consuming them and about to destroy that country.

I am now striving to live the life of a true Suni Muslim. In the future I intend to be careful not to sentence anyone who has not first been proven guilty. I must repeat that I am not a racist nor do I subscribe to the tenets of racism. I can state in all sincerity that I wish nothing but freedom, justice, and equality, life, liberty, and the pursuit of happiness for all people.

However, the first law of nature is self-preservation, so my first concern is with the oppressed group of people to which I belong, the 22 million Afro-Americans, for we, more than any other people on earth today, are deprived of these inalienable *human rights*.

But time is running out for America. The 22 million Afro-Americans are not yet filled with hate or a desire for revenge, as the propaganda of the segregationists would have people believe. The universal law of justice is sufficient to bring judgment upon the American whites who are guilty of racism. The same law will also punish those who have benefited from the racist practices of their forefathers and have done nothing to atone for the "sins of their fathers." Just look around on this earth today and see the increasing troubles this generation of American whites is having. The "sins of their fathers" are definitely being visited upon the heads of this present generation. Most intelligent American whites will admit freely today without hesitation that their present generation is already being punished and plagued for the evil deeds their forefathers committed when they enslaved millions of Afro-Americans in that country.

But it is not necessary for their victim—the Afro-American—to seek revenge. The very conditions the American whites created are already plaguing them into insanity and death. They are reaping what their forefathers have sown. "Their chickens are coming home to roost." And we, the 22 million Afro-Americans—their victims—need only to spend more time removing the "scars of slavery" from the backs and the mind of our own people, physical and mental scars left by four hundred years of inhuman treatment there in America at the hands of white racists.

The key to our success lies in *united action*. Lack of unity among the various Afro-American groups involved in our struggle has always been the reason we have failed to win concrete gains in our war against America's oppression, exploitation, discrimination, segregation, degradation, and humiliation. Before the miserable condition of the 22 million "second-class citizens" can be corrected, all the groups in the Afro-American community must form a united front. Only through united efforts can our problems there be solved.

How can we get the unity of the Afro-American community? Ignorance of each other is what has made unity impossible in the past. Therefore we need enlightenment. We need more light about each other. Light creates understanding, understanding creates love, love creates patience, and patience creates unity. Once we have more knowledge (light) about each other we will stop condemning each other and a *united front* will be brought about.

All 22 million Afro-Americans have the same basic goal, the same basic objective. We want freedom, justice, and equality, we want recognition and respect as *human beings*. We are not divided over objectives, but we have allowed our racist enemies to divide us over the *methods* of attaining these common objectives. Our enemy has magnified our minor points of difference, then maneuvered us into wasting out time debating and fighting each other over insignificant and irrelevant issues.

The common goal of 22 million Afro-Americans is respect as *human beings*, the God-given right to be a *human being*. Our common goal is to obtain the *human rights* that America has been denying us. We can never get civil rights in America until our *human rights* are first restored. We will never be recognized as citizens there until we are first recognized as *humans*.

The present American "system" can never produce freedom for the black man. A chicken cannot lay a duck egg because the chicken's "system" is not designed or equipped to produce a duck egg. The system of the chicken was produced by a chicken egg and can therefore reproduce only that which produced it.

The American "system" (political, economic, and social) was produced from the enslavement of the black man, and this present "system" is capable only of perpetuating that enslavement.

In order for a chicken to produce a duck egg its system would have to undergo a drastic and painful revolutionary change . . . or *REVOLUTION*. So be it with America's enslaving system.

In the past the civil rights groups in America have been foolishly attempting to obtain constitutional rights from the same Government that has conspired against us to deny our people these rights. Only a world body (*a world court*) can be instrumental in obtaining those rights which belong to a human being by dint of his being a member of the human family.

As long as the freedom struggle of the 22 million Afro-Americans is labeled a civil rights issue it remains a domestic problem under the jurisdiction of the United States, and as such, bars the intervention and support of our brothers and sisters in Africa, Asia, Latin America, as well as that of the well-meaning whites of Europe. But once our struggle is lifted from the confining civil rights label to the level of *human rights,* our freedom struggle has then become *internationalized.*

Just as the violation of *human rights* of our brothers and sisters in South Africa and Angola is an international issue and has brought the racists of South Africa and Portugal under attack from all other independent governments at the United Nations, once the miserable plight of the 22 million Afro-Americans is also lifted to the level of *human rights* our struggle then becomes an international issue, and the direct concern of all other civilized governments. We can then take the racist American Government before the World Court and have the racists in it exposed and condemned as the criminals that they are.

Why should it be necessary to go before a world court in order to solve America's race problem? One hundred years ago a civil war was fought supposedly to free us from the Southern racists. We are still the victims of their racism. Lincoln's Emancipation Proclamation was supposedly to free us. We are still crying for freedom. The politicians fought for amendments to the Constitution supposedly to make us first-class citizens. We are still second-class citizens.

In 1954, the U.S. Supreme Court itself issued a historic decision outlawing the segregated school system, and ten years have passed and this law is yet to be enforced even in the Northern states.

If white America doesn't think the Afro-American, especially the upcoming generation, is capable of adopting the guerrilla tactics now being used by oppressed people elsewhere on this earth, she is making a drastic mistake. She is underestimating the force that can do her the most harm.

A real honest effort to remove the just grievances of the 22 million Afro-Americans must be made immediately or in a short time it will be too late.

MARI EVANS

The Emancipation of George-Hector (a colored turtle)

STUDY QUESTIONS FOR COMPREHENSION

1. What relationship, if any, do you find between current events and the lines "head rared back to/ be/ admired"?
2. Explain the title.
3. Restate the poem in your own words.

George-Hector
. . . is
spoiled.
formerly he stayed
well up in his
shell . . . but now
he hangs arms and legs
sprawlingly
in a most langorous fashion . . .
head rared back to
be
admired.

he didn't use to
talk . . .
but
he does now.

From *American Negro Poetry* edited by A. Bontemps. Reprinted by permission of the author.

BEN CALDWELL

The King of Soul, or the Devil and Otis Redding

STUDY QUESTIONS FOR COMPREHENSION

1. This play is based on the Faust story. What similarities and what differences do you find?
2. What are the implications of the Devil's remark, "I can't harm you unless you let me"?
3. Why does Otis make a deal with the Devil?
4. Would the play be different if Otis Redding were not black?

CHARACTERS:

Otis	*Two Teen-aged Girls*
Otis' Mother	*Black Extras* (scene fillers)
Church Woman	*Two Black Men* (in bar)
Black Lawyer	*Pilot* (white)

The Devil (the sequence of his disguises) as the devil/A&R man/master of ceremonies/aircraft salesman/airport mechanic/policeman

SCENE 1

(We see a church in a Black community. Down South. A sign says, "Macon County Baptist Church." It's Sunday—services are over. We see a group of PEOPLE going, slowly, in different directions. Walking and talking, or just standing, enjoying the sun-bright morning. We

focus upon a conversation betwn two middle-aged WOMEN. One of them is the mother of a young MAN who sings in the church choir.)

WOMAN. It sure was a lovely service today. The reverend spoke just beautifully. You know that boy of yours sure can sing! My goodness! The sisters get happy everytime he opens his mouth! He sound like he got more God in him than all the rest of us.

MOTHER. Yes, Otis makes me so proud. I feel like I was blessed to birth him. He such a good boy, too—he worries so much 'bout me and his daddy, and his sisters and brothers—he wants so much for us. He's all the time talking about how much money he might make if he went and made some records. He wants to do so much. Well, sister, I'm gon' get on home and fix dinner for that family of mine. Give my love to all of yours.

WOMAN. Alright now.

(Fade out on this screen, and we go to:)

SCENE 2

(A barely lighted room. OTIS lays sleeping. He is startled awake (he is really dreaming) by a flash of red light that flickers like a fire. A figure, a WHITE MAN, is standing at the foot of his bed, like an apparition. His suit looks red, and has a high white collar like a priest's. (Throughout the play, which is Otis' life, we see the same WHITE MAN. We witness him as he changes costumes & disguises. He is the Devil. Keep your eye on the Devil.)

OTIS. What?! Who's there? What you' doin' in here?

DEVIL. Who I am is not important—you are the important one.

OTIS. Well, whoever you are, you got no business in here! *(Not frightened, but suspicious.)*

DEVIL. Don't be afraid, you're only dreaming—but the dream is real. I can't harm you unless you let me. I only want to make a deal with you.

OTIS. What kinda deal?

DEVIL. I'll explain. You want to do a lot of things for your family—for yourself. You want to move them out of this old house and into a new one. You want all kinds of things that you think will make you and your family happier, right?

OTIS. Yeah, you' right.

DEVIL. As I said, I wish to make a deal with you. I will see that you have all that you want, but I want something that you have.

OTIS. If you can give me everything, what could I possibly have that you want?

DEVIL. You have something I don't have . . . that's the thing I want.

OTIS. What?

DEVIL. I want your soul. Truthfully, I don't have one. And that's the only weight that will hold me here.

OTIS. That sounds stupid to me—how can I give you my soul?

DEVIL. If you agree to give it to me it's mine!

OTIS *(not serious)*. Okay you can have my soul! Now where's the house and cars?

DEVIL. It's not that easy. We must draw up a contract. I will give you all the things you want, and when that's done (to your satisfaction) you will willingly give me your soul.

OTIS. Suppose I take what you offer and then don't give you my soul?

DEVIL. Then your life would be forfeited as payment. But you're too honorable to do that. Is it a deal?

OTIS *(mumbled in his sleep)*. Yeah, uhhuh!

(The red light stops flickering, and the rm is dark again.)

OTIS *(loudly—now awake)*. Is somebody in here? Is somebody in here? Man, I musta been dreamin'.

HIS MOTHER'S VOICE *(calls from another rm)*. Otis, is somethin' the matter?

OTIS. No, ma, I'm alright. I just had some kinda funny dream. It woke me up.

(In a dim lighted corner we see the DEVIL-APPARITION change costume and wait for the scene to change.)

SCENE 3

(Small town "downtown" scene. Signs identify the various stores and buildings. Emerging from a store, laden with packages, is a big, young,

BLACK COUNTRY BOY. His strength is his handsomeness. He's accosted by (the Devil comes out of the shadows as) a well-dressed WHITE MAN.)

DEVIL. Say, young man, stop a moment! You're Reverend Redding's son aren't you? (OTIS *nods and says, "Yes."*) I've heard a lot about you, son. I want to do something for you. I want to help you make a lot of money.

OTIS *(anticipating a scheme).* I don't wanna be no prize-fighter, mister!

DEVIL. I don't mean fighting, boy, I mean with your voice.

OTIS *(some interest).* How?

DEVIL. My name is Mr. Jacobs. I represent Antis Records. You have a beautiful sound, Otis. If you were singing somewhere besides church you could make a lot of money.

OTIS. My daddy says my voice is God's gift—I'm supposed to share it! They enjoy my singing like I enjoy some of theirs—it would be like selling smiles! And my daddy says it's wrong to sing anything but church music.

DEVIL. Your daddy's wrong. He just doesn't know. Anything you do with your voice will be holy and spiritual—your father just doesn't know. Furthermore you can reach more people outside the church. You'll be sharing this God-gift to a much greater extent. I'm telling you, you can make a lot of money!

OTIS *(not quite persuaded).* I don't know. Hey, do I know you? I have the strongest feelin' that I've met you before—or somebody look 'xactly like you.

DEVIL. It wasn't me, but we're the same. But that's not important to me, the important thing is you. You can have all the things you want. Everything for your mother, and father, your brothers and sisters—see the world—you can leave this *little* town if you want to—buy a new house—a car! *Give me* your voice and I'll get you everything you want.

OTIS. I don't believe it, but I'd like to try it! It sure sounds good! What do I have to do besides say, "It's a deal"? *(They shake hands.)*

DEVIL. I'm going to have to work hard in order to sell you to the public, but we're both gonna make a lot of money—here's the deal. Our contract will state that after you've made *(He says this slowly to make the figure sound more impressive.)* *one million dollars,* all rights and royalties to your singing belong to me!

OTIS *(amazed).* A million dollars! *(Pause.)* Wait—how come only a million for me?

DEVIL. *Only* a million! Boy, what other opportunity would guarantee you a million dollars?

OTIS. But it just don't seem sensible to sell *my* voice completely for *just* a million dollars!

DEVIL. Look, you may be screaming your lungs out in that church from now to eternity and won't make anywhere near a million dollars. *(Pause.)* Now is it a deal?

OTIS. Yeah. Okay.

DEVIL. Good. Meet me here tomorrow, six o'clock, and I'll have all the papers. You're on your way, Otis.

(They part company. OTIS right. DEVIL left. The DEVIL hurriedly changes into his next costume of deception.)

SCENE 4

(We hear the final strains of "Satisfaction," the bedlam of a crowd screaming its appreciation. A WHITE MAN (the Devil in a tuxedo) rushes onto the stage, saying:)

DEVIL. How about that? How about that? Let's hear it! The great Otis! Let's bring him back out. Come on back, Otis!

(A tall BLACK MAN, in a bright/orange suit, comes back on stage. He is glistening with perspiration from his efforts, and breathing heavily. The WHITE MAN puts his arm over OTIS' shoulder, and puts the microphone to his face. The Devil is congenial.)

DEVIL. How 'bout that, Otis? They really love you out there. How does it feel to be the hottest thing in the country?

OTIS. Oh, Jack, it feels just great! I still can't believe it! I want to thank all my people—my fans—for all they've done for me. They're the ones truly responsible for my being here today!

DEVIL *(put-on sincerity).* I wanna tell you Otis, it's really a sign of greatness when you attribute your greatness to the people. *(Brief applause).* Tell me, what's the secret of that special sound of yours?

OTIS. Well, Jack, I believe it's sincerity. I just sing and sound the way I feel—and that's the truth. The things I sing I really feel them from my soul on out! No secret or no trick.

DEVIL *(put-on sincerity. Pretending to understand).* That's just beautiful, Otis. Ladies and gentlemen, Otis Redding! OTIS REDDING! One of the truly great ones!

(Applause, screams, as OTIS leaves the stage. The DEVIL goes to a dark corner, changes his disguise and waits.)

SCENE 5

(A record shop. Two teen-age GIRLS emerge with their record purchases.)

1ST. What you buy?

2ND. I bought Otis' new side. It's badddddd!

1ST. Oh yeah, Otis is *my* man! You see that house he bought for his mother?

2ND. Yeah. You seen him in person yet?

1ST. Yeah, girl, that is one big, good-looking nigger! You know what I wish I could do?

(She is telling her giggling GIRL FRIEND her wish, as they continue on their way out of sight. The DEVIL is in the shadows, watching and waiting.)

SCENE 6

(An angry BLACK MAN is pacing the floor. He has a piece of paper in his hand. OTIS is seated, looking dejected. The MAN is saying:)

LAWYER. As your lawyer I should have known about this from the very beginning. A contract like this is not only illegal, it's immoral! How did you go for a thing like this? (OTIS *shrugs.*) Oh I know—this isn't the first time a white man has shown a poor Black boy a picture of success and made him pay a ridiculously high price for it.

OTIS. But isn't there something we can do about it? It's my voice. Mine! I can say I don't wanna sing for that m.f. no more! I can say I changed my mind. *It's my voice!* I'll keep on singing! For someone to *own* my voice is damn near as ridiculous as someone owning my sou . . . see what you can do about it, huh?

LAWYER. We'll see what the courts have to say about it.

SCENE 7

(Court corridor. OTIS, his lawyer, MR. JACOBS, stand as a group.)

DEVIL. A bargain is a bargain—you weren't man enough to live up to it.

LAWYER. What the hell you mean! That was an unfair, unethical, contract. You were taking unfair advantage of this man!

DEVIL. If it wasn't for me he wouldn't be where he is today! I didn't twist his arm and make him sign. I explained everything to him. I performed a service in return for his agreement to the terms of the contract.

LAWYER. What the hell is your gripe, Mr.? You've made a few million from singing, and you can't carry a goddamned tune! You . . . the judge allowed you the rights and royalties to *all* of Otis' past recordings! Stopped all future recordings—what more do you want? Why should you make it all?

OTIS *(interrupting)*. Well, you got the records, but the things I'm gon' do gon' make the things I've done seem like nothing. I still got my voice! You won the records, but I still got my voice!

DEVIL. The only "voice" you have is what I have on records! To me, the real value of the things you've done comes after you're gone. Remember Sam? What I have will be all that's left of you! *(The DEVIL rushes to a dark corner and changes his disguise.)*

LAWYER *(in disgust)*. Ain't that a bitch! Well, that m.f. has a temporary victory. You can still make plenty of money. He has no claim to your live appearances. And maybe we'll get that injunction on future recordings settled soon. A few appearances around the country and you can make enough to finance your own record company.

(They are about to leave—DEVIL approaches carrying attaché case.)

DEVIL. Mr. Redding! Mr. Redding! I'd like to speak to you a moment. *(OTIS and the LAWYER stop to listen.)* I represent the Fall-T Aircraft Company. I have a proposition, which you'll probably find very interesting. *(Shows picture.)* Your own personal aircraft. A twin-engined jet. You no longer have to be bothered with airline schedules. You make your own schedule. A private jet is a convenience and an asset to the modern businessman. All the top names have one today.

OTIS. Sounds good. Look, contact my lawyer tomorrow and he'll take care of the deal.

DEVIL. Thank you, Mr. Redding. I think you'll be pleased. *(Smiling.)*

(They leave. The DEVIL returns to the dark corner to change again.)

SCENE 8

(We see a WHITE MAN in a phone booth, talking to someone. We hear the airport/airplane sounds.)

PILOT. Yes. I'm at the airport now. I have to have the battery changed. No, it's just a minor thing. The mechanic, here, says he'll take care of it. It'll be ready to take off as soon as you get to the airport. Alright. Okay. Yeah, the weather's bad, but I think we'll have a good trip. *(To MECHANIC—who is the Devil in another disguise.)* You'll take care of Mr. Redding's plane?

DEVIL *(slightly sinister)*. Yes, I'll take care of Mr. Redding's plane.

SCENE 9

(The same two TEEN-AGERS are dancing to the music from a radio—a soul station—the music is interrupted by a bulletin.)

ANNOUNCER. Rhythm & Blues singer Otis Redding was believed

killed, today, when his private, twin-engine jet crashed into icy-cold Lake Monona, in Wisconsin. It's an unconfirmed report, let's hope it's not true. We'll give you details as we receive them.

(Starts playing records again. Second record finishes and the ANNOUNCER says, sadly:) Ladies and gentlemen, a great voice has been silenced. The king of soul is dead. The report has been confirmed. Otis Redding was killed when his jet aircraft crashed, early today, in Wisconsin. He was truly, appropriately called "the king of soul." Otis was soul. The existence of this intangible was proven by Otis' sound. You know, like you don't believe there's a voice like Otis' til you hear it. And it sounds like what began as perfection—needed no cultivation. You got to believe in soul once you've heard Otis. He's gone, but the inspiration of his soulful voice, singing his songs, still belongs to us. It's really a great, great, and tragic loss.

(The DISC JOCKEY plays "Try a Little Tenderness." The two TEEN-AGERS are seated on the floor, beside the radio, showing their sorrow in silence. The lights and the sound fade, as the DEVIL is huddled in his corner, changing his costume for another appearance.)

SCENE 10

(Sad, sorry PEOPLE dressed in black. Some of them are crying. The DEVIL is on the scene in a policeman's uniform. We hear the people's comments.)

PEOPLE. "I ain't never seen so many flowers." "Yeah, they sure put him away nice." "I didn't know he was so big!" "He looked like that statue of that Egyptian king, Khafre."

OTIS' MOTHER *(escorted by other members of the family.)* Remember how the house used to seem just to vibrate when he use to sing. It sounds like I can still feel Otis' presence.

(The DEVIL disappears into darkness, and we don't see him again.)

SCENE 11

(Dimly lighted bar. Two MEN seated on high stools, drinking. They are loudly discussing the singer's death.)

1ST MAN. That's right, man, whitey is a cold motherfucka!

2ND MAN. Aw man you' crazy! You always get some crackpot ideas! What the white man gon' kill Otis Redding for?

1ST MAN. Anytime a Black man start doing something for his people whitey kill 'im—one way or another!

2ND MAN. What was Otis Redding doing for his people? All he was doing was singing and making a lotta money!

1ST MAN. WE WAS PROUD OF HIM, IF NOTHING ELSE! Look at what they did to Muhammad Ali!

2ND MAN. They just took his title, they didn't kill him! If whitey so cold why didn't he kill him?

1ST MAN. They tryin' like hell to kill him! Financially! They cut-off his livelihood! And tryin' to put him in jail! They tryin' to kill his proud, strong Black image! They tried to make it look like the white man giveth, and the white man taketh away. But the champ had enough sense to say the only way you take this title is in the ring where he won it. He made Black children say, "I'm the greatest!" He made the world realize that Black is beautiful and strong!

2ND MAN. I can't see anything they'd have to gain by killing Otis—he was making a lot of money for them.

1ST MAN. He makin' more money for them now that he's dead, cause now they don't have to pay him! That's part of their game! The white man sells *you*, and you only get a part of the money! He even got the nerve to take the lion's share! Otis was moving in the direction to get more of it—or all of it! Didn't you read where he was startin' his own record company? And he was gon' manage other talent! Now to the white man it's hard enough to take a nigger makin' *some* money, but when that nigger want *all* the money—when he start goin' for himself—competing—the white man say, "He's got to go!"

(2ND MAN is beginning to give these ideas serious consideration.)

1ST MAN. Another thing, like I say, the white man was sellin' Otis—Otis was a product to the white man—like cornflakes! That's all! He want to make as much money off his "product" as he can. What increases the value of the product more than a great demand for it? What creates more of a demand for a great singer's records than his death? And whitey has no scruples, 'specially when it comes to the dollar!

2ND MAN. You soundin' foolish again—why the man gon' get rid of somebody makin' as much money for them as Otis was? Otis was young, and still had a lotta songs in him.

1ST MAN. Man, that whitey know he can find another young, hungry, Black soulbrother, to take Otis' place! Like he change car styles every year—same quality, different body!

(2ND MAN is considering these points of view seriously again.)

1ST MAN *(reminiscing).* Yeah, man, Otis was sayin' somethin'. I could just look at my woman, sometimes, and feel and understand what Otis meant when he sang, "I Can't Turn You Loose." I've often thought about the good and bad about my woman when he sang "Respect" and "Security."

It made me think about this jive-ass, frustrating country when he sang, "I Can't Get No Satisfaction." All Otis' music had a message. Tellin' us 'bout ourselves, in a way. Make you happy, or sad, or sorry. Made you "feel" and "think." Made you examine yourself, and try to get yourself together. Yeah, man, don't tell me whitey didn't want him out of the picture. For more reasons than one.

2ND MAN. You know, I think you right! It'd be good if we didn't have to have *no* dealings with the devil!

1ST MAN. Yeah.

(They drink their drinks in silence. Jazz comes from the jukebox. The lights dim to black, ending the play.)

CHARLES MURRY

Patterns, Currents, and Visions

STUDY QUESTIONS FOR COMPREHENSION

1. What does Charles Murry mean by the lines "Dark beautiful people circumventing the realities of bondage"?
2. Define "viability," "transcend," and "parochial."
3. What are the lies of history?

Patterns only the tired hands and bright eyes
of my mother could understand.
Dark beautiful people circumventing the realities
of bondage.
Moving toward viability and survival.
As dark maidens intimately nurse the embryo
of a new nation,
ebony warriors transcend the ruined, parochial
minds of western civilization.

Currents of blackness gyrating through
the congested intersections of my mind.
Visions of reverence and messages of relevancy
overwhelming the lies of history:
Chakka, the cotton fields, Prisons like Harlem.
Culture and Heritage cleansing the soul,
retiring the dreadful burden of ignorance.

D'ARMY BAILEY

Equal— but Separate?

STUDY QUESTIONS FOR COMPREHENSION

1. Is D'Army Bailey a separatist or an integrationist?
2. What does the author mean by "functional coalitions"?
3. Explain the phrase the "dogma of the elite" which appears toward the end of the essay.

For a good part of the 1960's large numbers of blacks and a minority of whites were making concerted efforts to create a more open and equitable society. These efforts involved individuals and groups who assumed there were ways other than racial exclusion of preserving personal, cultural and group integrity within a diverse citizenry. They assumed the appreciation of one's unique experience did not require a denigration or avoidance of the unique experiences of others. Moreover, they felt that the ethnocentric attitudes which grew out of the arbitrary, often vicious separation of blacks and whites could best be overcome through the free interchange of people, ideas and experiences. To some, these assumptions are no longer valid. They are now calling instead for outright separation of the races.

An attempt at fairly assessing the separatist phenomenon should include a brief look at its development.

Separatism is a product of the disillusionment and bitterness attending the collapse of the Civil Rights Movement—a campaign dedicated to political, economic and social integration. Promises of change and faith in a coming era of decency, backed by the high-sounding rhetoric of our national spokesmen, were doubtless responsible for the incredibly peaceful, patient nature of the Movement. It should have been obvious that the cruel deception, inten-

From *Civil Liberties,* February 1969. Reprinted by permission of *Civil Liberties* and D'Army Bailey.

tional or not, was bound to explode with devastating consequences. And so it did. Violence in the South and vacillation in the North made it clear that the promise of equality was a pious shibboleth; the promise of freedom, devious bombast. For those who were personally involved in the Movement, the end was traumatic.

PRIDE BLACK AND WHITE

When the Movement broke down, there was a thorough re-evaluation of the human rights campaign. The conclusion was that most white Americans—northern and southern alike—are fiercely proud of their race and determined to preserve its prerogatives.

These facts had already been proved by the violent resistance to school desegregation and fair employment in the southern and border states. They were increasingly being shown in the northern states in ways which, if less violent, were nonetheless as determined and as hostile. Additionally, the pivotal issues were the same in all regions of the country.

Given those circumstances, integration was bound to lose ground to new priorities. For many blacks it was a matter of pride—there was no point in pleading against continuing rejection. For others it was a matter of necessity. Since blacks apparently could not participate as equal partners within American society, the only effective alternative was the development of separate, self-sustaining black enclaves, which would yield a relative equality of bargaining power. Thus, there arose the demands for black power and racial separation.

For the most part, the development was inevitable, and the emotional appeal is obvious. However, it is the rationality of separatism that should concern us here. If the separatist design is unsupportable as a rational proposition, its continued pursuit for nonrational reasons is strategically unwise and self-indulgent. Can the black man achieve his goals through separatism?

Our primary goal is a fairer distribution of economic, political and social power. Our other goals are less tangible but no less important—the general recognition of the equal worth and dignity of blacks and our right to move freely whenever, wherever and however we choose.

The separatist has concluded that blacks can no longer expect whites voluntarily to yield a fair share of their power, and that without power blacks cannot attain equality and dignity. The conclusion is sound up to that point. But the separatists go further. They have concluded also that the only effective way of achieving power is through the formation of myriad black interest groups—educational, economic, political and social—from which all whites are excluded. Theoretically, exclusion eliminates divisiveness and distraction. The separatists assume blacks as a group necessarily have a unique and common interest in the struggle for power and influence and, therefore, are more likely to pursue a unified strategy aimed at common goals. They assume blacks will gain pride and a sense of dignity from involvement in an effective black power block.

FUNCTIONAL COALITIONS

But the assumption is more doctrinal than functional. It is based on several fallacies.

To begin with, for many blacks the struggle for power and influence is more personal than racial in nature. The sources of power vary with the individual's expectations, and so do the methods by which power can be obtained. Goals are as similar and dissimilar among blacks as among whites. For example, like whites, some blacks seek political power. The functional strategies of the aspiring black politician will not differ markedly from those of his white counterpart. That is to say, a politician of any color will assess the makeup of his constituency and their desires, then formulate a program broad enough to gain wide approval. If his constituency is racially mixed, as is the case in most major cities, a separatist program is unlikely to succeed. The situation will not be altered by the increasing numerical strength of blacks in major urban areas since it can be anticipated that cities, as political units, will increasingly incorporate adjacent suburban areas, thus reinforcing white influence in inner city politics. Similarly, the alliances and directions of the black businessman, except in marginal business ventures aimed exclusively at the black community, will be determined more by sound managerial and fiscal policies than by race.

The desirability of functional coalitions applies as well to group efforts within the community. Most of the roots of the problems affecting blacks lie outside the black community. Therefore, the search for solutions cannot be confined within black areas. A community council on housing or education, for example, must be equipped with the resources and technical expertise to pursue remedies in the federal, state and local hierarchies; the communications media; financial institutions; the courts; and, where necessary, the streets. Even the best organized black community cannot alone amass sufficient resources and technical expertise to pursue such remedies effectively. And wherever the remedy is pursued, there will have to be power blocks working jointly outside as well as inside the affected community.

The idea of functional coalitions as an alternative to separatism differs from other notions of black-white cooperation in that blacks would not rely upon the magnanimity and direction of whites. Instead the directions would first be defined by individuals and groups within the community, and the support of particular groups of whites, liberal or otherwise, would come out of common interest in the specific goals. None of these coalitions would be static. They would shift across ideological, class and ethnic lines according to new strategies, goals and opportunities. A racial litmus test forecloses the strategic options and therefore represents the height of irrationality.

RACE NOT DETERMINANT

Separatism is inappropriate also as a means of developing pride and a sense of dignity. Pride and dignity, like power, depend on both personal and impersonal factors. The personal factors are largely unrelated to race and exist among blacks to an extent no greater and no less than among whites. As impersonal factors they involve the individual's feelings about being identified with a particular group. Whether the individual is proud or ashamed of the identification depends largely on his evaluation of the status, achievements and potential of his group.

Insofar as the achievements of blacks are concerned, educators and historians have been grossly remiss in conveying a fair sense of the significant roles which blacks have played in shaping this country. But the problem is not to be remedied by racial separation. The need is for a more balanced historical perspective. And, as I noted earlier, racial pride and dignity require that blacks obtain a proportionate share of economic and political power. For a minority population this requires strategic placement and functioning within major social institutions.

We must certainly recognize that the notion of separatism opens the way to dangerous distortions by those who already believe the best way of dealing with the race problem is by cordoning off an already powerless black community.

There are other disturbing features of the separatist movement. Inherent in it has been an almost authoritarian demand for conformity and uncritical acceptance of its main doctrines. Those who have bothered to differ in the slightest have been summarily dismissed as tools of the white establishment or worse. There is no constituency to which the separatist is accountable. The dogma of the elite has been substituted for notions of participatory democracy.

As is the case with all such elites, however, the separatists will not reign long. Which is not to say that a better society will automatically follow the demise of separatism. It may well be that neither functional coalitions nor anything else can draw us from this racial abyss. If all else fails, blacks will no doubt decide to tear down the entire society. Entire because, like it or not, the destinies of blacks and whites in America are inextricably woven. The ultimate equality may be the equality of desolation, blacks and whites together.

HAYWOOD BURNS

Reply

STUDY QUESTIONS FOR COMPREHENSION

1. Is Haywood Burns a separatist or an integrationist?
2. Do Burns's goals for the Blacks differ from D'Army Bailey's?
3. What is Burns's attitude toward using authoritarian methods to attain any goal?

Dear Brother D'Army,

America has always been a separatist society. Whether by slave code, the lash, the lynch mob, Jim Crow laws or subtle, covert discrimination, white separatism has held the black man apart from full and equal participation in this society. The traditional wisdom has been that Americans, when challenged with their democratic credo, would ultimately resolve their "dilemma" in favor of fairness. The Movement provided just such a challenge—it dared white America to be what it said it already was. In the wake of the disillusionment and despair that followed the fragmentation of the Movement, America has been forced to acknowledge the truth about itself—it is racist.

This is a truth that many black people have known for a long time, but most hoped that the society was capable of transformation. Most still do. But those who do not (and the evidence so far seems to be on their side) feel that the most rational response for the racially oppressed is group initiative along racial lines. You question the logic of their position. However, given the history of this nation, it seems to me that the burden of proof must now shift to the man who maintains that black freedom can be achieved "within (the) major social institutions." If the society is racist, he must tell us how its institutions can transcend its racism, and if they cannot, how it is "rational" to insist that black people's goals can be achieved by working within them. There are those who, even though they may believe with you that the social system is capable of the necessary change, refuse to sacrifice another generation of our children upon the altar of this hope.

IMPULSE NOT NEW

I think it is a mistake to view the separatist impulse as merely a response to America's intransigence when challenged by the Movement of the 60's. It is as well a reaction to America's failure to respond to more than 300 years of black protest. It is a response to a constant strain in our past, to the voices of our prophets of nationalism—Cuffe, Delany, Singleton, Bishop Turner, DuBois, Garvey, Muhammad and Brother Malcolm. These voices have been muted by historians, who have stressed the integrationist strain in black protest or ignored black protest altogether, but they nonetheless echo namelessly in the collective consciousness of our people. The black experience in recent years makes consideration of the separatist alternatives all the more relevant. I say "alternatives" because although space did not permit you to distinguish among them in your article, "separatists" come in many varieties: principally those who wish to leave the United States to establish a new nation, those who wish land (e.g., five states) within the United States, and those who want black hegemony over the existing black enclaves within this country. I believe it was to this last group that you addressed your attention and therefore I will do the same.

You were critical of those who "have concluded . . . that the only effective way of achieving power" for black Americans is through organizing black groups. In the sense that "only" means that such organization is a necessary prerequisite for community empowerment, I agree with this point of view. All the lessons of history seem to me to indicate that the black American can never expect to achieve true power until the black community comes together and achieves some level of self-realization. This is necessary for overcoming the fractured nature of our community which has been our historical legacy, for understanding ourselves, and for affirming those aspects of our experience that have sustained us through the dark night of the Diaspora. It is necessary for defining as a group the problems we face as a group and arriving at ways by which these problems may be solved.

Your separatist man who believes that "exclusion eliminates divisiveness and distraction" is made of black straw. I do not know an intelligent separatist who takes that position. The point of coming together is to work out through group introspection some of the problems that plague the black man by reason of his blackness, recognizing that there are bound to be differences and that all men—regardless of color—are subject to the foibles of Man. Authoritarianism and dogmatism among separatists must be dealt with for the evils they are.

POLITICAL INTEREST CONFINED

I had difficulty also with your discussion of the politics and economics of separatists. Presumably, the true separatist, if he favors enclaves, will not want to represent a community outside the enclave, and so will gear his program to his community alone. Annexation of suburbs as cities become majority black seems unlikely in most places because of the legal complications involved and because of white suburban resistance to assuming the tax burden of the inner city. But whether or not the enclave is part of a larger city, the demand will still be for political control of the enclave. I agree with you that organization of the black community has little to recommend it in the economic realm if it is only going to substitute black profiteering for white profiteering. However, the major thrust in this area has been toward the creation of new economic forms which will benefit the community.

Of course, there will have to be functional coalitions. Our world is much too interdependent for any group hermetically to seal itself off. On different scales, any of the three kinds of separatism would have to engage in interaction with others for mutual benefit. But what is the value of coalition until the black community has reached a certain coherence and defined its problems?

It is true that "separatism" through a certain sophistry and distortion can be used by white racists against the black community, but then so can "integration." The problem as I see it is not one of a war of absolutist doctrines of "separatism" versus "integration," but of finding ways for the black community to achieve power so that it can help shape the terms upon which black-white interaction will take place. It is in this context that individual choices, which are the hallmark of the open society, will then be freely made.

Paradoxical as it may seem, I believe that if there yet remains hope that America will ever become something other than a separatist society, the hope lies in black people, coming together to pursue their own liberation.

Yours in the struggle,
Haywood Burns

MARGARET BOURKE-WHITE

The Louisville Flood, 1936

STUDY QUESTIONS FOR COMPREHENSION

1. Even though the photograph on the next two pages was taken in 1936, do you find it still meaningful?
2. Note the words included in the photograph.
3. What idea is Margaret Bourke-White communicating through this photograph?
4. Why do you suppose this picture has been used as an example of excellence in photography?

WORLD'S HIGHE

Courtesy of Margaret Bourke-White

JOHNIE SCOTT

Intent

If, in the beginning,
there was love
(and love moved as
a man stepping from
stone to stone to
finally cross the river)

If, in the beginning,
there was a clear eye
(and thought formed
as if man were moving
from star to star,
and finally to destiny)

If, in the beginning,
there was purpose
(and silence grew
as though plants were
flourishing in some
proverbial garden)

Then why, as we live,
do we hate and not love
(while rivers grew
to swollen proportions
and logjams built
mounds of filth)

Then why, as we live,
does the unwanted child cry
(above dark hills
hang suspended blue
stars and a child asks,
Why does a slum have stars?

Then why, as we live,
is there chaos within sanity
(silence
has always been
a deafening sound;
it is a peace that frightens)

If there was Intent, and it was good
though good is blinded and men staggered on;
If there was meaning, and this had a value,
though feelings are blotted and cares fly away;
If there was happiness, and this brought tears,
though the people cry out, shame and sorrow reign;
If there was Intent, and it was good,
then why this emptiness and blue stars,
like so many hanging lanterns, above a slum?

Writing Assignments for Part Six

1. Using reference materials in the library, write a report on a current problem faced by a particular group of Indians.
2. Research the current situation of the agricultural worker, and write either a report or an essay on what you find.
3. Write an essay in which you discuss the view that man's moral progress lags far behind his technological progress.
4. If you were the President of the United States or the mayor of your city, what steps would you take to end discrimination?
5. Have you ever been involved in or witnessed a situation in which discrimination or injustice was clearly present? What was your reaction? How was the situation resolved?
6. React to the poem "Intent" by Johnie Scott.
7. Man's inhumanity to man occurs not just against certain races, religions, or national groups, but in the course of daily events. If you have witnessed or experienced cruelty of one human being to another, describe the experience.
8. Respond in any form you wish (poem, short story, personal narrative, description) to the theme of this section.

PART SEVEN / *War and Mankind*

Yes; quaint and curious war is!
You shoot a fellow down
You'd treat, if met where any bar is . . .
Thomas Hardy

PEANUTS
Tm. Reg. U. S. Pat. Off.—All rights reserved
Copr. 1964 by United Feature Syndicate, Inc.
I DON'T WORRY ABOUT THE WORLD COMING TO AN END ANY MORE..

THE WAY I FIGURE IT, THE WORLD CAN'T COME TO AN END TODAY BECAUSE IT IS ALREADY TOMORROW IN SOME OTHER PART OF THE WORLD!
11-26

ISN'T THAT A COMFORTING THEORY?

I'VE NEVER FELT SO COMFORTED IN ALL MY LIFE!
SCHULZ

War

STUDY QUESTIONS FOR COMPREHENSION

1. According to the author, what are the causes of war?
2. What is the difference between the reasons advanced for war and the real causes?
3. How are disputes settled within countries?

Since the dawn of history, men have fought against other men. Any struggle in which two large groups try to destroy or conquer each other is a war. There have been many kinds of wars. Families have fought against families, tribes against tribes, followers of one religion against followers of another. In modern times, wars have been fought between nations or groups of nations. Armies and navies once were almost the only factors in determining the outcome of wars. Now, civilians must join in the war effort if it is to succeed.

Wars have always caused great suffering and hardship. Most people hate war, yet for hundreds of years war has been going on somewhere in the world nearly all the time. War is a man-made disaster. Earthquakes and floods *happen* to mankind, but man *makes* war himself. To understand why wars go on when nearly everyone wants peace, we must look into the nature of war.

CAUSES OF WAR

In modern times, no nation or group chooses war if it can get what it wants peacefully. The fighting starts when a nation wants something so badly that it is willing to go to war to get it Sometimes war results from a disagreement between two nations, and sometimes from a desire for conquest. Some basic causes may be a desire for more land, a desire for more wealth, a desire for more power, or a desire for security.

War for land to live on. In ancient times, men often fought so that they could get enough to eat. When the pasture lands in Central Asia dried up, hungry tribesmen would make war on their neighbors in order to get new lands. The neighbors sometimes fought back. More often they gave up their lands and tried to seize those of a still weaker tribe.

Much of the fighting that went on between early American pioneers and American Indians was this kind of war. The Indians wanted to roam freely over the land, hunting, trapping, or fishing. The pioneers wanted to clear the land and plant it in crops. Indian fighting was dangerous, and no one who already had a good farm was likely to go out and fight the Indians for another. But landless men from abroad preferred the dangers of war to the horrors of poverty.

This type of war has not entirely disappeared, but it is no longer common or important. The early war for land to live on usually had these two important characteristics: those who did the fighting made the decision to fight, and the fighters wanted something for themselves.

War for wealth. The peoples of ancient empires fought many wars for wealth. The decision to fight was made by the ruler and his advisers. The fighting was often done by hired armies. A king who sought to conquer new lands did not mean to drive the people out of the lands. Generally he just wanted to collect taxes from the people in the territory he invaded.

When Alexander the Great led his armies against the Persian Empire, the common people of the invaded lands paid little attention, except to hope that their own property would not be destroyed. It usually made little difference to them which king collected taxes. Wars were fought solely by rulers and their armies.

In the Middle Ages, there were many wars for wealth. Often one noble would try to seize the property of another. He would use his own soldiers and perhaps hire other leaders and their soldiers to help him. Sometimes the conqueror of a city would take a large money payment in return for leaving the city in peace.

War for power. The great European nations fought wars throughout the world to gain or increase their power. These wars united the people and strengthened the governments. Wars of conquest based on the ideas of a super-race or of a superior economic system are often wars to extend the power of a government.

War for security. Most countries fear the possibility of attack, and maintain armed forces to defend themselves. Sometimes this fear may be directed toward a particular country. In that case a nation may decide to choose its own time and strike the first blow. Or it may decide to conquer some weaker neighbor, and thus increase its own resources as a defense against attack.

DIFFERENCES BETWEEN CAUSES AND REASONS

When a nation makes war, its government always states the *reasons* for the war. This is necessary if the people are to be united in the war effort. But the reasons given for a war need not be the same as its *causes*. For example, the Government of the United States pointed to the British interference with American shipping and the impressment of American seamen as reasons for the War of 1812. A cause which was not stated was the desire on the part of some Americans to extend the United States into lands held by the British and their Spanish allies in North America. This was one of the important *causes* of the war, but it was not stated as a *reason*. The causes of war may be selfish, base, or even wicked, but the reasons stated are usually lofty and noble. Both sides in a war may show reasons which they consider to be valid.

WAR MEANS ABSENCE OF LAW

War is not the only kind of struggle in which there may be some right on both sides. Almost every case that comes to trial before a court has this same quality. In a suit over property, both sides can usually show a claim of some sort. The court has to decide which is the *better* claim. If there were no court, both persons claiming the property might feel justified in fighting for it.

In frontier days many Westerners carried guns and settled their disputes by fighting. Until courts and police forces were established, they had no other way to settle quarrels in which both sides were partly right. People often joined forces against horse thieves and other "bad men," but they could not handle quarrels between honest men who disagreed about their rights.

Today a similar problem exists among nations. The people in any country are likely to see their own interests more clearly than they can see the interests of people in another country. People's own desires seem so reasonable and so important that the desires of people in another country are likely to look selfish and unreasonable. Laws and courts can take care of such disputes *within* a country, but there has as yet been no effective law *between* countries. That is why the use of force to settle a dispute is a *crime* within a country and a *war* between countries. War can exist only where there is no effective law.

DEPRESSION AND WAR

Some economists and historians think there is a close connection between war and economic depression. They argue that in a worldwide depression every country tries to protect itself at the expense of other countries. Each nation wants to cut down unemployment at home, and tries to make sure that little is bought from abroad which could be made by its own workers at home. This can easily be done by raising tariffs. It is sometimes called a way of "exporting unemployment" to other countries.

The chief concern of any government during a depression is to get people back to work. One way to do this is by building armaments. If anger can be stirred up against another country, or if people can be made to feel that they are in danger of attack, funds for military preparation are readily voted. Besides, the armed forces themselves give employment to many.

A modern democracy, such as the United States, would never risk war in order to end a depression or put people to work. But war may provide more employment and give many people a larger share of food, clothing, and other good things than they can have in depression. For this reason, a long depression makes war seem less dreadful to those who have lost all hope, and may drive them to follow such leaders as Adolf Hitler.

METHODS OF WARFARE

Changes in the ways of waging war have had a great effect on the way people live. Some historians think that the idea of human equality came to be widely accepted because guns took the place of spears, swords, and arrows as the chief weapons of war. They point out that an armored knight in feudal days was more than a match for dozens of men who had no armor. But, these historians point out, the minutemen of Lexington and Concord, with guns in their hands, were equal or nearly equal to the same number of British soldiers. Following their theory, the historians go on to point out that when one fighting man became the equal of another, some men decided that voting was an easy way to tell how a fight over a given issue would come out. The idea of human equality gained strength when people accepted each person's right to cast a vote that was just as important as any other person's vote.

Modern warfare has moved away from the days when soldiers with rifles were the most important part of an army. War has been mechanized until it is in large part a contest in producing machinery. In Thomas Jefferson's day, it made sense to protect "the right to keep and bear arms," so that people could overthrow a tyrannical government. Today, the private citizen cannot possibly keep the kinds of arms that would serve this purpose.

As the methods of warfare have changed, the cost of war has increased. For example, the War of 1812 cost the United States about $117,079 each day. But World War II cost the nation about $250,000,000 each day.

THE ATOMIC BOMB

The atomic bomb, used by the United States against Japan in 1945, has brought another great change into warfare. After the invention of the bomb, it seemed probable that future wars would be short and terribly destructive. No one doubted that great cities could be destroyed and millions of people killed within a few hours. The only question was whether the nations of the world could change their habits fast enough to keep war from breaking out. Most scientists agreed that a full-scale atomic war might destroy civilization as we know it.

TOTAL WAR

Even as late as the 1700's, most wars were fought by hired professional armies. The French Revolution produced the idea of the "nation in arms." To protect their young republic, thousands of volunteers became soldiers, and the "mass armies" of France surprised and dismayed the old-fashioned generals of Europe. After that, France drafted all able-bodied men at certain ages to protect the country.

In World Wars I and II, the members of the fighting forces were not the only persons drafted and organized by the various governments. Whole nations were mobilized for civilian defense and aid to warfare, with much government control over manufacturing, transportation, farming, and mining. Total war has come to mean the use for war purposes of all the natural resources and man power of a country.

IS WAR "NORMAL"?

Democratic countries take it for granted that peace is normal, and that war means something has gone wrong. But it is hard to say just where peace ends and war begins. Nations may be on unfriendly terms for years, building up their armies and navies, falling farther and farther under the sway of militarism, seeking allies, and trying to win control of each other's markets, without any actual clash of armed forces. It is debatable whether these countries are really at peace. They might be considered to be merely observing a rest period between wars.

GERALD M. FEIGEN

Letter to the Editor

Editor—I wish to make a comment about Vietnam from the point of view of a surgeon. What I have to say applies to both sides and all sides. I want to talk about the wounded—the young men who lie dying on the moist earth; youth beginning, youth ending, without fruition; youth and bullets that tear out a hole as big as a basketball, and spill away the life force.

The enemy, to both sides, is a hostile stranger who must be destroyed. In the distance he is a faceless shadow, lurking behind the seared bushes; he must be killed before he kills you. Once he is wounded, his status changes. Now your doctors ease his pain with morphine, dim the bright mask of death nearby; now your doctors dress his wounds, try to reassemble his disarray. So the wound is the equalizer, and either side is the other.

Generals on both sides pore over maps; frowning in concentration, they plan the push. They decide. A unit of young men, not quite ready for life, are made ready to die. On the way they are terrified; there is total uncertainty. They go on. They are fighting for their country, but also for their lives. Soon the pressure mounts to near panic, and the statistics begin to operate. A scream and a thud, a scream and a thud—cryout of young men caught by mortar shells dropped into silly looking pipes. The silence is filled with unbearable noise, and each man moves according to his programming, until the daymare or the nightmare is over, and he can crawl into sleep or be tumbled into death.

The near dead lie gasping, passing in review their too-short lives. If they've seen their wounds they stare in frightened wonder. How can the clock ever work again, with all those little wheels and springs twisted in crimson puddles? The great gobs wrenched from their

From the *San Francisco Chronicle*, March 4, 1966.

bodies leave hopeless gaps, hastily covered. They lie alone, badgered by flies, drifting between desperate fear and unconsciousness.

The old men who plan things are safe and "wise," their wisdom failing their young agents on the battleground. The old men justify, qualify, ratify, and prophesy. They must suspect that political differences can no longer be solved by military action, but until they admit it to themselves and establish a conference table, they are letting the young men die, suddenly, without dignity; they are letting the young men fall to the maggoty ground to dribble away the promise, the dream, and the cherished life.

The insides of both sides look the same on the jungle dirt.

Gerald M. Feigen, M.D.

DON L. LEE

Hero

(a poem for brig. general frederic davison,
if he can dig it)

little willie
a hero in
the american tradition.
a blk/hero.
he
received the:
bronze star: which read "meritorious action,"
(his momma had to look the word up)
good conduct medal,
combat infantry badge,
purple heart,
national defense service medal,
vietnam campaign ribbon,
& some others i can't even spell.

little willie
a hero in

the american tradition.
a blk/hero.
he
received his medals

p
o
s
t
h
u
m
o
u
s
l
y
.
.
.

LEO TOLSTOY

Advice to a Draftee

STUDY QUESTIONS FOR COMPREHENSION

1. What advice do you suppose Tolstoy would give to today's potential draftee?
2. Explain Tolstoy's statement that one's actions should be based on morality rather than on the consequences of one's act.
3. Explain Tolstoy's answer to the question, "How can you refuse to do what everyone else does?"

In my last letter I answered your question as well as I could. It is not only Christians but all just people who must refuse to become soldiers—that is, to be ready on another's command (for this is what a soldier's duty actually consists of) to kill all those one is ordered to kill. The question as you state it—which is more useful, to become a good teacher or to suffer for rejecting conscription?—is falsely stated. The question is falsely stated because it is wrong for us to determine our actions according to their results, to view actions merely as useful or destructive. In the choice of our actions we can be led by their advantages or disadvantages only when the actions themselves are not opposed to the demands of morality.

We can stay home, go abroad, or concern ourselves with farming or science according to what we find useful for ourselves or others; for neither in domestic life, foreign travel, farming, nor science is there anything immoral. But under no circumstance can we inflict violence on people, torture or kill them because we think such acts could be of use to us or to others. We cannot and may not do such things, especially because we can never be sure of the results of our actions. Often actions which seem the most advantageous of all turn out in fact to be destructive; and the reverse is also true.

The question should not be stated: which is more useful, to be a good teacher or to go to jail for refusing conscription? but rather:

what should a man do who has been called upon for military service —that is, called upon to kill or to prepare himself to kill?

And to this question, for a person who understands the true meaning of military service and who wants to be moral, there is only one clear and incontrovertible answer: such a person must refuse to take part in military service no matter what consequences this refusal may have. It may seem to us that this refusal could be futile or even harmful, and that it would be a far more useful thing, after serving one's time, to become a good village teacher. But in the same way, Christ could have judged it more useful for himself to be a good carpenter and submit to all the principles of the Pharisees than to die in obscurity as he did, repudiated and forgotten by everyone.

Moral acts are distinguished from all other acts by the fact that they operate independently of any predictable advantage to ourselves or to others. No matter how dangerous the situation may be of a man who finds himself in the power of robbers who demand that he take part in plundering, murder, and rape, a moral person cannot take part. Is not military service the same thing? Is one not required to agree to the deaths of all those one is commanded to kill?

But how can one refuse to do what everyone does, what everyone finds unavoidable and necessary? Or, must one do what no one does and what everyone considers unnecessary or even stupid and bad? No matter how strange it sounds, this strange argument is the main one offered against those moral acts which in our times face you and every other person called up for military service. But this argument is even more incorrect than the one which would make a moral action dependent upon considerations of advantage.

If I, finding myself in a crowd of running people, run with the crowd without knowing where, it is obvious that I have given myself up to mass hysteria; but if by chance I should push my way to the front, or be gifted with sharper sight than the others, or receive information that this crowd was racing to attack human beings and toward its own corruption, would I really not stop and tell the people what might rescue them? Would I go on running and do these things which I knew to be bad and corrupt? This is the situation of every individual called up for military service, if he knows what military service means.

AARON BOHROD

Military Necessity

The painting on the next page is of a village crucifix in France which is strung with Signal Corps wires.

STUDY QUESTIONS FOR COMPREHENSION

1. What is the significance of Bohrod's title, "Military Necessity"?
2. What message about war and mankind do you think Bohrod is trying to communicate?
3. How do you react to the painting? Can you determine *why* you respond as you do?

I can well understand that you, a young man full of life, loving and loved by your mother, friends, perhaps a young woman, think with a natural terror about what awaits you if you refuse conscription; and perhaps you will not feel strong enough to bear the consequences of refusal, and knowing your weakness, will submit and become a soldier. I understand completely, and I do not for a moment allow myself to blame you, knowing very well that in your place I might perhaps do the same thing. Only do not say that you did it because it was useful or because everyone does it. If you did it, know that you did wrong.

In every person's life there are moments in which he can know himself, tell himself who he is, whether he is a man who values his human dignity above his life or a weak creature who does not know his dignity and is concerned merely with being useful (chiefly to himself). This is the situation of a man who goes out to defend his honor in a duel or a soldier who goes into battle (although here the concepts of life are wrong). It is the situation of a doctor or a priest called to someone sick with plague, of a man in a burning house or a sinking ship who must decide whether to let the weaker go first or shove them aside and save himself. It is the situation of a man in poverty who accepts or rejects a bribe. And in our times, it is the situation of a man called to military service. For a man who knows its significance, the call to the army is perhaps the only opportunity for him to behave as a morally free creature and fulfill the highest requirement of his life—or else merely to keep his advantage in sight like an animal and thus remain slavishly submissive and servile until humanity becomes degraded and stupid.

For these reasons I answered your question whether one has to refuse to do military service with a categorical "yes"—if you understand the meaning of military service (and if you did not understand it then, you do now) and if you want to behave as a moral person living in our times must.

Please excuse me if these words are harsh. The subject is so important that one cannot be careful enough in expressing oneself so as to avoid false interpretation.

April 7, 1899

e. e. cummings

my sweet old etcetera

STUDY QUESTIONS FOR COMPREHENSION

1. Do you find the appearance of cummings's poem disturbing?
2. Do you find that your concept of the word *etcetera* changes as you read the poem?
3. What point do you think cummings is making in this poem?

my sweet old etcetera
aunt lucy during the recent

war could and what
is more did tell you just
what everybody was fighting

for,
my sister

isabel created hundreds
(and
hundreds) of socks not to
mention shirts fleaproof earwarmers

etcetera wristers etcetera my
mother hoped that
i would die etcetera
bravely of course my father used
to become hoarse talking about how it was
a privilege and if only he
could meanwhile my

self etcetera lay quietly
in the deep mud et

cetera
(dreaming,
et
  cetera, of
Your smile
eyes knees and of your Etcetera)

J. DAVID SINGER

Political Science of Human Conflict

STUDY QUESTIONS FOR COMPREHENSION

1. What does Singer mention at the beginning of his essay as being specifically necessary before a nation can wage war?
2. What must the populations of warring nations be prepared to give up?
3. What forces exist that cause the leaders of warring nations to continue hostilities?

Military power must be based upon, and supplemented by, a mobilized national population. If the national society is to provide the men, the money, and the material willingly—or even passively—with which to make any threat of military force credible, the population must be persuaded that a genuine threat is posed by the adversary of the moment. Furthermore, the citizenry must be persuaded to accept such ancillary costs of preparedness as a serious erosion of civil liberties, and in the mid-twentieth century, the additional burden of genetically harmful radioactivity.

Since none of these are traditionally thought of as inherent in the human condition (though even this set of norms may be changing), the national political elites find it necessary to paint an increasingly treacherous, if not omnipotent picture of the opposing nation(s) in the conflict. The consequence need not necessarily be Lasswell's "garrison state," but it inevitably becomes some approximation thereof. That is, as the symbols of legitimacy are constantly associated with, and invested in, the preparedness program and its parallel activities, organized or individual resistance to the train of events becomes ever more costly and difficult.

The tragedy is, of course, that at about the time the political elites discover what they have set in motion, it is extremely costly to seek to slow or reverse it. They discover that their domestic pay-off structure is full of rewards for continuing to feed the hostility and the jingoism, and loaded with penalties if they hesitate to do so. Normally, the would-be peacemaker loses out (at the polls, in the smoke-filled rooms, or whatever the path to political power) to the sabre-rattler and the demagogue. As a consequence, the holder or seeker of domestic power finds himself seriously inhibited from "doing business" with the enemy. Bargaining is seen as appeasement, *quid pro quo* concessions represent capitulation, and serious negotiation may well be denounced as treason.

The irony, of course, is that a similar pattern is reproduced within the society of the other conflicting nation. The two national systems not only produce this positive feedback process *within* themselves, but by their consequent external behavior produce exactly what is required to strengthen and accelerate it within the other. The distribution of power among the subnational groups is ultimately such that those who favor the "hard line" acquire a strangle hold over the domestic political process. Not only are the probabilities of a "co-existence" faction achieving national office extremely low, but those already in office find it increasingly necessary to placate and reinforce the more aggressive groups in order to retain legitimacy. The result is, of course, a tacit and indirect alliance between the "hard-line" groups in each of the nations, with the titular power-holders trapped in a pay-off matrix (admittedly of their own making in some measure) in which punishment for co-operative diplomatic gestures comes from both their own national subgroups and their opposite numbers in the other nation.

JOHN MOFFITT

The Second Coming

STUDY QUESTIONS FOR COMPREHENSION

1. Why does Moffitt not capitalize the pronoun when he refers to the Lord?
2. Why does Moffitt feel that war is opposed to the principles of Christianity?
3. What point is Moffitt conveying in this poem?

Were you there,
Were you there,
When they crucified
My Lord?
When they struck
His holihood,
When they nailed him
To the rood,
When they drew
His blood?
(I was there,
I was there,
And I saw him
Hanging there,
Felt the thunder
In my soul
Smite the thunder
In the air.)

Were you there,
Were you there,
When he stood

From *This Narrow World* by John Moffitt (New York: Dodd, Mead and Company, 1958).

Beside the tomb,
In the garden
In the morning,
Risen from
Gehenna's womb?
(I was there,
I was there,
And I saw him
Standing there,
Saw his lonely
Patient smile,
Fairer than
All things fair,
And I heard him
Plight his word
To return
Among us here.)

Were you there,
Were you there,
When he kept his
Pledge to men,
When he came
To earth again?
When they cast him
In the dust,
When they broke
His trust,
When they sealed
A nation's doom
In the name
Of kingdom come,
When they dropped
The cobalt bomb?
(I was there,
I was there,

And I saw him
Weeping there,
Saw the pitiless
Sharp crown
Pressing close
About his hair,
And I saw
The seraphim
As they swung
Their swords of flame,
And I saw
The victims' feet
All around
The Judgment Seat,
And I felt
The wrath of God
Like a vast
Devouring cloud,
And I watched
The world go down
In a churning
Cloud of dust,
To the bottom
Of the pit.
And my Lord,
And my Lord,
Rose and
Followed it.)

ARTHUR HOPPE

Star of Wonder, Star of Light

STUDY QUESTIONS FOR COMPREHENSION

1. Why are parts of "Star of Wonder, Star of Light" in italics?
2. What point is the author making?
3. Relate the main idea in "Star of Wonder, Star of Light" to that expressed in the poem "The Second Coming" by John Moffitt.

ST. LUKE 2:7—And she brought forth her firstborn son, and wrapped him in swaddling clothes, and laid him in a manger; because there was no room for them in the inn.

And it came to pass that Joseph and his espoused wife, Mary, being great with child, came unto their own city to be taxed. And lo, a star appeared in the East.

It was first spotted by three radarmen tending their electronic scanners on a hillside blockhouse which was an integral station in the Distant Early Warning (DEW) Line. "Unidentified object, bearing two-seven-oh, elevation three-oh," chanted one. They woke the lieutenant. He checked the tapes. It wasn't Midas or Samos or Echo II or Discoverer VI. He woke the colonel, who woke the general, who said: "Sound the red alert, start the emergency countdown, and get me the President."

And thus it came to pass that the horns wailed and Joseph and Mary were in confusion, for the city was strange unto them. The people of the city were afraid. And they ran to and fro. And Joseph feared for Mary his wife.

"No, Mr. President," the general was shouting over the red telephone. "We don't know what the hell it is. We're checking. NASA confirms it isn't one of ours. It must be one of theirs."

And lo, the star approached from the East toward the city. And in the city this sign was viewed with wonder and alarm. And husbands sought their wives. And mothers sought their children. And some remained in the houses, sorely afraid, seeking comfort in each other. And some ran into caves they had dug in the earth. And they, too, were sorely afraid.

"Three minutes, forty-five seconds . . . Three minutes, forty seconds . . ." The steel hatches over the underground silos in Wyoming and Kansas and Idaho slid silently open. The blast doors around each underground launching pad clanged shut. And each technician watched his dials and checked his readings and did his duty.

And in the city, Joseph and Mary took refuge in a doorway. But an officer came unto them and spoke unto them saying that they could not remain in this place. And they must seek shelter in a cave.

"If it's theirs," said the President, rubbing his temples with his fingertips, "they'll be trying to knock out our first strike capability. If so, we've got to get our missiles in the air first. How much time have we got?" "It's closing fast," said one of the three Joint Chiefs of Staff. "One minute, thirty seconds . . . One minute, twenty-five seconds . . ."

And lo, the star hovered over the city.

"Fire!" said the President. "And God help us."

And thus it came to pass that Joseph and his wife, Mary, sought entrance to a cave. But their way was barred by a man, armed as if for war. And he spake angrily unto them, saying:

"There is no room in the shelter."

HENRY REED

Naming of Parts

STUDY QUESTIONS FOR COMPREHENSION

1. Reed refers to several parts of the gun. What is his purpose in referring to those parts that the soldiers do not yet have?
2. Why is Spring chosen as the setting for the poem?
3. Can you sum up Reed's essential point?

To-day we have naming of parts. Yesterday,
We had daily cleaning. And to-morrow morning,
We shall have what to do after firing. But to-day,
To-day we have naming of parts. Japonica
Glistens like coral in all of the neighbouring gardens.
  And to-day we have naming of parts.

This is the lower sling swivel. And this
Is the upper sling swivel, whose use you will see,
When you are given your slings. And this is the piling swivel,
Which in your case you have not got. The branches
Hold in the gardens their silent, eloquent gestures,
  Which in our case we have not got.

This is the safety-catch, which is always released
With an easy flick of the thumb. And please do not let me
See anyone using his finger. You can do it quite easy
If you have any strength in your thumb. The blossoms
Are fragile and motionless, never letting anyone see
  Any of them using their finger.

And this you can see is the bolt. The purpose of this
Is to open the breech, as you see. We can slide it
Rapidly backwards and forwards: we call this
Easing the spring. And rapidly backwards and forwards
The early bees are assaulting and fumbling the flowers:
    They call it easing the Spring.

They call it easing the Spring: it is perfectly easy
If you have any strength in your thumb: like the bolt,
And the breech, and the cocking-piece, and the point of balance,
Which in our case we have not got; and the almond-blossom
Silent in all of the gardens and the bees going backwards and forwards,
    For to-day we have naming of parts.

ARNOLD TOYNBEE

War Is Not the Normal Condition of Man

STUDY QUESTIONS FOR COMPREHENSION

1. What are the historical facts that Toynbee uses to disprove the frequent statement that "Man has always made war in the past; therefore, Man will always make war"?
2. The author states that war is an institution which "cannot be operated without a political organization and an economic surplus." Explain.
3. Toynbee says that wars can be prevented. How?

Is war man's normal condition? Is it perhaps even a built-in element of human nature?

Of these two possibilities, the second is of course more serious than the first, but the first is serious enough by itself to be fatal, if true. Man has now been overtaken by a consequence of his gift for technology. He has invented the atomic weapon. If war is a normal condition of man, human life is not going to go on existing on this planet much longer. The genus Homo is soon going to "join the majority," as the Romans used to put it in their inscriptions on tombstones.

First, then, is war a normal condition of man? One fact that seems to tell in favor of this hypothesis is that wars have not ceased since the end of the Second World War. Mankind has waged two world wars within the span of one lifetime, and before the end of the Second World War two atomic bombs had been dropped on human beings. Yet it seems that we have not had enough.

For instance, the American people, who passed the neutrality legislation of 1935 in the hope of being able to keep out of the coming war in Europe and became involved against their will, have since embarked on a war of their own. The theater is Vietnam: and Vietnam is as remote from the United States as any theater of war could be. What does this mean? Does it mean that Americans, being human, could not refrain for long from indulging in an activity that is part of the normal condition of man?

The evidence might seem to point that way, and it is not an isolated case. Ethiopians and Somalis, Indonesians and Malaysians, Israelis and Arabs, have all been behaving like the Americans and the Vietcong.

This is all true and all depressing. Yet the evidence of history, including current history, points the other way, I believe, when this evidence is looked at as a whole.

It is true that, since the end of the Second World War, there have been a number of local wars. But it is also true that, during those 20 years, there has been no war between any of the three superpowers, no world war, and no war in which the atomic weapon has been used. The reason surely is that the significance of this invention has been recognized, and this has led the governments and the peoples, since then, to keep their warfare within bounds, even though it has not deterred them from going on playing the very dangerous game of making war within these limits. If war were man's normal condition, the normal sequel to the Second World War would have been for the United States and Russia to go to war with each other, and for China then to go to war with the survivor, if there was one.

Roman history gives us a longer view than our own generation gives. The Romans closed the doors of the temple of the god Janus when Rome was at peace, and those doors are recorded only once to have been closed (and then for only a year or two) before they were closed in the reign of Augustus. Thus the pre-Augustan chapter of Roman history might seem to be evidence that war is the normal condition of man.

The next chapter, however, is evidence to the contrary. Augustus established peace throughout the Mediterranean world, and the Augustan peace was preserved for a quarter of a millennium.

Within that period there were, of course, one or two short civil wars over the succession to the imperial throne; there were one or two minor wars with the Parthian Empire, which was Rome's only civilized nextdoor neighbor, and there was intermittent police action against the barbarians beyond the Roman Empire's frontiers. All the same, this was on the whole an age of peace for the western end of the Old World. The years 31 B.C.–235 A.D. stand out, in this respect, in sharp contrast to the preceding millennia. Those 265 years of peace prove that, after all, war is not the normal condition of man in that part of the world.

The same tale is told by the histories of Switzerland and Norway. In the sixteenth century the Swiss were the most warlike nation in Europe. They served as mercenary soldiers in the armies of all the belligerent Western European powers. The French Government had to hire Swiss infantry because the French peasantry were then reluctant to go to war. Yet the French peasant conscript soldiers overran Europe in the Napoleonic wars, whereas the Swiss turned into the most peaceful nation in Europe. By now, Switzerland has been a neutral state for a century and a half.

As for the Norwegians, their Vikings once raided all the coasts of Europe, right around into the Mediterranean. Yet in 1940, when Norway was attacked without provocation by Germany, Norway had been at peace for 126 years without a break. In 1940 there was no one alive in Norway who had ever met any living Norwegian, even in his grandparents' generation, who had had a personal experience of war. If war were really the normal condition of man, all Norwegians would have become pathological cases by the beginning of the present century.

The history of the eastern end of the Old World tells the same story even more emphatically. During the millennium ending in 221 B.C., the Chinese world was as full of wars as the contemporary Mediterranean world. But, since the political unification of China in 221 B.C., China has normally been at peace down to this day, with some exceptional bouts of internal disorder of the kind that punctuated the shorter-lived Roman peace. At this moment, China is reunited and this large section of man's habitat is at peace. A survey of Chinese history gives the impression that peace, not war, is the normal condition of man.

In face of these historical facts, it is impossible to maintain that war is the normal condition of man. There have been bouts of war, but bouts of peace have followed them sooner or later, and, in Eastern Asia at any rate, these bouts of peace have been much longer. In China for more than 21 centuries beginning in 221 B.C., civil servants, scholars and businessmen all had a higher social status than soldiers. Then why is China militant today? There is an obvious special reason: From 1840 to 1945, China was attacked, stamped on, humiliated and fleeced by one warlike foreign country after another—first by Britain, then by France, and finally by Japan, a parvenu country which had borrowed its civilization from China. A century of such treatment would be enough to make a saint turn savage.

But perhaps war, even if it is not the normal state of man, is a latent element in human nature which is capable of coming to the surface at any time. To test this proposition, we have to be clear about our use of words. We shall go wrong if we say "war" when we really mean "pugnacity" or "aggressiveness."

It may be true that without pugnacity and aggressiveness there cannot be war, but the converse does not hold good. There can be pugnacity and aggressiveness without war. Many animals are pugnacious, yet man is the only known animal that makes war; and, as far as we know, man has been making war only for about the last 5,000 years—that is to say, for only about half of one per cent of the probable time during which the genus Homo has existed.

Pugnacity and aggressiveness may well be built-in elements in human nature. They are probably built into every species of living creature, from the tiger and the slug to the amoeba. Self-assertion is of the essence of life. This self-assertion is perpetually being challenged, because there are more self-assertive creatures than one. When self-assertion meets counter-self-assertion, pugnacity and aggressiveness are the sparks that the encounter sets flying. In mammals of many species, including man, one of the common forms of rivalry is the competition between males for the possession of females. But a fight between two bull seals for a cow, or between two men for a woman, is quite different from a war between two human armies.

War is not just pugnacity boiling over; it is an institution governed by rules. This is one reason why man is unique in being a war-making animal. Pugnacity cannot be institutionalized without the application of human reasoning power (though reason has never been put to a more irrational use). More than that, this institution cannot be operated without a political organization and an economic surplus.

One of the distinctive features of this canalization of pugnacity is that, in war, the pugnacity is impersonal. A soldier on one side has no personal quarrel with any soldier on the other side. The quarrel is not between individuals; it is between communities. Soldiers Hans and Kurt cannot have any animus against the unknown soldiers Arthur and Edward; but, as German soldiers, they can and do have an animus against Britain when Germany and Britain are at war. No state, no war.

War can be waged only by states, and it takes at least two states to wage it. In a world in which there is just one state—a world state embracing the whole of society—international war is an impossibility. There can still be civil wars, revolutions, insurrections, riots, disorders, because social justice is never likely to be perfect, and because man is a pugnacious animal.

But the histories of the Roman and Chinese empires—and of the British Empire in India, too—show that these domestic disturbances do not produce anything like so much slaughter and suffering as in international wars.

We rightly speak of "the Roman peace," in spite of our awareness that this peace was not unbroken. It was an age of peace compared to what had gone before and to what was to come after. The British peace in the Indian subcontinent lasted for just 100 years ending in 1947, and it was interrupted only by the mutiny of the British East India Company's Indian army in 1857. Yet, during that century, anything like the present war in the subcontinent would have been impossible. What has made this possible now is the partition of the unitary British Indian Empire into two sovereign states.

We also know how the Roman peace and the Chinese peace were created and maintained—by the suppression of the sovereignty of the local states that had been the previous warmakers. Sovereignty was transferred from the local states to the Roman and the Chinese world states. Each of these two empires was a world state in the sense that each embraced virtually the whole of the civilized world that came within its horizon.

Since civilization has become global now, and since the whole surface of our planet has become a single arena for warmaking purposes, the world state that we have to build must be on a literally worldwide scale. This is within our power organizationally and technologically; many private business organizations are operating efficiently on a worldwide scale already. The obstacle is not organizational or technological; it is psychological.

We are clinging to the institution of local sovereign states, because this war-breeding form of political organization is one of Western man's old bad habits. And Western institutions, good and bad alike, are being copied all over the world today by non-Western peoples who have been fascinated by Western civilization because of its power and wealth. What we all need to do now is to copy the war-preventing types of political organization represented by the Roman and the Chinese world states.

Deprive our countries of their sovereignty in order to give a monopoly of sovereignty to a new world state with which we have no hallowed associations and for which we therefore feel no affection or loyalty? Would this be tolerable? Well, it would at least be more tolerable than seeing our national states wiped off the map in a common annihilation.

The states of the United States are no longer sovereign in fact, though they retain a nominal sovereignty by a tactful fiction. Yet the states of the Union continue to be important institutions as members of a federation. It is now the turn of the United States itself—and of Russia, China and the rest of the world's present 125 sovereign states, down to Andorra and San Marino—to subordinate themselves voluntarily to a world-wide federal state created jointly by them all.

Self-subordination or self-extinction? Which are we going to choose? If we plead that we are not free to choose, history will give us the lie. We are free, so we are responsible. Our fate is in our own hands.

"I never was much good at taking tests."

Two Songs

STUDY QUESTIONS FOR COMPREHENSION

1. To which of the following two songs do you react favorably? Unfavorably? Why?
2. These two songs were written over one hundred years apart. How does "The Willing Conscript" reflect changes in attitude that have occurred because of the passage of time?
3. As different as these songs are, how can you tell that both authors love their country?

JULIA WARD HOWE

The Battle Hymn of the Republic

Mine eyes have seen the glory of the coming of the Lord:
He is trampling out the vintage where the grapes of wrath are stored;
He hath loosed the fateful lightning of his terrible swift sword:
His truth is marching on.

I have seen him in the watch-fires of a hundred circling camps;
They have builded him an altar in the evening dews and damps;
I can read his righteous sentence by the dim and flaring lamps:
His day is marching on.

I have read a fiery gospel, writ in burnished rows of steel:
"As ye deal with my contemners, so with you my grave shall deal;
Let the Hero, born of woman, crush the serpent with his heel,
Since God is marching on."

He has sounded forth the trumpet that shall never call retreat;
He is sifting out the hearts of men before his judgment-seat:
O, be swift, my soul, to answer him! be jubilant, my feet!
Our God is marching on.

In the beauty of the lilies Christ was born across the sea,
With a glory in his bosom that transfigures you and me;
As he died to make men holy, let us die to make men free,
While God is marching on.

He is coming like the glory of the morning on the wave,
He is wisdom to the mighty, he is honor to the brave,
So the world shall be his footstool, the soul of wrong his slave,
Our God is marching on!

TOM PAXTON

The Willing Conscript

Oh Sergeant I'm a draftee and I've just arrived in camp,
I've come to wear the uniform and join the martial tramp,
And I want to do my duty but one thing I do implore,
You must give me lessons, Sergeant,
For I've never killed before.

To do my job obediently is my only desire,
To learn my weapon thoroughly and how to aim and fire,
To learn to kill the enemy and then to slaughter more
I'll need instructions, Sergeant,
For I've never killed before.

Now there are rumors in the camp about our enemy;
They say that when you see him he looks just like you and me
But you deny it, Sergeant, and you are a man of war;
So you must give me lessons
For I've never killed before.

Now there are several lessons that I haven't mastered yet—
I haven't got the hang of how to use the bayonet.
If he doesn't die at once, am I to stick him with it more?
  Oh I hope you will be patient,
  For I've never killed before.

And the hand grenade is something that I just don't understand,
You've got to throw it quickly or you're apt to lose your hand,
Does it blow a man to pieces with its wicked, muffled roar?
  Oh, I've got so much to learn, because I've never killed before.

Well, I want to thank you, Sergeant, for the help you've been to me,
You've taught me how to kill, and how to hate the enemy,
And I know that I'll be ready when they march me off to war.
  And I know that it won't matter that I've never killed before,
  I know that it won't matter that I've never killed before.

ALBERT EINSTEIN

Only Then Shall We Find Courage

STUDY QUESTIONS FOR COMPREHENSION

1. Does Einstein believe that it is possible for America to maintain its supremacy in nuclear weapons?
2. Does Einstein believe that there is a defense system possible against nuclear war?
3. What is Einstein's proposal for peace?
4. Does Einstein's use of the term "law and order" differ from the way the term "law and order" is used today?

Often in evolutionary processes a species must adapt to new conditions in order to survive. Today the atomic bomb has altered profoundly the nature of the world as we know it, and the human race consequently finds itself in a new habitat to which it must adapt its thinking.

In the light of this new knowledge, a world authority and an eventual world state are not just *desirable* in the name of brotherhood; they are *necessary* for survival. In previous ages a nation's life and culture could be protected to some extent by the growth of armies in national competition. Today we must abandon competition and secure co-operation. This must be the central fact in all our considerations of international affairs; otherwise we face certain disaster. Past thinking and methods did not succeed in preventing world wars. Future thinking *must* prevent wars.

Modern war, the bomb, and other discoveries present us with revolutionary circumstances. Never before was it possible for one nation to make war on another without sending armies across borders. Now, with rockets and atomic bombs, no center of population

From *Einstein on Peace* (New York: Simon & Schuster, 1960), pp. 383–385. Reprinted by permission of the Estate of Albert Einstein.

on the earth's surface is secure from destruction by a single surprise attack.

America has a temporary superiority in armaments, but it is certain that we have no lasting secret. What nature tells one group of men, she will tell in time to any group interested and patient enough in asking the questions. But our temporary superiority gives this nation the tremendous responsibility of taking the lead in mankind's effort to surmount the crisis.

Being an ingenious people, Americans find it hard to believe that there is no foreseeable defense against atomic bombs. But this is a basic fact. Scientists do not even know of any course of action which promises us any hope of adequate defense. The military-minded cling to old methods of thinking, and one Army department has been surveying possibilities of going underground and, in the event of war, placing factories in places like Mammoth Cave. Others speak of dispersing our population centers into "linear" or "ribbon" cities.

Reasonable men, in considering these new aspects of warfare, refuse to contemplate a future in which our culture would attempt to survive in ribbons or in underground tombs. Neither is there any reassurance in such proposals as keeping a hundred thousand men alert along the coasts scanning the sky with radar. There is no radar defense against the V-2, and should a "defense" be developed after years of research, it is not humanly possible for any defense to be perfect. Should one rocket with an atomic warhead strike Minneapolis, that city would look almost exactly like Nagasaki. Rifle bullets kill men, but atomic bombs kill cities. A tank is a defense against a bullet but there is no defense in science against the weapon which can destroy civilization.

Our defense is not in armaments, nor in science, nor in going underground. Our defense is in law and order.

Henceforth, every nation's foreign policy must be judged at every point by one consideration: Does it lead us to a world of law and order or does it lead us back toward anarchy and death?

PETER KELSO, age 11

Sleep and Dreams

Go perfect into peace,
  Peace mighty-majestic and molded, mounted
  Upon the satin whipped waves of the heavens.
  Roam in orchards of twilit apples, and
  Drawn by a million vermilion stallions,
  Shadow dappled across the fields of legend—
Go perfect into peace.

Go perfect into peace,
  Grave and golden,
  Free of fiery fury.
  Bathed in the glowing tears of dawn,
  Night-washed, night-webbed—
Go perfect into peace.

Writing Assignments for Part Seven

1. Find one article favoring the United States' position in Indochina and one article opposed to U.S. intervention in Indochina. Summarize both articles.
2. Write an essay in which you discuss what action an individual can take that may affect the policies of a democratic government.
3. Which of the selections in this section do you find most interesting or most persuasive? Support your statement by specific references to the text. You may wish to group certain selections: for instance, "The Second Coming," "Military Necessity," and "Star of Wonder."
4. Write an essay in which you discuss the psychological effect of nuclear war.
5. Write a letter to a congressman (or any other important public figure) persuading him to take specific actions toward peace.
6. Describe in as vivid detail as possible a person, a place, or a scene that is connected in some way with war.
7. Write an autobiographical or biographical sketch related to your own or a friend's war experiences.
8. Respond to any one or more selections in this section in any form you choose: a poem, a short story, a narration, a description, an essay.

PART EIGHT / *The Future: What Do We Face?*

Thou canst not stir a flower without troubling of a star.
Francis Thompson

The Works of Nature

Courtesy of Edward Shuster

Courtesy of Standard Oil Collection
University of Louisville Photographic Archives

The Works of Man

DON MARQUIS

what the ants are saying

The following poem appeared in 1927 in a book by Don Marquis, "the lives and times of archy and mehitabel." *archy is a cockroach who uses a newspaper editor's typewriter at night, and, since he has to jump on each key, he cannot, of course, use capital letters.*

Even in the 20's some had the foresight that man was destroying his land.

STUDY QUESTIONS FOR COMPREHENSION

1. To which areas of the world does archy refer?
2. What reason does archy give for man's destruction of the land?
3. Is archy optimistic about the future?

dear boss i was talking with an ant
the other day
and he handed me a lot of
gossip which ants the world around
are chewing over among themselves

i pass it on to you
in the hope that you may relay it to other
human beings and hurt their feelings with it
no insect likes human beings
and if you think you can see why
the only reason i tolerate you is because
you seem less human to me than most of them
here is what the ants are saying

it wont be long now it wont be long
man is making deserts of the earth
it wont be long now
before man will have used it up
so that nothing but ants
and centipedes and scorpions
can find a living on it
man has oppressed us for a million years
but he goes on steadily
cutting the ground from under
his own feet making deserts deserts deserts

we ants remember
and have it all recorded
in our tribal lore
when gobi was a paradise
swarming with men and rich
in human prosperity
it is a desert now and the home
of scorpions ants and centipedes

what man calls civilization
always results in deserts
man is never on the square
he uses up the fat and greenery of the earth
each generation wastes a little more
of the future with greed and lust for riches

north africa was once a garden spot
and then came carthage and rome
and despoiled the storehouse
and now you have sahara
sahara ants and centipedes

toltecs and aztecs had a mighty
civilization on this continent

but they robbed the soil and wasted nature
and now you have deserts scorpions ants and centipedes
and the deserts of the near east
followed egypt and babylon and assyria
and persia and rome and the turk
the ant is the inheritor of tamerlane
and the scorpion succeeds the caesars

america was once a paradise
of timberland and stream
but it is dying because of the greed
and money lust of a thousand little kings
who slashed the timber all to hell
and would not be controlled
and changed the climate
and stole the rainfall from posterity
and it wont be long now
it wont be long
till everything is desert
from the alleghenies to the rockies
the deserts are coming
the deserts are spreading
the springs and streams are drying up
one day the mississippi itself
will be a bed of sand

ants and scorpions and centipedes
shall inherit the earth

men talk of money and industry
of hard times and recoveries
of finance and economics
but the ants wait and the scorpions wait
for while men talk they are making deserts all the time
getting the world ready for the conquering ant
drought and erosion and desert

because men cannot learn

rainfall passing off in flood and freshet
and carrying good soil with it
because there are no longer forests
to withhold the water in the
billion meticulations of the roots

it wont be long now it won't be long
till earth is barren as the moon
and sapless as a mumbled bone

dear boss i relay this information
without any fear that humanity
will take warning and reform

archy

SUSAN LANDOR

South Bayshore, 1969— "A Thing of Beauty Is a Joy Forever"

Courtesy of the Sierra Club

RACHEL CARSON

From *Silent Spring*

STUDY QUESTIONS FOR COMPREHENSION

1. What is Rachel Carson's purpose in describing this hypothetical town?
2. What is Strontium 90?
3. What gave rise to the enormous growth of man-made or synthetic chemicals?

There was once a town in the heart of America where all life seemed to live in harmony with its surroundings. The town lay in the midst of a checkerboard of prosperous farms, with fields of grain and hillsides of orchards where, in spring, white clouds of bloom drifted above the green fields. In autumn, oak and maple and birch set up a blaze of color that flamed and flickered across a backdrop of pines. Then foxes barked in the hills and deer silently crossed the fields, half hidden in the mists of the fall mornings.

Along the roads, laurel, viburnum and alder, great ferns and wildflowers delighted the traveler's eye through much of the year. Even in winter the roadsides were places of beauty, where countless birds came to feed on the berries and on the seed heads of the dried weeds rising above the snow. The countryside was, in fact, famous for the abundance and variety of its bird life, and when the flood of migrants was pouring through in spring and fall people traveled from great distances to observe them. Others came to fish the streams, which flowed clear and cold out of the hills and contained shady pools where trout lay. So it had been from the days many years ago when the first settlers raised their houses, sank their wells, and built their barns.

Then a strange blight crept over the area and everything began to change. Some evil spell had settled on the community: mysterious maladies swept the flocks of chickens; the cattle and sheep sickened and died. Everywhere was a shadow of death. The farmers spoke of much illness among their families. In the town the doctors had become more and more puzzled by new kinds of sickness appearing among their patients. There had been several sudden and unexplained deaths, not only among adults but even among children, who would be stricken suddenly while at play and die within a few hours.

There was a strange stillness. The birds, for example—where had they gone? Many people spoke of them, puzzled and disturbed. The feeding stations in the backyards were deserted. The few birds seen anywhere were moribund; they trembled violently and could not fly. It was a spring without voices. On the mornings that had once throbbed with the dawn chorus of robins, catbirds, doves, jays, wrens, and scores of other bird voices there was now no sound; only silence lay over the fields and woods and marsh.

On the farms the hens brooded, but no chicks hatched. The farmers complained that they were unable to raise any pigs—the litters were small and the young survived only a few days. The apple trees were coming into bloom but no bees droned among the blossoms, so there was no pollination and there would be no fruit.

The roadsides, once so attractive, were now lined with browned and withered vegetation as though swept by fire. These, too, were silent, deserted by all living things. Even the streams were now lifeless. Anglers no longer visited them, for all the fish had died.

In the gutters under the eaves and between the shingles of the roofs, a white granular powder still showed a few patches; some weeks before it had fallen like snow upon the roofs and the lawns, the fields and streams.

No witchcraft, no enemy action had silenced the rebirth of new life in this stricken world. The people had done it themselves.

This town does not actually exist, but it might easily have a thousand counterparts in America or elsewhere in the world. I know of no community that has experienced all the misfortunes I describe. Yet every one of these disasters has actually happened somewhere, and many real communities have already suffered a substantial number of them. A grim specter has crept upon us almost unnoticed, and this imagined tragedy may easily become a stark reality we all shall know.

What has already silenced the voices of spring in countless towns in America? . . .

The history of life on earth has been a history of interaction between living things and their surroundings. To a large extent, the physical form and the habits of the earth's vegetation and its animal life have been molded by the environment. Considering the whole span of earthly time, the opposite effect, in which life actually modifies its surroundings, has been relatively slight. Only within the moment of time represented by the present century has one species —man—acquired significant power to alter the nature of his world.

During the past quarter century this power has not only increased to one of disturbing magnitude but it has changed in character. The most alarming of all man's assaults upon the environment is the contamination of air, earth, rivers, and sea with dangerous and even lethal materials. This pollution is for the most part irrecoverable; the chain of evil it initiates not only in the world that must support life but in living tissues is for the most part irreversible. In this now universal contamination of the environment. chemicals are the sinister and little-recognized partners of radiation in changing the very nature of the world—the very nature of its life. Strontium 90, released through nuclear explosions into the air, comes to earth in rain or drifts down as fallout, lodges in soil, enters into the grass or corn or wheat grown there, and in time takes up its abode in the bones of a human being, there to remain until his death. Similarly, chemicals sprayed on croplands or forests or gardens lie long in soil, entering into living organisms, passing from one to another in a chain of poisoning and death. Or they pass mysteriously by underground streams until they emerge and, through the alchemy of air and sunlight, combine into new forms that kill vegetation, sicken cattle, and work unknown harm on those who drink from once pure wells. As Albert Schweitzer has said, "Man can hardly even recognize the devils of his own creation." . . .

For the first time in the history of the world, every human being is now subjected to contact with dangerous chemicals, from the moment of conception until death. In the less than two decades of their use, the synthetic pesticides have been so thoroughly distributed throughout the animate and inanimate world that they occur virtually everywhere. They have been recovered from most of the major river systems and even from streams of groundwater flowing unseen through the earth. Residues of these chemicals linger in soil to which they may have been applied a dozen years before. They have entered and lodged in the bodies of fish, birds, reptiles, and domestic and wild animals so universally that scientists carrying on animal experiments find it almost impossible to locate subjects free from such contamination. They have been found in fish in remote mountain lakes, in earthworms burrowing in soil, in the eggs of birds—and in man himself. For these chemicals are now stored in the bodies of the vast majority of human beings, regardless of age. They occur in the mother's milk, and probably in the tissues of the unborn child.

All this has come about because of the sudden rise and prodigious growth of an industry for the production of man-made or synthetic chemicals with insecticidal properties. This industry is a child of the Second World War. In the course of developing agents of chemical warfare, some of the chemicals created in the laboratory were found to be lethal to insects. The discovery did not come by chance: insects were widely used to test chemicals as agents of death for man.

The result has been a seemingly endless stream of synthetic insecticides. . . .

What sets the new synthetic insecticides apart is their enormous biological potency. They have immense power not merely to poison but to enter into the most vital processes of the body and change them in sinister and often deadly ways. Thus, as we shall see, they destroy the very enzymes whose function is to protect the body from harm, they block the oxidation processes from which the body receives its energy, they prevent the normal functioning of various organs, and they may initiate in certain cells the slow and irreversible change that leads to malignancy. . . .

. . . From the town of Hinsdale, Illinois, a housewife wrote in despair to one of the world's leading ornithologists, Robert Cushman Murphy, Curator Emeritus of Birds at the American Museum of Natural History.

> Here in our village the elm trees have been sprayed for several years [she wrote in 1958]. When we moved here six years ago, there was a wealth of bird life; I put up a feeder and had a steady stream of cardinals, chickadees, downies and nuthatches all winter, and the cardinals and chickadees brought their young ones in the summer.
>
> After several years of DDT spray, the town is almost devoid of robins and starlings; chickadees have not been on my shelf for two years, and this year the cardinals are gone too; the nesting population in the neighborhood seems to consist of one dove pair and perhaps one catbird family.
>
> It is hard to explain to the children that the birds have been killed off, when they have learned in school that a Federal law protects the birds from killing or capture. "Will they ever come back?" they ask, and I do not have the answer. The elms are still dying, and so are the birds. *Is* anything being done? *Can* anything be done? Can *I* do anything? . . .

Gordo by Gus Arriola

Fighting to Save the Earth from Man

STUDY QUESTIONS FOR COMPREHENSION

1. Define *ecology* and *ecosystem*.
2. Define *biosphere*.
3. Give one or more examples of man's thoughtless use of nature that have had disastrous effects.
4. Does the author suggest that man is deliberately destroying his environment?

The great question of the '70s is: Shall we surrender to our surroundings or shall we make our peace with nature and begin to make reparations for the damage we have done to our air, to our land and to our water?

—State of the Union Message

Nixon's words come none too early. The U.S. environment is seriously threatened by the prodigal garbage of the world's richest economy. In the President's own boyhood town of Whittier, a part of metropolitan Los Angeles, the once sweet air is befouled with carbon monoxide, hydrocarbons, lead compounds, sulfur dioxide, nitrogen oxides, fly ash, asbestos particulates and countless other noxious substances. The Apollo 10 astronauts could see Los Angeles as a cancerous smudge from 25,000 miles in outer space. Airline pilots say that whisky-brown miasmas, visible from 70 miles, shroud almost every U.S. city, including remote towns like Missoula in Montana's "big sky" country. What most Americans now breathe is closer to ambient filth than to air.

The environment may well be the gut issue that can unify a

polarized nation in the 1970s. It may also divide people who are appalled by the mess from those who have adapted to t. No one knows how many Americans have lost all feeling for nature and the quality of life. Even so, the issue now attracts young and old, farmers, city dwellers and suburban housewives, scientists, industrialists and blue-collar workers. They know pollution well. It is as close as the water tap, the car-clogged streets and junk-filled landscape—their country's visible decay, America the Ugly. . . .

The real problem is much bigger than the U.S. By curbing disease and death, modern medicine has started a surge of human overpopulation that threatens to overwhelm the earth's resources. At the same time, technological man is bewitched by the dangerous illusion that he can build bigger and bigger industrial societies with scant regard for the iron laws of nature. French Social Anthropologist Claude Lévi-Strauss compares today's human condition to that of maggots in a sack of flour: "When the population of these worms increases, even before they meet, before they become conscious of one another, they secrete certain toxins that kill at a distance—that is, they poison the flour they are in, and they die."

Ultimately, both men and maggots need the help of an emerging science of survival—ecology. . . .

Ecology is often called the "subversive science." Only 70 years old, it avoids the narrow specialization of other sciences—and thus appeals to generalists, including people with a religious sense. Ecology is the systems approach to nature, the study of how living organisms and the nonliving environment function together as a whole or ecosystem. The word ecology (derived from the Greek root *oikos*, meaning "house") is often used in ways that suggest an attitude rather than a discipline. Anthropologists and psychiatrists have adapted it to their work. . . . But few yet grasp its subtle meanings—as Senator Ted Stevens of Alaska proved last summer. Arguing for fast development of his state's oil-rich North Slope, Stevens referred to his dictionary. "Ecology," he declared, "deals with the relationship between living organisms." Then he added triumphantly: "But there are no living organisms on the North Slope."

Stevens missed the whole point: the arctic ecosystem is full of life (including Eskimos) but is so vulnerable to pollution that the North Slope threatens to become a classic example of man's mindless destruction. The intense cold impedes nature's ability to heal itself; tire marks made in the tundra 25 years ago are still plainly visible. What most worries ecologists, in fact, is man's blindness to his own utter dependency on all ecosystems, such as oceans, coastal estuaries, forests and grasslands. Those ecosystems constitute the biosphere, a vast web of interacting organisms and processes that form the rhythmic cycles and food chains in which ecosystems support one another.

The biosphere is an extraordinarily thin global envelope that sustains the only known life in the universe. At least 400 million years ago, some primeval accident allowed plant life to enrich the atmosphere to a life-supporting mixture of 20% oxygen, plus nitrogen, argon, carbon dioxide and water vapor. With uncanny precision, the mixture was then maintained by plants, animals and bacteria, which used and returned the gases at equal rates. The result is a closed system, a balanced cycle in which nothing is wasted and everything counts. For example, about 70% of the earth's oxygen is produced by ocean phytoplankton—passively floating plants and animals. This entire living system modified temperatures, curbed floods and nurtured man about 5,000,000 years ago. Only if the biosphere survives can man survive.

To maintain balance, all ecosystems require four basic elements: 1) inorganic substances (gases, minerals, compounds); 2) "producer" plants, which convert the substances into food; 3) animal "consumers," which use the food; and 4) "decomposers" (bacteria and fungi), which turn dead protoplasm into usable substances for the producers. As the key producers, green plants alone have the power to harness the sun's energy and combine it with elements from air, water and rocks into living tissue—the vegetation that sustains animals, which in turn add their wastes and corpses to natural decay. It is nature's efficient reuse of the decay that builds productive topsoil. Yet such is the delicacy of the process that it takes 500 years to create one inch of good topsoil.

The process is governed by distinct laws of life and balance.

One is adaptation: each species finds a precise niche in the ecosystem that supplies it with food and shelter. At the same time, all animals have the defensive power to multiply faster than their own death rates. As a result, predators are required to hold the population within the limits of its food supply. The wolf that devours the deer is a blessing to the community, if not to the individual deer. Still another law is the necessity of diversity. The more different species there are in an area, the less chance that any single type of animal or plant will proliferate and dominate the community. Even the rarest, oddest species can thus be vital to life. Variety is nature's grand tactic of survival.

Man has violated these laws—and endangered nature as well as himself. When a primitive community ran out of food, it had to move on or perish. It could harm only its own immediate environment. But a modern community can destroy its land and still import food, thus possibly destroying ever more distant land without knowing or caring. Technological man is so aware of his strength that he is unaware of his weakness—the fact that his pressure upon nature may provoke revenge.

By adding just one alien component to a delicate balance, man sometimes triggers a series of dangerous changes. Nature immediately tries to restore the balance—and often overreacts. When farmers wipe out one pest with powerful chemicals, they may soon find their crops afflicted with six pests that are resistant to the chemicals. Worse, the impact of a pesticide like DDT can be vastly magnified in food chains. Thus DDT kills insect-eating birds that normally control the pests that now destroy the farmers' crops. The "domino theory" is clearly applicable to the environment.

In South Africa, for example, a campaign was waged against hippopotamuses. Deemed useless beasts that merely cluttered up rivers, they were shot on sight. Result: the debilitating disease called schistosomiasis has become as great a public-health hazard in certain areas as malaria was 50 years ago. As usual, the missing links in the chain of events were discovered the hard way. It turns out that hippos keep river silt in motion as they bathe. When they heave themselves up riverbanks to dry land, they also go single file and act like bulldozers, making natural irrigation channels. Without the animals, the rivers quickly silted up; without the overflow channels, periodic floods swept like scythes over adjacent lands. The altered conditions favored a proliferation of schistosomiasis-carrying water snails.

Such harsh intrusions on wildlife constitute only one way in which man abuses nature. Another is through his sheer numbers. From an estimated 5,000,000 people 8,000 years ago, the world population rose to 1 billion by 1850, 2 billion about 1930, and now stands at 3.5 billion. Current projections run to 7 billion by the year 2000. . . . Stanford Population Biologist Paul Ehrlich grimly warns that the biosphere cannot sustain that many people. As Ehrlich puts it: "There can only be death, war, pestilence and famine to reduce the number." . . .

Modern technology is already pressuring nature with tens of thousands of synthetic substances, many of which almost totally resist decay—thus poisoning man's fellow creatures, to say nothing of himself. The burden includes smog fumes, aluminum cans that do not rust, inorganic plastics that may last for decades, floating oil that can change the thermal reflectivity of oceans, and radioactive wastes whose toxicity lingers for literally hundreds of years. The earth has its own waste-disposal system, but it has limits. The winds that ventilate earth are only six miles high; toxic garbage can kill the tiny organisms that normally clean rivers.

In a biospheric sense, the U.S. bears a heavy responsibility. According to Paul Ehrlich, "Each American child is 50 times more of a burden on the environment than each Indian child." Although the U.S. contains only 5.7% of the world's population, it consumes 40% of the world's production of natural resources. In 70 years of life, the average American uses 26 million gallons of water, 21,000 gallons of gasoline, 10,000 lbs. of meat, 28,000 lbs. of milk and cream, as well as $8,000 worth of school buildings, $6,000 of clothing and $7,000 of furniture. To compound the problem, a Gallup poll shows that 41% of Americans consider the ideal family size to be four or more children.

The result of massive production is massive filth. Every year,

Americans junk seven million cars, 100 million tires, 20 million tons of paper, 28 billion bottles and 48 billion cans. Just to collect the garbage costs $2.8 billion a year. The U.S. also produces almost 50% of the world's industrial pollution. Every year, U.S. plants discard 165 million tons of solid waste and gush 172 million tons of smoke and fumes into the air. Moreover, chemicals have replaced manure as fertilizers, while vast cattle feedlots have moved closer to cities. Result: animal wastes now pollute drinking water and pose a sanitation problem equivalent to that of almost a billion people.

The truth is that Americans have done far too little to tame the polluting effects of technology. Even the far reaches of Puget Sound are burdened with pulp-mill discharges. Mining companies spew so many wastes over tiny East Helena, Mont. (pop. 1,490) that the lettuce there contains 120 times the maximum concentrations of lead allowed in food for interstate shipment. Tourists are beginning to leave Appalachia nowadays; poisonous acid from strip mines has seeped into the water table.

The nation's 83 million cars cause 60% of the air pollution in cities. Fully aware of the pressure to reform, Detroit will introduce 1971 models that exhale only 37% as much carbon monoxide as did 1960 models. To achieve this, however, requires increased engine heat, which in turn will increase the nitrogen oxide emissions. And nitrogen oxides are particularly dangerous: under sunlight, they react with waste hydrocarbons from gasoline to form PAN (peroxyacl nitrate), along with ozone, the most toxic element in smog.

"We now have 50% more nitrogen oxides in the air in California," says Ecologist Kenneth E. M. F. Watt. "This has a direct bearing on the quality of light hitting the surface of the earth. At the present rate of nitrogen buildup, it's only a matter of time before light will be filtered out of the atmosphere and none of our land will be usable." Tougher auto-emission standards in California will start reducing the nitrogen problem next year. But Watt argues that California's air pollution is already so bad that it may start a wave of mass deaths by 1975—perhaps beginning in Long Beach. He also blames pollutants for the rising number of deaths from emphysema in Southern California. Trouble may well loom for Los Angeles, which sits in a smoggy bowl that often contains only 300 ft. of air. Almost every other day, the city's public schools forbid children to exercise lest they breathe too deeply. . . .

The U.S. is far from alone in these battles with pollution and waste. The smog in Tokyo is so dense that some residents are asking: Is it worth owning a car when there is no blue sky to drive it under? The tidy Swiss are horrified to discover that their three crystalline lakes—Geneva, Constance and Neuchâtel—are turning murky with effluent from littoral cities and industries; the trout and perch in them are nearly gone. In Italy, trash is neatly collected in plastic bags and then thrown like confetti over the landscape. Norway's legendary fjords are awash with stinking cakes of solid wastes.

Pollution respects no political boundaries. The Rhine flows 821 miles past the potash mines of Alsace, through the industrial Ruhr Valley to the North Sea. Known as "Europe's sewer," the river is so toxic that even hardy eels have difficulty surviving. The Dutch, who live at the river's mouth, have a stoic slogan: "Holland is the rubbish bin of the world." In Sweden, when black snow fell on the province of Smaland, authorities suspected that thick soot had wafted from across the sea.

Where do most of the pollutants end up? Probably in the oceans, which cover 70% of the globe. Yet even the oceans can absorb only so much filth; many ecologists are worried about the effects on phytoplankton. . . . Other ecologists fear that the oceans will become so burdened with noxious wastes that they will lose their vast power of self-purification. . . .

Some environment experts visualize future dramas of disaster that seem to border on science fiction. A few scientists feel that the outpouring of carbon dioxide, mainly from industry, is forming an invisible global filter in the atmosphere. This filter may act like a greenhouse: transparent to sunlight but opaque to heat radiation bouncing off the earth. In theory, the planet will warm up. The ice-caps will melt; the oceans will rise by 60 ft., drowning the world's coastal cities.

Other scientists argue the exact opposite: they point out that the earth's average temperature has dropped by .2° C. since 1945, though the carbon dioxide content of the air keeps increasing every year. To explain this phenomenon, many ecologists think that various particles in the atmosphere are reflecting sunlight away from the earth, thus cooling the planet. Since about 31% of the world's surface is covered by low clouds, increasing this cover to 36% through pollution would drop the temperature about 4° C.—enough to start a return to the ice age.

This is no idle speculation. Various experts feel that major volcanic eruptions in the past have thrust enough particles into the air to affect global climate. When Krakatoa exploded in 1883, the temperature at the surface of the earth was reduced for several years. The new worry, though, is that such particles will not shower to the ground in rain or snow. The supersonic transport will fly at 60,000 ft., where there is no atmospheric turbulence or weather to bring pollutants down to earth. Even assuming that the plane has a fumeless engine, the water vapor in its exhaust may accumulate in the stratosphere, reflecting sunlight away from the earth.

Man's inadvertence has even upset the interior conditions of the earth's crust. One of the most respected U.S. geophysicists, Gordon F. J. MacDonald, reports that wherever huge dams are built, the earth starts shuddering. The enormous weight of the water in the reservoirs behind the dam puts a new stress on the subsurface strata, which are already in natural stress. In consequence, giant sections of the earth's crust sheer past one another and the earth quivers. MacDonald warns that earthquakes may result (and did near Denver) from one of the newest antipollution techniques: injecting liquid chemical wastes into deep wells.

If technology got man into this mess, surely technology can get him out of it again. Not necessarily, argues Anthony Wiener of the Hudson Institute. Wiener sees technological man as the personification of Faust, endlessly pursuing the unattainable. "Our bargain with the Devil," he says, "is that we will figure out the consequences of whatever we do. We may have a 100% probability of solving all those problems as they arise. But as we solve them, we may find that our only remedies will create more of the same problems."

One example is the mighty Aswan High Dam project, built on the Upper Nile River with Soviet aid. When an international team of ecologists studied the effects of the dam, they were shocked. For one thing, waterweeds are clogging the shoreline of Lake Nasser behind the dam. The weeds may well speed evaporation through transpiration to the point where the lake lacks enough water to drive the gigantic generators.

The dam has also stopped the flow of silt down the Nile, which in the past offset the natural erosion of the land from the Nile delta. As a result, down-stream erosion may wash away as much productive farm land as is opened up by new irrigation systems around Lake Nasser. Without the nutrient-rich silt reaching the Mediterranean, the Egyptian sardine catch declined from 18,000 tons in 1965 to 500 tons in 1968. As a final penalty, irrigation projects on the delta plain have allowed a moisture-loving snail to thrive. Since it carries schistosomiasis, most of the delta people have had that agonizing liver and intestinal disease.

An example closer to home: though President Nixon prescribes an increased dose of technology to cure pollution, his medicine may well have side effects. Consider his $10 billion plan to build new primary and secondary municipal water-treatment plants. While such plants do make water cleaner, they also have two serious faults. Unlike more expensive tertiary treatment plants, they do not exterminate man-killing viruses, like those that cause infectious hepatitis. They also convert organic waste into inorganic compounds, especially nitrates and phosphates. When these are pumped into rivers and lakes, they fertilize aquatic plants, which flourish and then die. Most of the dissolved oxygen in the water is used up when they decompose. As a result, lakes "die" in the sense that they become devoid of oxygen, bereft of fish, choked by weeds. In short, by solving one problem (dirty water), the sewage plants create another (eutrophication).

Behind the environment crisis in the U.S. are a few deeply ingrained assumptions. One is that nature exists primarily for man to conquer. Many thinkers have traced the notion back to early Judaism and Christianity. *Genesis 1:26* is explicit on the point that God gave man "dominion over the fish of the sea, and over the birds of the air, and over the cattle, and over all the earth." The ecological truth is

EDWARD SHUSTER

Patrick's Point

Courtesy of Edward Shuster

SUSAN LANDOR

Santa Barbara Beach Contaminated by Oil Spillage, February 1969

quite different. The great early civilizations—Babylonian, Sumerian, Assyrian, Chinese, Indian and perhaps Mayan—over-exploited the basic resource of land. In the end, says LaMont Cole, "they just farmed themselves out of business."

Another ready assumption is that nature is endlessly bountiful. In fact, the supply of both land and resources is finite. Martin Litton, a director of the Sierra Club, says: "We are prospecting for the very last of our resources and using up the nonrenewable things many times faster than we are finding new ones." Litton reaches this alarmist conclusion: "We've already run out of earth, and nothing we can do will keep humankind in existence for as long as another two centuries."

No less troubling is the belief that economic growth is worth any effort. Until recently, neither capitalist nor Communist seriously questioned the whirling-dervish doctrine that teaches, in René Dubos' words, "Produce more than you can consume so that you can produce more." This leads to ecological mismanagement. For example, says Barry Commoner: "Every day we produce 11,000 calories of food per capita in the U.S. We need only 2,500 calories." At the same time, while most of Latin America is suffering from protein deficiency, the U.S. is taking thousands of tons of protein-rich anchovies from the Humboldt Current off Peru and Chile. The anchovies are ground up for chicken feed in Arkansas—food energy that could have gone more wisely to hungry human beings. Worse, some of the fish meal is made into cat food. "And," says Commoner, "we don't even eat the cats!"

What most appalls ecologists is that technological man is so ignorant of his impact. Writing in *Foreign Affairs,* Britain's Lord Ritchie-Calder recently pointed out that neither the politicians nor the physicists who developed the first atomic bomb were fully aware of the consequences of radioactive fallout. The men who designed the automobile helped to annihilate distance as a barrier between men. Yet the car's very success is turning cities into parking lots and destroying greenery in favor of highways all over the world. Each year the U.S. alone paves over 1,000,000 acres of oxygen-producing trees.

"Once you understand the problem," says Barry Commoner in one of his gloomier moments, "you find that it's worse than you ever expected." Yet even LaMont Cole, a charter member of the doomsday school of ecologists, is not entirely discouraged: "There has been so much progress in the past five years that if I'm not careful I'm liable to become a little optimistic."

There is certainly no lack of hopeful ideas for balancing the environment, and the most encouraging change to date is the groundswell of U.S. public opinion. The nation is at least starting to combat gross pollution. Even so, real solutions will be extremely difficult and expensive. To wean farmers away from pesticides and chemical fertilizers, for example, would cause at least a temporary decline in farm productivity and a hike in food prices. Fortunately, ecologists are developing reasonable replacements; there is nothing wrong with organic fertilizers or the prechemical method of crop rotation. Much is also being learned about the biological control of pests. To kill the leaf hopper *Dikrella,* which destroys grapes and is now immune to DDT, California ecologists have employed a tiny wasp—and the cost of controlling leaf hoppers has declined by 87% since the wasp buzzed into action.

Ideally, the entire environment should be subjected to computer analysis and systems control. Whole cities and industries could measure their inputs and outputs via air, land and water. By making cost-benefit choices—for example, between new plants and old marshes—they could balance the system. But this is a far-off dream. Far more knowledge is needed about how ecosystems work. Even the simplest is so complex that the largest computer cannot fully unravel it. Yet a promising start is being made in Colorado, where Ecologist George Van Dyne is running a key project under the International Biological Program to discover how a grasslands ecosystem responds to various stresses. Van Dyne and 80 other scientists are trailing every imaginable creature on the Western prairie and gathering data for a computer-modeling scheme that may become a landmark in ecological forecasting.

Government's first priority is to enact environmental standards —and then enforce the law. Regulatory agencies should do far more to assess new products and policies before they harm man and nature. At all levels, governments must join in regional attacks on air and river pollution that cross political boundaries. At the federal level, the maze of agencies with conflicting environmental responsibilities must be reordered. While the Agriculture Department pays farmers to drain wetlands, for example, the Interior Department pays to preserve them. Worse, the farm-subsidy program encourages the misuse of toxic chemicals, one-crop farming that destroys ecological diversity, and mechanization that drives jobless rural laborers into packed cities. Federal highway builders, the Army Corps of Engineers—all such official land abusers—need retraining in ecological values.

To relieve city congestion, Washington should subsidize more new towns and rural redevelopment. Especially in a technological society that so burdens nature, it should do more to limit population. It is obvious that few Americans will imitate Paul R. Ehrlich and some of his young disciples, who have tried to set a dramatic example by having vasectomies. Instead, the Government might well offer new incentives: bigger tax deductions for small families and even singles, for example, or higher old-age benefits for couples who have no more than two children. If all parents had two children, the U.S. population would remain stable.

Industry has a vital role: first to minimize pollution, and then to work toward recycling all wastes. There is profit in the process. Paper, glass, and scrap copper have long been re-used. Fly ash can be recaptured and pressed into building blocks; reclaimed sulfur dioxide could ease the global sulfur shortage. The oil industry could do a profound service for smoggy cities by removing the lead from gasoline (motorists would pay 2¢ more per gallon). The packaging industry would benefit all America by switching to materials that rot —fast. By one estimate, burning scrap paper and garbage in efficient incinerators could generate 10% of the nation's electricity. Such incinerators already provide central steam heating for Paris. To be sure, big changes might raise consumer prices and cut profits. But businessmen should also consider a greater profit: rescuing the environment.

Basic to all solutions is the need for a new way of thinking. So far, the key to so-called progress has been man's ability to focus his energies on a single problem, whether fighting a war or going to the moon. But thinking in compartments is the road to environmental disaster. Americans must view the world in terms of unities rather than units. To recognize the interdependence of all creatures is to see all kinds of follies—from the one-occupant cars that choke highways to the tax policies that discourage mass transit and land preservation.

The biggest need may be a change in values; the whole environmental problem stems from a dedication to infinite growth on a finite planet. Pessimists argue that only a catastrophe can change that attitude—too late. By contrast, Barry Commoner and others put their faith in man's ability to reform when confronted by compelling facts. It is also possible that ecologists can eventually stir enough people to an emotion as old as man—exaltation. Ecology, the subversive science, enriches man's perceptions, his vision, his concept of reality. In nature, many may find the model they need to cherish. The question is: How many?

Consumption of Resources

AMERICANS:

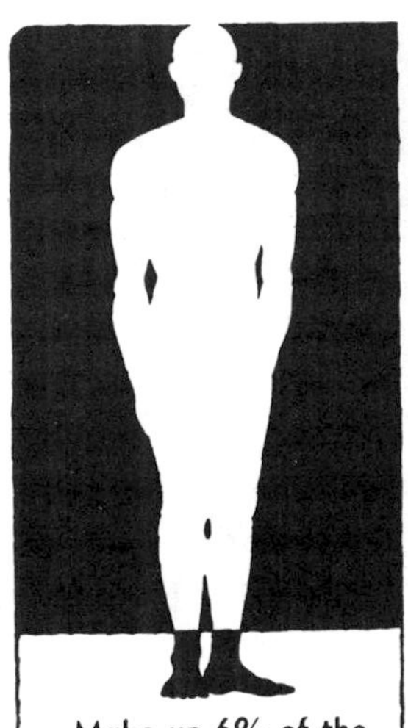

Make up 6% of the world's population.

Consume 35% to 50% of world's resources.

Produce 50% of the world's pollution.

Courtesy of Enterprise Science Service

MARY PRATT

Directions

STUDY QUESTIONS FOR COMPREHENSION

1. What does Mary Pratt mean by the term "reconstructed ground"?
2. Where in the poem does Mary Pratt contrast the short time it takes for man to destroy what nature has taken eons to develop?
3. What are the "new maps (of hell)"?

I can hardly tell you
a sensible way to come,
the map keeps changing so—
new freeways spring up overnight,
then the old roads are too slow.
(But come where the parking lots are in bloom,
come under the trees by the asphalt.)

Last night as I drove home
I saw a fire of roots
burning like tangled wires
in the triangular darkness
of an intersection:
remnants of a landmark,
some trees where roads crossed.
The fire still burns
green against my lids,
but it's hard to remember
the way those roots
dug into the earth
or the look of the earth itself.

Out here we live on reconstructed ground:

our houses are built on it
after the bulldozer retreats
leaving its clean striations.
Or apartments loom like ectoplasm
in the scraped orchard—
awkward, unlikely, not readily rented—

If there is a frontier, I suppose
it's those last patches of green
(orchard and rising hills,
lizard roots, rabbit leaves)
uneconomic as they seem.

Hard to persuade, though:
Old di Napoli,
leaving something for his children,
sold his orchard before he died,
saw the trees cut down,
taken for firewood,
the roots dug up and burned.

Not an unusual pace

(though in the Cretaceous
the flowering trees appeared—
magnolias—then plums, apricots;
still later, in the Tertiary,
the feeding creatures)

And there my father stands,
touchy, private, his own man,
making his landscape anonymous:
the smoke goes up from burning maple,
spreads a pall for miles,
and people in the new developments
call the councilman.

Geology accelerates,
becomes cartography,
striking it rich;
these old mapmakers
make new maps (of hell)
to keep up with the growth.

(Hard to persuade:

—But I cried out in the leaved darkness
as if I had waked, sighting land,
and like a navigator looked to find
awkward and incredible, the Bear
among the trees, guiding me home.)

"We've a warrant for your arrest."

Reprinted from *Atlas* Magazine (April 1970). From Franklin—*Daily Mirror,* London.

ROY BONGARTZ

It Walks Like a Man

STUDY QUESTIONS FOR COMPREHENSION

1. According to Bongartz, what is the main distinction between man and Brute?
2. How serious is Bongartz?
3. The mechanical man is still in the experimental stage. Do you think he will be a common sight by the year 2000?

Scientists must be a frustrated lot, never content with things as they are—especially not content with our own human minds and bodies. No sooner did they trade in our brains for computers than they began inventing machines to replace our bodies. Now on the way are robots 20 feet tall and ten times stronger than Charles Atlas; man, who so far is still tolerated, raises a casual finger or points a toe, and the machine just as casually builds a bridge, dashes enemy soldiers to the ground, or does the frug.

One such walking machine, at General Electric Co., is called the Beyond-road-utility-tool-extender, or Brute. When its creator, engineer Ralph Mosher, climbs up into its head, hooks himself up to it, and turns it on, it will do nearly anything he does (except that if Mosher falls down, Brute has a terrible time getting up again). If Mosher wiggles his hips, Brute wiggles *its* hips. Already, on an earlier model, Mosher proved the mastery of machine over man by beating two little Schenectady girls, aged 5 and 6, at hoop spinning.

Brute will have arms with hands, and legs with interchangeable feet (snow feet for winter, balloon feet for walking in moon dust, flipper feet for water skiing), and will march along at 35 miles an hour. A parade of them, bulletproof, fireproof and, presumably,

Reprinted by permission from *The Nation*, June 14, 1965.

painted in various colors from pink through dark brown, could stage a coast-to-coast freedom march and be as fresh when they arrived as when they left—assuming no hard-losing segregationists stretched wires across the way to trip them up. But Southern farmers might like some Brutes of their own to replace those long-regretted slaves—the machines could be delivered with ingratiating smiles painted on their heads. A man in an easy chair in Brute's head, making the merest suggestion of those tiresome old cotton-picking motions, could have his plantation harvested in no time.

In fact, everybody will need a Brute. A Marine Corps colonel, for example, says, "Brute can do anything a Marine can do, and ten times better." (When a Marine Brute goes out on Saturday night to pick up a girl, that's just what it means.) It is also this colonel's idea that a Brute could chase guerrillas through the jungle, catch them and dash their brains out. "To make the picture of demoralization complete," he says, "Brute might have painted on its front some unearthly device such as a mauve-and-green heikei crab." What attracts everybody about Brute is that you don't have to learn how to run it; you just climb into its head and go about your business, whatever it may be. Brute amplifies your motions and your muscles, and you get a lot more done that way. For example, you could merely brush your teeth while Brute at the same time scrubbed down thirty-two cars—provided you had the cars arranged in two semi-circular tiers of sixteen each. And be careful taking out that bridgework.

A gardener's Brute would, of course, come with a very big green thumb. A watchmaker could make a watch while his Brute simultaneously made a new clock for the railroad station tower—of course it would be stem-wound. In the same way, a hobbyist could make a ship model while Brute made a fine 60-foot schooner—the only question being how to launch it from that big bottle.

By a feedback system, an operator feels any resistance that his machine encounters—such as that met by a boy-operated Brute trying to pull a girl-operated Brute into the woods for a walk after a picnic. Even holding hands, boy and girl Brutes would produce a good deal of clanking. But the police would love to have Brutes—they could reach down and pick up a speeding car with one hand, and rattle the occupants around inside to teach them a lesson. In a

Brute, a lifeguard could be anywhere on the beach, in a few seconds, with a dozen fast strides—but take it easy on the artificial respiration. Even a baby with a rattle could be placed in Brute's head—as long as the Brute had a 50-gallon steel drum full of rocks to play with. And a somewhat older child can help build our Great Society; give a little boy a sand pail and a shovel, hook him up, leave him alone all day, and by supper time you'll have enough basement dug out for a new Brute-Hilton. Nevertheless, in spite of future perfecting of the machines, some professions will probably always have to do without the help of Brute: diamond cutters, barbers, gynecologists.

Though aged Brutes can be left to rust like old cars, it may be wiser to farm them out to Arizona communities with plenty of sunshine and Three-in-One oil, lest they become restive and vengeful; it should be remembered that even an elderly Brute has the strength, if angered, to pick up a handful of uncooperative social security officials and slam them against the side of the welfare office. But today, Brute is still young, so young, in fact, that it is still attached by umbilical cord to an electric outlet, and may well end up with an Oepidus complex toward the power and light company.

The trouble, of course, is that Brute was made in man's own image. He stands upright on two legs; it might have been much better if he walked on all fours. If man had been less egotistical, he might have designed Brute after some animal other than himself. An anteater, a fish, a sloth perhaps. Maybe just an ordinary dog. But then there would be the technical problems which, with man, do not arise, such as making Brute wag his tail or bark. Brute is on the way in and man is on the way out, but man still figures because—without a man in its head—a machine, even today, cannot figure out *what is coming next*. Engineer Mosher says it is impossible to "construct a machine versatile enough by itself to make its way through sand, mud, strewn rocks, swamp or forest—and to do this without knowing what was coming up next. The most advanced computer system couldn't accomplish it. But a man can do this." What Mosher is saying is simply that man has but one thing left with which to compete with the machine—his ability to worry. If we lose that, or if Brute learns to worry on his own, then Brute takes over altogether.

There's something to worry about.

EDGAR HEFFLEY

No Help Wanted: Cybernation

STUDY QUESTIONS FOR COMPREHENSION

1. Many people maintain that if a man wants to work, he can always find a job. How would you evaluate such a statement?
2. What are the kinds of activities that you associate with the word *leisure*?
3. If you were fairly certain that the nation's industries would have no need for your services ten years from now, what changes would you make in your present goals?
4. What do you think the author had in mind when he referred to the "chamber of horrors" that might result from a failure to control the forces unleashed by the modern technological revolution?

Two revolutions have been engulfing human beings throughout the world since World War II. Neither revolution is new as a world phenomenon. What is new is the intensity and the magnitude of each.

One is a social revolution that is touching even the remotest parts of the world, a world caught in a violent conflict of opposing ideologies and outmoded social institutions. This social revolution is characterized by peaceful petition, civil disobedience, and civil disorder in the more politically stable countries, as in the case of the United States, and by bloody revolutions and violence in the more underdeveloped parts of the world, as in the case of Cuba and the Congo. Whatever form the disturbance takes, the social goals are the same. People everywhere are determined to put an end to social injustice with its attendant poverty, cultural deprivation, and human degradation.

The other revolution is a technological one. It is a revolution that offers hope for the realization of social justice. But, unless controlled, this technological revolution may produce a chamber of horrors for much of mankind and quite probably the total annihilation of the human race in a nuclear holocaust.

Though both revolutions present mankind with serious implications for the future, there is a particular aspect of the latter revolution that is not too widely publicized or understood, in spite of the fact that most people are confronted daily with its effects. Cybernation is a term that few people outside of scientific or academic circles are familiar with, yet it is cybernation that perhaps poses the most immediate threat to all of us. The term cybernation means the processes of communication and control in man and machines, according to Norbert Wiener, the man who invented the term. It refers to integrated systems of production utilizing automation and computers. In the first case we have the automatic producers of material objects and, in the other, the sophisticated analyzers and interpreters of complex data. According to Donald N. Michael, author of *Cybernation: The Silent Conquest,* "Cybernated systems perform with a precision and rapidity unmatched in humans." It is not too much of an exaggeration, if the experts are correct, to suggest that within ten years the United States could produce most of its manufactures and a large part of its services utilizing such systems and without the necessity of employing many millions of the present labor force. The effects of automation and computers upon the labor force are already presenting the people of the United States with serious social and economic problems. One of the most critical questions that it raises is the question of our future ability to provide gainful employment for most of our labor force. If reasonably full employment of the labor force is an unattainable goal, then a dramatic change in American social institutions must be effected if we are to survive a total social disintegration.

The disturbing effects of cybernation are already apparent in some recent statistics which Michael cites in *Cybernation: The Silent Conquest,* a report to the Center for the Study of Democratic Institutions, published in 1962:

> *Blue-Collar Adults* In the highly automated chemical industry, the number of production jobs has fallen 3% since 1956 while output has

> soared 27%. Though steel capacity has increased 20% since 1955, the number of men needed to operate the industry's plants—even at full capacity—has dropped 17,000. Auto employment slid from a peak of 746,000 in boom 1955 to 614,000 in November. . . . Since the meat industry's 1956 employment peak, 28,000 workers have lost their jobs despite a production increase of 3%. Bakery jobs have been in a steady decline from 174,000 in 1954 to 163,000 last year. On the farm one man can grow enough to feed 24 people; back in 1949 he could feed only 15.

According to the same report, in the six years prior to this article labor union statements claimed that 1,500,000 fewer workers have been employed in manufacturing.

The prospect of displaced blue collar workers finding employment in the service industries is not very encouraging either. Again citing the same report, in New York alone automatic elevators have already displaced 40,000 operators. Also, the R. H. Macy Co. is trying out its first electronic sales girl. This machine is smart enough to dispense 36 different items in 10 separate styles and sizes. It accepts one- and five-dollar bills in addition to coins and returns the correct change, plus rejecting counterfeit currency.

Many middle management jobs in government and industry are being and will continue to be eliminated by computers capable of thinking problems through with a logic superior to that of which most humans are capable. It appears that those jobs which will be done by humans in the future will generally require a superior education and training. If most Americans in the future find little opportunity for the employment of skills and training of the traditional types, if gainful employment at all, then obviously at least two changes will have to take place. One, Americans will have to change their attitudes about what should be the basis for a member of society receiving an equitable share of what is produced; and, two, they will have to find a solution to the problem of how to utilize their leisure time. Both will require a rethinking of personal goals and a search for answers to the rather old human question of the meaning of human existence.

HERBERT A. OTTO

New Light on the Human Potential

STUDY QUESTIONS FOR COMPREHENSION

1. Herbert Otto believes that human beings use what percentage of their ability?
2. What are Otto's examples indicating that man has tremendous capabilities he does not use?
3. What does Otto mean by "negative conditioning"?

William James once estimated that the healthy human being is functioning at less than 10 per cent of his capacity. It took more than half a century before this idea found acceptance among a small proportion of behavioral scientists. In 1954, the highly respected and widely known psychologist Gardner Murphy published his pioneering volume *Human Potentialities.* The early Sixties saw the beginnings of the human potentialities research project at the University of Utah and the organization of Esalen Institute in California, the first of a series of "Growth Centers" that were later to be referred to as the Human Potentialities Movement.

Today, many well-known scientists such as Abraham Maslow, Margaret Mead, Gardner Murphy, O. Spurgeon English, and Carl Rogers subscribe to the hypothesis that man is using a very small fraction of his capacities. Margaret Mead quotes a 6 per cent figure, and my own estimate is 5 per cent or less. Commitment to the hypothesis is not restricted to the United States. Scientists in the U.S.S.R. and other countries are also at work. Surprisingly, the so-called human potentialities hypothesis is still largely unknown.

What are the dimensions of the human potential? The knowledge we do have about man is minimal and has not as yet been brought together with the human potentialities hypothesis as an organizing force and synthesizing element. Of course, we know more about man today than we did fifty years ago, but this is like the very small part of the iceberg we see above the water. Man essentially remains a mystery. From the depths of this mystery there are numerous indicators of the human potential.

Certain indicators of man's potential are revealed to us in childhood. They become "lost" or submerged as we succumb to the imprinting of the cultural mold in the "growing up" process. Do you remember when you were a child and it rained after a dry spell and there was a very particular, intensive earthy smell in the air? Do you remember how people smelled when they hugged you? Do you recall the brilliant colors of leaves, flowers, grass, and even brick surfaces and lighted signs that you experienced as a child? Furthermore, do you recall that when father and mother stepped into the room you *knew* how they felt about themselves, about life, and about you—at that moment?

Today we know that man's sense of smell, one of the most powerful and primitive senses, is highly developed. In the average man this capacity has been suppressed except for very occasional use. Some scientists claim that man's sense of smell is almost as keen as a hunting dog's. Some connoisseurs of wines, for example, can tell by the bouquet not only the type of grape and locality where they were grown but even the vintage year and vineyard. Perfume mixers can often detect fantastically minute amounts in mixed essences; finally there are considerable data on odor discrimination from the laboratory. It is also clear that, since the air has become an overcrowded garbage dump for industrial wastes and the internal combustion engine, it is easier to turn off our sense of smell than to keep it functioning. The capacity to experience the environment more fully through our olfactory organs remains a potential.

It is possible to regain these capacities through training. In a similar manner, sensory and other capacities, including visual, kinesthetic, and tactile abilities, have become stunted and dulled. We perceive less clearly, and as a result we feel less—we use our dulled senses to close ourselves off from both our physical and interpersonal environments. Today we also dull our perceptions of how other people feel and we consistently shut off awareness of our own feelings. For many who put their senses to sleep it is a sleep that lasts unto death. Again, through sensory and other training the doors of perception can be cleansed (to use Blake's words) and our capacities reawakened. Anthropological research abounds with reports of primitive tribes that have developed exceptional sensory and perceptive abilities as a result of training. Utilization of these capacities by modern man for life-enrichment purposes awaits the future.

Neurological research has shed new light on man's potential. Work at the UCLA Brain Research Institute points to enormous abilities latent in everyone by suggesting an incredible hypothesis: The ultimate creative capacity of the human brain may be, for all practical purposes, infinite. To use the computer analogy, man is a vast storehouse of data, but we have not learned how to program ourselves to utilize these data for problem-solving purposes. Recall of experiential data is extremely spotty and selective for most adults. My own research has convinced me that the recall of experiences can be vastly improved by use of certain simple training techniques, provided sufficient motivation is present.

Under emergency conditions, man is capable of prodigious feats of physical strength. For example, a middle-aged California woman with various ailments lifted a car just enough to let her son roll out from under it after it had collapsed on him. According to newspaper reports the car weighed in excess of 2,000 pounds. There are numerous similar accounts indicating that every person has vast physical reserve capacities that can be tapped. Similarly, the extraordinary feats of athletes and acrobats—involving the conscious and specialized development of certain parts of the human organism as a result of consistent application and a high degree of motivation—point to the fantastic plasticity and capabilities of the human being.

Until World War II, the field of hypnosis was not regarded as respectable by many scientists and was associated with stage performances and charlatanism. Since that time hypnosis has attained a measure of scientific respectability. Medical and therapeutic applications of hypnosis include the use of this technique in surgery and anesthesiology (hypnoanesthesia for major and minor surgery), gynecology (infertility, frigidity, menopausal conditions), pediatrics (enuresis, tics, asthma in children, etc.), and in dentistry. Scores of texts on medical and dental hypnosis are available. Dr. William S. Kroger, one of the specialists in the field and author of the well-known text *Clinical and Experimental Hypnosis,* writes that hypnotherapy is "directed to the patient's needs and is a methodology to tap the 'forgotten assets' of the *hidden potentials* of behavior and response that so often lead to new learnings and understanding." (My italics.) As far as we know now, the possibilities opened by hypnosis for the potential functioning of the human organism are not brought about by the hypnotist. Changes are induced by the subject, utilizing his belief-structure, with the hypnotist operating as an "enabler," making it possible for the subject to tap some of his unrealized potential.

The whole area of parapsychology that deals with extrasensory perception (ESP), "mental telepathy," and other paranormal phenomena, and that owes much of its development to the work of Dr. J. B. Rhine and others is still regarded by much of the scientific establishment with the same measure of suspicion accorded hypnosis in the pre-World War II days. It is of interest that a number of laboratories in the U.S.S.R. are devoted to the study of telepathy as a physical phenomenon, with research conducted under the heading "cerebral radio-communication" and "bioelectronics." The work is supported by the Soviet government. The reluctance to accept findings from this field of research is perhaps best summarized by an observation of Carl G. Jung's in 1958:

> (Some) people deny the findings of parapsychology outright, either for philosophical reasons or from intellectual laziness. This can hardly be considered a scientifically responsible attitude, even though it is a popular way out of quite extraordinary intellectual difficulty.

Although the intensive study of creativity had its beginnings in fairly recent times, much of value has been discovered about man's creative potential. There is evidence that every person has creative abilities that can be developed. A considerable number of studies indicate that much in our educational system—including conformity pressures exerted by teachers, emphasis on memory development, and rote learning, plus the overcrowding of classrooms—militates against the development of creative capacities. Research has established that children between the ages of two and three can learn to read, tape record a story, and type it as it is played back. Hundreds of children between the ages of four and six have been taught by the Japanese pedagogue Suzuki to play violin concertos. Japanese research with infants and small children also suggests the value of early "maximum input" (music, color, verbal, tactile stimuli) in the personality development of infants. My own observations tend to confirm this. We have consistently underestimated the child's capacity to learn and his ability to realize his potential while *enjoying* both the play elements and the discipline involved in this process.

In contrast to the Japanese work, much recent Russian research appears to be concentrated in the area of mentation, with special emphasis on extending and enlarging man's mental processes and his capacity for learning. As early as 1964 the following appeared in *Soviet Life Today,* a U.S.S.R. English language magazine:

> The latest findings in anthropology, psychology, logic, and physiology show that the potential of the human mind is very great indeed. "As soon as modern science gave us some understanding of the structure and work of the human brain, we were struck with its enormous reserve capacity," writes Yefremov (Ivan Yefremov, eminent Soviet scholar and writer). "Man, under average conditions of work and life, uses only a small part of his thinking equipment. . . . If we were able to force our brain to work at only half its capacity, we could, without any difficulty whatever, learn forty languages, memorize the large Soviet Encyclopedia from cover to cover, and complete the required courses of dozens of colleges."
>
> The statement is hardly an exaggeration. It is the generally accepted theoretical view of man's mental potentialities.
>
> How can we tap this gigantic potential? It is a big and very complex problem with many ramifications.

Another signpost of man's potential is what I have come to call the "Grandma Moses effect." This artist's experience indicates that artistic talents can be discovered and brought to full flowering in the latter part of the life cycle. In every retirement community there can be found similar examples of residents who did not use latent artistic abilities or other talents until after retirement. In many instances the presence of a talent is suspected or known but allowed to remain fallow for the best part of a lifetime.

Reasons why well-functioning mature adults do not use specific abilities are complex. Studies conducted at the University of Utah as a part of the Human Potentialities Research Project revealed that unconscious blocks are often present. In a number of instances a person with definite evidence that he has a specific talent (let's say he won a state-wide contest in sculpture while in high school) may not wish to realize this talent at a later time because he fears this would introduce a change in life-style. Sometimes fear of the passion of creation is another roadblock in self-actualization. On the basis of work at Utah it became clear that persons who live close to their capacity, who continue to activate their potential, have a pronounced sense of well-being and considerable energy and see themselves as leading purposeful and creative lives.

Most people are unaware of their strengths and potentialities. If a person with some college background is handed a form and asked to write out his personality strengths, he will list, on an average, five or six strengths. Asked to do the same thing for his weaknesses, the list will be two to three times as long. There are a number of reasons for this low self-assessment. Many participants in my classes and marathon group weekends have pointed out that "listing your strengths feels like bragging about yourself. It's something that just isn't done." Paradoxically, in a group, people feel more comfortable about sharing problem areas and hang-ups than they do about personality resources and latent abilities. This is traceable to the fact that we are members of a pathology-oriented culture. Psychological and psychiatric jargon dealing with emotional dysfunction and mental illness has become the parlance of the man in the street. In addition, from early childhood in our educational system we learn largely by our mistakes—by having them pointed out to us repeatedly. All this results in early "negative conditioning" and influences our attitude and perception of ourselves and other people. An attitudinal climate has become established which is continually fed and reinforced.

As a part of this negative conditioning there is the heavy emphasis by communications media on violence in television programs and motion pictures. The current American news format of radio, television, and newspapers—the widely prevalent idea of what constitutes news—results from a narrow, brutalizing concept thirty or forty years behind the times and is inimical to the development of human potential.

The news media give much time and prominent space to violence and consistently underplay "good" news. This gives the consumer the impression that important things that happen are various types of destructive activities. Consistent and repeated emphasis on bad news not only creates anxiety and tension but instills the belief that there is little except violence, disasters, accidents, and mayhem abroad in the world. As a consequence, the consumer of such news gradually experiences a shift in his outlook about the world leading to the formation of feelings of alienation and separation. The world is increasingly perceived as a threat, as the viewer becomes anxious that violence and mayhem may be perpetrated on him from somewhere out of the strange and unpredictable environment in which he lives. There slowly grows a conviction that it is safer to withdraw from such a world, to isolate himself from its struggles, and to let others make the decisions and become involved.

As a result of the steady diet of violence in the media, an even more fundamental and insidious erosion in man's self-system takes place. The erosion affects what I call the "trust factor." If we have been given a certain amount of affection, love, and understanding in our formative years, we are able to place a certain amount of trust in our fellow man. Trust is one of the most important elements in today's society although we tend to minimize its importance. *We basically trust people.* For example, we place an enormous amount of trust in our fellow man when driving on a freeway or in an express lane. We trust those with whom we are associated to fulfill their obligations and responsibilities. The element of trust is the basic rule in human relations. When we distrust people, they usually sense our attitude and reciprocate in kind.

The consistent emphasis in the news on criminal violence, burglarizing, and assault makes slow but pervasive inroads into our reservoir of trust. As we hear and read much about the acts of violence and injury men perpetrate upon one another, year after year, with so little emphasis placed on the loving, caring, and humanitarian acts of man, we begin to trust our fellow man less, and we thereby diminish ourselves. It is my conclusion the media's excessive emphasis on violence, like the drop of water on the stone, erodes and wears away the trust factor in man. By undermining the trust factor in man, media contribute to man's estrangement from man and prevent the full flourishing and deeper development of a sense of community and communion with all men.

Our self-concept, how we feel about ourselves and our fellow man and the world, is determined to a considerable extent by the inputs from the physical and interpersonal environment to which we are exposed. In the physical environment, there are the irritants in the air, i.e., air pollution plus the ugliness and noise of megapolis. Our interpersonal environment is characterized by estrangement and distance from others (and self), and by the artificiality and superficiality of our social encounters and the resultant violation of authenticity. Existing in a setting that provides as consistent inputs multiple irritants, ugliness and violence, and lack of close and meaningful relationships, man is in danger of becoming increasingly irritated, ugly, and violent.

As work in the area of human potentialities progressed, it has become ever clearer that personality, to a much greater degree than previously suspected, functions in response to the environment. This is additional confirmation of what field theorists and proponents of the holistic approach to the study of man have long suspected.

Perhaps the most important task facing us today is the regeneration of our environment and institutional structures such as school, government, church, etc. With increasing sophistication has come the recognition that institutions are not sacrosanct and that they have but one purpose and function—to serve as a framework for the actualization of human potential. It is possible to evaluate both the institution and the contribution of the institution by asking this question: "To what extent does the function of the institution foster the realization of human potential?"

Experimental groups consistently have found that the more a person's environment can be involved in the process of realizing potential, the greater the gains. It is understandable why scientists concerned with the study of personality have been reluctant to consider the importance of here-and-now inputs in relation to personality functioning. To do so would open a Pandora's box of possibilities and complex forces that until fairly recently were considered to be the exclusive domain of the social scientist. Many scientists and professionals, particularly psychotherapists, feel they have acquired a certain familiarity with the topography of "intra-psychic forces" and are reluctant to admit the reality of additional complex factors in the functioning of the personality.

It is significant that an increasing number of psychologists, psychiatrists, and social workers now realize that over and beyond keeping up with developments in their respective fields, the best way to acquire additional professional competence is through group experiences designed for personal growth and that focus on the unfolding of individual possibilities. From this group of aware professionals and others came much of the initial support and interest in Esalen Institute and similar "Growth Centers" later referred to as the Human Potentialities Movement.

Esalen Institute in Big Sur, California, was organized in 1962 by Michael Murphy and his partner, Dick Price. Under their imaginative management the institute experienced a phenomenal growth, established a branch in San Francisco, and is now famous for its seminars and weekend experiences offered by pioneering professionals. Since 1962 more than 100,000 persons have enrolled for one of these activities.

The past three years have seen a rapid mushrooming of Growth Centers. There are more than fifty such organizations ranging from Esalen and Kairos Institutes in California to Oasis in Chicago and Aureon Institute in New York. The experiences offered at these Growth Centers are based on several hypotheses: 1) that the average healthy person functions at a fraction of his capacity; 2) that man's most exciting life-long adventure is actualizing his potential; 3) that the group environment is one of the best settings in which to achieve growth; and 4) that personality growth can be achieved by anyone willing to invest himself in this process.

Human potentialities is rapidly emerging as a discrete field of scientific inquiry. Exploring the human potential can become the meeting ground for a wide range of disciplines, offering a dynamic synthesis for seemingly divergent areas of research. It is possible that the field of human potentialities offers an answer to the long search for a synthesizing and organizing principle which will unify the sciences. The explosive growth of the Human Potentialities Movement is indicative of a growing public interest. Although there exist a considerable number of methods—all designed to tap human potential—work on assessment or evaluation of these methods has in most instances not progressed beyond field testing and informal feedback of results. The need for research in the area of human potentialities has never been more pressing. The National Center for the Exploration of Human Potential in La Jolla, California, has recently been organized for this purpose. A nonprofit organization, the center will act as a clearing house of information for current and past approaches that have been successful in fostering personal growth. One of the main purposes of the center will be to conduct and coordinate basic and applied research concerning the expansion of human potential.

Among the many fascinating questions posed by researchers are some of the following: What is the relationship of body-rhythms, biorhythms, and the expansion of sensory awareness to the uncovering of human potential? What are the applications of methods and approaches from other cultures such as yoga techniques, Sufi methods, types of meditation, etc.? What is the role of ecstasy and play vis-à-vis the realizing of human possibilities? The exploration of these and similar questions can help us create a society truly devoted to the full development of human capacities—particularly the capacities for love, joy, creativity, spiritual experiencing. This is the challenge and promise of our lifetime.

ANNE SEXTON

The Addict

Sleepmonger,
deathmonger,
with capsules in my palms each night,
eight at a time from sweet pharmaceutical bottles
I make arrangements for a pint-sized journey.
I'm the queen of this condition.
I'm an expert on making the trip
and now they say I'm an addict.
Now they ask why.
Why!

Don't they know
that I promised to die!
I'm keeping in practice.
I'm merely staying in shape.
The pills are a mother, but better,
every color and as good as sour balls.
I'm on a diet from death.

Yes, I admit
it has gotten to be a bit of a habit—
blows eight at a time, socked in the eye,
hauled away by the pink, the orange,
the green and the white goodnights.
I'm becoming something of a chemical
mixture.
That's it!

My supply
of tablets

has got to last for years and years.
I like them more than I like me.
Stubborn as hell, they won't let go.
It's a kind of marriage.
It's a kind of war
where I plant bombs inside
of myself.

Yes
I try
to kill myself in small amounts,
an innocuous occupation.
Actually I'm hung up on it.
But remember I don't make too much noise
And frankly no one has to lug me out

and I don't stand there in my winding sheet.
I'm a little buttercup in my yellow nightie
eating my eight loaves in a row
and in a certain order as in
the laying on of hands
or the black sacrament.

It's a ceremony
but like any other sport
it's full of rules.
It's like a musical tennis match where
my mouth keeps catching the ball.
Then I lie on my altar
elevated by the eight chemical kisses.

What a lay me down this is
with two pink, two orange,
two green, two white goodnights.
Fee-fi-fo-fum—
Now I'm borrowed.
Now, I'm done.

Drug Traffic

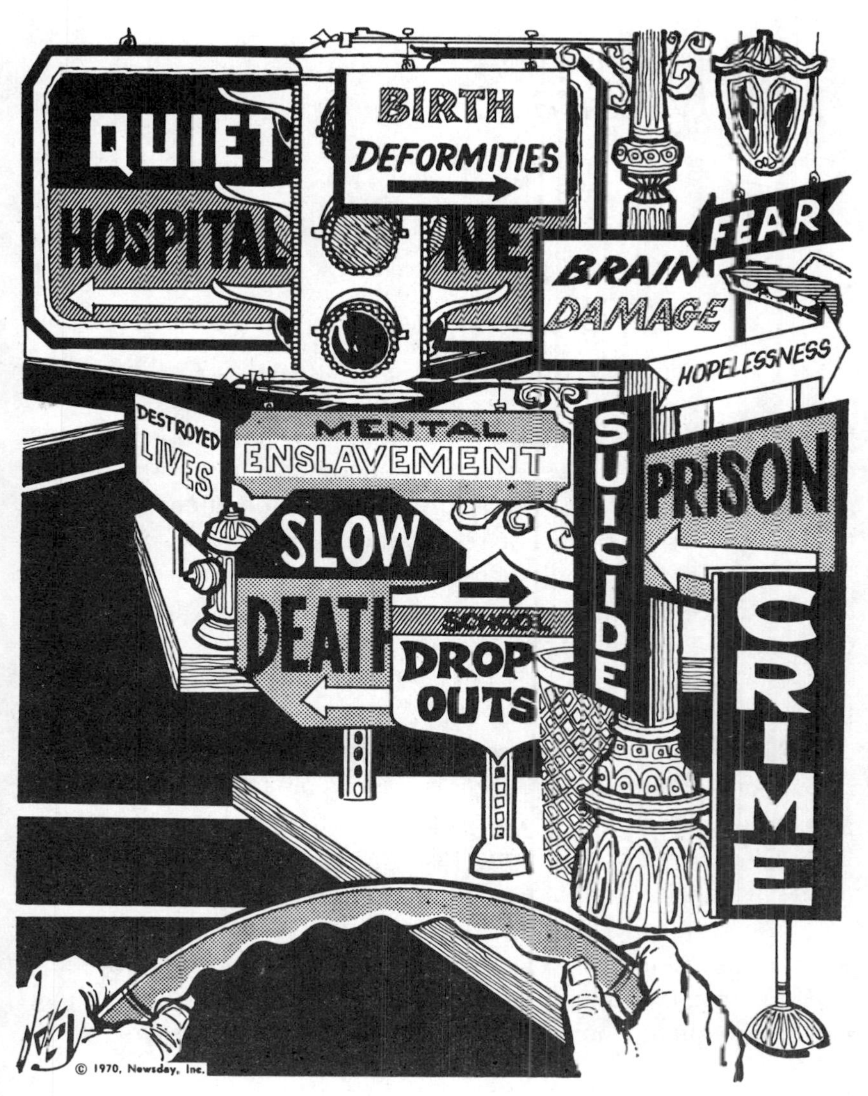

Tom Darcy—Reprinted by permission of Newsday, Inc.

RUSSEL V. LEE, M.D.

Drugs: The Stampede into Hysteria

STUDY QUESTIONS FOR COMPREHENSION

1. Which drug, according to Dr. Lee, is the worst of all that man uses to escape reality?
2. Is it primarily addiction or deprivation that causes the antisocial behavior of drug addicts?
3. Does Dr. Lee favor the use of drugs?

In recent years we have heard much about the abuse of drugs. Most of it is nonsense. We have been stampeded into a hysteria which has resulted in absurd laws and absurd penalties for offenses that are trivial insofar as their effect on society is concerned.

It is time that people generally knew more about these many drugs that are used largely to escape reality and to formulate a program based on knowledge and scientific facts.

The worst of all drugs in this category is, of course, alcohol. And it is socially and legally respectable.

Alcohol ranks fourth in some areas as a cause of death (San Francisco is one of the worst areas); it is responsible for over 50 per cent, perhaps as high as 65 per cent, of fatal automobile accidents, over 50 per cent of the arrests in most cities, 10 per cent of admissions to mental hospitals.

There are probably over five million alcoholics of the severe type in the country and five million more for whom it is a problem. The alcoholic is a difficult person to handle; he is noisy, often pugnacious, frequently homicidal, in all ways a social nuisance.

Reprinted from the *San Francisco Chronicle,* June 14, 1970, by permission of the author and publisher.

This is not true of the other drugs concerning which so much hullabaloo is raised. In fact, the morphine addict who has a sufficient dose is likely to be a very pleasant fellow. But by long association and because of the fiasco of prohibition in the large cities, we have come to tolerate alcohol and there are negligible programs for its control.

The race has had long experience with opium and now with its derivatives, codeine, morphine and heroin. There are areas where opium is an accepted, normal part of the day's ration (and this has gone on for centuries), and continued by the individual for years without the terrible consequences alleged to be inevitable.

But the outstanding characteristic of these drugs is that they are terribly addictive. An unfortunate who is "hooked" will do literally anything to get a "fix." The absolute necessity felt by the individual to get these drugs places him at the mercy of the supplier. And supplying the addicts is the source of millions, perhaps a few billions, of dollars for the criminal element who control the market.

Most addicts are "manufactured," i.e., deliberately put on the habit by a peddler who knows that after they have become addicted to his free drugs, they will be willing to pay heavily for future supplies. Our great number of addicts results from this.

In the days before the calamitous Harrison Anti-Narcotic Act, when addicts could buy the drug freely at low cost, the problem was nothing compared to today. In countries like Great Britain, where it can be prescribed by a physician, or bought at a pharmacy at a reasonable price, there are few addicts.

The Harrison Anti-Narcotic Act is largely responsible for our present deplorable state. The officials of the Federal Bureau of Narcotics violently resist rational efforts to change the present ridiculous situation. The money spent on law enforcement, on the imprisonment officers is worse than wasted. It does great harm.

Insofar as the opium derivatives are concerned, the control should be entirely in medical hands. Doctors should be permitted to treat addiction, to prescribe drugs or, probably better, arrange for the administration of these drugs at a minimal fee to those who are hopelessly addicted.

It is not primarily addiction; it is deprivation that does the harm. The deprived addict will do and does do almost anything to get the drugs. Shoplifting, car theft, burglary, robbery, and prostitution are engaged in to get the drug. It may cost the addict $50 a day to keep supplied. This may mean he must steal $500 worth of merchandise because the fence must get his.

On the other side, if the heroin or morphine addict is given as much as he needs (the actual cost is negligible), he causes no trouble. Nothing like the alcoholic. Society would be better off to do this. It would put the underworld peddlers and the unnecessary enforcement officers out of business. With no financial incentive to produce addicts, the number would decline.

It has been shown that jail sentences, commitment to Lexington or Ft. Worth (treatment centers) seldom cures. Actually, addiction is a youthful disease. Many get off the habit in their middle thirties and forties and cause no trouble thereafter.

The substitution of methadone (a synthetic that takes the place of heroin) should be routine and should be free. A rational, scientific medical approach to the problem of "hard" addiction is overdue.

The other drugs of this new subculture of ours are relatively new and quite different both in effect and in social significance from heroin or alcohol. Each needs separate discussion.

Marijuana—"grass"—is closely related in physiological effect and botanically to hashish which has been used in Asia and North Africa for more than a hundred years. The active principle of hashish and marijuana is known chemically and is a potent, dangerous substance. But like the nicotine in tobacco, also a virulent poison, very small amounts are actually absorbed by smoking a "joint" or even several.

It has a quite pleasant, mildly intoxicating effect. It seems to remove some of the inhibitions to some forms of variant social behavior but never results in the wild, uncontrollable behavior of alcoholic drunkenness. It is not addictive in the sense of heroin but the users get to like it and may use it occasionally only for a let down.

Marijuana is deplored because it is said to lead to the use of "hard" drugs. There is apparently no physiological tendency for this to happen, but it is certainly true that among users of grass one is more likely to meet users of other drugs except, curiously, alcohol. The two seldom go together.

LSD is a strange drug. Perhaps it has some of the metaphysical effects attributed to it by its devotees. Perhaps it does act on consciousness and release creativity. The evidence is contradictory.

Certainly on a "trip" the user has a strange experience and a different kind of consciousness. Certainly he escapes reality in a real way, and certainly in many cases even permanent psychological damage is done.

There are instances of the activation of latent psychosis. There is plenty of evidence that it changes motivations in ways that may lead to self-destruction. It is not a drug for people to play with. It may have important uses in psychiatry—some say it cures alcoholism—but the evidence is not in.

GEORGE WALD

Speech at MIT

The following is a speech given on March 4, 1969, at the Massachusetts Institute of Technology by Dr. George Wald of Harvard, a Nobel Prize winner in physiology and medicine.

STUDY QUESTIONS FOR COMPREHENSION

1. Explain why Wald believes that the Vietnam situation is only one part of a larger problem.
2. What is Wald's position on the draft?
3. What, in Wald's view, is the only point of government?
4. Contrast Wald's position with that implied by Senator Russell's comment.

All of you know that in the last couple of years there has been student unrest breaking at times into violence in many parts of the world: in England, Germany, Italy, Spain, Mexico and needless to say, in many parts of this country. There has been a great deal of discussion as to what it all means. Perfectly clearly it means something different in Mexico from what it does in France, and something different in France from what it does in Tokyo, and something different in Tokyo from what it does in this country. Yet unless we are to assume that students have gone crazy all over the world, or that they have just decided that it's the thing to do, there must be some common meaning.

I don't need to go so far afield to look for that meaning. I am a teacher, and at Harvard, I have a class of about 350 students—men and women—most of them freshmen and sophomores. Over these past few years I have felt increasingly that something is terribly wrong—and this year ever so much more than last. Something has gone sour, in teaching and in learning. It's almost as though there were a widespread feeling that education has become irrelevant.

A lecture is much more of a dialogue than many of you probably appreciate. As you lecture, you keep watching the faces; and information keeps coming back to you all the time. I began to feel, particularly this year, that I was missing much of what was coming back. I tried asking the students, but they didn't or couldn't help me very much.

But I think I know what's the matter, even a little better than they do. I think that this whole generation of students is beset with a profound uneasiness. I don't think that they have yet quite defined its source. I think I understand the reasons for their uneasiness even better than they do. What is more, I share their uneasiness.

What's bothering those students? Some of them tell you it's the Vietnam War. I think the Vietnam War is the most shameful episode in the whole of American history. The concept of War Crimes is an American invention. We've committed many War Crimes in Vietnam; but I'll tell you something interesting about that. We were committing War Crimes in World War II, even before the Nuremburg trials were held and the principle of war crimes stated. The saturation bombing of German cities was a War Crime. Dropping atom bombs on Hiroshima and Nagasaki was a War Crime. If we had lost the war, some of our leaders might have had to answer for those actions.

I've gone through all of that history lately, and I find that there's a gimmick in it. It isn't written out, but I think we established it by precedent. That gimmick is that if one can allege that one is repelling or retaliating for an *aggression*—after that everything goes. And you see we are living in a world in which all wars are wars of defense. All War Departments are now Defense Departments. This is all part of the double talk of our time. The aggressor is always on the other side. And I suppose this is why our ex-Secretary of State, Dean Rusk —a man in whom repetition takes the place of reason, and stubbornness takes the place of character—went to such pains to insist, as he still insists, that in Vietnam we are repelling an aggression. And if that's what we are doing—so runs the doctrine—anything goes. If the concept of war crimes is ever to mean anything, they will have to be defined as categories of acts, regardless of alleged provocation. But that isn't so now.

I think we've lost that war, as a lot of other people think, too.

The Vietnamese have a secret weapon. It's their willingness to die, beyond our willingness to kill. In effect they've been saying, you can kill us, but you'll have to kill a lot of us, you may have to kill all of us. And thank heavens, we are not yet ready to do that.

Yet we have come a long way—far enough to sicken many Americans, far enough even to sicken our fighting men. Far enough so that our national symbols have gone sour. How many of you can sing about "the rockets' red glare, bombs bursting in air" without thinking, those are *our* bombs and *our* rockets bursting over South Vietnamese villages? When those words were written, we were a people struggling for freedom against oppression. Now we are supporting real or thinly disguised military dictatorships all over the world, helping them to control and repress peoples struggling for their freedom.

But that Vietnam War, shameful and terrible as it is, seems to me only an immediate incident in a much larger and more stubborn situation.

Part of my trouble with students is that almost all the students I teach were born since World War II. Just after World War II, a series of new and abnormal procedures came into American life. We regarded them at the time as temporary aberrations. We thought we would get back to normal American life some day. But those procedures have stayed with us now for more than 20 years, and those students of mine have never known anything else. They think those things are normal. Students think we've always had a Pentagon, that we have always had a big army, and that we always had a draft. But those are all new things in American life; and I think that they are incompatible with what America meant before.

How many of you realize that just before World War II the entire American army including the Air Force numbered 139,000 men? Then World War II started, but we weren't yet in it; and seeing that there was great trouble in the world, we doubled this army to 268,000 men. Then in World War II it got to be 8 million. And then World War II came to an end, and we prepared to go back to a peacetime army somewhat as the American army had always been before. And indeed in 1950—you think about 1950, our international commitments, the Cold War, the Truman Doctrine, and all the rest of it—in 1950 we got down to 600,000 men.

Now we have 3.5 million men under arms: about 600,000 in Vietnam, about 300,000 more in "support areas" elsewhere in the Pacific, about 250,000 in Germany. And there are a lot at home. Some months ago we were told that 300,000 National Guardsmen and 200,000 reservists—so half a million men—had been specially trained for riot duty in the cities.

I say the Vietnam War is just an immediate incident, because so long as we keep that big an army, it will always find things to do. If the Vietnam War stopped tomorrow, with that big a military establishment, the chances are that we would be in another such adventure abroad or at home before you knew it.

As for the draft: Don't reform the draft—get rid of it.

A peacetime draft is the most un-American thing I know. All the time I was growing up I was told about oppressive Central European countries and Russia, where young men were forced into the army; and I was told what they did about it. They chopped off a finger, or shot off a couple of toes; or better still, if they could manage it, they came to this country. And we understood that, and sympathized, and were glad to welcome them.

Now by present estimates four to six thousand Americans of draft age have left this country for Canada, another two or three thousand have gone to Europe, and it looks as though many more are preparing to emigrate.

A few months ago I received a letter from the Harvard Alumni Bulletin posing a series of questions that students might ask a professor involving what to do about the draft. I was asked to write what I would tell those students. All I had to say to those students was this: If any of them had decided to evade the draft and asked my help, I would help him in any way I could. I would feel as I suppose members of the underground railway felt in pre-Civil War days, helping runaway slaves to get to Canada. It wasn't altogether a popular position then; but what do you think of it now?

A bill to stop the draft was recently introduced in the Senate (S. 503), sponsored by a group of senators that ran the gamut from

McGovern and Hatfield to Barry Goldwater. I hope it goes through; but any time I find that Barry Goldwater and I are in agreement, that makes me take another look.

And indeed there are choices in getting rid of the draft. I think that when we get rid of the draft, we must also cut back the size of the armed forces. It seems to me that in peacetime a total of one million men is surely enough. If there is an argument for American military forces of more than one million men in peacetime, I should like to hear that argument debated.

There is another thing being said closely connected with this: that to keep an adequate volunteer army, one would have to raise the pay considerably. That's said so positively and often that people believe it. I don't think it is true.

The great bulk of our present armed forces are genuine volunteers. Among first-term enlistments, 49 percent are true volunteers. Another 30 percent are so-called "reluctant volunteers," persons who volunteer under pressure of the draft. Only 21 percent are draftees. All re-enlistments, of course are true volunteers.

So the great majority of our present armed forces are true volunteers. Whole services are composed entirely of volunteers: the Air Force for example, the Navy, almost all the Marines. That seems like proof to me that present pay rates are adequate. One must add that an Act of Congress in 1967 raised the base pay throughout the services in three installments, the third installment still to come, on April 1, 1969. So it is hard to understand why we are being told that to maintain adequate armed services on a volunteer basis will require large increases in pay; that they will cost an extra $17 billion per year. It seems plain to me that we can get all the armed forces we need as volunteers, and at present rates of pay.

But there is something ever so much bigger and more important than the draft. That bigger thing, of course, is the militarization of our country. Ex-President Eisenhower warned us of what he called the military-industrial complex. I am sad to say that we must begin to think of it now as the military-industrial-labor union complex. What happened under the plea of the Cold War was not alone that we built up the first big peacetime army in our history, but we institutionalized it. We built, I suppose, the biggest government building in our history to run it, and we institutionalized it.

I don't think we can live with the present military establishment and its $80 billion a year budget, and keep America anything like we have known it in the past. It is corrupting the life of the whole country. It is buying up everything in sight: industries, banks, investors, universities; and lately it seems also to have bought up the labor unions.

The Defense Department is always broke; but some of the things they do with that $80 billion a year would make Buck Rogers envious. For example: the Rocky Mountain Arsenal on the outskirts of Denver was manufacturing a deadly nerve poison on such a scale that there was a problem of waste disposal. Nothing daunted, they dug a tunnel two miles deep under Denver, into which they have injected so much poisoned water that beginning a couple of years ago Denver began to experience a series of earth tremors of increasing severity. Now there is a grave fear of a major earthquake. An interesting debate is in progress as to whether Denver will be safer if that lake of poisoned water is removed or left in place. (N.Y. Times, July 4, 1968; Science, Sept. 27, 1968.)

Perhaps you have read also of those 6000 sheep that suddenly died in Skull Valley, Utah, killed by another nerve poison—a strange and, I believe, still unexplained accident, since the nearest testing seems to have been 30 miles away.

As for Vietnam, the expenditure of fire power has been frightening. Some of you may still remember Khe Sanh, a hamlet just south of the Demilitarized Zone, where a force of U.S. Marines was beleaguered for a time. During that period we dropped on the perimeter of Khe Sanh more explosives than fell on Japan throughout World War II, and more than fell on the whole of Europe during the years 1942 and 1943.

One of the officers there was quoted as having said afterward, "It looks like the world caught smallpox and died." (N.Y. Times, Mar. 28, 1968.)

The only point of government is to safeguard and foster life. Our government has become preoccupied with death, with the business of killing and being killed. So-called Defense now absorbs 60 percent of the national budget, and about 12 percent of the Gross National Product.

A lively debate is beginning again on whether or not we should deploy antiballistic missiles, the ABM. I don't have to talk about them, everyone else here is doing that. But I should like to mention a curious circumstance. In September, 1967, or about 1½ years ago, we had a meeting of M.I.T. and Harvard people, including experts on these matters, to talk about whether anything could be done to block the Sentinel system, the deployment of ABM's. Everyone present thought them undesirable; but a few of the most knowledgeable persons took what seemed to be the practical view, "Why fight about a dead issue? It has been decided, the funds have been appropriated. Let's go on from there."

Well, fortunately, it's not a dead issue.

An ABM is a nuclear weapon. It takes a nuclear weapon to stop a nuclear weapon. And our concern must be with the whole issue of nuclear weapons.

There is an entire semantics ready to deal with the sort of thing I am about to say. It involves such phrases as "those are the facts of life." No—they are the facts of death. I don't accept them, and I advise you not to accept them. We are under repeated pressure to accept things that are presented to us as settled—decisions that have been made. Always there is the thought: let's go on from there! But this time we don't see how to go on. We will have to stick with those issues.

We are told that the United States and Russia between them have by now stockpiled in nuclear weapons approximately the explosive power of 15 tons of TNT for every man, woman and child on earth. And now it is suggested that we must make more. All very regrettable, of course; but those are "the facts of life." We really would like to disarm; but our new Secretary of Defense has made the ingenious proposal that now is the time to greatly increase our nuclear armaments so that we can disarm from a position of strength.

I think all of you know there is no adequate defense against massive nuclear attack. It is both easier and cheaper to circumvent any known nuclear defense system than to provide it. It's all pretty crazy. At the very moment we talk of deploying ABM's we are also building the MIRV, the weapon to circumvent ABM's.

So far as I know, the most conservative estimates of Americans killed in a major nuclear attack, with everything working as well as can be hoped and all foreseeable precautions taken, run to about 50 millions. We have become callous to gruesome statistics, and this seems at first to be only another gruesome statistic. You think, Bang! —and next morning, if you're still there, you read in the newspapers that 50 million people were killed.

But that isn't the way it happens. When we killed close to 200,000 people with those first little, old-fashioned uranium bombs that we dropped on Hiroshima and Nagasaki, about the same number of persons was maimed, blinded, burned, poisoned and otherwise doomed. A lot of them took a long time to die.

That's the way it would be. Not a bang, and a certain number of corpses to bury; but a nation filled with millions of helpless, maimed, tortured and doomed persons, and the survivors of a nuclear holocaust will be huddled with their families in shelters, with guns ready to fight off their neighbors, trying to get some uncontaminated food and water.

A few months ago Sen. Richard Russell of Georgia ended a speech in the Senate with the words: "If we have to start over again with another Adam and Eve, I want them to be Americans; and I want them on this continent and not in Europe." That was a United States senator holding a patriotic speech. Well, here is a Nobel Laureate who thinks that those words are criminally insane. (Prolonged applause.)

How real is the threat of full-scale nuclear war? I have my own very inexpert idea, but realizing how little I know and fearful that I may be a little paranoid on this subject, I take every opportunity to ask reputed experts. I asked that question of a very distinguished professor of government at Harvard about a month ago. I asked him what sort of odds he would lay on the possibility of full-scale nuclear war within the foreseeable future. "Oh," he said comfortably, "I think I can give you a pretty good answer to that question. I estimate the probability of full-scale nuclear war, provided that the situation remains about as it is now, at 2 percent per year." Anybody can do the simple calculation that shows that 2 percent per year means that the chance of having that full-scale nuclear war by 1990 is about one in three, and by 2000 it is about 50-50.

I think I know what is bothering the students. I think that what we are up against is a generation that is by no means sure that it has a future.

I am growing old, and my future so to speak is already behind me. But there are those students of mine who are in my mind always; and there are my children, two of them now 7 and 9, whose future is infinitely more precious to me than my own. So it isn't just their generation; it's mine too. We're all in it together.

Are we to have a chance to live? We don't ask for prosperity, or security; only for a reasonable chance to live, to work out our destiny in peace and decency. Not to go down in history as the apocalyptic generation.

And it isn't only nuclear war. Another overwhelming threat is the population explosion. That has not yet even begun to come under control. There is every indication that the world population will double before the year 2000; and there is a widespread expectation of famine on an unprecedented scale in many parts of the world. The experts tend to differ only in the estimates of when those famines will begin. Some think by 1980, others think they can be staved off until 1990, very few expect that they will not occur by the year 2000.

That is the problem. Unless we can be surer than we now are that this generation has a future, nothing else matters. It's not good enough to give it tender loving care, to supply it with breakfast foods, to buy it expensive educations. Those things don't mean anything unless this generation has a future. And we're not sure that it does.

I don't think that there are problems of youth, or student problems. All the real problems I know are grown-up problems.

Perhaps you will think me altogether absurd, or "academic," or hopelessly innocent—that is, until you think of the alternatives—if I say as I do to you now: we have to get rid of those nuclear weapons. There is nothing worth having that can be obtained by nuclear war:

nothing material or ideological, no tradition that it can defend. It is utterly self-defeating. Those atom bombs represent an unusable weapon. The only use for an atom bomb is to keep somebody else from using one. It can give us no protection, but only the doubtful satisfaction of retaliation. Nuclear weapons offer us nothing but a balance of terror; and a balance of terror is still terror.

We have to get rid of those atomic weapons, here and everywhere. We cannot live with them.

I think we've reached a point of great decision, not just for our nation, not only for all humanity, but for life upon the Earth. I tell my students, with a feeling of pride that I hope they will share, that the carbon, nitrogen and oxygen that make up 99 percent of our living substance, were cooked in the deep interiors of earlier generations of dying stars. Gathered up from the ends of the universe, over billions of years, eventually they came to form in part the substance of our sun, its planets and ourselves. Three billion years ago life arose upon the Earth. It seems to be the only life in the solar system. Many a star has since been born and died.

About two million years ago, man appeared. He has become the dominant species on the Earth. All other living things, animal and plant, live by his sufferance. He is the custodian of life on Earth. It's a big responsibility.

The thought that we're in competition with Russians or with Chinese is all a mistake, and trivial. Only mutual destruction lies that way. We are one species, with a world to win. There's life all over this universe, but in all the universe we are the only men.

Our business is with life, not death. Our challenge is to give what account we can of what becomes of life in the solar system, this corner of the universe that is our home and, most of all, what becomes of men—all men of all nations, colors and creeds. It has become one world, a world for all men. It is only such a world that now can offer us life and the chance to go on.

PETER VIERECK

Game Called on Account of Darkness

Once there was a friend.
He watched me from the sky.
Maybe he never lived at all.
Maybe too much friendship made him die.

When the gang played cops-and-robbers in the alley,
It was my friend who told me which were which.
Now he doesn't tell me any more.
(Which team am I playing for?)

My science teacher built a telescope
To show me every answer in the end.
I stared and stared at every star for hours.
I couldn't find my friend.

At Sunday school they said I breathe too much.
When I hold my breath within the under
Side of earth, they said I'll find my friend.
. . . I wonder.

He was like a kind of central-heating
In the big cold house, and that was good.
One by one I have to chop my toys now,
As firewood.

Every time I stood upon a crossroads,
It made me mad to feel him watch me choose.
I'm glad there's no more spying while I play.
Still, I'm sad he went away.

W. T. STACE

Man Against Darkness

STUDY QUESTIONS FOR COMPREHENSION

1. Rephrase in your own words Stace's main point.
2. Stace claims that religion is not necessary in order for man to lead a moral life. Why does he say that it is more desirable that morality stem from man's mind rather than from an external source such as an organized religion? Do you agree or disagree?
3. What does the author mean by the "Great Illusion"? By "minor illusions"? What are some of the illusions by which you live or *have* lived?

The Catholic bishops of America recently issued a statement in which they said that the chaotic and bewildered state of the modern world is due to man's loss of faith, his abandonment of God and religion. For my part I believe in no religion at all. Yet I entirely agree with the bishops. It is an oversimplification to speak of *the* cause of so complex a state of affairs as the tortured condition of the world today. Its causes are doubtless multitudinous. Yet allowing for some element of oversimplification, I say that the bishops' assertion is substantially true.

Jean-Paul Sartre, the French existentialist philosopher, labels himself an atheist. Yet his views seem to me plainly to support the statement of the bishops. So long as there was believed to be a God in the sky, he says, men could regard him as the source of their moral ideals. The universe, created and governed by a fatherly God, was a friendly habitation for man. We could be sure that, however great the evil in the world, good in the end would triumph and the forces of evil would be routed. With the disappearance of God from the sky all this has changed. Since the world is not ruled by a spiritual being, but rather by blind forces, there cannot be any ideals, moral or otherwise, in the universe outside us. Our ideals, therefore, must proceed only from our own minds; they are our own inventions. Thus the world which surrounds us is nothing but an immense spiritual emptiness. It is a dead universe. We do not live in a universe which is on the side of our values. It is completely indifferent to them.

There is a popular belief that some particular scientific discoveries or theories, such as the Darwinian theory of evolution, or the views of geologists about the age of the earth, or a series of such discoveries, have done the damage. It would be foolish to deny that these discoveries have had a great effect in undermining religious dogmas. But this account does not at all go to the heart of the matter. Religion can probably outlive any scientific discoveries which could be made. It can accommodate itself to them. The root cause of the decay of faith has not been any particular discovery of science, but rather the general spirit of science and certain basic assumptions upon which modern science, from the seventeenth century onward, has proceeded.

The founders of modern science—for instance, Galileo, Kepler, and Newton—were mostly pious men who did not doubt God's purposes. Nevertheless they took the revolutionary step of consciously and deliberately expelling the idea of purpose as controlling nature from their new science of nature. They did this on the ground that inquiry into purposes is useless for what science aims at: namely, the prediction and control of events. To predict an eclipse, what you have to know is not its purpose but its causes. Hence science from the seventeenth century onward became exclusively an inquiry into causes. The conception of purpose in the world was ignored and frowned on. This, though silent and almost unnoticed, was the greatest revolution in human history, far outweighing in importance any of the political revolutions whose thunder has reverberated through the world.

For it came about in this way that for the past three hundred years there has been growing up in men's minds, dominated as they are by science, a new imaginative picture of the world. The world, according to this new picture, is purposeless, senseless, meaningless. Nature is nothing but matter in motion. The motions of matter are governed, not by any purpose, but by blind forces and laws. Nature in this view, says Whitehead—to whose writing I am indebted in this part of my paper—is "merely the hurrying of material, endlessly, meaninglessly." You can draw a sharp line across the history of Europe dividing it into two epochs of very unequal length. The line passes through the lifetime of Galileo. European man before Galileo —whether ancient pagan or more recent Christian—thought of the world as controlled by plan and purpose. After Galileo, European man thinks of it as utterly purposeless.

It is this which has killed religion. Religion could survive the discoveries that the sun, not the earth, is the center; that men are descended from simian ancestors; that the earth is hundreds of millions of years old. These discoveries may render out of date some of the details of older theological dogmas, may force their restatement in new intellectual frameworks. But they do not touch the essence of the religious vision itself, which is the faith that there is plan and purpose in the world, that the world is a moral order, that in the end all things are for the best. This faith may express itself through many different intellectual dogmas, those of Christianity, of Hinduism, of Islam. All and any of these intellectual dogmas may be destroyed without destroying the essential religious spirit. But that spirit cannot survive destruction of belief in a plan and purpose of the world, for that is the very heart of it. Religion can get on with any sort of astronomy, geology, biology, physics. But it cannot get on with a purposeless and meaningless universe.

If the scheme of things is purposeless and meaningless, then the life of man is purposeless and meaningless too. Everything is futile, all effort is in the end worthless. A man may, of course, still pursue disconnected ends, money, fame, art, science, and may gain pleasure from them. But his life is hollow at the center. Hence the dissatisfied, disillusioned, restless spirit of modern man.

Along with the ruin of the religious vision there went the ruin of moral principles and indeed of all values. If there is a cosmic purpose, if there is in the nature of things a drive toward goodness, then our moral systems will derive their validity from this. But if our moral rules do not proceed from something outside us in the nature of the universe—whether we say it is God or simply the universe itself—

then they must be our own inventions. Thus it came to be believed that moral rules must be merely an expression of our own likes and dislikes. But likes and dislikes are notoriously variable. What pleases one man, people, or culture displeases another. Therefore morals are wholly relative.

Another characteristic of our spiritual state is loss of belief in the freedom of the will. This also is a fruit of the scientific spirit, though not of any particular scientific discovery. Science has been built up on the basis of determinism, which is the belief that every event is completely determined by a chain of causes and is therefore theoretically predictable beforehand. It is true that recent physics seems to challenge this. But so far as its practical consequences are concerned, the damage has long ago been done. A man's actions, it was argued, are as much events in the natural world as is an eclipse of the sun. It follows that men's actions are as theoretically predictable as an eclipse. But if it is certain now that John Smith will murder Joseph Jones at 2:15 P.M. on January 1, 1963, what possible meaning can it have to say that when that time comes John Smith will be *free* to choose whether he will commit the murder or not? And if he is not free, how can he be held responsible?

It is true that the whole of this argument can be shown by a competent philosopher to be a tissue of fallacies—or at least I claim that it can. But the point is that the analysis required to show this is much too subtle to be understood by the average entirely unphilosophical man. Because of this, the argument against free will is generally swallowed whole by the unphilosophical. Hence the thought that man is not free, that he is the helpless plaything of forces over which he has no control, has deeply penetrated the modern mind. We hear of economic determinism, cultural determinism, historical determinism. We are not responsible for what we do because our glands control us or because we are the products of environment or heredity. Not moral self-control, but the doctor, the psychiatrist, the educationist, must save us from doing evil. Pills and injections in the future are to do what Christ and the prophets have failed to do. Of course I do not mean to deny that doctors and educationists can help. And I do not in any way mean to belittle their efforts. But I do wish to draw attention to the weakening of moral controls, the repudiation of personal responsibility which, in the popular thinking of the day, result from these tendencies of thought.

No civilization can live without ideals, or to put it in another way, without a firm faith in moral ideas. Our ideals and moral ideas have in the past been rooted in religion. But the religious basis of our ideals has been undermined, and the superstructure of ideals is plainly tottering. None of the commonly suggested remedies on examination seems likely to succeed. It would therefore look as if the early death of our civilization were inevitable.

Of course we know that it is perfectly possible for individual men, very highly educated men, philosophers, scientists, intellectuals in general, to live moral lives without any religious convictions. But the question is whether a whole civilization, a whole family of peoples, composed almost entirely of relatively uneducated men and women, can do this. Of course, if we could make the vast majority of men as highly educated as the very few are now, we might save the situation. And we are already moving slowly in that direction through the techniques of mass education. But the critical question seems to concern the time lag. Perhaps in a few hundred years most of the population will, at the present rate, be sufficiently highly educated and civilized to combine high ideals with an absence of religion. But long before we reach any such stage, the collapse of our civilization may have come about. How are we to live through the intervening period?

I am sure that the first thing we have to do is to face the truth, however bleak it may be, and then next we have to learn to live with it. Let me say a word about each of these two points. What I am urging as regards the first is complete honesty. Those who wish to resurrect Christian dogmas are not, of course, consciously dishonest. But they have that kind of unconscious dishonesty which consists in lulling oneself with opiates and dreams. Those who talk of a new religion are merely hoping for a new opiate. Both alike refuse to face the truth that there is, in the universe outside man, no spirituality, no regard for values, no friend in the sky, no help or comfort for man of any sort. To be perfectly honest in the admission of this fact, not to seek shelter in new or old illusions, not to indulge in wishful dreams about this matter, this is the first thing we shall have to do.

I do not urge this course out of any special regard for the sanctity of truth in the abstract. It is not self-evident to me that truth is the supreme value to which all else must be sacrificed. Might not the discoverer of a truth which would be fatal to mankind be justified in suppressing it, even in teaching men a falsehood? Is truth more valuable than goodness and beauty and happiness? To think so is to invent yet another absolute, another religious delusion in which Truth with a capital T is substituted for God. The reason why we must now boldly and honestly face the truth that the universe is non-spiritual and indifferent to goodness, beauty, happiness, or truth is not that it would be wicked to suppress it, but simply that it is too late to do so. In the end we cannot do anything else but face it. Yet we stand on the brink, dreading the icy plunge. We need courage. We need honesty.

Now about the other point, the necessity of learning to live with the truth. This means learning to live virtuously and happily, or at least contentedly, without illusions. And this is going to be extremely difficult because what we have now begun dimly to perceive is that human life in the past, or at least human happiness, has almost wholly depended upon illusions. It has been said that man lives by truth, and that the truth will make us free. Nearly the opposite seems to me to be the case. Mankind has managed to live only by means of lies, and the truth may very well destroy us.

The illusions by which men have lived seem to be of two kinds. First, there is what one may perhaps call the Great Illusion—I mean the religious illusion that the universe is moral and good, that it follows a wise and noble plan, that it is gradually generating some supreme value, that goodness is bound to triumph in it. Secondly, there is a whole host of minor illusions on which human happiness nourishes itself. How much of human happiness notoriously comes from the illusions of the lover about his beloved? Then again we work and strive because of the illusions connected with fame, glory, power, or money. Banners of all kinds, flags, emblems, insignia, ceremonials, and rituals are invariably symbols of some illusion or other. The

British Empire, the connection between mother country and dominions is partly kept going by illusions surrounding the notion of kingship. Or think of the vast amount of human happiness which is derived from the illusion of supposing that if some nonsense syllable, such as "sir" or "count" or "lord" is pronounced in conjunction with our names, we belong to a superior order of people.

There is plenty of evidence that human happiness is almost wholly based upon illusions of one kind or another. But the scientific spirit, or the spirit of truth, is the enemy of illusions and therefore the enemy of human happiness. That is why it is going to be so difficult to live with the truth.

There is no reason why we should have to give up the host of minor illusions which render life supportable. There is no reason why the lover should be scientific about the loved one. Even the illusions of fame and glory may persist. But without the Great Illusion, the illusion of a good, kindly, and purposeful universe, we shall *have* to learn to live. And to ask this is really no more than to ask that we become genuinely civilized beings and not merely sham civilized beings.

I can best explain the difference by a reminiscence. I remember a fellow student in my college days, an ardent Christian, who told me that if he did not believe in a future life, in heaven and hell, he would rape, murder, steal, and be a drunkard. That is what I call being a sham civilized being. On the other hand, not only could a Huxley, a John Stuart Mill, a David Hume, live great and fine lives without any religion, but a great many others of us, quite obscure persons, can at least live decent lives without it.

To be genuinely civilized means to be able to walk straight and to live honorably without the props and crutches of one or another of the childish dreams which have so far supported men. That such a life is likely to be ecstatically happy I will not claim. But that it can be lived in quiet content, accepting resignedly what cannot be helped, not expecting the impossible, and thankful for small mercies, this I would maintain. That it will be difficult for men in general to learn this lesson I do not deny. But that it will be impossible I will not admit since so many have learned it already.

Man has not yet grown up. He is not adult. Like a child he cries for the moon and lives in a world of fantasies. And the race as a whole has perhaps reached the great crisis of its life. Can it grow up as a race in the same sense as individual men grow up? Can man put away childish things and adolescent dreams? Can he grasp the real world as it actually is, stark and bleak, without its religious or romantic halo, and still retain his ideals, striving for great ends and noble achievements? If he can, all may yet be well. If he cannot, he will probably sink back into the savagery and brutality from which he came, taking a humble place once more among the lower animals.

RONALD N. BRACEWELL

Is Another World Ringing Our Number?

STUDY QUESTIONS FOR COMPREHENSION

1. How does the first paragraph break down the resistance of those readers who scoff at the possibility of life in outer space?
2. What argument does Bracewell advance to dispel the fears many have of contact with creatures from outer space?
3. What does Bracewell say about the language barrier between earth people and visitors from space?

"That which makes me of this Opinion, that those Worlds are not without such a Creature endued with Reason, is that otherwise our Earth would have too much the Advantage of them, in being the only part of the Universe that could boast of such a Creature." —Christianus Huygens, Dutch astronomer, *New Conjectures Concerning the Planetary Worlds, Their Inhabitants and Productions* (c. 1670).

Many people think there is intelligent life out in space somewhere. This is not just an idea of our times, but is a topic which must have come up over and over again in man's discussions. I can picture my ancestors sitting around the campfire and speculating about tribes residing beyond some impassable mountain range or on the bright objects in the heavens above them. Do not think that such talk would have withered for want of facts to go on. There would have been folklore of tribes in other places and rumors brought back by hunters; there might even have been in the group a member who could report having seen and talked to a visitor from a celestial body. There would have been doubters, those who thought their tribe was the only tribe, but it is well to remember that the people of the Mediterranean once thought their land was the center of the universe, then it was the Earth, then the sun, and all were wrong.

Recent scientific discoveries have revived interest in life in space, and in this article I will tell about some current lines of thought and contribute some ideas of my own. First, a little more history.

In the late 1500's a good deal of speculation was provoked by Copernicus, who in the year of his death published his view of a sun-centered planetary system. This idea, which demoted the earth from a central and unique position, directly suggested the possibility of other inhabited earths, and the theme was vigorously developed by Giordano Bruno. For this heresy he was burnt by the church in Rome in 1600.

Bruno's views had no basis in observational fact such as science has now taught us to require, nor is there any observation on record today that evidences the existence of life outside the earth strongly enough to compel assent. In fact the popularity not too long ago of the theory that planets resulted from the grazing collision of a passing star with our sun, a demonstrably rare occurrence, countered the idea of a plurality of worlds. Happily the collision theory has now been discredited. Other avenues of investigation have made it likely that the planets were formed out of a primordial gas cloud, from which the sun itself was formed, by condensation and accretion. In this view the planets are composed of fragments that were not pulled into the sun. Observations of the birth of stars such as our sun now taking place elsewhere in our galaxy form a basis for this.

Now if planets are the more or less normal byproduct of star formation, it makes an enormous difference to the discussion. For various reasons based on telescopic observations, astronomers now generally consider it probable that planets are commonplace companions of the tens of billions of stars like our sun that compose our galaxy, although I should warn that, as yet, no planet outside our own solar system has been directly observed. Nevertheless, I personally judge it to be more likely than not that there is intelligent life elsewhere in our galaxy, outside our solar system. I do not exclude the possibility that we are the only intelligent beings; however, if I adopt that assumption there is really nothing more to say, whereas the opposite view leads to interesting trains of thought.

For example, of the other intelligent communities in space, some will be more advanced than we and some less; but when we bear in mind the accelerating pace of technology and science we see that those who are ahead of us will be very much ahead of us indeed in their understanding of and control over their physical environment. Western civilization of 200 years ago was impressive compared with that of primitive areas, but perhaps not much more so than Roman civilization had been. Recent centuries have witnessed enormous strides by comparison and recent decades even greater ones. (It will be perceived that I am referring here to man's understanding and control of the physical world we live in and not to matters of morals, politics, and many areas of the humanities which have remained relatively static.) No one can say what will be achieved a century hence. The cost of food, clothing, and housing may be brought within the reach of all, disease may be eliminated, the weather brought under control, and staggering things done that we can hardly conceive of now. And yet, there will be, somewhere in the galaxy, communities that passed through our level of technology —chemical fertilizers, electric power, radio, bombs, satellites, computers, molecular biology—a million years ago. Picture them today if you can.

If we made contact with such people it would be a shattering experience. They could tell us the physics and chemistry that are waiting in the future for us to discover laboriously at great cost. I don't see why they couldn't tell us how to deal with serious diseases. Of course it is most unlikely that their biological makeup would make them subject to the same ills as we suffer, but we could give them a standard six-year course in medicine (compressible to a few minutes of running time when suitably digitized onto a magnetic computer tape), and reasonably expect them to figure out what our troubles are.

Some people worry that it would be dangerous for us to encourage contact on the grounds that the natives who ran out on the beach to greet the European seafarers often suffered. The visitors might carry us away and breed us for beef cattle, they say, or steal our mineral resources. But I think that it would be cheaper for them to synthesize steak chemically on their own planet and to replenish depleted minerals from uninhabited worlds closer to home. Remember that the great European sea voyages of discovery were made by people hardly superior in any way to the peoples they visited except in ability to sail. But the cost and difficulty of interstellar voyages are such as to invalidate simple comparison with the contacts between civilizations that were made on the earth in recent centuries.

The chief commodity of interstellar trade, and probably the only one, will be information. It would be nice to have an artifact from another planet, a piece of art, or perhaps some seeds, but we will be able to get their poetry and music by radio and I suppose even sculpture could be reduced to a digital code that would permit reconstitution at the far end. I don't know whether color television will improve to the point where paintings can be transmitted faithfully, but perhaps the other party will not be too interested. They will be interested, however, in the hard knowledge that we have accumulated, even if they are far more advanced than we are. After all, we make expeditions to ancient sites of human habitation and painfully piece together the scanty evidence as we attempt to form a picture of life at the time. No matter how primitive the inhabitants may have been, if we could revive one he could help us immeasurably with what we are trying to do. In the same way, we have accumulated a lot of information about our earth and solar system which would make contact with us very much more attractive than exploration of an uninhabited planet where such detailed data would be impossible to acquire.

Assuming then that it is desirable to make contact with our more advanced neighbors, how should we go about it? It seems certain that the party that takes the initiative in a project like this is the one with the superior technology. After all, Columbus discovered America and the red Indians did not discover Europe. Therefore, instead of sending signals we should be looking for the signals that may be beamed at us. A good deal of thought has been devoted to the method of signalling that might be adopted by a community desiring to attract our attention, and there are weighty arguments favoring microwave radio. (Powerful light beams from lasers have been suggested but careful consideration reveals problems.)

Should we therefore be tuning in on possible transmissions from planets belonging to neighboring stars? The answer to this question depends on one thing we do not know and that is the distance to the nearest superior community. So for the purposes of discussion I take three cases in turn: the distance is (a) 10 light years or less, (b) between 10 and 100 light years, and (c) more than 100 light years.

Even 10 light years is a very long way, but we certainly do not expect to find neighbors closer than this because we know very well the dozen or so stars in the spherical volume of space extending out from our sun to a distance of 10 light years, and there are only two or three which, for one reason or another, cannot be rejected out of hand as likely candidates for life.

It takes a radio signal one year to travel one light year, so it takes 20 years to send out a message and receive a reply over this distance, assuming the called party replies without delay. We can see that the communication will hardly be like a telephone conversation—it will be more like shipwrecked sailors on different coral islands communicating by sea bottle. The fact that 20 years is a substantial fraction of a human lifetime does not in any way diminish the significance of the contact. It can certainly make an impact on our civilization, but it will not be through spokesmen who enjoy interlocution.

If they are there, at about the 10 light year distance, and if their technology is ahead of ours, I suspect that they already know about us, and I would confidently expect unmistakable messages to be received from them in due time. Possibly not in a hurry, though; it might pay them to give us a few decades beyond their first detection that we had discovered radio to give us time to make the further discoveries of the ionosphere, semiconductor devices, and radio astronomy and to develop the large radio telescopes without which we could hardly make it worth their while to page us.

We do not know exactly how intelligent life came to be on our own planet but we do know that for a billion years there were trees and a few reptiles and that civilization has been a recent very brief episode. Therefore, if one picks at random some star possessing a planet with conditions suitable for life, it is still entirely possible that in fact no life exists, or that life exists but no technology, and only in some cases could one expect to find a technological community. For this reason we cannot expect that the nearest community more advanced than ourselves is on the nearest suitable planetary system. It is not impossible, but the chances are slim.

So it is more realistic to think about the situation where the nearest superior community is an order of magnitude farther away, say up to 100 light years. Now in this case the distance and the round trip travel time for electromagnetic communication are truly staggering. You may wonder whether radio communication can even span such a gap, but that question can be answered with confidence from experience with the reception of radio waves of natural origin from parts of the galaxy that are even more distant. The time scale of information exchange makes the human lifetime of even less significance, but the earlier remarks about the irrelevance of this remain the same.

The overriding difficulty as it appears to me now is how to make the initial contact. Once established, a radio link will work perfectly, but how do you tune in on a station whose wavelength is unknown? On top of this, we must use beamed antennas that can be pointed at a star from which we wish to receive, but which cannot simultaneously receive from other directions. In the sphere of 100 light years radius centered on our sun there are over a thousand stars which, in our present state of knowledge, we cannot eliminate as candidates for habitation. Perhaps one of them is beaming a signal at us. If so, let us hope that the signal is not turned off by the time we get around to listening to that star and let us hope that they are still waiting, a century later, when our reply arrives.

The prospects of success in this situation seem so gloomy that I cannot imagine that this can be the technique by which newly-emerging technologies are inducted into the galactic chain of communication. There must be a better trick. Don't forget, when we do make our contact, it will not be the first time that such a thing has happened. There may be a lively traffic in information circulating about the galaxy at this moment, and the members of this galactic community will have exchanged their experiences on detection and induction of new civilizations. In comparison with the facts our current deliberations are no doubt childish; still it behooves us to think about the matter because the intrinsic difficulties are such that the technique for contact may have to lean heavily on our alertness.

In trying to see how the residents of another planet would do it, I have reasoned that two-way question-and-answer communication is indispensable to setting up agreement on codes and programs. Unless they can reduce the contact process to a time interval over which a human being can maintain attention, they risk complete failure. After all we have no institutions that can plan a hundred years ahead, and they can guess that. The answer seems to be to send a messenger. Now this need not be an individual of their race, although their biological engineering may well have proceeded to the point where a subrace of interstellar messengers has been bred. It would be completely unacceptable to us, but perhaps not to them, to breed human brains in bottles, with eyes and arms but no bodies or legs, but possibly one can do the equivalent with solid state devices. One way or another, it is clearly possible in principle to pack an enormous amount of information into a modest interstellar probe, about the size of a football, and to send it into the vicinity of our planetary system. It would take a long time in transit, but on arrival could make contact certain by emitting loud signals at close range on radio wavelengths that, from direct monitoring, it knows we use. From two-way interchanges with this messenger probe we could obtain satisfying quantities of information, including a late edition of their leading encyclopedia, the whereabouts of home base, and the wavelength on which acknowledgment was awaited.

Whatever the form of government on this other world, no

doubt they have a budget, and I can envisage a program under which, within the resources available, they launch one probe a year to each of the 1,000 most likely surrounding stars in turn and repeat at 1,000-year intervals. Of course, most of the messenger probes would be doomed to extinction, and it would be a long program that would pay off only occasionally. One of their messengers to our solar system may have been broadcasting in the neighborhood of earth in the Middle Ages when we had no radio, and the next may be due in 500 years time. Or it may be due soon. I don't expect that the visiting machine would be supplied with the massive rocket needed for descending to the earth's surface because the radio contact alone would suffice—landing a nice tape recorder at great expense in pre-radio days would have been pointless. The purposes of their program would be optimized by spending their available resources on the largest number of adequate probes.

Some fascinating discussions have taken place over the question of how to communicate with someone whose language you don't know. Strange as it may seem, the science fiction authors are right. The visitors will speak English. Just as we can decipher texts in extinct languages, even though the speakers are all dead, so will English be readily decipherable, and all the more so if we supply the mechanical visitor something as helpful as the digitized contents of a big dictionary (preferably illustrated). Naturally there will be words that will be baffling to the messenger; it can ask us about them.

If our nearest technological neighbor is farther away than 100 light years, the problems are multiplied. If the closest one is at say 1,000 light years, then from the dimensions of the galaxy, about 100,000 light years in diameter, it can be calculated that the total number of technological communities in the whole galaxy would be only about 10,000. This low number (compared with the tens of billions of stars in the galaxy) could mean that intelligent life is intrinsically rare, only one solar system in a million having it, or it could mean that the longevity of technological societies is limited. For example, it could be that a goodly fraction of societies that develop atomic science promptly bomb themselves back to the stone age. In either case, the round trip communication time severely limits the degree of meaningful contact that could build up, except perhaps between small groups of durable communities here and there.

The thoughts developed in this article depend heavily on the discovery of radio less than a hundred years ago, and for the most part could not have been entertained at all in 1869. So, while the prospects for immediate interstellar communication do not seem too bright, still we should allow for the further discoveries about the physical world that nature undoubtedly has in store for our world and that may change the picture again. We need to be inventive, alert, and—above all—patient.

HAROLD GILLIAM

Celebration for a Small but Important Planet

We celebrate the Earth.
We celebrate the seas that gave birth to life.

We celebrate the green plants that gave us breath.

We celebrate the waters that flow upon the land
and the air that envelops the planet.
We celebrate the ocean, fount of all life.

We celebrate the microscopic diatoms
that float in the green waters
and create life-giving oxygen.

We celebrate the great whales as they rise and sound
in their hemispheric migrations,
the shoals of salmon that cruise the far seas
and come home again for the act of procreation
in the streams of their birth.

We celebrate the ground swells that rise into ridges
curve concavely into white churning thunder,
bursting on the headlands, spreading on the beaches.

We celebrate the bays and estuaries and marshes
where the waters of the land meet those of the sea,
where life emerged into the sun
and made its first halting advance on the shore.

We celebrate the great storms
born of the impact of warm and cool air masses
far out on the moving ocean,
lashing the coasts with rain,
washing the cities, making fertile the valleys,
whitening the mountain slopes
and the high granite ridges.

We celebrate the seasons.
We shall observe the vernal and autumnal equinoxes.
We shall hold high festival at the winter solstice,
when the sun begins its long return northward,
at the summer solstice, when the sun is at climax,
the days are long and bright,
and the currents of life are at the flood.

We celebrate the sunrise
and the dew of morning on the grass.

We celebrate the coming of night
and the rising of the constellations.

We celebrate the grassy prairies and the dry plains
and the deserts where life is thin
and the ribs of the Earth show through.

We celebrate the migrations of the flocks,
and the rhythms that send them down the semispheres
from arctic to tropics and back again with the sun.

We celebrate the trees,
each wind-sculptured cypress of the ocean shore,
each redwood of the ferny coastal canyons,
each laurel and oak and shining-leaved eucalyptus,
each maple and aspen and high-pointed fir.

We celebrate the soil, its millions living organisms,
its microbes and minerals,
its fungi and worms and bacteria

that nourish the living plants,
providing food for animals and men.

We celebrate the rich valleys
where grapevines grow in furrowed fields
and peaches ripen to sweetness in the summer sun.

We celebrate the bending grasses and the grains,
the chaparral on the hillsides,
the acrid odors of sage and manzanita,
the ferns of damp canyons
and the mesquite of inland deserts.

We celebrate the poetry of the Earth.
We see perfection
in the parabolic flight of a single white egret,
in the flock of a million shearwaters
skimming the offshore waves,
in the trajectory of a mountain waterfall,
in the symmetry of an oak leaf.

We pledge ourselves to the defense of the Earth,
of its air, of its waters,
of the life that moves upon it.
We shall defend it from the assaults of machinery,
from the noxious gasses, the toxic wastes,
the subtle poisons . . .
from ourselves.

We shall come to the Earth
not with devices of destruction
but with respect and humility,
to guide our machines reverently upon the land.

We pledge ourselves to preserve,
from encroaching pavement and omnivorous bulldozers,
the soils on which our food is grown,
the wild beaches of the ocean shore
and of rivers and lakes,

some forests where the whine of the chain saw
will never be heard, some valleys
where animals graze undisturbed in the sun.

We shall respect the processes of the Earth,
the long cyclic chemistry that restores the soil
and renews the waters
and replenishes the ambient air.

We shall abet the forces of renewal. We shall conserve the
precious materials of the planet.
We shall waste nothing.
We shall return organic materials to the soil,
recycle the metals and the paper and the water.

We shall preserve ample areas of our land,
around our cities as well as in far places,
not for development or exploitation,
but for the replenishment of the species,
that we may learn from Nature
its rich complexity and diversity,
its checks and balances,
its perennial search for new possibilities,
that we may perceive supernal beauty,
feel a sense of community with all living things,
and create a society in harmony with the Earth.

We shall take time from frenetic urban pursuits
to contemplate a cloud, a tree, or leaves of grass,
to behold Creation
as it takes place before us each day,
that we may know wonder and exaltation
and join with all men, our brothers,
in celebration of the fellow creatures
with whom we share this planet.

We cherish the hope that men may lay down their arms
and join in reverence for the Earth
to build anew the habitations of the human spirit.

We invoke the prayer of the Navajo:
"That we may walk fittingly
where birds sing, where the grass is green,
Our Mother the Earth, Our Father the Sky."

We join with the Taoist poet:
"I shall dwell among green mountains . . .
My soul is serene."

We sing with the Psalmist:
"The heavens declare the glory of God,
And the firmament showeth his handiwork."

For all these we give thanks—
for the turning planet,
for the flowing waters,
for the moving air,
for all plants and trees,
for all creatures that move upon the land,
through the waters and the air.

We celebrate the nourishing Earth,
our home and the abode of our children forever.

NAUM GABO

Translucent Variation on a Spheric Theme

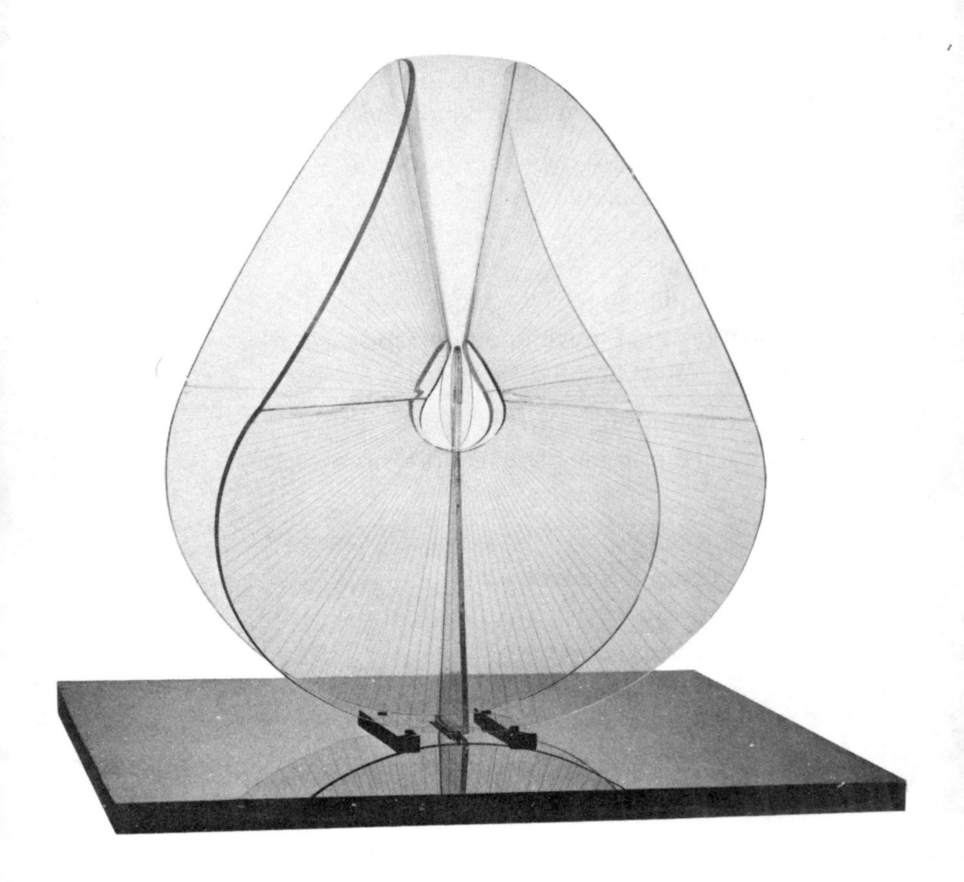

1951 version of 1937 original. The Solomon R. Guggenheim Museum, New York City

EDWARD SHUSTER

City

Courtesy of Edward Shuster

Man is capable of creating order and beauty.
Man is capable of creating disorder and ugliness.
Which will he choose in the future?

Writing Assignments for Part Eight

1. Write a report upon the latest developments in the exploration of outer space.
2. Write a report upon what changes automation has brought about in a U.S. industry.
3. Do you think that population should be controlled by law?
4. If you knew you would not be permitted to have children, what changes would you make in your plans for the future?
5. A man at the turn of the century worked from sixteen to eighteen hours a day. A man thirty years from now will work perhaps five. Write an essay in which you discuss the problems and promises of such added leisure time.
6. Write a report on Rachel Carson.
7. What can be done to prevent the desolation suggested in the excerpt from Rachel Carson's *Silent Spring*?
8. In an essay, take a position on Wald's contention that competition between nations leads to destruction, that "We are one species, with a world to win."
9. In any form you wish, discuss the possibility that "another world is ringing our number."
10. Write an essay in which you support or refute Stace's argument as expressed in "Man Against Darkness" that a movement toward atheism is a movement toward maturity.
11. Respond, in any form you wish (poetry, short story, personal narrative, description) to any of the problems touched upon in this section.
12. Can you imagine, in some specific ways, how, on a day-to-day basis, you could more fully realize your own human potential. Use any written form you wish.